The Black Athlete
as Hero

ALSO BY JOSEPH DORINSON

Kvetching and Shpritzing: Jewish Humor in American Popular Culture (McFarland, 2015)

Paul Robeson: Essays on His Life and Legacy (McFarland, 2002; paperback 2004)

The Black Athlete as Hero

American Barrier Breakers from Nine Sports

JOSEPH DORINSON

McFarland & Company, Inc., Publishers
Jefferson, North Carolina

This book has undergone peer review.

LIBRARY OF CONGRESS CATALOGUING-IN-PUBLICATION DATA

Names: Dorinson, Joseph, 1936– author.
Title: The Black athlete as hero : American barrier breakers
from nine sports / Joseph Dorinson.
Description: Jefferson, North Carolina : McFarland & Company, Inc., Publishers, 2022 |
Includes bibliographical references and index.
Identifiers: LCCN 2022032923 | ISBN 9781476678863 (paperback : acid free paper) ∞
ISBN 9781476645964 (ebook)
Subjects: LCSH: African American athletes—Political activity—History. |
Sports—Political aspects—United States—History. | African American athletes—
Biography. | Heroes—United States—Biography. | African Americans—
Social conditions—History. | Racism against Black people—History. | Social classes—
United States—History. | United States—Race relations—History. | BISAC:
SOCIAL SCIENCE / Ethnic Studies / American / African American &
Black Studies | SPORTS & RECREATION / History
Classification: LCC GV706.32 .D867 2022 | DDC 796.089/96073—dc23/eng/20220805
LC record available at https://lccn.loc.gov/2022032923

BRITISH LIBRARY CATALOGUING DATA ARE AVAILABLE

ISBN (print) 978-1-4766-7886-3
ISBN (ebook) 978-1-4766-4596-4

Front cover: Kareem Abdul-Jabbar, then known as Lew Alcindor (Malcolm W. Emmons);
(insets top, left to right) Fritz Pollard (Brown University), Joe Louis
and Jackie Robinson (Library of Congress); (insets bottom, left to right)
Florence Griffith Joyner (Ronald Reagan Library), and Tiger Woods (Tim Hipps)

Printed in the United States of America

*McFarland & Company, Inc., Publishers
Box 611, Jefferson, North Carolina 28640
www.mcfarlandpub.com*

Table of Contents

Part Six—Basketball

Section 7—Golf, Hockey, Gymnastics

Acknowledgments

I dedicate this book to my parents, Peter and Rita Dorinson, and to three of my favorite authors, Peter Golenbock, Bill Rhoden and David Maraniss, for their inspiration and mastery of sports history, biography, and politics.

To borrow a phrase from the eminently quotable Yogi Berra, I would like to thank the many folks who made this book necessary. I salute my father, Peter Dorinson, who boxed in the U.S. Army as "Soldier Boy" Dorinson during World War I and later as a professional. He nurtured my love of all sports. Although his six-day-a-week work schedule prevented his attendance at my various games, we spent quality time on Sundays, talking and watching sports. He took me to my first Yankee Stadium double-header in 1946, which the Yankees won and where my mother fainted from excessive heat and oppressive smoke. A fine raconteur, my dad regaled me with recollections of Babe Ruth, Benny Friedman, and Jack Johnson, whom he considered the greatest—rather than Muhammad Ali, a reasonable judgment since he died in 1963. I owe my father life, love, and a future as a sports historian. My mother, however, stressed academics, urging me to become a writer. Thanks mom, belatedly. She died of heart trouble in 1976; so, sadly, my parents perished before I published.

If it takes a village to educate single child, the author of this book had to stand on the shoulders of Giants, not to mention Dodgers and Yankees. Friends from the old and new Brooklyn neighborhoods, summer camps, Stuyvesant High School, Columbia University, Long Island University, Danforth Associates of New York, Florida Basketball Fraternity, and Madison-Marine-Homecrest Civic Association—too numerous to cite by name—all merit my profound gratitude. And they know who they are.

The idea for this book germinated in 1997, when I co-directed with my late colleague Joram Warmund a three-day conference to honor Jackie Robinson. As the-co-organizer of—and participant in—several subsequent academic conferences on Paul Robeson, Basketball, Baseball, and my beloved borough of Brooklyn—all with a sports component—I befriended and benefited from prominent journalists, mellifluous broadcasters, inspirational educators, and prolific authors: Dave Anderson, Hal Bock, Robert W. Creamer, Peter Golenbock, Jules Tygiel, Lester Rodney, Maury Allen, Jean Jensonne, Mike Hermann, Joseph Boskin (my mentor), Peter Levine, Bob Lipsyte, Bill Rhoden, Stan Isaacs, Bill Mardo, Bob Peterson, Bonnie DeSimone, Dave Maraniss, Tom Boswell, George Willis, Bob Herzog, Lee Lowenfish, Stan Isaacs, Ira

Berkow, Pete Hamill, Marty Glickman, Stanton Green, Mike D'Innocenzo, Larry Lester, Richard Zamoff, Bijan Bayne, and Jimmy Breslin, among other luminaries.

Through the above contacts, I met Dolph Schayes, "Fuzzy" Levane, Kareem Abdul-Jabbar, Ralph Branca, Ed Charles, Monte Irvin, Larry Doby, Joe Black, Spike Lee, Gene Hermanski, Bob Feller, Bobby Bragan, Enos Slaughter, Stan Musial, Bill Russell, Joe Black, Joe Pignatano, Johnny Podres, Donn Clendenon, Ozzie Smith, Warren Spahn, Lou Brock, Frank Robinson, Duke Snider, Bobby Thomson, Tommy Hawkins, and a favorite of my youth: "Old Reliable" Tommy Henrich.

The literary giants mentioned above plus Sam Smith, Brad Snyder, David K. Wiggins, David Halberstam, Dave Zirin, Martin Duberman, and Howard Bryant provided a roadmap in this quest. SABR (Society for American Baseball Research) offered excellent biographical information, as did other digital sources (such as *The Undefeated*, which proved invaluable). I could never have completed this manuscript without the efforts of Long Island University's excellent technical support staff, spearheaded by Stewart Alleyne, along with Tom Weis and Leon Hubbard under the aegis of the able Delicia Gaines.

Former Negro Leaguers Max Manning, Armando Vazquez, and Ted "Double Duty" Radcliffe in 1999. Manning was a hard-throwing right-handed pitcher for the Newark Eagles from 1939 to 1948, taking time out to fight in World War II. Vazquez was a Cuban good-fielding first baseman who played five years in the Negro leagues with the Indianapolis Clowns and New York Cubans. Unwilling to return to Castro's Cuba, Vazquez remained in New York City, where he worked on the custodial staff of P.S. 163 on 97th Street in Manhattan. Radcliffe, nicknamed "Double Duty" by Damon Runyon, who had seen him pitch one game of a double-header and catch the other, played in the Negro leagues from 1928 to 1946, enjoying several strong seasons on the mound (author collection).

At the John Henry "Pop" Lloyd Conferences in Atlantic City, I found inspiration in Negro League baseball history, courtesy of organizers Larry Hogan (no relation to the Maryland governor but equally engaging), Michael Everett, and Belinda Manning, the daughter of Negro League pitching ace Max Manning. That experience introduced me to the important work of Larry Lester, Susan Rayl, Leslie Heaphy, Dick Clark, Robert Ruck, James A. Riley, and some wonderful Negro League veterans like Jimmy Dean, Bob Scott, Armando Vazquez, Jim Robinson, Max Manning, Ted "Double Duty" Radcliffe, and the last of the then living Harlem Renaissance basketball stars, John "Wonder Boy" Isaacs.

Constrained by COVID-19, I had to improvise. Cut off from travel to libraries, I had to rely on digital sources, *The New York Times*, SABR, Google—even Wikipedia, I must admit, proved useful. Obituaries of prominent athletes imparted valuable information as well as inspiration. When Rafer Johnson, the 1960 Olympic decathlon champion, died, I felt compelled to add his biographical sketch to the track and field section. In addition, Kurt Streeter's magnificent eulogy in the December 7, 2020, edition of the *New York Times* illuminated my mission with amazing felicity and grace. His words sing.

> Death stalks us always. It is a bitter truth we tend to shove from our thoughts in typical times. But during a Covid, we cannot. It is before our eyes daily, in the news in our communities, sometimes in our homes. We lose beloved public figures every year, of course. But this year, we lost them with an awful and steady rhythm....
>
> Sports was not immune. Who can forget the helicopter crash in January that killed Kobe Bryant, his daughter Gianna and seven of their friends....? Their obituaries reminded us of athletic greatness, better days and brilliance too often overlooked. Joe Morgan, Don Shula and John Thompson....
>
> Our personal sports icons have a way of living alongside us, enduring and powerful in their memories. We marvel at their talent, their ability to perform during the tensest moments. Their victories and bitter losses become signposts marking the march of time.

Finally, to family members who have endured my preoccupation with this book, I offer apologies coupled with gratitude for your support, love, and patience. To my bride of 52 years, Eileen Levine (village queen) Dorinson; daughter Hilary Dorinson and partner Corey Resnick; daughter Paula; son Robert and wife Valerie Dorinson; grandchildren in order of birth, Leila, Hailey, Rebecca, Brodie, and Jesse, I sing your praise along with the heroes in this book.

Introduction:
Hero Defined

What is a *hero*? If the events of 9/11 helped us to redefine this concept, so did the recent COVID-19 pandemic. First responders, health professionals, and medical researchers have stepped up on the heroic ladder. Long silent, athletes have also joined this special group as they speak out on social issues engendered by the murders of innocent victims at the hands of police and militia who are supposed to protect the people, not violate their rights under law.

Author Ernest Hemingway defined a hero as one who exhibits "grace under pressure." Mythology expert Joseph Campbell put 1,000 faces on this mythical figure. Departing from his Marxist roots and its emphasis on class struggle, philosopher Sidney Hook refocused on "the hero in history" as the primary agent of change. Myriad interpretations flowered from the heroic life concept leaving lay readers both baffled and beguiled. Contemporary *kitsch* culture has blurred the distinction between the heroic life and media-forged fantasies that equate celebrities with heroes.

The rise of antiheroes in twentieth-century history, literature, and film added to this quandary.[1] In "The Second Coming," William Butler Yeats lamented that the best in his era lacked "all conviction" while the worst were "full of passion and intensity." Current world politics prove the prescience of the good Irish poet as racist reactionary xenophobes have risen to power by evoking "fear and trembling."

Potentially, this is the best of times for sports heroes. The field of dreams lures all-star athletes with astronomical sums of money for their specialized talents. Money, however, measures only one facet of the good life. When death summoned concussive victims in football like Dave Duerson and Junior Seau (both by suicide) and basketball's Kobe Bryant by helicopter crash, the media encouraged soul-searching analysis. Victims of drug abuse like baseball's Doug Caminiti and basketball's Len Bias also evoked disbelief coupled with lamentation for athletes who die young. Watching the once magnificent Muhammad Ali light the Olympic torch in 1996 with unsteady hands filled viewers with pity and sadness. Excessive blows to his head and the ravages of Parkinson's disease that ensued compelled us into contemplation of the price of glory. We continue to grapple with this incongruity.

African American athletes have put their stamp on other people's lives to be sure, but a debate rages about whether this influence is salutary or not. In football and basketball, they have achieved extraordinary success, now accounting for roughly 65 percent of all players in the NFL and 73 percent in the NBA. Is this dominance rooted in genes or beans, nature or nurture, heredity or environment? In 2000, one author, Jon Entine, tackled this issue in a book, *Taboo: Why Black Athletes Dominate Sports and Why We are Afraid to Talk about It*. Entine leans heavily towards genetics with heavy emphasis on long-distance runners in Kenya and basketball players in the USA. The so-called elephant in this room is the mind-body duality harking back to Descartes, only this time in racial tropes. Consequently, white supremacists, emerging from their rocks of late, cling to their spurious claim of mental superiority if not physical parity. Some Black social critics view athletes of color as modern gladiators who entertain affluent white spectators for their pleasure and the profits of corporate giants. Their fear is that a dichotomy of brain and brawn works to the detriment of Blacks, as Hoberman complained.[2]

Author John Hoberman added his research to this combustible mix in his book *Darwin's Athletes: How Sport Has Damaged Black America and Preserved the Myth of Race*. His explosive conclusion is that success in sports precludes advancement in other, more intellectual pursuits. The emphasis on the sporting life pits physical supremacy (popularly associated with Blacks) against intellectual supremacy (popularly associated with whites), thus fanning the flames of lingering racism. Hoberman further argues that the sports arena represents a metaphorical prison, which denies access to middle-class avenues of success by funneling African Americans into a narrow channel. By confining Blacks to athletic prowess, the establishment propels them into a state of perpetual subordination at street level. He even dismisses Jackie Robinson's achievements as overplayed.[3]

My thesis will demonstrate that Hoberman's book, though well researched and forcefully written, is off-base. What the Texas-based writer fails to appreciate is the vital, indeed pivotal role Black athletes played in shoring up group identity and penetrating the barriers of a once unyielding caste system. A good example of this double enhancement is illustrated in the heroic and controversial life of Paul Robeson. Before this great athlete became a national figure by way of football at Rutgers, Blacks were stereotyped as the inversion of America's "Protestant ethic." They appeared as either docile or savage, faithful or tricky, pathetic or comical, childish or oversexed. This public perception distorted the Black persona while reinforcing segregation in most sports as well as in society. In order to survive, Black athletes had to conform, i.e., act in accommodation to the social order. This required submission to white coaches coupled with a code of moral respectability.

For Blacks, the sports opportunity structure in the nineteenth century was limited to horse racing, boxing, and baseball (briefly). Success, however limited, not only bolstered race pride but also led to wealth acquisition and property ownership.[4] Three-time Kentucky Derby winning jockey Isaac Murphy purchased large tracts of land. Unfortunately, alcoholism led to death at an early age.[5] The first Black to enter Major League Baseball—prior to Jackie Robinson—Moses "Fleet" Walker owned a hotel, an opera house, and several movie houses in Steubenville, Ohio. It also may have saved his life. In a street brawl, Walker beat a white man to death. An all-white jury, perhaps influenced by his celebrity, found him not guilty. Booted out of baseball by Hall of Famer Cap Anson, Walker concluded that Blacks could only survive separate from whites. In his book *Our Home Colony*, Walker warned against integration, using the metaphor of a volcano to describe the volatility of forced relations between the races. Thus, he advocated avoidance.[6]

This book attempts to address complex as well as burning issues, stoked by electoral politics in 2016 and 2020 with the focus on Black heroes in sports. As a baby born during the Great Depression, I grew up laden with Mel Brooksian "high anxiety." Escape from near Armageddon led me to the daily sports pages. New York City was once blessed with an abundance of newspapers with excellent sports coverage. There, a reader found clarity, certainty, and comfort. Scores were finite. Pitchers lasted nine innings minus pitch-counts. Hitters and fielders with outstanding performance numbers usually stayed with one team until retirement or injury intervened. If one lived in New York City, one could root for three teams: the Giants of Manhattan, Dodgers of Brooklyn, or Yankees of the Bronx. In 1936, the year I was born, my favorite Yankee team dominated American baseball. Fans basked in "reflected glory" as I did in troubled times. Poverty plagued youngsters who lived in low-income projects like this author could feel enriched by identification with a favorite team.

Media hyped local teams and resident heroes with nicknames like "The Sultan of Swat," "The Bronx Bombers," "Leo the Lip," "The People's 'Cherce,'" "The Brooklyn Bums," "The Big Cat," and "The Fighting Irish," as well as team nicknames such as "Blackbirds," "Beavers," "Violets," "Rams," and "Red Men," prior to political correctness. Young fans communed at the local candy store, once the hub of urban teenage culture, to debate, celebrate, or denigrate players and teams and to share memories. As I grew older, however, I began to view the world, including sports, through "a glass, darkly" as Saint Paul put it starkly. In 1947, the advent of Jackie Robinson proved pivotal. Before his arrival, most sporting events were lily-white. Despite our American creed, embedded in Jefferson's exalted language, not everyone was created equal. Racism continued to fester. Robinson's presence illuminated the absence of his African American peers. With heightened awareness, I began to look for other Black heroes to undermine white bigotry.

Philadelphia Phillies manager Ben Chapman's barrage of racist invective visited on Robinson filled me with rage. Though a staunch Yankees fan, I also rooted for Robinson and the Black players who followed: Larry Doby, Satchel Paige, Roy Campanella, Don Newcombe, Junior Gilliam, Willie Mays, Monte Irvin, Joe Black, Sandy Amoros, and finally, Elston Howard. My social consciousness was also raised in after-school programs and summer camps, thanks to my progressive parents who provided a positive environment at home and away. At Camp Kinderland, I encountered two giants of African American culture, W. E. B. Dubois and Paul Robeson, the subject of a subsequent chapter. Consequently, I learned that stereotypical racial figures like Stepin Fetchit, Uncle Ben, and Aunt Jemima were not only wrong, but also degrading. Moreover, my Negro classmates at Gaynor JHS 49 reinforced positive interaction. In one incident, a white student, unhappy with my call, sucker-punched me while I umpired a punch ball game in the school gym. Milford Dyches, a Black classmate, came to my defense as I groaned in pain. Milford put a hurt on my attacker. Though this incident occurred 70 years ago, I still savor that memory of support and comradery.

Fast forward to my college years. My failure as a pre-med and pre-law student propelled me into history, always a favorite subject. And my parents into bereavement. Inspired by charismatic Columbia professor James P. Shenton's brilliant lectures, I learned salient truths about race, class, ethnicity, and gender in American history. He encouraged me to pursue graduate study, where I floundered in search of a dissertation topic. I assayed several subjects—American Peace movements, a settlement house on the Lower East Side, immigration, and ethnic leadership—in quest of the academy's holy grail, a PhD. None of these topics found fruition because my preferred study—sports history—lacked academic favor or cachet in the late 1950s and early 1960s.

Nevertheless, sports always appealed to me as fan, as scholar, and as teacher. Combined with civil rights activism—NAACP and CORE at Columbia, voting rights in Georgia under the aegis of Dr. King and his SCLC associates—the subject of Black heroes beckoned. In 1970, a group of young Turks, as it were, in the history department of Long Island University's Brooklyn Campus formed a cabal, as critically labeled, in our history department to modernize the curriculum. Despite opposition from the history chair, we—Gary Marotta, Frank Jonas, John Reilly, Joram Warmund, and this writer—introduced courses in American Social History, African American History, and Women's History. Later, we added Holocaust History, Film History, Psychohistory, and Sports History. I led the charge for change, which most of our students welcomed. Only a few resisted. When a veteran African American professor of French History initially refused to teach the course outside his specialty when our specialists departed for greener pastures (he later relented), I volunteered to teach African American History and did so for 10 years after Professors Eisenberg and Marotta left. Facing a challenge with the rise of Black militancy, I engaged in a risky gambit during our initial class. In white chalk on a blackboard, I posed a question: "Can a white boy teach black history?" Students responded with a mixed bag of pros and cons. At the end of our verbal give-and-take, I urged patience and fortitude. Give me your definitive answer, I counseled, at semester's end. In most cases, the responses were highly positive. One year, a student balked at my use of the word "boy," unaware of my intended irony. My involvement in African American culture culminated in the late 1990s with two major conferences at LIU Brooklyn on Jackie Robinson and Paul Robeson, which subsequently morphed into two co-edited books on these giant figures in American history.

Searching for a proper paradigm to explain the dynamic linking Black leadership with sports heroes, I found a good fit in C. Eric Lincoln's exemplary study of Black nationalism, delineating the rise of Black Muslims. Professor Lincoln posited three basic types of response: accommodation, avoidance, and aggression by "a minority group living in an environment of constant prejudice and discrimination."[7] Obviously, these modalities of action do not operate as isolates in a vacuum. Subject to societal change, they sometimes blend and traverse boundaries. Concentrating on sports figures, I was drawn to those athletes who mirrored W. E. B. Dubois's concept of two "divided souls" as key to unlocking deep painful truths embedded in African American history. DuBois explained the dilemma of "two souls, two thoughts, two unreconciled strivings, two warring ideals in one dark body whose dogged strength alone keeps it from being torn asunder."[8] Emerging from the Platonic cave, I finally saw the light.

Elected to departmental chair of history at Long Island University in 1985, I promised to secure an African American professor. As mentioned above, one initially reluctant colleague, a senior African American professor, lacking sufficient student enrollees for his course in French History, finally agreed to teach the Black History course, successfully as well. When he left to serve as campus provost, I recruited a young Black female scholar in 1991 to teach this course. Thirty years later, Dr. Kim Jones continues in that capacity and now offers courses in Slavery and the Diaspora, and Women's History. I also hired several outstanding African American scholars to profess history: Professors Craig Wilder, Clarence Taylor, and Sol Levy, who after leaving LIU, went on to stellar careers in academe at other institutions.

In 1976, I taught the first course in sports history at LIU Brooklyn. Success exceeded my expectations. It attracted students from various disciplines across the academic spectrum. At least two weeks were devoted to sports at LIU Brooklyn, to the delight of our scholar-athletes. I finally found my *métier*. After delivering several well-received papers at the annual American Popular Culture Conferences, I began to publish articles and book reviews in the then virgin field. Popular Culture Association president and co-founder Ray Browne urged me to convert one paper on "Black Heroes in Sports" to an article for the *Journal of Popular Culture*'s winter issue in 1993. That entry provided the template and roadmap for this book.

That article also propelled me to the annual John Henry "Pop" Lloyd Conference in Atlantic City, New Jersey, on October 8, 2000, as keynote speaker, at the request of co-directors Lawrence Hogan and Mike Everett to honor Negro League veterans in the context of African American culture. Focused mainly on baseball, these awards were presented to legendary blues musician David "Honeyboy" Edwards, author Robert Peterson, scholar/activist Richard Lapchick, and former Harlem Ren hoop star and Atlantic City Mayor James Usry. At the culminating dinner on Saturday evening, I had to improvise. Defective audio equipment and protracted prior presentations proved challenging. Unwilling to read my paper except for pertinent quotes, I extemporized the salient points. Encouraged by attentive listeners, I sensed that the audience composed of baseball notables, scholars, and fans was tuned into my words, which flowed in rhythmic cadence. I ad-libbed references to luminaries in the audience who had overcome personal obstacles and racial barriers. As I brought the lecture to a dramatic climax, fighting back incipient tears, I received a standing ovation. The local newspaper imparted my message coupled with a photograph on the front page. The caption cited my message[9]:

> Keynote speaker Joseph Dorinson tells the crowd at the 8th John Henry "Pop" Lloyd Awards ceremony that black heroes such as Jackie Robinson and Muhammad Ali deserve not only recognition, but respect and constant memory.

At this dinner, a parent of one of my students, a baseball player at LIU Brooklyn, conferred high praise in a single word: "Awesome!" It remains, clichés aside, my finest hour and a prime motivation for this book.

Another pivotal experience occurred in a visit to Dodger Stadium. My wife and I flew to Los Angeles to visit our daughter Hilary, then enrolled in a master's degree program in Occupational Therapy at USC. A second goal was to raise money for a major conference at LIU Brooklyn, honoring Jackie Robinson, 50 years after he broke the color barrier in modern Major League Baseball. We met with the director of public relations, former Notre Dame and LA Laker star Tom Hawkins, the first African American basketball player at Notre Dame and one of the few Black executives in sports at that time (1997). Tommy Hawkins took us on a tour of Dodger Stadium before we talked business. I brought a letter of introduction from LIU's former athletic director and provost, Buck Lai, who had played Minor League Baseball in the Dodger organization and helped to set up the Vero Beach training facility to accommodate players of color, frequent victims of race discrimination in the past. Hawkins perused the letter, which essentially was a pitch for financial support; Hawkins had been briefed in advance. He indicated that Peter O'Malley, current owner of the Dodgers, refused to support our conference. When I asked why, Hawkins explained the reason. Our keynote speaker, Roger Kahn, roiled the O'Malley family when he last appeared in Los Angeles. A local reporter asked Kahn what he thought of the Dodger owners. He replied: "Walter was a scoundrel but his son Peter was too dumb to be a scoundrel." Sensing my discomfort, Hawkins mentioned that he wrote a poem about Jackie Robinson shortly after his mother's death. I urged the Dodger executive to show me the poem. Hawkins went into an adjacent room and returned with a sheet of paper containing the poem.

As Tom Hawkins read the poem, my wife and I—moved by the poignant words—wept salty tears. I asked Tom for permission to take the poem to our conference, insisting that it was worth more money than any O'Malley donation. At the opening ceremony on April 3, 1997, thrust into a master of ceremony role due to the absence of our university president, recovering from surgery, I read the poem, "Jackie, Do They Know? An Ode to Jackie Robinson," again fighting back tears.[10]

Do they know what you did Jackie Robinson when you broke that color line? Do they Know the worlds that you opened when the Dodgers asked you to sign?

Do they know the humiliation that you suffered through the years or how it felt to "stomach" the threats and constant racial jeers?

Do they know the competitive compassion with which you played the game or the host of insults you endured when they defiled your name?

Do they know that you rose above it with majestic winning style, escorting a perennial bridesmaid down the coveted championship aisle?

Do they that you were a "Black Moses" with a soul of raging fire, a man who firmly Stood his ground with undiminished desire?

Do they know that you had all the tools, talents, "smarts," and skill, well blended With civility plus an unshakable iron-clad will?

Do they know when you left the game no grass grew under your feet, you continued pioneering using the executive suite?

Do they know with respect and reverence, we document your deeds. Careful to water And nourish your bountiful well-sown seeds?

Do they know that in the hall of fame you regally reside, having scaled the heights of
The "grand old game" and humanity with pride?

Do they know that you left us early, age fifty-three when you passed? But, in that half-century,
What a legacy you amassed?

Warmly received, Hawkins's poem graced our Jackie Robinson book. The heroic life of Jackie Robinson provides the spark that illuminates this book just as it inspired Tommy Hawkins and so many other writers, athletes, and fans.

Recently, prolific author Howard Bryant added another important concept to advance this journey. His notion of "the Heritage," which he succinctly defined as control, helps us to understand the role of the Black sports hero in our history.[11] Rooted in Jackie Robinson's enduring touchstone "A life is not important except in the impact it has on other people's lives," my choices presented in the narrative that follows are predicated not only on great athleticism but most certainly on impact. The chapters are organized on a particular sport rather than as biographical sketches *per se*. It proved impossible to include every extraordinary Black athlete with extended biographies. Therefore, I selected those athletes who made a difference and for whom I have a particular affinity. Another reason prompted several choices. As I indicated to a *New York Times* reporter in 1998, we have a serious problem with memory loss. We live in a throwaway culture that discards its heroes. As Daniel Boorstin lamented, celebrities have eclipsed heroes in our troubled times. Will we remember the recently departed Lou Brock, Bob Gibson, Joe Morgan, Elgin Baylor, and Irv Cross? The latter was a star NFL player who became the first Black to anchor a network sports show on CBS.[12] Can we retrieve them if they fall into obscurity? This book attempts to answer that question.

SECTION ONE

BOXING

1

Jack Johnson, Joe Louis, Ray Robinson, and Muhammad Ali

Jack Johnson and His Predecessors

The Black athlete as hero often delivers a mixed message. Part of this ambivalence is due to the absence of historical context. Aggressive in the arena, he or she avoided conflict in early American society, fraught with slavery during which outstanding boxers, fighting to entertain plantation owners, gained certain privileges, even freedom. In the postbellum period, still repressed by external restraints such as Jim Crow laws and mores, some Black athletes exploded in rage. Hailed by one group, usually insiders, they alienated others. Before the civil rights movement gained traction on the 1960s, Black athletes—women as well as men—had to abide by almost impossible standards while in pursuit of possible dreams, grappling with enormous social psychological tension throughout their quest.

Black boxing culture was cultivated under some form of slavery or servitude in antebellum America. The first to gain recognition in the so-called sweet science was Bill Richmond. Born in 1763 and raised in Staten Island, he immigrated to England as servant to General Earl Percy, who provided him with education and vocational training as a cabinetmaker. As a boxer in Percy's mother country, Richmond gained status; as husband to an Englishwoman, he came into money, sufficient to operate a school for boxers. He fought until age 57, winning the admiration of British workers and earning notice from poet Lord Byron.[1] His death in 1829 at age 66 evoked sadness among fans across the class divide.

One of his acolytes, Tom Molyneux, rose from slavery in South Carolina after beating a fellow slave. Relocated to New York City, he won several matches among his peers, free Black men. Migration to London offered new challenges, including a bout with British champ Tom Cribb. Raucous fans and a biased referee probably caused a sure victory to eventuate in defeat in the 40th round following a low blow from the bloodied Cribb. Despite defeat, Molyneux won fame and glory rather than stripes and degradation from brutal masters in America. Dissipation aborted his career and shortened his life to 41. Back in the USA, boxing before the Civil War, Bill Rhoden argues, became a diversion for slave-owners "to dull the revolutionary instinct."[2] In short, all sports became an escape into "avoidance."

Reconstruction—"The Great Black Hope"—got off to a promising start after the

10

Civil War ended. Although "forty-acres and a mule" failed to materialize, Blacks enjoyed security under military rule in five designated districts. Legal protection issued from a series of constitutional amendments and Congressional legislation. Consequently, Blacks gained political power, which incurred the wrath of white bigots. Stirred to action, several white supremacist groups formed, most significantly and lethally the Ku Klux Klan. No strangers to violent intimidation by Southern whites and abandoned by several northern pre-war abolitionists, Blacks suffered the erosion of power, politically as well as economically. That descent accelerated after the presidential election of 1876, leading to the so-called Compromise of 1877. Southern Democrats sacrificed their presidential candidate, Samuel J. Tilden of New York, on the altar of power-greed, enabling Republican candidate Rutherford P. Hayes to become president though Tilden won a majority of the popular vote. A dispute over the vote count in three Southern states—South Carolina, Florida, and Louisiana—left 20 electoral votes in doubt and led to a protracted stalemate. A secret meeting in West Virginia resulted in a 15-man commission, consisting of eight Republicans and seven Democrats, putting Hayes over the top. In return, white southerners were promised economic investment, political independence, and most significantly, the removal of military rule, leaving Blacks minus protection and vulnerable to a form of economic servitude—in a word, powerless.[3]

In this regressive historical context, Black athletes had to either submit to the white power structure or rebel. The latter choice, as Jack Johnson would soon discover, was fraught with peril. On the other side of the color divide, whites enjoyed their so-called redemption. To maintain dominance, whites used power to change the rules of engagement, which author Bill Rhoden aptly dubs "the Jockey Syndrome," a reference to the short-lived success that Black jockeys experienced in horse racing.[4] A prime example can be found in the brilliant but turbulent and tragic career of Jack Johnson. Elite white boxers, especially title holders such as John L. Sullivan, also avoided Black challengers, the cases of George "Little Chocolate" Dixon, Joe Walcott (the original), and Joe Gans notwithstanding.

One year after the infamous Compromise of 1877, John Arthur (known as Jack or "Li'l Arthur") Johnson was born in Galveston, Texas, on March 31, 1878, one of the nine children born to former slaves Tina and Henry Johnson. Growing up in Texas, Johnson claimed that as a member of an integrated gang, he did not experience the ugly stain of racism. He played and frolicked with white children without incident. Johnson dropped out of school after only five years of education. Discovered by Leo Posner, head of the Galveston Athletic Club, Johnson learned to box. Dodging legal constraints on bouts of this blood sport, Johnson won a few, lost a few, and had several draws and no decisions through 1901. In 1902, however, he won five out of six fights, battling to a draw in the only non-win. He had experienced a reversal of fortune the year before when a seasoned veteran, Jewish light heavyweight Joe Choynsky, knocked him out in round three of their bout. Both combatants went to jail for defying a Texas law that banned boxing. While in jail, Choynsky successfully tutored Jack Johnson in the fine art of defense as well as offense in boxing. A 6'2" 200-pound counter-puncher with a devastating right uppercut, Li'l Arthur lost only three fights from 1902 to 1908, surviving a wicked left hook by Sam Langford, a welterweight in 1906. Langford was a brilliant Black boxer who repeatedly tried to break the color barrier in boxing for a title bout in his weight division. And failed. More relentless, Johnson defeated former heavyweight champ Bob Montgomery in 1907.

Johnson relentlessly pursued heavyweight champ Tommy Burns for a title match. Burns finally agreed. Twenty thousand fans paid to see the challenger Johnson methodically pummel Burns. Jack Johnson's 1908 defeat of Tommy Burns in Australia signaled a new era that caught white America off guard. Fighting all challengers, he survived a knockdown of middleweight champ Stanley Ketchel and returned the favor with a knockout punch in the 12th round.[5]

Set against a grim background of lynching and Jim Crow laws, Johnson's achievements coupled with his style established a new code of behavior.[6] He beat white boxers methodically and disdainfully. Outside the boxing arena, he flaunted sexuality with white women. He triggered scandal. Fearless, Johnson flouted all the rules of accommodation. He drove big cars unconstrained by speed limits. He consorted with white women, many engaged in commercial affection. Clad in custom-tailored suits, shirts adorned by diamond-studded

Jack Johnson in 1910, more than a year after he pursued heavyweight champion Tommy Burns around the world in an effort to goad the white fighter into a bout. When they finally met, in Sydney, Australia, on December 26, 1908, Johnson won the heavyweight crown in dominant fashion, toying with Burns until the fight was stopped in the 14th round. Johnson then held the title from 1908 to 1915. Photograph by E.S. Caywood (Library of Congress).

cufflinks, he partied through nights, and burnished the sexual stereotype and trope of Black hypersexuality by padding his genitals with gauze bandages to enhance the size of his phallic power while training for the next fight.[7] The first modern media star, Johnson played a pivotal role, Professor Gerald Early maintains, in serving as catalyst for the "New Negro" who emerged during the Harlem Renaissance.[8]

If the two-decade roller-coaster Progressive Era ushered in many vital reforms, it also witnessed a resurgence of violent racism. White supremacy, like its 2020 avatar, was a poor loser. The behavior of author Jack London offers a dramatic case in point. A professed socialist on the one hand and a devout racist on the other, London cried out for a white avenger, a "Great White Hope"—as did many other "dear hearts and (un)gentle people." That so-called savior of white supremacy arrived in the person of Jim Jeffries, former champ. Johnson's 1910 one-sided victory over Jeffries ignited race riots initiated by enraged white men like London, the other Jack of the literary trade. For him and myopic millions, Johnson loomed as the "Bad Nigger," a recurrent figure in American folklore.[9] Fearful Blacks offered words of caution. Booker T. Washington preferred the Tuskegee Way, i.e., the non-threatening accommodationist way. *The Age*, a Black newspaper, urged Johnson to "conduct himself in a modest manner." Fear of violence and threats of reprisal disturbed the Black bourgeoisie.[10] Among the Black masses, however, Johnson's victory offered cause to rejoice. Black pride surged. Celebrants cut out his pictures and collected money from wagers—$75,000 worth. Poets wrote paeans of praise. Another Black paper, the *Birmingham Reporter*, wrote: "Stand up, thou brawny Son of African lineage and let the world see thee!"[11]

Hailed as a race hero, Johnson deflated white supremacy. Yet his fight with Jeffries unleashed the worst elements of race feeling. His one-sided triumph on July 4 ignited riots in Houston and Fort Worth, Texas. This drama brought to Broadway by Howard Sackler elicited white guilt in 1968. As portrayed by a then svelte James Earl Jones, the great Black boxer appeared sympathetic. In 1910, however, harassment, vilification, and jail awaited the heavyweight champion.[12] Charged with violating the Mann Act for transporting his future wife over state lines for immoral purposes, Johnson was charged with three counts of unlawful sexual intercourse, two counts of debauchery, and two counts of crime against nature. Judge Kenesaw Mountain Landis presided. An all-white jury found Johnson guilty. He was sentenced to prison for one year plus one day. Thus, a law "meant to stop organized crime," author Brad Herzog tartly opined, "was used to

In this photograph, Jack Johnson stands ready to counterpunch the next "White Hope," Jim Jeffries, in 1910, two years into what would be an eight-year reign as world heavyweight champion. He surrendered the crown to Jess Willard in 1915 after allegedly violating the Mann Act. Johnson was adored by fans, white as well as Black, before and after his death by automobile accident in 1946 on the way to attend the Joe Louis–Billy Conn fight in Yankee Stadium (author collection).

stop Johnson."[13] While appealing his sentence, Johnson fled Chicago with a Negro base-ball team heading to Montréal. From there, he sailed to France and spent seven years on the lam. He continued to fight as well as entertain in Europe, though he was expelled from England. A lavish lifestyle drained his assets, propelling him into a bout in Cuba with 33-year-old Jess Willard for a $30,000 payout. Johnson led the 6'6" 250-pound Willard for the first 25 rounds. Then, per a prearranged plan (according to Johnson), he took a dive, losing by a knockout in round 26. Overweight and rusty at age 37, Johnson tired in the late rounds in the brutal heat. He lost the heavyweight title in his ninth contest as champion.[14]

The return of America's "native son" on April 5, 1915, ended his exile and his reign as champ. Divided in their reaction, some Blacks cheered; many waited for the other shoe to drop. The vast majority probably hoped that race hatred would abate. Hostility to Jack Johnson's lifestyle was no secret. Many fans of Johnson could take consolation in the rumor, fanned by Johnson himself, that he "took a dive" as he allegedly shielded his eyes from the Cuban sun.[15] The jury is still out on Johnson's ultimate persona. Lawrence Levine labels him a folk hero, while David Wiggins delineates his double-edged image. Ill-mannered, defiant, and incorrigible, Papa Jack married three white women, consorted with white prostitutes, belittled Black women. He also punctured the myth of Anglo-Saxon supremacy.[16] Going back to his heyday, one observes a strange confluence of opinion linking two alleged opponents, Booker T. Washington and W.E.B. DuBois. Both agreed that Jack Johnson's immoral behavior impeded race progress, but DuBois saw a positive element as well in boosting race pride and possibility. DuBois attributed the hatred of Johnson to his greatness as a boxer and "unforgivable blackness."[17] Was he an embarrassment to them or a rival for the affection of Black folks? Disturbed by this cognitive dissonance, I turned to Randy Roberts for relief. In his masterful biography, *Papa Jack*, we learn that Johnson always put himself first. Belittling successful Blacks and seeking the company of white prostitutes, Johnson manifested a deep ambivalence, indeed rage. He also accomplished much. He overcame hate, oppression, and outcasting. Defying a long-standing Negro preference for Republicans, he stumped for Al Smith in 1928 and supported FDR in subsequent elections. He defended the CIO as a "champion of peace, prosperity and happiness for millions of people." During World War II, he encouraged an all-out effort. He prodded Black men to enlist from his perch on New York City's 42nd Street. Dressed like a dandy, he lectured on war and peace at Herbert's Museum.

Glamorized in Howard Sackler's 1968 play, Johnson's wrenching ambivalence eluded the liberal author. Deep down, it appears, the best boxer in history wanted to be white, yet he hated the white world. A bundle of contradictions, he evoked mixed feelings among African Americans.[18] Upon Johnson's release from prison in 1921, Harlem residents greeted him like a conquering hero. Down and out during the Great Depression, he acted the "freak" in Chicago during the World's Fair where he fought children for a dollar, giving them a bang for a buck. He became an entertainer in vaudeville, Shakespeare, and bullfighting.[19]

He died as he lived—recklessly. Following a circus tour, he headed for the Louis-Conn rematch, 1946. Driving up Route 1 to New York, near Raleigh, North

Carolina, he lost control. Johnson and a friend, Fred Scott, were thrown from the car. Johnson died several hours later. No fighter attended his funeral. I remember as a 10-year-old reading about it in the papers and pressing my father for information. My dad, a former fighter, called him the greatest fighter he had ever seen, a judgment reaffirmed by ring historian Nat Fleischer. Arthur Ashe called him "the most significant black athlete in history."

Joe Louis

If Jack Johnson acted out aggressively, his successor in the boxing arena, Joe Louis, followed an accommodationist route. Born on May 13, 1914, in Alabama, the fifth child of seven, Joe Louis Barrow had roots in the Deep South. His parents were sharecroppers. He started to pick cotton at age four and did not learn to read until age nine. After his father left, his mother remarried. The reconstituted family, a kind of Brady Bunch in black, moved to Detroit. Joe carried ice and joined a violent gang. Channeling his aggression safely, he became an amateur boxer. In two years, he won 50 fights, 43 by knockout. He lost only four.[20]

Handled by two Black managers, John Roxborough and Julian Black, Joe turned pro. In his first money fight on July 4, 1934, Louis earned $50 in victory. He defeated the next 12 opponents—all white—handily. Beating Primo Carnera in 1935, Joe Louis gained national recognition and a match with former champ Max Baer. He destroyed Baer in four rounds. A hero in Harlem, Joe Louis lifted his people everywhere. In 1936, perhaps over-confident and under-trained, Louis lost to Hitler's Nordic darling, Max Schmeling. Undaunted in defeat, Louis came back. He wrested the crown from Jim Braddock on June 23, 1937, setting the stage for what pundits call the most significant—if not the greatest—fight of the twentieth century.

Two months earlier, Adolf Hitler had annexed Austria and was preparing to blitz Eastern Europe. Seventy thousand screaming fans packed Yankee Stadium on that memorable summer night. Who can forget the stentorian sounds of announcer Clem McCarthy as he described the blows: "A left and a right. Schmeling is down…!" I can hear it now. Reports indicate that two-thirds of radio listeners throughout America had their ears glued to this broadcast. In two minutes and four seconds and 41 blows, Schmeling and fascism—symbolically—went down for the 10-count. Mighty Joe had evened the score.[21] In the ring at least, it was democracy's finest hour.

Unlike Johnson, Louis played the humble hero. He did not pursue white women—at least openly. Recent research has revealed a liaison with famed skater/actress Sonja Henie. A model of discretion, Louis neither bragged nor taunted. All he said in response to critics who thought Billy Conn too fast for the "Brown Bomber" was: "He can run, but he can't hide." His fists did the talking. Epithets like the "Brown Bomber" followed as badges of honor: "Dark Destroyer," "Tan Torpedo," "Sepia Slugger." Blacks identified with him. Deified by Langston Hughes and celebrated in song, he became a folklore hero. President Roosevelt felt his biceps.[22] He fostered patriotism, generated pride, and dispelled prejudice. "A breaker of stereotypes and a destroyer of norms," writes Lawrence Levine, he entered America's pantheon.[23]

Defeat or near defeat deflated his admirers, indeed filled them with panic. Lena Horne recalled how she suffered after the first Schmeling fight while on the road with Noble Sissle's band. She wept hysterically, and the band members cried too.[24] The same panic surfaced when, five years later, Louis almost lost to Conn. Victories, however, brought reassurance and joy. Clearly, Louis resonated throughout Negro America anticipating the Martha and the Vandellas hit "Dancing in the Street." Jubilation followed triumph.

"Mercy, Mercy," warbled Fats Waller. But Joe Louis brought justice as well in two fists of loaded dynamite. Professor Levine argues that Joe Louis enabled Blacks to shed their trickster mask. They could now fight in center ring. While John Henry evoked fantasy, Joe Louis was for real. His mass appeal spread after 1939. *Ring* magazine honored him. In 1940, he jeopardized his standing by endorsing the Republican Wendell Willkie for president. Following FDR's triumph in the political arena, Louis returned to the boxing arena, where his clout carried more weight. When war came, he was ready, enlisting as a common soldier. In this capacity from 1942 to 1945, his heroic stature grew. His unselfish commitment to our noble cause, despite the continued stain of segregation, brought millions of Blacks to the banner. Louis evoked God and country: he was the "people's choice." Elevated by "divine grace," a mark of heroic, indeed charismatic leadership, Louis crested as an American David.[25]

The success of Joe Louis elevated African Americans. Richard Wright captured that ascent when he wrote: "From the symbol of Joe's strength, they took strength, and in that moment all fear, all obstacles were wiped out, drowned."[26] In 1940, Paul Robeson cut a record that combined the singular talents of lyricist Richard Wright, composer and conductor Count Basie, and his own mellifluous basso profundo. When he felled the Nazi Superman, Louis moved from champion to idol as "a hero of democracy."[27]

Lamentably, Louis's later years proved problematic. Despite his still unsurpassed record of a 12-year reign as heavyweight champion with 25 victories notched on his belt, Joe plunged into a dark hole of depression propelled by financial woes, drug abuse, and mental decline. He was married and divorced three times. In 1956, he owed the IRS over one million dollars. Louis worked as a greeter in Las Vegas. A series of heart attacks led to his death on April 12, 1981. Lacking the aggression of other Black athletes, he did not join the civil rights movement, opting for a role of accommodation. When his estate left too little to pay for his funeral, financial help came from Frank Sinatra and another benefactor, Max Schmeling. His son, Joe Louis, Jr., who became a lawyer, likened his tragic father to fictional salesman Willy Loman, who "was never aware that he had lost his territory." Louis's last wife adopted his "love children" and supported him through drug addiction and mental illness.[28] He was buried with full honors at Arlington National Cemetery. Conservative economist Thomas Sowell offered a powerful tribute[29]:

> What made Joe Louis a unique figure was not simply his great talent as an athlete. He appeared at a time when blacks were not only at a low economic ebb—but were the butt of ridicule. In this kind of world Joe Louis became the most famous black man in America.

What he did as a man could reinforce or counteract stereotypes
that hurt and held back millions
of people of his race. How he
fared in the ring mattered more
to black Americans than the fate
of any other athletes in any other
sport, before or since. He was all
we had…. Joe Louis was a continuing lesson to white Americans that to be black did not mean
to be a clown or a lout, regardless
of what the image-makers said.
It was a lesson that helped open
doors that had been closed for too
long.

Heavyweight champion Joe Louis leans against the
ropes in 1942 while taking a break from pre-fight
training at Greenwood Lake, New York. Learning
from Jack Johnson's woes, Louis adopted a less con-
frontational style as the humble champion. Louis,
who held the heavyweight crown longer than any
other fighter, won the hearts and minds of patriotic
Americans by defeating Max Schmeling with a dramatic first-round knockout in a return bout in 1938.
Frank Sinatra eulogized the Champ and helped pay
for Louis's funeral on April 18, 1981, attended by 2,500
mourners to celebrate their hero, who started work on
an Alabama cotton field and carried a nation's hopes
on his shoulders. Photograph by Carl Van Vechten
(Library of Congress).

Sugar Ray Robinson

In the first draft of this
book, the man many pundits
identify as the greatest fighter,
pound for pound, did not
appear. Prodded by an astute
first reader, I realized my error
of omission and those of more
prominent sports historians
like Brad Herzog and Richard
O. Davies. Bert Sugar, Kenneth
Shropshire, Dave Anderson,
Don Dunphy, Pete Hamill, Ira Berkow, Will Haygood, and Muhammad Ali, however, knew better. Unlike Joe Louis, Kenneth Shropshire observed, Sugar was "flamboyant, audacious…like Johnson, but without his hostile, provocative edge." He gave
the press "a good story."[30]

That good story began in Alley, Georgia, on May 3, 1921, where and when
Walker Smith, Jr., was born. Like the family of Joe Louis, the Smiths moved to
Detroit, Michigan, as part of the "Great Migration" following World War I. Economic opportunity beckoned. A former farmer, Walker Smith, Sr., worked two jobs
to support his wife and three children. After his parents separated when he was 11,
Walker Jr. moved with his mom and two older sisters first to a poor section—"Hell's
Kitchen"—on Manhattan's West Side and subsequently to Harlem. In order to qualify for an AAU tournament at age 15, Walker borrowed a birth certificate along with
a membership card belonging to a friend named Ray Robinson. The "Sugar" epithet was added when his mentor at the Salem Crescent Gym and future manager
George Gainford praised his "sweet" style of boxing in 1939. Rather than dancing in
Times Square for money or hanging out with a gang for kicks, Ray—prodded by his
mother—honed his boxing skills at the Salem Methodist Episcopal Church under

the aegis of Mr. Gainford. The newly minted Sugar Ray Robinson liked the sound of his name and kept it.[31]

As a Golden Glove competitor, Ray won the New York featherweight title in 1939 and the lightweight crown in 1940, turning professional at age 19. After he turned pro, Robinson rang up 40 consecutive victories, including 29 knockouts.[32] His first defeat came at the hands of Jake LaMotta, but he would avenge this loss three months later and five more times during his stellar career although "the Raging Bull" outweighed him by more than 10 pounds. LaMotta joked: "I fought Sugar Ray so often, I almost got diabetes." He later added to his comedy routine another quip. After being dethroned as middleweight champ, LaMotta remarked: "If the referee held up another 30 more seconds, Sugar Ray would have collapsed from hitting me."[33]

Robinson was drafted into the United States Army on February 27, 1943, linking up with former Detroit neighbor Joe Louis. This dynamic duo became a team during World War II, entertaining troops with boxing exhibitions. Unlike Ali, they supported the war effort—up to a point. When they encountered racism at a segregated air force base in Mississippi—Black soldiers were barred from their exhibition—Louis and Robinson balked. And a commanding general honored their protest and prevented a mini-rebellion.[34] In another incident at Alabama's Camp Siebert, 600,000 troops gathered before departing for Europe. When Joe entered a telephone booth reserved for whites, an irate MP poked Louis in the ribs with a "billy club." Refusing to accommodate the bigot, Louis questioned the man. Losing it, the MP raised his club to strike the heavyweight champion, whereupon Robinson jumped into the fray, choking and biting the offender. Other MPs separated the brawlers. Realizing that the intended victim was Joe Lois, they froze. "Call the lieutenant!" one panicky policeman bellowed. Taken to a jailhouse because Robinson had assaulted an MP, they were released by a colonel who bawled out the bullies. At the colonel's behest, Louis and Robinson rode through the streets in an open car to show that they were unbeaten and to prevent a riot.[35] These incidents may have contributed to Robinson's mysterious disappearance from military duty.

Still shrouded in mystery is an incident about which Robinson refused to offer a detailed description. A few facts are known. Robinson fell down a flight of stairs at Brooklyn's Fort Hamilton barracks. A week later, suffering from an attack of amnesia, Sugar Ray awoke in Staten Island's Halloran General Hospital. A person had found him on a city street. An EEG examination revealed a post-traumatic cerebral disturbance, comparable to an attack of epilepsy. Considering the many fights that Robinson had already engaged in, a concussion could be a likely cause of this trauma. During this period, Robinson's military unit had shipped out to Europe. Did Robinson deliberately go AWOL, as some critics (e.g., the vitriolic sportswriter Dan Parker) charged? Other critics called him a deserter and a coward. Whatever the cause, Ray Robinson received an honorable discharge on June 3, 1944.[36]

Robinson returned to the boxing arena. Unwilling to make a Faustian bargain with mob-controlled promoters, Robinson was denied a legitimate shot at title bouts, even though he defeated former and future welterweight champions Fritzie Zivic and Marty Servo. Finally, he got his chance and defeated Tommy Bell in a

15-round decision for the title in 1946. Before his first defense against Jimmy Doyle, he had a premonition that he would kill his opponent. Reluctant to fight, Sugar Ray consulted a priest who approved the fight. Knocked out in the eighth round, Doyle never regained consciousness from brain injuries and died the following day, traumatizing Robinson. Seeking atonement, Robinson donated 50 percent of his purse to Doyle's mother in order to honor her son's wish to buy her a house. At the coroner's inquest, asked if he intended to get Doyle in trouble, Ray candidly remarked about the brutal business of boxing: "Mister it's my business to get him in trouble."[37] From 1943 to 1951, Robinson racked up a 91-fight winning streak when he decided to move up to the next weight division in quest of another title. Unable to hold two titles simultaneously like his idol Henry Armstrong, who had acquired three to the dismay of mobbed-up promoters who applied a new rule to bar that practice, Robinson vacated the welterweight belt and went after an old foe, Jake LaMotta.

All of their prior fights were closely contested. Robinson had added incentives for winning decisively. The middleweight title was up for grabs. *New York Times* sportswriter James P. Dawson wrote a vivid account of Robinson's sweet revenge. Unlike his five previous bouts with "The Bronx Bull," Sugar Ray "battered" his opponent "into submission" in the 13th round. Because LaMotta refused to go down, Referee Frank Secora stopped the fight, saving Jake's life (preventing another Jimmy Doyle–like demise) and his pride. Held on Valentine's Day, 1951, this fight attracted 14,802 paying customers, grossing $180,619.[38] Not only did Sugar Ray cop the middleweight crown from frequent foe LaMotta, but he also gained a measure of revenge for French hero Marcel Cerdan, who had lost his title to the "Bronx Bull" in a fierce brawl in Detroit on June 16, 1949, and his life on October 28, 1949, in a plane crash on the way to America for a return bout.[39]

As an American in Paris, Robinson became a conquering hero when he arrived on November 18, 1950. He won two fights within a month, winning both by technical knockouts. In its January 1, 1951, issue, *Time* magazine captured the rapture of French journalists as they watched Ray Robinson and his nine-person entourage entering the Hotel Claridge on the Champs-Élysées. They followed him strolling along this famous boulevard, frequenting shops, practicing his French, and eyeing the girls who danced at the Lido. Robinson inspired a new confection of sweet rice: in his honor, they were called "Sugar Cakes."[40]

After defeating Jake LaMotta, Robinson enjoyed a second tour of Europe in 1951. He returned to the Hotel Claridge again, this time with both more stuff—32 trunks, 15 suitcases, three radio sets, 140 jazz records, six punching bags, 10 pairs of boxing gloves—and a posse of 14 (or 17, depending on your source): wife, trainer, cornermen, friends, barber, cook, chauffeur, masseuse, golf instructor, "gofers," a bodyguard, plus a 4′6″ dwarf named Jimmy Kapoura, an interpreter who knew five languages. His wardrobe consisted of 12 lightweight business suits, five overcoats, and 100 neckties. At the invitation of and cost to his European promoter Charlie Michaelis, Robinson also brought along his purple-pink Cadillac automobile.[41]

Mobbed, autographed, and photographed by Gordon Parks, Ray Robinson had a police escort as he drove his Cadillac on the Champs Élysées to cheering crowds. Paris had always been hospitable to Blacks who visited or migrated to their beloved

"City of Lights." During his 1939 stay in Paris, Edwin "Duke" Ellington enjoyed his freedom and caviar. Josephine Baker, Richard Wright, and James Baldwin also shared that felicitous experience. Robinson befriended Maurice Chevalier and Georges Carpentier. At a charity event, he spoke briefly in French and gave President Vincent Auriol's wife a $10,000 check from the Damon Runyon Cancer Foundation to a comparable French fund to combat cancer. Then, he planted a double kiss on each cheek of France's First Lady. Subsequently, after defeating the French welterweight champion, Kid Marcel, Robinson donated purse money from the fight to the French cancer fund. He raised three million francs for retired actors at the Palais de Chaillot displaying talent as a drummer and tap dancer. He earned a new epithet: "*Le Sucre Merveilleux*" or "Marvelous Sugar."[42]

Robinson fought in Belgium, Germany, Italy, and Britain. *Time* magazine put Sugar Ray on its June 25, 1951, cover in anticipation of a title fight with Randy Turpin in Britain. Indifferent to rigorous training, Robinson entered the bout as a heavy favorite, but his opponent pulled off a major upset by decision in 15 rounds. Insouciantly, Sugar Ray returned for rest and relaxation in Paris and on the French Riviera before returning to America for a rematch at New York City's Polo Grounds. Better prepared, Robinson was ahead on points until a cut above his left eye, probably caused by a head-butt in their first fight, bled profusely. Realizing the danger, Robinson aggressively pursued the aggressor. With a hard right, he decked Turpin. The muscular British boxer rose, vulnerable to Robison's heavy artillery. Mercilessly battered, helpless on the ropes, Turpin was saved by referee Ruby Goldstein's intervention, declaring a technical knockout with eight seconds remaining in round 10.[43]

Eager to emulate his idol Henry Armstrong, who captured titles in three different weight divisions, Ray Robinson challenged light heavyweight champion Joey Maxim, who accepted. Slated for Yankee Stadium on June 23, 1952, the fight was postponed due to a heavy rainstorm until June 25, one of the hottest days in New York City history. Maxim outweighed Robinson by 18 pounds; Robinson had superior skill. The stifling heat—105 degrees under the lights—knocked out the referee in the 10th round and exhausted Robinson in rounds 11, 12, and 13. Ahead on points, winning 10 rounds, Sugar Ray could not continue; he had lost 16 pounds and the quest for a third title. A die-hard Robinson fan, I heard the fight on the radio and moaned for my fallen idol. A delirious Robinson, drenched in a life-saving cold shower, shouted, "I'm not crazy! You may think I am, but God beat me tonight!"[44]

After this disappointing loss, snatched from the jaws of victory, Robinson also had a 22-month hiatus from boxing to take a turn in show business as a tap dancer. He returned to the ring to reclaim his middleweight title after six warm-up bouts in a what would become a recurrent pattern, knocking out Carl "Bobo" Olson in the second round on December 9, 1955. Two years later he lost the title to Gene Fullmer, only to regain the lost crown four months later with a fifth round knockout. He lost the title a third time to Carmen Basilio in a 15-round brawl and reclaimed the title in another brawl that lasted 15 rounds in 1958. By this time, at age 37, Robinson's once magnificent skills had eroded. When he fought a journeyman Paul Pender in 1960, the bookies pegged Robinson four to one to win. The aging Robinson tired in the last five rounds giving the younger (by nine years) Pender the edge in a split decision 148–142 and 147–138, while Robinson led one card by a vote of 146 to 122. To the surprise of many, Pender won the rematch, also in a split decision. Prudently, Pender retired while still champion in 1963. As for Sugar Ray, he continued to fight until 1965 because—having blown $4 million—Robinson needed the money. When cream puff puncher (according to Pete Hamill) Joe Archer beat the boxer, once proclaimed the best boxer pound for pound in November 1965, Ray Robinson hung up his gloves.[45]

In retirement, though broke, Robinson continued to reap honors. Madison Square Garden held a Sugar Ray Robinson Night on December 10, 1965. Given a trophy, he had no place to rest it on in his sparsely furnished Manhattan apartment on Riverside Drive. Two years later, Robinson was inducted into *Ring* magazine's Hall of Fame. Well-connected friends found acting roles for him in film and on TV in the lean years that followed. Sugar Ray and his third wife, Millie, moved to Los Angeles,

"Sugar Ray" Robinson, né Walker Smith, Jr., is shown here in what is believed to be his last fight at Madison Square Garden, February 1962. The only fighter who could knock out an opponent while back-pedaling, a highly touted amateur, he went on to become one of the greatest boxers, pound for pound, of all time, capturing both welterweight and middleweight titles, the latter a record five times. Robinson retired in 1965 with a record of 173 wins, 19 losses, and six draws. Photograph by Orlando Fernandez of the *New York World-Telegram* (Library of Congress).

where he established a youth foundation for inner-city youngsters, which proved beneficial to future star athletes like Florence Griffith Joyner and Freeman McNeil. Even after his death in the "cruelest month," on April 12, 1989, due to diabetes and Alzheimer's disease, Robinson was honored posthumously with induction into the International Boxing Hall of Fame.

In a 1998 documentary, author Jack Newfield discussed Sugar Ray Robinson's "dark side." Far from perfect, Robinson's flaws were revealed. He had sexual liaisons with multiple lady friends. When his second wife, Edna Mae, complained about these infidelities, he beat her. Their son, Ray Robinson, Jr., suggested that his mother's inability to bear more children resulted from his father's violent outbursts. He too suffered physical abuse as well as neglect from his famous father. Sadly, Ray Jr. told boxing writer Thomas Hauser,[46] "Dad would have three rooms in the Hotel Theresa where he kept his girls. And when he got caught, it precipitated violence. I think one of the reasons my mother had so many miscarriages was because of the abuse she suffered from my father. I can recall him hitting her on several occasions for no reason at all." Ronnie Smith, Robinson's son from his first marriage, which was annulled in 1939, recalled: "My dad was a dad to lots of children, except his own."[47] Another critic, Sam Lacey, the first Black Native American member of the Baseball Writers Association, did not mince words or mute displeasure over the famous fighter: "I have said many times that Sugar Ray Robinson was the greatest athlete in any given field I have had the pleasure of observing. I have also said that he can be one of the most disgusting figures one is compelled to meet in this business."[48] Boxing writer W.C. Heinz called Robinson "a great con man." Carmen Basilio, twice Ray's opponent for the middleweight crown, detested him as an arrogant S.O.B, primarily because Robinson ignored him at a meeting.[49]

So, given this score sheet, how do we assess Mr. Robinson? Hero or anti-hero? Perhaps both. His active libido and violent eruptions conjure up comparison with other outstanding athletes like Jim Brown, discussed later in this book. Many great figures in history suffer from hubris, beset with tragic flaws. Unlike Brown, who retired at the pinnacle of his game and went on to successful ventures after retirement, Robinson stayed in the ring too long and suffered physically, economically, and mentally. Yet how can one disregard the amazing record in the ring? Sugar Ray Robinson engaged in 202 bouts, winning 175, 109 by knockouts, drawing six times, and losing 19 times, mostly in the twilight of a once brilliant career.[50]

Biographers Will Haygood and Kenneth Shropshire, both keenly aware of Robison's flaws, conclude their balance sheet in favor of *Le Sucre Merveilleuse*. At his funeral on April 19, 1989, attended by 2,500 mourners, one of the early speakers, Mike Tyson, broke down and cried. Shropshire vividly captures the moment when Jesse Jackson, robed more like an Oxford don in academic regalia than a preacher, touched on Robinson's unique gifts. He noted the passing of that last celebrity of the "Magnificent Four": Jesse Owens, Joe Louis, Jackie Robinson, and now Sugar Ray Robinson. Listen[51]:

> Sugar, Mr. Personality, boxer, negotiator, actor, entrepreneur, pretty, sweet, tough. He was as authentic to America as jazz. Sugar Ray was an original art form. He took us beyond racism and fear. He wasn't just a boxer. Sugar took care of people; God will take care of Sugar.
>
> Champions win events. Heroes win people. Champions are of short duration—you can be stripped of champion stature. Heroes cannot be. Heroes are needed. They give us security and confidence. Sugar had charisma and special gifts from God.
>
> He was part of the American quilt. His patch in that quilt had nonnegotiable integrity.... He was born on the bottom, but he left on the top. He went from "guttermost" to "uppermost."

Kenneth Shropshire closes his excellent book with a nuanced evaluation of Mr. Robinson. True, Sugar Ray had trouble with women, money, and retirement, but he recognized the power of celebrity and its commodification. Minus the mob, knowing his star value, he made demands and negotiated contracts with promoters, opponents, and radio and TV executives, thus paving the way for athletes to follow. He does not serve as a role model like Jackie Robinson, Bill Russell, Hank Aaron, or LeBron James to be sure, but he provides cautionary life lessons for all athletes—white as well as black—rising to the top.[52]

Muhammad Ali

Bob Dylan heralded the start of a new era in 1963 with the apt song "The Times They Are a-Changing." Plagued by income tax woes and declining health, Joe Louis fell out of favor in the 1960s, a turbulent decade of "jangling discord" and generational conflict. Images collided in this decade with love beads, miniskirts, long-haired men, short-haired women, bombs in Birmingham, marches to Selma, setting sun in Alabama, rising sun in Japan. Out of these cultural collisions came a hero who was both black and beautiful, born Cassius Clay. In the wake of assassinations of the Kennedy brothers, Malcolm X, and Dr. King, our nation desperately needed heroes of uncommon clay. Heightened cynicism fed a renewed penchant for conspiracy theories. A popular culture author with an expertise in hero scholarship, Marshall Fishwick detected profound changes that spurred opposition to poverty, virginity, power elites, and apple pie. Even God became a target for cynics.[53] Sports historians Douglas A. Noverr and Larry E. Ziewacz dubbed this era "The Super Sixties," highlighting an that had entered common coinage preceding a plethora of nouns, including "super" rage against the establishment after the youthful president, who had pleaded for "super" sacrifice, had been assassinated.[54]

In the early sixties, a "super" bad dude occupied center stage in boxing when "Sonny" Liston demolished Floyd Patterson in first-round knockouts in 1962 and 1963. Rising as a counterforce, Cassius Clay, born in Louisville, Kentucky, on January 13, 1942. He grew up in a solid nuclear family: father, mother, and brother. With the support of an Irish policeman, he began to box seriously. In 1960, he won the light heavyweight gold medal at the Rome Olympics. A syndicate of smart investors in Louisville financed the young slugger's entry into the professional ranks. Clay rewarded their support with a string of 19 consecutive wins. Matched against the seemingly invincible and heavily favored "Big Bad" Sonny Liston, he scored a stunning seventh round technical knockout on February 24, 1964.

After this major or super upset, Clay announced his conversion to Islam, marked by a new name, Muhammad Ali. Sportswriters, broadcasters, and fellow fighters like former champ Floyd Patterson mocked this transformation in disbelief. Ignoring advice "to settle down and fly right," Ali remained defiant and unbeatable. A return bout with Sonny Liston resulted in a first round knockout from, as some ringsiders alleged, a phantom punch. In many subsequent fights Ali felled many opponents: Chuvalo, Cooper, London, Mildenberger, Williams, Terrell, Foley, and Patterson. Because former champ Patterson persisted in calling him Clay, Ali toyed with the hapless Floyd, prolonging the bout with "trash talk" and a merciless beating.[55]

Then, refusing to enter military service and the "Viet-Nam Quagmire," Ali alienated the establishment. In an unprecedented move, they—the New York State Athletic Commission and the World Boxing Association—dethroned Ali. Former champs Gene Tunney and Jack Dempsey branded him un–American.[56] An elderly white federal judge in Houston, Texas, sentenced Ali to five years in prison and fined him $10,000. Although he remained out of jail pending appeals, he was denied the right to box and his passport was revoked. Joyce Carol Oates wrote about Ali in *ESPN Sports Century*, inviting comparison with Charlie Chaplin and

Paul Robeson, earlier victims of persecution.[57] Like Joseph Campbell's 1,000-faced mythical hero, Ali went into exile, thereby losing everything—title, income, freedom, face—except his rebellious, defiant, aggressive principles. Sports historian David Wiggins illuminates Ali's predicament. In departing from the traditional model of American hero, Ali eschewed "aw shucks" humility. From the outset of his career, Muhammad was flamboyant, immodest, and defiantly confident. As writers Robert Lipsyte and Jonathan Eig have demonstrated, Ali's libido, prior to fights, was never curtailed. Indeed, he refused to put his "soul on ice" like Jake LaMotta while training. Whereas other fighters remained celibate during "Lent for Boxers" to harvest more testosterone, Ali flaunted his multiple assignations with wives and mistresses.[58]

Exalting in his blackness, Ali exposed American hypocrisy on race. At this critical juncture in exile, Muhammad opted for avoidance as well as aggression. Not a complete separatist despite his ties to Elijah Muhammad and sons, Ali believed in possibilities. Perhaps aware of his own deficits as a functional illiterate, he overcompensated. Black Panther co-founder Eldridge Cleaver touted Ali as a genuine revolutionary. Agnostic on this assertion, I think it more accurate to view Ali as a catalyst for the athletic revolt that followed culminating in the attempted Olympic boycott in 1968.

Exiled involuntarily, Ali returned to the ring. Beaten by Frazier and Norton, he was given little chance to dethrone the then svelte gladiator George Foreman. Ten years after the triumph over Sonny Liston and seven years after yielding the title, he went to Zaire in search of redemption. Using a brilliant but high-risk strategy—the fabled rope-a-dope—Ali conserved his energy while Foreman spent his. Aware that Foreman was a bully, he started the fight with an aggressive attack rather than his signature dance. He spent most of the first six rounds fending off Foreman's attempted assault while resting on the ropes. Duped into exhaustion, Foreman succumbed to a barrage of blows in the seventh round. As Ali hovered over the fallen champ, an ebullient, enraptured Howard Cosell boomed out Bob Dylan's apt song "Forever Young."

Ali became legend. Children chanted

Muhammad Ali in 1967. As Cassius Clay, he gained prominence by winning the light-heavyweight title in the 1960 Rome Olympiad. After turning pro, he defeated the heavily favored incumbent, Sonny Liston, for the heavyweight title in 1964. Following his triumph, Clay converted to Islam and acquired a new moniker, Muhammad Ali. When he refused to enter the U.S. Army to fight in Vietnam, he was dethroned, put on trial, convicted, and given a prison sentence. Photograph by Ira Rosenberg (Library of Congress).

his name and pundits proclaimed his fame. And his many enemies lapsed into silence. Sportswriter Maury Allen hoisted Ali to the mountaintop of sports giants alongside Joe Louis, Joe DiMaggio, Jackie Robinson, Ted Williams, Jackie Robinson, and Bill Russell.[59] Ali, however, never lost his mass appeal or common touch. I vividly remember greeting him on Seventh Avenue in 1973 after teaching an evening class. Clad in a white Jay Gatsby suit with his trainer/advisor Drew "Bundini" Brown and entourage in tow, several steps behind, smiling, shaking hands, exuding charisma, he glided up towards me and illuminated the dark streets with his incandescent presence. Ace reporter Jimmy Cannon identified him with the decade that defined America. The author and would-be athlete hailed this electrifying bronze god who generated such wonderful powers. Extremely photogenic, he loved people, and the camera loved him in return.[60] He drew strength from people—all people from the high and mighty to the lowliest autograph seeker.

How does one pin him down? Journalist Jack Newfield saw him as man-child, con man, entertainer, poet, draft-dodger, rebel evangelist, champion. Full of contradictions like Walt Whitman's everyman, he contained multitudes. He also had exquisite timing. In 1974, President Nixon resigned in disgrace. In that same year, Ali returned to grace. Resilient, a veritable phoenix, he later came back in triumph to avenge prior losses to Frazier, Norton, and Spinks. Immodestly but arguably accurately, Ali rated the greatest champions. He placed himself first with Jack Johnson in second place, and Joe Louis number three.[61]

Perceptions differ. Race continues to plague the American collective conscience. Ali denigrated Joe Frazier and other "uglies." Ali alienated white fans, this writer included, with braggadocio and arrogance. He violated the traditional canon of heroic behavior, taunting his opponents, flaunting his gifts. As people became aware of the "better angels" of Ali's nature, they seemed to view him in a different light. Because of Ali, Reggie Jackson swelled with race pride. Unlike Jack Johnson, Ali preferred Black companions, male as well as female. He gloried in his blackness. While Joe Louis reacted to history, Muhammad Ali made history. As author Jeffrey Sammons observed, he chose mastery over drift. He changed his name (if not legally). He converted to Islam. He opposed the war in Vietnam. Defiantly Black, he stood up for his beliefs.[62] Clearly, Ali avoided the total isolation of Jack Johnson and the premature canonization of Joe Louis. He could not—did not—break away. A true believer in American possibility, Ali embodied Black heroism as he blazed a unique path to glory.[63]

Preeminent anthropologist Claude Levi-Strauss argued that popular hero myths serve to resolve unwelcome contradictions in order to restore equilibrium. In this vital task, the hero functions as healer, savior, deliverer, scapegoat, and quester. Heroes mediate among competing forces in society with which they must also synchronize.[64] In the Jim Crow era, Black hero/leaders had to embody role models who were both attractive and non-threatening. Hence, they experienced the constraints of accommodation and the temptations of avoidance. Such behavior was bound to alienate younger blacks as Booker T. Washington had pricked W.E.B. DuBois. World War II erected a door of opportunity through which Joe Louis and Jackie Robinson ran.

Two African American pioneers, Muhammad Ali and Rosa Parks, engage in friendly discourse in 1994. The two fought the good fight in two different arenas—transportation and boxing—with their eyes firmly fixed on the prize: civil rights, social justice, and splendor in the ring we call America (Library of Congress).

Indeed, it was Muhammad Ali who synthesized the operative modes of "Triple A" behavior, combining—at different stages of his amazing career—acceptance, avoidance, and aggression.[65] In addition to his role as magnificent fighter, Ali was mensch for all seasons. When he learned from a telecast that a Jewish center for handicapped seniors faced termination, he donated $100,000 on December 2, 1975. Author Oates noted that Ali, "once an icon-breaker," became an "American icon" known throughout the world, a brand name symbolizing "'success.'"[66] A hero for the best reasons, he spearheaded the revolt of Black athletes. In that surge for social justice coupled with self-respect, he achieved apotheosis. Like his heroic precursors, he was, to echo philosopher Friedrich Nietzsche, "a fighter against his times." Quoting Ali, President Obama eulogized this ultimate fighter[67]:

"I am America, I am the part you won't recognize. But get used to me—black, confident, cocky; my name, not yours; my religion, not yours; my goals, my own. Get used to me." That's the Ali I came to know as I came of age—not just as skilled a poet on the mic as he was a fighter in the ring, but a man who fought for us. He stood with King and Mandela; stood up when it was hard; spoke out when others wouldn't. His fight outside the ring cost him his title and his public standing. It would earn him enemies on the left and the right, make him reviled, and nearly send him to jail, but Ali stood his ground. And his victory helped us get used to the America we recognize today.

SECTION TWO

TRACK AND FIELD

2

Jesse Owens, Harrison Dillard and Mal Whitfield, and Rafer Johnson

Like boxing, track and field competition has a long historical tradition in the pre–Columbian world, harking back to ancient civilizations. Unlike boxing, however, track and field did not provide clear professional outlets for socio-economic mobility. Consequently, underprivileged Americans, recent immigrants, and minority groups gravitated to boxing, while track and field competitors got caught up in the quest for national pride and personal glory after the modern Olympics resumed in 1896, thanks largely to the efforts of Baron De Coubertin. Defeated by Germany, the baron's beloved France desperately needed a face-lift. Through athletic competition, he believed that an Olympic revival could restore pride, promote patriotism, and gain prestige trough the medium of sports. Inspired by a heady mix of French revival, pan-Hellenism, muscular Christianity, and a desire for international accord, Coubertin soldiered on.[1]

Other countries followed that trajectory. Germany is a good as well as bad example. As author Richard Mandel has demonstrated, Adolf Hitler used the Berlin Olympics to gain legitimacy for his heinous Fascist regime, to the detriment of world peace. Successful in that quest, Hitler miscalculated the impact of Jesse Owens and fellow Black athletes on destroying the myth of Aryan supremacy. Sadly, sprinter Eddie Tolan, who had competed successfully in the 1932 Olympics, did not experience a triumphant return befitting a sports hero as Harry Levette acidly lamented in "Eddie Tolan Is the Fastest Human—But":

> He can run like hell, but—he's a nigger right on.
> He wins honor for America but nothing for himself.
> He must plot right, passing up eating places while he's hungry.
> Begging for somebody to take his part so he can inch along.
> The better he does the worse it hurts.
> Like Cullen, he can exclaim: "I who have burned my hands upon a star."[2]

Mack Robinson, Jackie's older brother, won a silver medal in the 1936 Olympics in the 200-meter race. Upon his return to Pasadena from Oregon University in 1938, Mack was rewarded with a job as a street cleaner. Defiantly, Mr. Robinson wore his Olympic jacket while sanitizing the streets. And he lost that job along with all other Black workers, fired by the city government in retaliation to an order by a judge that called for the integration of local public swimming pools.[3]

28

African American women, trailing their male counterparts, began engaging in competitive sports in the 1920s. Confronting stereotypes regarding femininity, sexuality, class, and race, they had a late start. Historically, harking back to the ancient Greeks, males claimed sports as their domain. Supported by their own segregated communities and religious organizations, Black women entered the sporting arena for individual as well as collective achievement. They had to overcome working-class and gender constraints in a racially charged environment. Opportunities for mobility through sports through intercollegiate competition, two "hot" wars plus a "cold" one, political engagement, and civil rights activism—all contributed to salutary change throughout the twentieth century. Author Jennifer H. Lansbury charts that dramatic progress in her informative book.[4] Of particular relevance is her chapter on Alice Coachman where she cogently argues for this almost forgotten figure with these trenchant words[5]:

> Coachman was the first African American female athlete of national and international fame to compete routinely against white women, and her career was seminal for two different reasons. On the one hand, her career showed that a black woman track athlete celebrated by white American society was a distinct possibility. It also demonstrated, on the other, that black women athletes would push back when confronted with the stereotypes of white society.

Of course, as the first female athlete to win gold, taking top honors for the high jump in the 1948 London Olympics, Coachman earned her spurs as a hero.

Later, as this section will show, African American athletes played a critical role in Olympic competition with the Soviets during the Cold War with a more positive outcome for both the country and its Black citizenry. In addition, women made their indelible mark in sports history by way of track and field competition on the world stage. They too performed as surrogate warrior in the Cold War waged largely in arenas and stadiums devoted to sports. In a real sense, these tightly contested events may have prevented "hot" wars. To put a different spin on Carl von Clausewitz's famous dictum, sports is "merely a continuation of politics by other means."

One unsung hero, Fred Thompson, deserves mention. Like other subjects in this book, Fred, aged five, was raised by an aunt when his parents broke up. A product of Brooklyn public schools and higher education in Manhattan and Queens, Thompson became a successful lawyer, rising to assistant state attorney general. I met him through a mutual friend, Ernie Brod, when he worked as a lawyer for the Federal Trade Commission. Fred Thompson gave up a lucrative law practice in 1974 to head the Colgate Women's Games. He also founded, funded, and coached the Atoms Track Club in Brooklyn's Bedford Stuyvesant community center, which became a refuge for young, poor women from broken homes. He inspired many to succeed in track and field. In its first 15 years, "the club produced 50 college graduates," author Bernard D. McFadden observed. "They became teachers. Lawyers, nurses, psychologists, entrepreneurs—and mothers."[6] A bachelor with no biological children of his own, Fred Thompson became a father figure for a multitude of young women—including one devoted protégé, Lorna Forde, who cared for him in his home as the end approached. Fred Thompson was truly a man for all seasons.

Jesse Owens

Both Jesse Owens and Joe Louis chose to compete in individual rather than team sports where segregation limited recognition for Blacks. Biographer William J. Baker argues that "America's black community fixed its attention on both men, viewing them as leaders on the road to a new era of black achievement and recognition."[7] Whites seemed indifferent to Negro intellectuals and artists. Cerebral attainments always played second fiddle in a culture suffused, as Richard Hofstadter acidly observed, with anti-intellectualism. Therefore, the athletic arena would prove pivotal in gaining social acceptance. This put a tremendous burden on athletes as agents of self-esteem and group confidence. Editorials in the Negro press called for Black heroes.[8] Owens himself had idolized two heroes: one Black, the other white. Ironically, Charlie Paddock, the white role model, was a world-class athlete, while Booker T. Washington, his black counterpart in Owens's pantheon, was an educator. Thus, at age 15, Jesse fixed on athletics and hard work as his path to glory. Separation or avoidance in the Garvey mold did not appeal. Neither did the militancy or aggressive mode of W.E.B. DuBois. Owens opted for the pragmatic road of patience and accommodation.[9]

If 1936 proved glorious for Owens, it was a disaster for Louis. In a stunning upset, the "Brown Bomber" fell at Yankee Stadium, gunned down by the German heavyweight with the thick eyebrows, Max Schmeling. This left Jesse Owens holding the baton of his people's hopes. Headed for the Berlin Olympics, Owens and his fellow athletes girded for revenge.[10] At the Olympic Village, the Nazis paraded Schmeling around as a Teutonic knight/Aryan superman.

The Olympics opened on August 1 after Italy had occupied Ethiopia at the behest of that sawdust Caesar, Benito Mussolini. The Nazis had marched into the Rhineland, the Japanese into Manchuria; Franco had returned to Spain. Fascism seemed invincible all over as democracies crumbled. Led by Fascist sympathizer Avery Brundage, American officials spurned pleas to boycott the Berlin Olympics. The United States fielded a team of 66 athletes, including 10 (or 18) Blacks.[11] The Nazis scorned the Americans for relying on the "black auxiliaries" who won six of eleven individual gold medals.

Jesse Owens dominated the 1936 Olympiad. On August 3, he drew the inside lane for the 100-meter finals. With a burst of speed, Owens hit the tape at 10.3 seconds, winning the first of four gold medals. In the long jump, he faced elimination after two efforts. On the final try, he went past 25 feet to qualify. On the last jump in the medal competition, Owens set a new Olympic record with a leap of 26 feet 5¼ inches for his second gold. Arthur Daley described Jesse "as the phenomenon from Ohio State [who] rocketed to his third crown, taking the 200 meters in world and Olympic record time [20.7 seconds]."[12]

The last medal that Owens won was tainted by controversy. Wishing to placate Hitler, Avery Brundage persuaded American officials to replace Marty Glickman and Sam Stoller, two Jews, with Jesse Owens and Ralph Metcalfe, two Blacks. Till the day he died, Glickman, who became one of America's preeminent sportscasters, contended that Brundage and Coach Cromwell colluded in this move because they both belonged to the pro–Nazi America First Committee.[13] Whatever the motives, the Owens-Metcalfe-Draper-Wycoff 400-meter relay team set a new world record of

39.8 seconds. Jesse Owens went home with four gold medals, a conquering hero. He had driven four spikes into the myth of the master race and Nazi invincibility.

Ironically, lynching claimed 26 Black lives in the United States from 1935 to 1936. Owens remained a symbol of a dream deferred. He failed to challenge the caste system. Sadly, Owens never graduated from Ohio State. To be sure, he derived material benefits from his athletic prowess, but he also was pressed into carnival exhibitions in which he raced against professional baseball players and, worse, horses. Like Joe Louis, Jesse Owens tried to set a good example. He persisted in preaching the pieties of success made in America. True to the spirit of Booker T. Washington, he urged patience and accommodation. When Professor Harry Edwards organized a boycott of the 1968 Olympics, Owens labored mightily to thwart this effort. Though he received respect because of his glorious records and advanced age, Owens also became the target of snickers when he tried to play the race card in 1968.[14]

At twilight time, Jesse Owens was frequently on the run. Biographer Baker chronicles his efforts to cope with mid-life crisis: frenetic globe-trotting, endless lecture tours, frantic womanizing, embroidered remembrance of 1936, and heavy cigarette smoking that no

Jesse Owens sprints for gold in the 200-meter race at the1936 Berlin Olympics. In garnering four gold medals, a first for an American athlete, Owens destroyed Hitler's myth of Aryan supremacy. Unwilling to go to Sweden after his triumph in Berlin, Owens was punished by Avery Brundage, head of the American Olympic committee, which abruptly ended his amateur career. *Sport* magazine ranked Owens in the top five. President Ford awarded Jesse Owens the Presidential Medal of Freedom in 1976. A heavy cigarette smoker, Owens developed a fatal case of lung cancer. He died at age 66 on March 31, 1980 (Library of Congress).

doubt contributed to his fatal lung cancer.[15] A true believer, Owens defended a system that had experienced radical change during World War II leaving him frozen in time professing a faith, revived by President Reagan, that did not quite mesh with reality.

Harrison Dillard and Mal Whitfield

No trophies were displayed in the dining room.[16] They were packed away. Dillard comments: "I always saw sports as a way to better myself through education and

I worked at that." Writing in the *Cleveland Press* about Owens after he died in 1980, Dillard recalled how he snuck in to watch Jesse Owens run and jump. "He was lean and lithe, with skin the color of coffee and cream. I watched wide-eyed as he glided up to the bar and leaped and slid over it easily in the effortless manner that has never been equaled to this day."[17] Three years later, Jesse Owens was starring in Berlin. When he returned, young Harrison at age 13 cheered for Jesse as he passed in an open car. Jesse waved and said, "Hi."

William Harrison "Bones" Dillard was born, one of four children, in Cleveland on July 8, 1923. His parents were sharecroppers who moved to Cleveland during "The Great Migration." His father worked in construction; his mother was a housemaid. Harrison, as he preferred to be called, had rickets as a child. At age 10, he weighed only 50 pounds; hence, his nickname "Bones." As a child, he jumped over abandoned old car seats in the streets to practice hurdling.[18] Inspired by Jesse Owens, he gravitated to track and attended the same Eastern Technical High School. Owens subsequently persuaded Dillard to become a hurdler and gave him a pair of track shoes in 1941.[19] Dillard won Ohio's state titles in high hurdles and track, both at 100 yards.

After high school, Dillard earned a scholarship to Baldwin-Wallace College, Ohio, in 1941. At 5'10" and 157 pounds, he trained hard and majored in economics. War interrupted his studies. Harrison entered the U.S. Army with the 92nd Infantry Division, also known as the "Buffalo Soldier," for 32 months. As part of a segregated force, he landed in Italy in 1944. He served in major combat duty for seven months. Fighting for a good cause, he was proud to be an African American in a Black outfit. Unfortunately, white soldiers incited hatred and libel, referring to the Black soldiers as thieves and rapists. Susceptible to these canards, Italians called Dillard's group "evil black soldiers" (*soldati neri cattivo*) or, as he recalled in his 2012 autobiography, *Bones*. He learned about survival, hatred, and triumph. Shortly after the war ended, Harrison ran four races in an Army track meet in Frankfurt, Germany, with General George Patton in attendance. In the interview with Daniel McGraw, Harrison Dillard admitted to being "scared shitless." Nevertheless, he went on to win four gold medals in the 200-meter dash, relay, and high and low hurdles. Not given to effusive praise, General Patton made an exception when he proclaimed, "He's the best god damned athlete I've ever seen."[20]

Dillard went back to college and won 82 consecutive races. He trained in the snow or in the women's gym. The streak ended when, in an Olympic trial run in 1948, Dillard banged his foot into four of seven hurdles and stopped at the eighth hurdle. Thus, Harrison failed to make the USA Olympic squad in his forte, the hurdles. Resilient and resolute, he trained for the 100-meter dash. In the trials, he managed a third place. Expected to finish fifth, he literally nosed out favorite Barney Ewell at 10.3 seconds in the first photo finish in Olympic history. He won a second gold as the third leg of the 400-meter relay. No parade greeted Harrison Dillard when he returned from his London triumph, just a pat on the back.

Eventually, Dillard broke 11 world and Olympic records plus copping 14 titles in national competitions. Dillard regained redemption in 1952. At Helsinki that year, Harrison won two gold medals, taking the 100-meter high hurdles and running the second leg of the 400-meter relay in 40.1 seconds, tying his mentor Jesse Owens for a (then) record of four gold medals.[21] In 1953, Harrison Dillard participated in the Maccabi Games and won gold one more time. The 1955 Sullivan Award was conferred on Harrison Dillard one year after his fellow Olympian from Ohio, Mal Whitfield, won that award.

Are athletes heroes? Responding to this question, the basic theme of this book, Dillard expressed doubts when compared to doctors, teachers, and great economists. But he added: "Jesse Owens was a hero because he performed his athletic feats in circumstances where they were important by throwing the lie in Hitler's face and right in his house. Jesse knew he was representing a way of thinking, of freedom and equality and he knew he had to perform at those 1936 games to back that up and he did."[22]

And Harrison Dillard did it in his own way in 1948 and 1952. Towards the end of Dillard's track career, Cleveland Indian owner Bill Veeck hired him to do public relations for his team and provided time off to train for the '52 Olympics. John Carlos attributed Dillard's "'incredible success' to hard work," an opinion echoed by his longtime friend Ted Theodore, who stated emphatically: "He outworked everybody."[23] Although he failed to qualify for the 1956 Olympics, he was a success in his life after athletics. Dillard sold life insurance, served as director of a Cleveland radio station, wrote a sports column for the *Cleveland Press* in the 1970s, and served as business manager for the Cleveland public schools for 26 years, retiring in 1993. He was also a track advisor and a spring-training instructor for the Yankees and Indians, coaching players on running. A family man to the end, Dillard lived with his wife Joy for more than 50 years and then, after her death in 2009, with his daughter Terri and granddaughter Izmailia until his death in 2019 at the age of 96. Harrison Dillard exemplified the "good life," and as Frank Litsky concluded in his obituary, "Dillard enjoyed being a role model."[24]

Born on October 11, 1924, in Bay City, Texas, "Marvelous" Mal Whitfield moved to Los Angeles with his family at age four, when his dad died. After his mom died eight years later, he went to live with his sister Betty. In 1932, he snuck into the Los Angeles Coliseum to watch Eddie Tolan defeat Ralph Metcalfe in the 100-meter race. That event inspired young Mal to run in a future Olympiad, as Whitfield recalled in a *Sports Illustrated* article. After graduation from Thomas Jefferson High School in 1943, he joined the air force as part of the celebrated but segregated Tuskegee Airmen, 100th Fighter Squadron of Group 332. After the war, Whitfield stayed in the service while attending Ohio State University in 1946. Every morning he woke up at 5:00 a.m. and went to bed at 12:30 a.m. Active during the Korean War, he flew 27 bombing missions while training in track as well, running on runways with a .45-caliber strapped to his side.[25] As a staff sergeant, he competed in the London Olympics of 1948, where he set an Olympic record when he won the gold medal at 1 minute and 49.2 seconds, minus the sidearm. Whitfield struck gold again in the 800-meter relay race. Four years later at Helsinki, he won gold in the 800 again but settled for silver in the relay. At 6'2" and 165 pounds, Mal raced with blazing speed. Because his chief rival, Arthur Wint, smoked cigarettes and drank whiskey, Whitfield had the edge.

Whitfield ultimately set six records. I witnessed one of these triumphs from the balcony of Madison Square Garden during the Millrose Games in New York

City. For 50 cents and a General Organization (GO) card, public school students were entitled to this true bargain for hockey and basketball games too. Continuing to rack up wins in his middle-distance races, Whitfield earned the moniker "Marvelous Mal." Honorably discharged in 1952, Whitfield completed his degree at California State, Los Angeles. In 1953, Whitfield became the first African American to receive the prestigious Sullivan Award as our country's outstanding amateur athlete.[26] Mal Whitfield was inducted into the Track and Field Hall of Fame in 1974 and the USA Olympic Hall of Fame in 1988.

In 1955, he became a "good will ambassador." While working for the State Department, he visited 130 countries. After his athletic career, Whitfield promoted sports and physical education in Europe, Africa, and the Middle East for the United States Information Agency. He coached neophyte athletes in 20 countries while he lived in Kenya, Uganda, and Egypt. The mayor of Nairobi called Whitfield the "Billy Graham of the sports world" because he spread the gospel of physical fitness. He also held sports advisory positions in Liberia and Nigeria. Many of the runners that he mentored, like Kenya's Kipchoge Keino and Ethiopia's Mamo Wolde, eventually earned Olympic medals. Runners from Burundi and Chad regarded Mal Whitfield "as the godfather."[27] Upon his return, he established the Mal Whitfield Foundation to promote sports, academics, and culture around the word. After a long, purposeful life, Whitfield "laid his burden down" on November 19, 2015. He was 91.

Daughter Fredricka Whitfield recalled Mal's infectious sense of humor and his compassion. Now a major journalist with CNN, Fredricka remembers the family— parents Mal and Nola plus older siblings (all the children were born in Africa) Malvin Jr. and Nyna—piling into a Land Rover and motoring through the bustling streets of downtown Mogadishu, Somalia. Her father pointed out life, in stark contrast to their 24-7 guarded high-walled ocean beach compound for the family of diplomats. A woman suffering from elephantiasis, probably caused by ingesting a parasite in bad water, sat on the sidewalk begging for money. Later, Fredricka understood her father's purpose, namely, to be aware, to appreciate, and to assimilate.[28] Mal taught his children: "You can do it." "All things are possible." "Run your own race." "We all matter." "There are no boundaries." "Keep moving." He endured until the last breath.

Rafer Johnson

While perusing the first draft of this book, I realized that many important athletes were omitted. After reading the obituary of Rafer Lewis Johnson, that omission became painfully clear. Author Bill Dwyre cited two of Johnson's admirers who pondered why Rafer did not receive the Presidential Medal of Freedom before his death on December 2, 2020, and offered plausible explanations. Ann Myers Drysdale, a pioneer athlete in her own right, explained: "With Rafer, it was never about him and always about someone else." Bill Plashke added that Johnson was the least self-promoting person who put the spotlight on others.[29] In the introduction to Johnson's autobiography, celebrated newscaster Tom Brokow recalled their collaboration on KNBC, a TV station in Los Angeles, where he befriended and defined

Rafer Johnson as a hero—"an icon of dignity and determination."[30] Thus, I decided to make amends by adding Rafer Lewis Johnson to atone for a palpable oversight.

My only personal encounter with Mr. Johnson occurred in the summer of 1961, when I traveled to Israel. Cousin Yair Safran suggested that we tour the country. During our journey we spotted a large crowd of adoring fans gathered around two very tall and handsome African Americans. As we neared the center of attraction, we realized that the two gentlemen were high jumper John Thomas and Rafer Johnson, coaches at the Maccabi Games as part of an American goodwill tour of the young country. Though Thomas was the first athlete to clear seven feet, he finished a disappointing third in the 1960 Rome Olympics one year prior, while at the same Olympiad Rafer Johnson attained the pinnacle of success, winning the decathlon. I vividly remember these two magnificent athletes, radiant in the August sun, adored by a large crowd of Israelis.

Rafer Johnson was born the second of six children to cotton picker Louis Johnson and Alma Gibson Johnson in Hillsboro, Texas, on August 18, 1935 (1934 in another source), 55 miles south of Dallas, where he spent most of his early years in abject poverty plus stifling segregation. Rafer recalled life in Texas as painful: "I don't care if I never see Texas again. There's nothing about it I like. If my family had stayed in Texas, I not only wouldn't have represented the United States in the Olympic Games, I wouldn't have gone to college."[31]

To improve their lives, Rafer's family moved to central California, where they were the only Blacks in a largely Swedish community. At first, California living proved difficult; the family resided in a railroad boxcar near a cannery. Conditions improved, however, with the help of a California businessman. Johnson excelled in sports. Rafer played football, baseball, and basketball and ran track at Kingsbury High School. As a halfback on the gridiron, Johnson averaged nine yards per carry, leading his team to three league titles. As a hoopster, he averaged 17 points per game. In baseball he averaged .400. Sculpted like an Adonis at six feet three inches, 200 pounds, Johnson prudently chose track and field after he witnessed Bob Mathias in neighboring Tulare dominating the decathlon competition.

So Rafer Johnson sought to emulate his idol, Bob Mathias, Olympic gold medalist at the London and Helsinki games. As a junior in high school, Johnson won the AAU junior decathlon title, but finished third in the senior competition the following year.[32] Fearing football injury, he then concentrated on track and field as he prepared for college. Accepted to UCLA, Johnson competed in the 1955 Pan-American Games in Mexico City as a Bruin. He won—in his fourth decathlon. As a sophomore in 1956, he won his first national championship. Injuries, however, prevented him from beating his Olympic teammate, Milt Campbell, who won gold by 350 points. Rafer had to settle for silver.[16]

Six months after beating his Soviet challenger Kuznetsov in Moscow by 405 points, Johnson was named 1958's *Sports Illustrated* Sportsman of the Year. Shortly after his triumph in Moscow, Rafer and his brother Jimmy were driving to their sister's high school graduation when a reckless driver trying to pass a truck caused their car to fishtail into a concrete barrier. Rafer suffered intense back pain, putting his quest for Olympic gold in jeopardy. An assistant coach at UCLA, Craig

Dixon, advised weightlifting as physical as well as occupational therapy. This regimen plus two shots of Novocain enabled Johnson to compete in the Olympic trials at the University of Oregon, where he won, setting a world record of 8,683 points on July 9, 1960.[33]

Not only did Johnson prove invincible in future decathlons but also he was quite popular. Elected as student body president his senior year, Rafer had the distinction of being the first African American pledge to a predominantly Jewish fraternity. Facing mounting competition from his UCLA teammate C. K. Yang and Vasili Kuznetsov, a Soviet star, Johnson went into overdrive to win gold at the 1960 Rome Olympics. Prior to that pivotal event, Johnson and Yang broke Kuznetsov's world record at Eugene, Oregon with Rafer finishing first with 8,683 points. Before departing for Rome, a contingent of Olympic athletes were fêted at City Hall in New York. Rafer John was called upon to speak at the rally, where he succinctly stated: "It is the goal of each of us to win a gold medal. Naturally, that's not possible for all. But we hope to do the best job possible of representing our country." Impressed with his stature and eloquence, team officials designated Rafer Johnson as the captain of the United States Olympic team. As captain in Rome, Rafer Johnson became the first African American athlete to carry the United States flag at the Olympics, a symbol of racial progress and an antidote to Soviet propaganda as the Cold War raged.[34]

During the climax of the decathlon competition in Rome, Johnson led Yang, who represented his native Taiwan, by 55 points—a lead that was maintained by a pole vault of 13' 5.5", his personal best. To win, Rafer had to stay close to Yang in the 1,500-meter run, Yang's best event. He succeeded in finishing only six yards and 1.2 seconds behind Yang in a time of 4.47.7. Finishing with 8,392 points, he set an Olympic record (later superseded). At age 25, Johnson had fulfilled his quest and earned a high honor, the Sullivan Award, as the best American athlete of 1960. The Associated Press added to his laurels by naming Johnson their Athlete of the Year.[35]

While training for the 1960 Olympiad, he ran into Kurt Douglas, intent on breaking the blacklist in Hollywood with a film version of Howard Fast's stirring novel *Spartacus*. Unable to gain permission and retain amateur status, Johnson rejected an offer from Douglas to play an important role as an African gladiator that eventually went to Woody Strode, a teammate of Jackie Robinson on UCLA's football team. Later, however, Johnson enjoyed a career in film and television after graduating from UCLA.[36] Rejecting various offers to continue as a professional athlete, Johnson found a niche in film. He had minor roles in several films culminating in weightier parts in two Tarzan movies, in one of which Tarzan kills him because he is the bad guy. Better roles went to Sidney Poitier and Harry Belafonte. So, Rafer Johnson found a new calling in broadcasting.[37]

He also got involved in politics, which would cause a long bout of trauma. Impressed—unlike Jackie Robinson—with John F. Kennedy's stance on civil rights in the election campaign in 1960, Rafer voted for him. Later, he met Robert F. Kennedy at an awards dinner, which led to working for the Peace Corps under the Kennedys' brother-in-law, Sargent Shriver. Johnson forged a close lifelong bond with the Kennedy family. Eunice Shriver drew Rafer into a productive relationship with the

Special Olympics for people with disabilities. Rafer served in a leadership role for 50 years with the organization, which supported 34,500 athletes in Southern California as of 2020.[38]

Working for Robert Kennedy's campaign for the presidency in 1968, Johnson was present at the assassination in the kitchen of Los Angeles's Ambassador Hotel. Rosey Grier, a great defensive tackle, served as Bobby Kennedy's bodyguard; Rafer Johnson, a campaign volunteer as well as family friend, was invited to what promised to be a victory celebration. Instead, it turned deadly as Sirhan Sirhan, now rotting in jail, fired three bullets into Kennedy before he was apprehended by Grier, Johnson, and George Plimpton. As Johnson wrote about this horrific event, he recalled that he and Rosey Grier made sure that the assassin would not harm Ethel Kennedy and that no one would take vengeful action against the perpetrator.[39]

Los Angeles Mayor Tom Bradley recruited Rafer Jonson to help with the 1984 Olympiad as an executive. In that capacity, Johnson helped to select Peter V. Ueberroth to head this important operation. In turn, Johnson was named to carry the Olympic torch. Begun in New York City, where Rafer Johnson ignited the torch, the ceremony involved a transcontinental relay, in which famous athletes and their descendants carried this icon in selected cities, ending in Los Angeles. At that terminal point, Johnson was named to carry the torch into the Coliseum and around the track and ascend the 99 steps at a brisk pace up a 50-degree incline to the top, where the 49-year-old former athlete was supposed to turn, face the crowd, and light the flame while thousands cheered. During the rehearsal, Johnson's leg cramped, requiring a change of plans. Jesse Owens's granddaughter Gina Hemphill got the nod to circle the track and hand the torch in relay formation to Johnson, who ascended to complete the lighting ritual as thousands cheered.[40]

In his autobiography, Rafer Johnson describes the highs (like the one described above) and lows, like his dad's drinking problem. During the workweek, Lewis Johnson was fine, Rafer remembers wistfully, but on weekends his father was a violent, besotted man who beat his wife and children until his sons were big enough to defend her and themselves. Late in life, Johnson's father had to be banished from football games that his son Jim played at a Hall-of-Fame level—because of his boisterous behavior fueled by alcohol. Sober he was a role mode, but liquor turned a Dr. Jekyll into a Mr. Hyde. Separated from his wife and alienated from his children, Lewis Johnson's declining years were bitter and lonely, worsened by drink and Alzheimer's disease. Rafer attributed his father's behavior to an accumulation of racist indignities and "sorrow over his unrealized potential."[41] Rafer's mother, on the other hand, was sweet, supportive, loving, happy. Avoiding "demon rum," Rafer Johnson enjoyed a series of remunerative, satisfying jobs and had a long, successful marriage with Elizabeth "Betty" Thorsen, with whom he had two children, Josh and Jennifer. Until the day that he died, Rafer Johnson lived up to his mantra and chosen epitaph: "The guy tried to get it done." In the coda to his autobiography, Johnson added: "I'll be happy to be remembered as someone who was of service to his family and community and tried to be the best that he could be."[42]

3

Wilma Rudolph,
Tommie Smith and John Carlos,
the Joyner Connection, and Carl Lewis

Wilma Rudolph

Born prematurely on June 23, 1940, in St. Bethlehem, Tennessee, Wilma Rudolph was the 20th of 22 children of father Edward's two marriages and the second of her mother Blanche's first marriage. She weighed 4.5 pounds at birth. Impoverished, Wilma lived in a home minus electricity and plus an outhouse. She was constantly ill when young with double pneumonia, whooping cough, scarlet fever, and polio, which damaged her left leg.[1] Determined to overcome, she had physical therapy and leg massage. Because a local hospital for whites only refused to help Wilma, her mother, a domestic worker, spent her day off taking Wilma on a 90-mile round trip to Nashville for heat and water treatment for her damaged left leg.[2] Due to her health issues, she was home-schooled until the second grade. At 11 years old, she stopped using braces. She explained her remarkable recovery: "My doctors told me I would never walk again. My mother told me I would. I believed my mother."[3] Wilma hopped on one leg at age six. At eight years old, she wore a leg brace. At age 11, she started to play basketball in bare feet.[4] Educated in all-Black schools, she gravitated to sports as she explained: "My father pushed me to become competitive…. With so many children, when you did something with one, you always had another along. He felt that sports would help me overcome the problems."[5] Wilma tried out for the basketball team at age 13, and with her lightning speed earned the moniker "Skeeter" from Clinton Gray, her basketball coach.

In the summertime, Wilma attended a track camp at the invitation of Tennessee State University at Nashville coach Ed Temple. She became so proficient in track that at age 16, Wilma was invited to the 1956 Melbourne Olympics. This 89-pound teenager won a bronze medal in the 400-meter relay. After her high school graduation, she received an athletic scholarship to attend Tennessee State. Gaining 41 pounds, she relished the opportunity to make good in the Rome Olympiad of 1960 under women's coach Ed Temple and along with sister Tigerbelles. She did not disappoint. Despite a swollen ankle in practice, she ran a winning semifinal in 11.3 seconds and the final for gold at 11.0 seconds. In the 200 meters, she set an Olympic record at 23.2

seconds and scored another gold with a 24.0-second final. She pulled off a trifecta in the 400-meter relay (despite a poor baton pass to her) for her third gold medal. Jubilant, she later wrote: "I came away from the victory stand and I was mobbed. ... People were jumping all over me, putting microphones in my face, pounding my back, and I couldn't believe it."[6] She returned home, a mega-star, to complete her education in 1961 with a degree in education. Wilma crafted a new image for female athletes, as "foxes" (attractive women) not oxes (tomboys) in the trenchant phrase of Jennifer Lansbury. Her speed invited the nickname "skeeter" because she buzzed around the track like a mosquito and her beauty attracted the amorous attention of fellow Olympic athletes Ray Norton and Cassius Clay.[7]

Significantly, Wilma Rudolph refused to attend a Clarksville banquet in her honor unless it was integrated. The town's power elite conceded, and Wilma won a victory for civil rights by setting a precedent of racial inclusion. She addressed an adoring crowd with these words: "In every effort I have been motivated by one thing; to do justice to those who believe in me and to use my physical talents to the glory of God and the honor of womanhood."[8] Winning the 1961 Sullivan Award as America's outstanding athlete, however, did not come with a payoff; so, Wilma retired from track and became a teacher and coach at the schools she had attended. Rudolph taught second grade and coached track and basketball in Tennessee for $400 per month.

Wilma Rudolph meets with President John F. Kennedy in the Oval Office in 1961. The year before, the 20-year-old Rudolph won the 100- and 200-meter sprints and the 4×100-meter relay at the Olympics in Rome, becoming the first woman to take home three gold medals in a single Olympiad. Photograph by Abbie Rowe (John F. Kennedy Presidential Library and Museum, Boston).

Wilma's personal life became less fluid than her track efforts. She had her first child with boyfriend Robert Eldridge, whom she had met in elementary school. She married another man, William Ward, for a short period. After their divorce in 1962, she married her old boyfriend in 1983, the father of her first child, Yolanda, followed by three more children: daughter Djuanna and sons Robert and Xurry. After 13 years of marriage, they too divorced. Wilma participated in several businesses. She coached at DePauw University in Indiana and recruited minority students. Wilma Rudolph also established a foundation in her name that tutored young children with books on American heroes, in which she certainly belonged. Voted into several prestigious halls of fame, Wilma Rudolph was the first American woman to win three Olympic gold medals. Writing Wilma's obituary in the *New York Times*, Frank Litsky noted that Rudolph, "handsome, regal, 6 feet tall, charming, gracious … became America's greatest female sports hero since Babe Didrikson Zaharias a generation earlier."[9] Bud Greenspan turned her dramatic life into a two-hour prime-time television movie in 1977. Wilma was "the Jesse Owens of women's track and field," he said, "and like Jesse, she changed the sport for all time. She became the benchmark for little black girls to aspire."[10] Diagnosed with a malignant brain tumor in July 1994, she died on November 12. She was only 54 years old.

Tommie Smith and John Carlos

1968 was a year to remember. Student protests spread across the globe prompted by what many considered an unjust war in Vietnam. Youth culture seemed to dominate the early 1960s. Hippies wore love beads, danced to new music, and engaged in experimentation with mind-altering drugs. Males let their hair grow on their faces and heads while females shortened their tresses as well as their dresses. Both genders explored fluid identities, fortified with birth control devices. A brave new world of freedom from puritanical restraints beckoned. Then, tragedy struck with a discordant string of assassinations of public figures, starting with President John F. Kennedy in 1963. Two years later, Malcolm X was killed, three blocks from where I lived. That same year, we witnessed a race riot precipitated by a police action in Harlem. In April 1968, while rallying strikers in Memphis, Tennessee, Dr. King was killed, igniting riots in many American cities.[11] Discordant notes sounded globally with the Tet Offensive in Vietnam, the Prague Spring in Eastern Europe silenced by Soviet tanks, a general strike in France, and a police massacre of protesting students and discontented workers.[12] That same summer brought another tragedy to the apparently cursed Kennedy family as Robert Kennedy, a leading candidate for the Democrat nominee for president, was killed in a kitchen by Sirhan Sirhan.

As Americans girded on their athletic armor for the 1968 Olympics in Mexico City, a young scholar and former athlete, Harry Edwards, planned a boycott of the games. Born in East Saint Louis, Illinois, on November 22, 1942, he attended San Jose State College in California, where he hurled the discus. At 6'8" and 260 pounds, Harry cut an impressive figure. After he completed his PhD in sociology at Cornell, he returned to California to teach sociology, preach the gospel of social change, and advocate for the liberation of Black athletes.[13] He decided to organize a boycott of the 1968 Olympics and orchestrated a protest outside of New York City's completed Madison Square Garden over Pennsylvania Station. To achieve his goals, Edwards created—with the assistance of, among others, Tommie Smith and John Carlos—the Olympic Project for Human Rights (OPHR) to express Black pride and to raise social consciousness. OPHR demanded better treatment for Black athletes and Black people globally and that more Black coaches be hired. The apartheid countries of South Africa and Rhodesia should be uninvited from the Olympics, OPHR argued, and Olympians who did not boycott should use their platform for change.[14]

Ten days before the games began, Mexican soldiers shot into protesting students, killing 3,000. Deeply moved, Carlos and Smith decided to act. To understand their act of silent protest, one has to examine their formative years leading up to this pivotal moment. Tommie Smith was born in Clarksville, Texas, on D-Day, June 6, 1944, to cotton sharecroppers James R. and Dora Smith, a Native American. They lived on a farm with cows and hogs but minus furnishings and heat. Smith's family moved to California for a better life. Tommie remembers a white boy named Wesley who knocked an ice cream cone from his hands coupled with a racial slur. Three years later, Tommie exacted revenge, beating him up. In middle school, he rose to 6'2" on a slender frame, weighing only 155 pounds. A versatile athlete, Smith displayed dominance in basketball and track and field.[15] He ran 100 yards at a 9.9-second clip, the 200 at 21.1 seconds; he could long jump 24' 6" and high jump 6'5". In his senior year, he won the 440 in 47.3 seconds.

Smith enrolled at San Jose State on a triple scholarship in basketball, football, and track. Coach Bud Winter advised Smith to concentrate on one sport and improve his grades. Regarding politics, the white coach chose not to interfere. He let students "do their own thing." As a sophomore, Smith tied a world record in the 200 in 20 seconds and broke it in 1966 with a 19.5-second run. Participation in R.O.T.C. may have slowed a growing political consciousness.[16] John Carlos attended P.S. 90 and Frederick Douglass Junior High School (where I taught as a substitute in the early 1960s) and at a vocational high school. He wanted to get his wife and daughter out of Harlem. Upon arrival, John learned "that a black man couldn't get a beer in a bar in Austin." Football coaches called Black players who dropped passes the "N" word or "Boy."[17]

John Carlos grew up in Harlem and earned a scholarship to East Texas State. He brought an extraordinary track resume with a 9.2-second 100-yard dash and a 20.2-second 200-yard dash. His wife, Kim, and young daughter accompanied him to Texas. Racism proved that he had made a big mistake. The Carlos family returned to New York City, where John met Harry Edwards, the Reverend Andrew Young, and Dr. Martin Luther King, Jr.

"Why was this idea of an Olympic boycott so attractive?" Carlos asked Dr. King.

To which Dr. King replied, "It would be like a ripple in the water spreading the idea that people of color were disenchanted about their treatment and we could aspire to something better as a human race ... plus the visual power that ... it would create."[18]

Unrelated to the Olympics, Carlos asked: "Why are you going back to Memphis when they are threatening your life?"

King replied: "John, I have to go back to stand for those who won't stand for themselves." Dr. King had given clear direction and new purpose to the life of John Carlos.[19] That response convinced Carlos to enroll at San Jose State, where Edwards taught sociology. Edwards, at 6'8" and 260 pounds, carried weight, intellectually as well as physically. He was learned, aggressive, persuasive, and Black—in short, a charismatic professor. He promoted militancy in his classes, using Black lingo, profanity, and threats to make a point. Carlos transferred to San Jose State in 1967. As author Kenny Moore wrote: "Hoarse, abrasive, hugely talented, a fountain of jive,

Carlos was a master of the gunfighter braggadocio of sprinters."[20] He ignored rules while Smith walked the straight and narrow. Both Carlos and Smith were awed by Harry Edwards. Edwards organized campus protests employing "Black Power" to force change. He led a student group on campus to demand equal access to housing, social, and political organization with a threat to disrupt the first football game. Fearing a riot, San Jose State President Robert Clark called off the game. That decision drove California governor Ronald Reagan ballistic. Edwards then summoned Lee Evans, John Carlos, and UCLA's Lew Alcindor to a meeting to discuss a boycott of the 1968 Olympics. Smith recoiled initially. He wanted to shine in Mexico City. At that juncture, Edwards put forward his four-point agenda in OPHR.[21]

To quell this movement the U.S. Olympic Committee (USOC) under the imperial aegis of Avery Brundage called in Jesse Owens. His efforts to thwart their agenda suggested to some that the once famous sprinter was out of touch with militant youth. Owens argued that Black athletes should win respect of white Americans through their performance and not through politics. Not on the same page with this new generation, Jesse's friendly persuasion proved ineffective. Lee Evans thought he was an Uncle Tom.[22] Moreover, racists poured vitriol on protestors. Brundage did not help matters when he opined that the "Boys" were making a grave mistake.[23] Red baiting mounted along with vile, racist remarks, like the overused phrase "Go back to Africa!" As a countermeasure, Brundage reinstated South Africa but backed down when the Soviet bloc, African, and Caribbean nations threatened to withdraw. Years later, Jesse Owens confided to Carlos that although both wanted to accomplish "peace, love, and harmony among the races," Carlos's "strong way" was more effective. And Owens finally agreed with Carlos that if he, Jesse, had stood up a little more in 1936, Carlos and Smith would not have had to in 1968."[24]

The assassination of Dr. King on April 4 seemed to change everything. The protestors argued amongst themselves. Some decided to go, while others stayed home. Although Tommie Smith was arguably the best runner of his day, he feared tough competitors like John Carlos according to Carlos.[25] They were often at odds both before and after their silent protest on the medal stand. Boycott support from Dr. King along with Jackie Robinson, Bill Russell, Jim Brown, and later Lew Alcindor as well as Muhammad Ali made the boycott doable and challenged conventional wisdom that athletes cannot and should not engage in politics. As Carlos wrote, "Ali was gifted, young and black. And he was proud of all of these attributes." In praise of Ali, Carlos adds that he shared learning disorders with the great boxer but Ali used "his knowledge and fame for the greater good."[26] Carlos was ambivalent. Though he wanted to stay home, Carlos decided to go for a medal and protest simultaneously. Something had to be done, he felt, after Dr. King's death and the International Olympic Committee's failure to ban apartheid-riddled South Africa.[27]

Wishing to avoid disrespect for the American flag or a raucous outburst, Tommie Smith orchestrated a silent protest that involved black gloves, scarves, bare feet, beads, unbuttoned jacket, and bowed heads. In the morning final race on October 16, 1968, Smith won gold, Australian Peter Norman took silver, and a disinterested (so he later claimed) John Carlos won bronze. Both American athletes received their medals in black socks, minus shoes, to represent Black poverty. Smith wore a black scarf symbolizing Black pride. Carlos unzipped his jacket to identify with all U.S. blue-collar workers and added a necklace of beads to represent for those who were lynched or murdered en route to America on slave ships. Norman, a Caucasian from Australia sympathetic to the plight of minorities in Australia, joined in the protest by wearing the OPHR badge along with his friendly rivals. Because he forgot his glove in the Olympic Village, Carlos borrowed a glove from Smith, which he raised with his left hand. During the ritual playing of "The Star Spangled Banner," Smith and Carlos bowed their heads. These gestures elicited loud boos and caustic criticism. Television sports broadcaster Brent Musburger, probably a Brundage shill, denounced them as parasites and "a pair of black-skinned storm troopers."[28] Jesse Owens dismissed the "black fist" as "a meaningless symbol." "When you open it," he said, "you have nothing but fingers—weak empty fingers." Money counts because "that's where the power is."[29]

Hardship followed. Both Smith and Carlos were banished from the Olympics and booted out of international competition. When the Mexican government cancelled their visas, they were forced to leave the country and endure infamy back home. They received death threats. In the cacophony of denunciation, one voice offered solace. Writing in the *Washington Post*, Shirley Povich noted: "If it is unpatriotic in the view of most observers, the courage and dignity of their revolt gesture is inescapable. The mild revolutionists are rare."[30] By his own admission, Carlos's inability to earn money, curb gambling addiction, or control his depression and womanizing ruined his marriage. Mounting pressure got to his wife, Kim. She fell into a deep depression. Carlos claimed that his infidelity, documented by the FBI with photos (which he claimed were sent to his despondent wife) drove her over the cliff. She left their home and committed suicide in 1977. Both Smith and Carlos tried to make it in professional football, Smith with the Cincinnati Bengals and Carlos with the Philadelphia Eagles and the Montreal Alouettes. Blessed with great speed, neither could emulate Bob Hayes. Suffering from a knee injury and "hands of stone, Carlos had to leave Montreal, a city that he loved."[31]

Redemption came slowly. Like his mentor, Harry Edwards, Smith became a professor of sociology and physical education and a track coach at Oberlin College and later enjoyed a similar position in Santa Monica, California. He also coached. Having replaced Avery Brundage as Olympic executive, Peter Ueberroth invited Carlos to help organize the 1984 Olympics in Los Angeles. That led to other opportunities and a successful second marriage. Carlos became a track and field coach at Palm Springs High School. Awards and statues followed. In 2006, my golden opportunity to share a podium with John Carlos at the Annual Pop Lloyd Conference faded. Carlos joined Smith on a voyage to Australia to serve as pallbearers at Peter Norman's funeral. Their white comrade Peter Norman had died in Australia after a long bout of depression, alcoholism, and blacklisting. White bigots never forgave Norman for his part in the 1968 protest. Belatedly, Australian authorities realized their mistake. What they offered Peter Norman in atonement came too little, too late. Smith and Carlos, however, could never forget. Also belatedly in 2008, 40 years after the event, Smith and Carlos received the Arthur Ashe Award, ESPN's highest sports humanitarian honor.[32] Today, Carlos and Smith support Colin Kaepernick. Carlos wrote:

"In 1968 we were on a program for humanity—we are still on the same program today." More reticent than Carlos, Smith explained to *New York Times* reporter Ken Belson that he is not more involved because, at 76 years old, he is not in the streets. But he has mentored thousands of students and athletes during his academic career. His Tommie Smith Youth Initiative services 3,000 kids a year. Moreover, "there is only one me, so I can do only so much, but I will continue to do it until I die because this is one thing I was born for, to help my brother man."[33]

The Joyner Connection: Flo-Jo and Jackie Kersee

No woman ever ran a faster race than Florence Griffith Joyner or looked better in a racing outfit. Nevertheless, her early death at age 38 coupled with rumors about steroid use, though never proven, left a cloud and a question. How does one evaluate genuinely great athletes like Flo-Jo (her nickname), Barry Bonds, Sammy Sosa, and Alex Rodriguez, to name only a few, tainted by illegal drug use? Unlike those mentioned, our subject in this segment never failed a drug test. Born on December 31, 1959, the seventh of 11 children of Robert and Florence, senior, Florence Delorez Griffith was raised primarily in the Watts section of Los Angeles, California. She started to run at age seven and never stopped until her heart did on September 21, 1998. When she attended elementary school, Florence joined the Sugar Ray Robinson organization and ran track on weekends. At ages 14 and 15, she claimed victories in competitive races at Jordan High School in Los Angeles. She also competed in the long jump, setting records in both track and field

Admitted to California State at Northridge, she helped her team, coached by Bob Kersee, to win the national track championship. Due to financial exigency, however, Florence had to drop out to support her family as a bank teller. Following Coach Kersee, she returned to college at UCLA in 1980. Failed attempts to qualify for the 1980 Olympics, which the United States boycotted after the Soviet invasion of Afghanistan, prompted Florence to concentrate on her studies, which culminated in 1983 with a degree in psychology. After some more disappointing results, she worked hard to qualify for the 1984 Olympics, winning a silver medal in the 200-meter race. In 1987, she married Al Joyner, the Olympic gold medalist in the triple-jump contest. Not only did she marry that year, but Flo-Jo also picked up speed in subsequent track meets. Flo-Jo also worked with her now brother-in-law Bob Kersee as well as her husband. At various tune-up races prior to the Olympics, her times at both 100 and 200 meters improved, significantly, raising suspicion in some quarters.[34]

In the quarterfinals of the U.S. Olympic Team Trials, she broke the world record as she completed the 100-meter race in 10.49 seconds, with the help of a tailwind, which the racing establishment ignored. Flo-Jo's final run at 10.61 seconds startled spectators, as did her American record of 21.77 seconds in the 200 meters. Unhappy with her lack of endorsement and sponsorship opportunities, she hired a personal manager, which led to a change of coaches. In the Olympic trials, Flo-Jo defeated former world champ Evelyn Ashford 10.54 seconds to 11.26. Flo-Jo also won the 200 in 21.56 seconds. Additionally, she took gold in the 4 by 100 relay, making her one

Florence Griffith Joyner is greeted by President Ronald Reagan after her stellar Olympic performance. In the 1988 Seoul Games, Flo-Jo won gold medals in the 100- and 200-meter races, setting world records in both events. Sadly, she succumbed to an epileptic seizure on September 21, 1998, at age 38 (Ronald Reagan Presidential Library and Museum).

of the top female track performers of all time. Shortly thereafter, she retired and was rewarded with the coveted James E. Sullivan Award in 1988. Then, the money started to roll in from lucrative endorsements and successful business ventures. She designed uniforms for the NBA Indiana Pacers, applying her talents in design and color. She appeared on television, including on a soap opera. Her attempted comeback in track was thwarted by tendonitis. Flo-Jo was inducted into the Track Hall of Fame in 1995. Her storied life came to a sudden end in her sleep due to a severe epileptic seizure on a September night in 1998. No steroids were found in her system, only Tylenol and Benadryl. Alexandre de Mérode, chairman of the IOC medical commission, insisted that Flo-Jo was wrongfully targeted.[35]

Unlike her sister-in-law and Olympic teammate, Jackie Joyner-Kersee is alive, well, and contributing to society as a genuine hero/heroine. Born on March 3, 1962, to teenage parents, Jacqueline was actually named after America's first lady at that time, Jackie Kennedy. Growing up in East St. Louis, she had to overcome severe asthma and financial hardship among other hurdles on her road to glory.[36] Inspired by a biopic of Mildred "Babe" Didrikson Zaharias, which she viewed as a 13-year-old, she devoted time plus hard work to become arguably America's greatest female athlete with a social conscience. In her teens, she won the pentathlon championships in four straight years while also participating in basketball, volleyball, and basketball. In her junior year, she set the Illinois high school long jump record for women with a 6.68-meter jump. In 1994, Joyner-Kersee excelled in women's hurdles with records in 50, 55, and 60 meters.[37] Jackie Joyner attended UCLA on a full scholarship. There she starred in basketball and track and field. She played four years of basketball as a 5'10" forward, interrupted by one year of Olympic training for the 1984 games. As a Bruin hoopster, she scored 1,167 points and led her team to the West Regional Finals of the 1985 NCAA Women's Tournament. As a senior, she had her best year with 12.7 points, 9.1 rebounds, 2.1 steals, and 1.4 assists per game.

Track and field, however, made Jackie Joyner famous. In the Los Angeles Summer Olympics in 1984, she won the silver medal in the heptathlon, only five points behind the winner. Using defeat as a spur to higher achievement, Jackie won the heptathlon in the 1986 Goodwill Games with a record-setting of 7,148 points. After this accomplishment, she won the James E. Sullivan Award, signifying the best United States amateur athlete. If there was any doubt about Jackie Joyner's extraordinary athleticism, it was clearly dispelled in the 1988 Seoul Olympiad.

Joyner-Kersee won two gold medals: one in the heptathlon with a record-shattering 7,291 points, the second in the long jump with another Olympic record of 24' 3.25". At the 1991 World Championships, Jackie won the long jump easily but injured her hamstring, which precluded her participation in the heptathlon. Recovered and resilient, Joyner-Kersee reclaimed Olympic gold in the heptathlon in Barcelona's 1992 Olympics. In the long jump, her supremacy ended with a bronze medal. Four years later, she competed in the 1996 Atlanta Olympiad, where she finished third for another bronze in the long jump. Her last hurrahs proved more successful in the 1998 Goodwill Games, where she won again. Her pro career in basketball at age 36 proved less successful as did her try for Olympic medals in Sydney, Australia, which hosted the 2000 games. Over four separate Olympics, she won six medals— three gold, one silver, two bronze—and was named *Sports Illustrated for Women*'s top female athlete of the twentieth century, having supplanted her inspirational idol, Babe Didrikson.[38]

Jackie Joyner-Kersee won three gold, one silver, and two bronze medals in the long jump and heptathlon over four Olympiads stretching from 1984 to 1996. In addition, she won multiple world championships, despite a severe asthma condition. Jackie was named the **Greatest Female Athlete of All Time** by *Sports Illustrated for Women* (courtesy John Mathew Smith, www.celebrity-photos.com).

In retirement, Jackie Joyner-Kersee established a youth center foundation that bears her name and encourages underprivileged youth in her hometown to play sports. In 2007, she helped to set up Athletes for Hope in concert with other athletes—Andre Agassi, Muhammad Ali, and Mia Hamm—to foster education and charity among their peers. In 1986, she married her coach, Bob Kersee, who trained sprinter Florence Griffith Joyner, who in turn married Al, Joyner's brother. Their success—along with heartbreak—"was all in the family." Jeré Longman wrote that Joyner-Kersee's greatest achievement "was that she made it O.K. for women to sweat." Longman added: "Along with Wilma Rudolph and Billy Jean King … Joyner Kersee was a pioneer, boldly crossing what was an athletic desert for women. As she retires, that barren landscape has changed."[39]

Carl Lewis

Frederick Carlton "Carl" Lewis was born in Birmingham, Alabama, on July 1, 1961, to track coaches, William and Evelyn Lewis. Evelyn had been a hurdler at the Pan Am Games in 1951. Carl's sister became a successful long jumper, indicating a positive DNA marker for athletic prowess in the Lewis family. Raised in Willingboro, New Jersey, Carl and three siblings enjoyed a middle-class lifestyle. Their parents provided culture as well sports with exposure to theater, music, and dance. After moving to New Jersey, Carl's parents operated a local athletic club suggesting that environment shapes sports stars as well as genetics. Carl competed in track and field, coached by both parents. Thanks to a growth spurt of several inches in a single month, Carl used crutches until his body and bones could catch up. As a high school senior Carl broke a record with a 16' 8" long jump.[40]

Lewis opted to return to the South. He enrolled at the University of Houston, where he set track and field records under coach Tom Tellez. Like Jesse Owens, Lewis mastered the long jump as well as the sprints. In 1979, he recorded a long jump of 26' 8", which he bettered in 1980 to win the NCAA title with a 27' 4.5" leap. Although he made the U.S.A. Olympic team, he could not compete because President Jimmy Carter instituted a boycott after the Soviet Union invaded Afghanistan. So, Carl and other boycotters participated in an alternate venue, the Liberty Bell Classic, where he earned a bronze medal in his forte with a jump of 25' 5¾". Lewis, however, did win gold in the 4 by 100 relay. In Dallas that year, he ran the 100 in 10 seconds, third fastest ever. Consequently, Carl Lewis won the Sullivan Award for best amateur athlete in 1981. His long jump improved to 28 feet. Approaching the Los Angeles Olympics in 1984, he loomed at number one in the 100 meters and number six in the 200 meters. He scored a great triumph in Los Angeles, first winning gold in the 100 in 9.99 seconds and then clearing 28 feet in the long jump. Lewis had more jumps remaining (and fans wanted him to break Bob Beamon's record), but, unwilling to incur injury, he geared up for the 200, in which he finished with a flourish in 19.88 seconds. He garnered a fourth gold in the 4 by 400 relay, running a second leg and contributing a new world record in this event at 37.83 seconds.

Because he had matched Jesse Owens's 1936 record of four golds, Lewis expected adulation coupled with endorsements. Painfully disappointed, he failed to understand this baffling outcome. Edwin Moses had a clue to this snub. Lewis lacked humility. Lewis appeared arrogant, aloof, egotistical, and preening—almost effeminate with flattop hair and flamboyant attire—hence, unmarketable. Homophobia polluted the atmosphere as AIDS spread, adding to a decade of discontent. Coca-Cola withdrew an endorsement offer, and Nike cancelled Lewis while elevating "Air Jordan." Lacking "machismo," Carl Lewis did not fit the Madison Avenue prototype. "Carl-bashing" in *Sports Illustrated* did not help his cause. Despite this strange turn of events, the Dallas Cowboys drafted Carl Lewis to play wide receiver, hoping for another Bob Hayes, and the Chicago Bulls drafted him with their 208th pick in the 10th round of the NBA draft as the best athlete available even though Lewis did not play either sport in college.[41]

A drug-enhanced Canadian, Ben Johnson, challenged Carl's supremacy in sprints, scoring a 9.95-second win in a 100-meter race. Lewis slipped in the rankings to number three in the sprints and number two behind the U.S.S.R's Robert Emmiyan in the long jump. So, Lewis concentrated on his forte, the long jump. Johnson won the 100 in 9.83 seconds. Lewis suffered another setback when his father, William, died at age 60. Grief stricken, Carl buried a 1984 gold medal in his father's coffin, promising his mother a replacement in the upcoming Olympiad in Seoul, which he accomplished. Lewis continued to compete in Seoul in 1988, Barcelona in 1992, and Atlanta in 1996—his last hurrah. In Atlanta, he won gold in the long jump. Despite his 2003 admission that that he used banned substances during the Olympic trials of 1988, he remains active in track and field as an assistant coach. Inducted into the Hall of Fame in 2001 and named "Olympian of the Century" by *Sports Illustrated* that same year, he remains *sans souci*, insouciant and unapologetic.[42]

SECTION THREE

FOOTBALL

4

Duke Slater, J. Mayo Williams, and Other Pathbreakers in the College and Pro Ranks

Until recently, the two most popular sports in the United States were football and baseball. Like boxing, football sanctioned violence, but on a broader field with more contestants. Football derived from a Native American sport called Pasuckuakohowog, which featured teams from 500 to 1,000 players on each side trying to kick a ball into a goal on a field one mile in length and half a mile wide. Comparable to war with no holds barred, it resulted in multiple injuries, even death. Adorned in war paint, contestants played for hours, sometimes two days, followed by a celebratory feast. Historian Alden Vaughan described one game in his dissertation, later a book.[1]

Modern football, played at the college level beginning in 1869 in New Jersey, had a shorter field to be sure, but it was no less intense and war-like. Violence is embedded in the game and its language, notes Murray Rose, with references to "bombs, blitzes, zones, trenches, and traps."[2] Rose further asserts that football players exude heroic qualities such as confidence, strength, and mechanical precision, powered by technology. Time is not only money in the Ben Franklin equation but also essential in synchronization with industrialization and war.

Brutality was visited on the few Black players in the early years, compelling them to employ tactical self-preservation. Fritz Pollard and Paul Robeson would use their cleats to prevent injury from gang tackling. Jim Brown and Joe Perry used powerful forearms and agile legs to punish would-be violent tacklers. Later Johnny Bright was less fortunate, when a racist opponent from Oklahoma A&M, Wilbanks Smith, blindsided him with a punch that broke his jaw on October 20, 1951. Bright lost his chance to win the Heisman Trophy that year, finishing fifth. Wilbanks Smith escaped punishment for his foul deed, and he never apologized, though an NCAA rule change prohibited future such assaults.[3]

Muscular Christianity animated modern football. Excessive violence led to injury and death, forcing even "Macho-Man" President Theodore Roosevelt to call for rule reform. Thanks to the efforts of Walter Camp, Yale University's gift to football, reform as well as respectably returned to the gridiron. Pro football's ascendancy coincided with rising Cold War tensions and the proliferation of television coverage. Sports historian Dave Zirin cites the overtime playoff game between the

New York Giants and the Baltimore Colts as a pivotal point. The increased presence of Black stars altered the game and made African American players less likely to incur Johnny Bright's dark day of victimization on the gridiron. A level playing field, however, did not materialize quickly due to a phenomenon in most major sports called "stacking."

According to compelling research by sports sociologists, Blacks in football (and in other major sports) were confined to marginal positions based on stereotypical assumptions crudely based on either brains or brawn. Black players were predominantly found in physical positions requiring speed, aggression, instinct, and—in the words of the Allstate commercial—"good hands," while white players were disproportionately situated in positions of control, intelligence, stability, and leadership. Transitioning into integration, Blacks were confined to running back and split ends on offense. On defense, they were positioned as corner backs and defensive ends. Centrality counted. Whites dominated as quarterbacks and centers on offense and as middle linebackers on defense. Kickers and punters were white even though one of the best punters was Cleveland Brown Horace Gillom, who also played defensive end from 1947 to 1956. In 1975, for example, all 27 placekickers were white, and Blacks numbered only three of the 70 punters though 42 percent of the NFL players were Black. Furthermore, Jonathan Brower's research indicated that second-string players were likewise mostly white.[4]

This section profiles pioneers such as Fritz Pollard, Paul Robeson, Duke Slater, J. Mayo Smith, Jim Brown, and the Black quarterbacks who disproved such stereotypes that reflected residual racism. Subsequently, substantial progress has contributed to a more level playing field.

Early Pathbreakers

Glory road in football is generally reserved for powerful running backs, fleet pass-catching ends, and strong-armed quarterbacks. Sports literature seems disproportionately devoted to these position players on offense. Regarding the previous chapters, it would appear that this author fell prey to a similar pattern. In charting the passage of African American football stars, one finds a necessary corrective. Therefore, let us now praise famous linemen along with other defenders behind the line, featuring linebackers *and* defensive backs. What follows is an attempt to right wrongs and offer a more balanced perspective without neglecting the salutary impact of players at the glamour and glory positions on offense.

The first barrier-breakers of color, including offensive players, started their careers in college before the two-platoon system gained traction. Paul Robeson of Rutgers and Frederick Douglass "Fritz" Pollard played both ways at a very high level. Both faced violence on the field and endured segregation off the field. In the first half of the twentieth century, most Black athletes gravitated to historically Black colleges and universities (HBCUs) as opposed to predominantly white universities (PWIs). Our focus, however, highlights those who broke barriers that had impeded integration followed by a discussion of HBCUs' later influence.[5]

As a youngster, I was fascinated by the efforts of Black athletes to integrate American sports. College football at that time far exceeded pro football in popularity. Prior to World War II, a token number of Black players surfaced at PWIs.[6] Perhaps the two best known among them, Pollard and Robeson, are discussed at length in the next chapter. Another all-time great at both the college and pro levels, Duke Slater, has only recently received the recognition he deserves. Still others, like J. Mayo Williams, today better known as a pioneering record producer, and Gideon ("Charlie") Smith, the first African American varsity athlete in any sport at Michigan State (then Michigan Agricultural College), have yet to receive their due.

Williams, who played end for Brown University from 1916 to 1920 (missing a year to serve in World War I), was a track champion known on the gridiron for his speed and tackling ability. After earning honorable mention All-America honors in 1920, he turned pro, joining Canton for a game before moving on to Hammond for the remainder of the 1921 NFL season. Two years later, still with Hammond, Williams was named a first-team All-Pro. After six seasons, he was out of the game, landing with Paramount Records, where he signed Ma Rainey, Blind Lemon Jefferson, and Blind Blake, among others; later, after taking time away to coach the Morehouse football team, he signed Blind Willie McTell for Decca.[7]

Smith, a tackle, earned all-star nods from 1913 to 1915, then played a single game of professional football for the Canton Bulldogs, becoming the last African American to play before the formation of the NFL. He then enjoyed a successful head coaching career at HBCUs Virginia State and Hampton, spending 20 years at the latter, finishing more than 50 games above .500 and guiding his team to a Black college national championship.[8]

Bobby Marshall was a two-time All-American end who played both offense and defense for the University of Minnesota from 1904 through 1906. In his time on the gridiron, the Golden Gophers went 27–2 and outscored their opponents 1,283 to 63.[9] He played professional football for Twin Cities clubs after his graduation in 1907, but the NFL was then still some 13 years away. Nevertheless, at the age of 40, Marshall seized the chance to play for the new league in 1920, starting seven games and getting into nine with the 1920 Rock Island Independents. He resurfaced five years later with the Duluth Kelleys, playing in three games, starting two, at 45 years old. Marshall was also a top-notch baseball player, starring with the St. Paul Gophers team that defeated the Leland Giants in 1909, winning the unofficial Black championship.[10]

Fred "Duke" Slater played tackle at the University of Iowa from 1918 to 1922, earning two All-America and three All–Big Ten selections. After college, Slater played 10 years in the NFL, becoming the league's first African American lineman. At 6'1" and at least 210 pounds, he was an imposing, remarkably durable player who in a 10-year pro career missed only one game. (He sat out that contest against the Kansas City Blues because the league had agreed not to allow African Americans to take the field in Missouri.[11]) After returning to the University of Iowa for law school—while still active in the NFL—he became a prosecutor and eventually the first African American judge seated on the Cook County Supreme Court. He was part of the inaugural College Football Hall of Fame class (1951) and, decades late, was enshrined in Canton's Pro Football Hall of Fame in 2020.

John Shelburne, a slashing running back, interrupted his football and academic careers at Dartmouth to join the army in 1918. The next year, in his return to the gridiron, he was an All-American and graduated with academic honors. He played six games for the Hammond Pros in 1922, coached for a time at Lincoln University in Pennsylvania, then returned to his hometown, Boston, and spent 30 years as a social worker at the Robert Gould Shaw House.[12]

Sol Butler played multiple sports at Dubuque College (now the University of Dubuque), earning 19 varsity letters. A talented track and field athlete, he earned a spot on the 1920 U.S. Olympic team (but injured himself in his first event at the Antwerp games). On the gridiron, he became the first African American to quarterback a college team for four straight years.[13] After college, Butler played four years (1923–1926) in the NFL, taking the field for the Rock Island Independents, Canton Bulldogs, Akron Pros, and Hammond Pros. In 1925, he also played briefly for the Kansas City Monarchs, going 1–0 on the mound. He would later become a sports editor for the *Chicago Bee*.[14]

Dick Hudson was a back for St. Mary's (Minnesota) and perhaps briefly Creighton before playing with the NFL's Minneapolis Marines in 1923 and with the Hammond Pros in 1925 and 1926.[15] Two years later, in 1928, after playing a season with the University of Iowa, Harold Bradley got into two games with the NFL's Chicago Cardinals, becoming the league's second African American lineman.[16] Guard and back Dave Myers turned pro out of New York University in 1930, signing with the Staten Island Stapletons and starting six games (appearing in seven). The following year Myers was with the Brooklyn Dodgers, for whom he played six games, starting five.

University of Oregon back Joe Lillard joined the Chicago Cardinals in 1932 and played until 1933. He and Ray Kemp, who came out of Duquesne to play tackle for a year (1933) with Pittsburgh, have the dubious distinction of being the last two African Americans in the NFL until 1946.

Additional NFL college-recruited Black football players were barred from 1934 to 1946. One Penn State player who might have made All-Pro was Dave Alston, who played with his brother Harry. A superb scholar-athlete (a pre-med major), he had all the tools as a triple threat in his freshman year. Like Jim Thorpe, he passed accurately, ran with excellent speed, and averaged 60-plus yards a punt. As freshmen, Dave and Harry led PSU

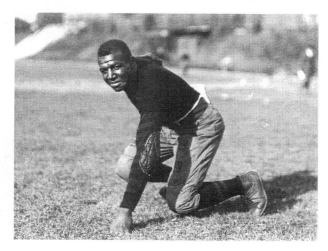

Duke Slater at the University of Iowa, circa 1920. An All-American as a Hawkeye, Slater went on to play professional football, return to Iowa for law school, and become a judge in Illinois (courtesy Frederick W. Kent Collection, University Archives, University of Iowa Library).

John Shelburne, shown here with fellow members of the 1920 Dartmouth football team, was an All-American running back who, after graduating with honors, played briefly in the NFL, suiting up with the Hammond Pros in 1922. He later moved back to his hometown of Boston and worked for 30 years as a social worker at the Robert Gould Shaw House (courtesy Dartmouth Digital Library Program).

to an undefeated season. Coach Bob Higgins called Dave Alston "the greatest player I ever coached." Dubbed the best sophomore football player in the nation by *Esquire* magazine, Dave died after a tonsillectomy on August 15, 1942, evoking the poet Whittier's somber observation: "For all sad words of tongue or pen, The saddest are these: 'It might have been!'"[17]

I recall following the exploits of Levi Jackson, the first football captain at Yale University, an elite Ivy League institution. Jackson seemed to personify the "American Dream." Born in Branford, Connecticut, on August 22, 1926, Jackson was a local hero.[18] Jackson watched his first football game in 1937 with eyes fixed on Heisman Trophy winner Clint Frank who led the Elis. Playing three major sports in high school, Levi moved to New Haven, where he was coached at Hillhouse High School by former Yale tackle, Reggie Root, class of '26. Root advised Jackson to apply to Yale, where Levi's father worked as master steward and chef in Pierson College.

World War II delayed Jackson's entry into college when the U.S. Army called. Playing on the army team, Jackson defeated the New York Giants 7–0 with a stunning 80-yard touchdown run. Offered a handsome contract by the vanquished Giants and a large football scholarship to play for Indiana University, Levi Jackson opted for Yale and the G.I. Bill, which covered $500 of his $600 yearly tuition.[19] As a lifelong Giants football fan, I regret Jackson's prudent decision, which negated the opportunity in 1945 to be Jackie Robinson's counterpart in football. At Yale, Jackson not only received a first-rate college education but he also crested as a football player.

In his first year, Levi gained 806 yards rushing from his fullback slot, fifth most in America, and helped propel the Elis to a 7–1- record and, most significantly, a victory over Harvard, Yale's major rival. As the first African American to play for Yale, Jackson received other unprecedented honors when he was unanimously elected captain and voted into a secret senior society. The youngest of six children, he had come a long way from obscurity to star among the prep school graduates not only with athletic attainments in a triad of varsity baseball, basketball, and football with 2,049 yards rushing but also with a triple major in sociology, psychology, and economics.

After graduating from Yale, Jackson (like Heisman Trophy winner Dick Kazmaier, one year later) again spurned pro football. Instead, he chose to work for the Ford Motor Company in Detroit. It turned out to be an excellent career move. He became an executive in 1962, retiring as a vice president in 1983. During his tenure at Ford, Jackson developed a minority dealership training program, specializing in urban affairs and labor relations. After the 1967 riots, Levi Jackson helped create jobs for inner-city residents. Levi Jackson died on December 7, 2000. He was 74.[20] Just as we remember Pearl Harbor on that day every year, a hero from Yale invites memory as well.

Ironically, as Jackson slipped from public prominence in recent years, his wife, Mary Winston Jackson, rose from anonymity. She married Levi in 1944. After matriculating in math and engineering classes, Mary rose to become NASA's first African American female engineer. In a move of reverse mobility, Mary stepped down a notch to manage programs designed to promote affirmative action in the employment of women and their promotion in NASA's science, engineering, and mathematics departments. Margot Lee Shetterly's 2016 book *Hidden Figures* (and the film by the same name) highlights Mary Jackson's effort along with Katherine Johnson and Dorothy Vaughan and delineates their work on the Mercury Project, enabling us to win the space race. Mary Jackson died on February 11, 2005. In her long, productive life, Mary Jackson won many honors, including the Congressional Gold Medal, posthumously awarded in 2019.[21]

The 1946 season marked a major turning point for the integration of professional football. The creation of a rival league, the All-American Conference (AAC), spurred a salutary search for new sources of talent among eager African American athletes, previously precluded by heinous Jim Crow laws and hoary customs. Cleveland lost its Rams franchise to Los Angeles after winning the NFL title in 1945. Ably filling that vacuum, the Browns of Cleveland, coached by Paul Brown, hired two Black stars, fullback-linebacker Marion Motley and guard Bill Willis, who contributed to their dynastic rule from 1946 to 1949 and enabled continued Browns dominance after the two leagues merged in 1950.[22]

Sports maven Paul Zimmerman cogently argued that Marion Motley was football's "GOAT" (greatest of all time).[23] Born in Leesburg, Georgia, on June 5, 1920, Motley moved north to Ohio with his family in 1923. Marion grew up in Canton, where he played football and basketball at McKinley High School before entering the all-Black South Carolina State College in 1939 and then transferring to Nevada University at Reno, where he starred in football from 1941 to 1943. A knee injury forced Motley, now 6'1" and 238 pounds, to drop out. In 1944, Marion joined the

U.S. Navy at Great Lakes, where he joined Coach Paul Brown. Under Brown's tutelage, Motley flourished as a fullback and linebacker. His last hurrah as a football star *cum* sailor was a thumping of Notre Dame 39–7. Discharged and ready to resume work in a steel mill, followed by a return to college to get his degree, Motley was summoned to Cleveland Browns training camp after initially being rejected by the imperious Coach Brown. Motley made the team and signed a contract calling for a $4,500 per year salary. Thanks to Motley's stellar play, particularly the designed draw play on a delayed hand-off as blitzing defenders tried to sack quarterback Otto Graham, the Browns won every title game in the short-lived AAC from 1946 to 1949.

The late Paul Zimmerman (a friend from Columbia College and a fellow busboy at Unity House, a Pennsylvania summer resort for garment workers) marveled at Marion Motley's skill as a great runner, outstanding blocker, and superb linebacker—in short, a winner with a 5.7-yards-per-carry average, besting his successor in Cleveland, Jim Brown, arguably the greatest runner in NFL history. In 1946, Motley averaged an amazing 8.2 yards per carry. That year, the Browns crested with a 14–2 record. The year of 1948 was even better. The Browns crested with a 15–0 record, including the title win over the Buffalo Bills 49–7. In those four AAC years, the Browns posted a 47–4–3 record with Marion Motley rushing for 3,024 yards. Racist encounters plagued Motley and his Black teammates including threatening letters that resulted in a forced exile from a game in segregated Miami in 1946, stoking Motley's fury. But he and Bill Willis persevered. Opponents stomped on the Black players and hurled insults, punctuated with the "N" word, and the officials did nothing. After the merger in 1950, Marion Motley ran for 188 yards in 11 carries, averaging 17 yards per carry against the hapless Pittsburgh Steelers, as 10,000 Black fans in attendance cheered. Motley was unanimously selected for first-team All-Pro.[24]

The mighty Motley reinjured his knee in 1951, which limited his ability in the twilight of his career. In 1953, Coach Brown suggested that Marion retire. After a comeback attempt failed, he was traded to the Pittsburgh Steelers in 1954, for whom he played linebacker for seven games before being released. In a shortened eight-year career, the great Motley amassed 4,720 rushing yards at 5.7 yards per carry, good enough for Football Hall of Fame entry in 1968 as the second African American player so honored. Unfortunately, he was deemed not good enough for a job in professional football following his retirement. The ungrateful Coach Brown, despite his effusive praise of Motley cited below, refused to hire him and insultingly told Marion to find work in the steel mills. His teammate, quarterback Otto Graham, who touted Motley as the best all-around fullback, even better than Jim Brown, also spurned his request for a coaching job when Graham headed the Washington Redskins. When new Cleveland owner Art Model hired some mediocrity to fill a position with the Browns, Motley fumed, suggesting that racism was in play. So, Hall of Famer Marion Motley, rated among the 12 best running backs in NFL history, worked at low-level jobs for the U.S. Postal Service System in Cleveland and for the Department of Youth Services in Akron, Ohio. Was this an appropriate coda for man that author Paul Zimmerman called the best player in the history of the sport?

Although Marion Motley died of prostate cancer on June 27, 1999, the debate goes on.[25]

Author Chris Murray quotes Paul Brown on Motley[26]:

> No one ever cared more about this team and whether it won or lost, no matter how many Yards he gained or where he was asked to turn, I've always believed that Motley could have gone into the Hall of Fame solely as a linebacker if we had used him only at that position. He was as good as the great ones.

Motley's fellow barrier-breaker, William Karnet "Bill" Willis, was born in Georgia on October 5, 1921. His family moved to Ohio the following year. After his father died in 1923, Willis was raised by his mother and grandparents. At Columbus East High School, he starred in track and field as well as football. To avoid invidious comparison with his older brother Claude, an all-state fullback at the same school, Bill opted to play as a lineman: tackle or end. After a one-year hiatus from school, encouraged by his high school coach, Bill Willis applied to Ohio State and was accepted in 1941. As a sophomore, Willis played middle-guard, nose-to-nose, against the opposing center. Undersized for a lineman at 210 pounds, Willis's blazing speed and high intelligence prevailed. Ohio State won the Big Ten Conference with a 9–1 record. While other Buckeye players left school for military service, Willis, classified 4-F due to varicose veins, remained. After a subpar season in 1943, Ohio State roared back in 1944 with a perfect record of nine wins and no losses. Bill's contributions to this undefeated season elicited recognition from United Press International and *Look* magazine when he was named to their respective All-Star teams. In the ensuing College All-Star game in Chicago, Willis was cited for his outstanding play.

Reunited with Coach Paul Brown in 1946 as a pro, Bill Willis enjoyed a sensational career, mostly on defense. Selected as an all-league player in every season he played in the All-America Football Conference and the NFL, Willis gained entry into the Pro Football Hall of Fame in 1977, nine years following Marion Motley's induction. In one of several racial incidents, he rescued Motley from a pile-up. As he recalled[27]:

> I started pulling guys off, saying: "OK boys, the play's over! Let go!" Well, they had a five-by-five type, a guy about 260 pounds, and he wheeled and said: "Keep your black hands off me!" I stepped back a pace in case he tried to reach me with a punch, but I was angry and I kept my hands on his shoulder pads…. I soon won the respect of my opponents. They learned that I could take it and dish it out, and I didn't really have to play dirty ball to hold my own. Speed was my greatest asset, but I could unleash a pretty solid forearm block and a rather devastating tackle.

Like Motley, Willis retired after the 1953 season and engaged in public service as director of the Ohio Youth Commission, a state agency designed to combat juvenile delinquency. He was inducted into the College Football Hall of Fame in 1971. Ohio State honored Willis by retiring his #99 jersey in 2007. As a pioneer in reintegration, he paved the way for others to follow. Therefore, when fellow African American Romeo Crennel was named head coach of the Cleveland Browns, Bill Willis rejoiced.[28]

The first African American football player to be immortalized by induction into the Pro Football Hall of Fame, Emlen Lewis Tunnell, was born on March 29, 1924, in Bryn Mawr, Pennsylvania. His parents divorced when Emlen was young. His mother, Catherine, raised her four children by working as housekeeper for wealthy residents of Philadelphia's Main Line elite families. In high school in 1940–41, Emlen played halfback. After graduation, Tunnell enrolled at the University of Toledo, where he played halfback. During the 1942 season, he suffered a broken neck in an attempt to tackle an opposing runner. When fully recovered, Emlen shifted gears and sports to help Toledo's basketball team gain entry to the 1943 National Invitation Tournament (more prestigious at that time than the NCAA tourneys) and reach the finals.

That same year Tunnell joined the war effort by serving in the U.S. Coast Guard from 1943 to 1946. A heroic figure during his football years, Emlen embodied that self-sacrifice as a lifesaver in military service. The first incident occurred on April 27, 1944, when a cargo ship was unloading 6,000 tons of explosives and gasoline at Papua, New Guinea's Aitape Harbor. Suddenly, Japanese aircraft unleashed a torpedo that blew a hole 27 feet by 27 feet in the starboard side of the ship. Tunnell used his bare hands to smother the flames, suffering severe burns himself, to save the life of a shipmate. The second incident occurred closer to home, in Newfoundland. Emlen jumped into freezing water to save a mate who fell overboard. As a ship steward, Tunnell was restricted to kitchen rather than combat duty. These two incidents went unnoticed until 2008, when Commander Bill McKinstry recognized Tunnell's name on the back of a photograph featuring a 1940s Coast Guard basketball team.[29] After leaving the Coast Guard, Tunnell pursued a college degree at the University of Iowa, where he played halfback and receiver. From 1946 to 1947, he starred, setting records for single-game receptions and touchdowns. He also played defensive back for the Hawkeyes. Dissatisfied with his role, Emlen left Iowa for his home in Pennsylvania. There, almost penniless, he decided to hitchhike to New York to try out for the New York Giants. Luckily, a Black trucker from the Caribbean, transporting bananas, evoking a Harry Belafonte chant, picked him up for what turned out to be a pivotal interview for both Tunnell and the Giants. Emlen had only a "buck fifty" in his pocket.[30] Exuding grit and confidence at this interview, Tunnell signed a contract and in so doing became the first African American to join the Giants. Playing with intelligence, intensity, ability, and speed, he became a game changer.

Tunnell's accomplishments on the football field can also be considered heroic. In a career spanning 167 games, he corralled 79 interceptions, ran 10 back for touchdowns, returned 258 punts for 2,209 yards, and averaged 16.2 yards per return. A career high 10 interceptions in 1949 heralded a new star, who converted defense into offense and set a precedent that all future defensive backs would try to emulate. In perhaps his banner year, 1952, Emlen produced seven interceptions, six recovered fumbles, 364 yards on kickoff returns, and league-leading 411 yards in punt returns. He made a key play in the 1958 NFL title game versus the Chicago Bears. With the Giants ahead 13–0 in the second quarter, the Bears elected to go for a first down near midfield, only needing one yard on fourth down. Emlen Tunnell rose to the occasion with a burst across the line to tackle J.C. Caroline for a one-yard loss, changing the momentum in favor of the Giants, who went on to clobber the Bears, 47–7.[31]

Tunnell closed out his Giants career as a player in 1958. That year I attended the final game of the season. The Giants needed a win to tie the Browns for league leadership and a playoff to determine which team would face the Baltimore Colts for the NFL championship. In a freezing snow-driven game, the Giants rallied for a 10–3 deficit to win on a last-minute 49-yard Pat Summerall field goal. Each team's punt returners, Emlen Tunnell and Bobby Mitchell, continually fumbled attempts to catch the slippery pigskin, proving that Tunnell was human after all. The following week, the Giants blanked the Browns, 10–0, holding the great Jim Brown to only eight yards rushing in seven attempts in another game marred by severely cold, snow-laced weather that engulfed my college roommate, Bob Boikess, and this writer.

In a hotly contested championship final that we watched from the comfort of our heated apartment, the Giants rallied from a 14–3 deficit to take the lead 17–14 and ball possession with less than three minutes left on the clock. On third down, quarterback Charlie Conerly handed the ball to left halfback Frank Gifford who, sweeping to his right for the four yards, was met by defensive end Gino Marchetti (who broke his right ankle on the tackle) and linebacker Bill Pellington, just nine inches short of the first-down marker. Or was it short? Frank Gifford, to this dying day, insisted that he had made the necessary yardage but that Marchetti's broken ankle caused an inaccurate "spot." Just before he died, Referee Ron Gibbs told his son, "You know, Joe, maybe Frank was right, maybe he did make the first down."[32]

Frank Gifford recalled how Emlen Tunnell catching a punt with soft hands reminded him of Willie Mays: "He had the softest hands I have ever seen and he wasn't all that fast, and yet he had those incredible returns of punts and kickoffs. He just had a great instinct of knowing where he was on the field at all times." Tunnell earned kudos from Giants coach Jim Lee Howell and teammates Harland Svare and Andy Robustelli. Giants co-owner John Mara praised him as a player, coach, and scout. But "more importantly," Mara said, "he was a wonderful human being, which is why he was the most beloved person in our organization."[33] Although his life was cut short by a heart attack during a practice session on July 22, 1975, Tunnell also garnered praise from the Green Bay Packers for whom he played from 1959 to 1961 under Coach Vince Lombardi. His last game as an active player, ironically, occurred in the 1961 title contest, in which the Packers clobbered the Giants, 37–0. After retirement he scouted for the Packers and, subsequently, the Giants. In 1965, he became the first Black assistant coach in the NFL. Two years later, he entered professional football's Valhalla, the Hall of Fame, the first African American inductee and first defensive player to be so honored. Even after his death Emlen Tunnell continued to muster honors. The U.S. Coast Guard belatedly awarded Tunnell the Silver Lifesaving Medal in 2011 for his heroic acts in 1944 and 1946, accepted by his sister Vivian and niece Catherine Robinson.[34] They are also naming a cutter and an athletic building after him on the Coast Guard Academy campus. Justice, however delayed, is justice served. Author Robert S. Cohen recently rated Tunnell the second greatest New York Giant of all time (after Lawrence Taylor). His soul goes marching on.[35]

Number three in Cohen's estimation is Roosevelt Brown. Born on October 20, 1932, in Charlottesville, Virginia—site of an ugly racial confrontation in 2017—Brown grew up in a segregated city. Too big to play trombone in the school band, he recalled, Roosevelt was persuaded by a coach to go out for football at Jefferson High School.[36] He attended Morgan State, an HBCU in Baltimore, Maryland, a veritable pipeline, along with other Black colleges, to the pros. *The Pittsburgh Courier* had closely followed his career and in 1952 selected Brown as a first-team All-American offensive tackle. The article in which he was honored caught the attention of New York Giants executives and scouts. Drafted number 321 in the 27th round, Rosey signed for $3,000 and a ticket to training camp. A diamond in the rough, Brown needed experience as well as polish. Veteran Giants tackle Al DeRogatis (later an expert radio announcer) had to teach rookie Brown the correct stance.[37] With broad shoulders tapering down to a 29-inch waist, this 6'3" 245-pound Adonis learned quickly. Aided by tremendous speed generated from powerful legs and a work ethic that would make ardent Calvinists quake with envy, Roosevelt Brown carved out quite a 13-year career, during which he missed only four games.

Brown's principal role from the left-tackle position was to protect Giants quarterbacks from blitzing linemen and to open holes for Giants running backs. On Frank Gifford's longest run from scrimmage in 1959 for 79 yards against the Washington Redskins, witnessed by this author from a seat in Yankee Stadium, Brown opened a hole with a crushing block, then proceeded apace with Gifford to wipe out the last defender just short of "pay-dirt." Gifford admitted that Rosey Brown made it possible for the famous halfback (turned wide-out receiver after a devastating blindsided tackle by Eagles linebacker Chuck Bednarik) to reach the Hall of Fame.[38] Brown amassed many honors during his career. He made eight All-Pro teams and 10 Pro Bowls. He helped the Giants to win six division titles in six years and one NFL championship in 1956. As a vendor for Harry P. Stevens Co. in Yankee Stadium that year for football as well as baseball, I remember it well. Roosevelt Brown was voted into the Hall of Fame in 1975 and named to the NFL's 75th anniversary as well as the 100th anniversary team. After retirement he worked for the Giants as an assistant coach and scout. Operating in a mode of accommodation, Brown rarely complained. Strangely, when lodged in Negro-only residences with teammate Emlen Tunnell in the early 1950s, he enjoyed the absence of curfews and supervision, freeing up Emlen and himself for enjoyable parties fueled by beer. He said: "It made me kind of angry when segregation ended, and we had to stay with white boys."[39]

Plagued by chronic phlebitis, Brown had to retire from active play in 1963 as the once formidable Giants began a long spiral downward. As as scout, however, he selected excellent choices like John Mendenhall and Leonard Marshall for a team in need of a rebuild. Brown, who never earned more than $20,000 in any year, put love of the game above financial remuneration: "You have to enjoy it. You have to have the game in your hearts. They can't pay us enough for what we go through on the field."[40] Roosevelt Brown's big heart failed him while gardening at his New Jersey home on June 9, 2004. His death left a large hole in the hearts of Giants fans. Even in defeat in the classic battle with Baltimore in 1958, Roosevelt found solace in what he believed was the greatest game ever played.[41]

Dick "Night Train" Lane was born on April 16, 1927, in Austin, Texas, to a pimp and a hooker. Wrapped in newspapers, he was thrust into a dumpster. Left to die, Richard was only three months old. People who heard him crying mistook him for a cat. Found and adopted by a generous if stern woman named Ella Lane, Richard joined four other children. To make ends meet, he did odd jobs: shining shoes, helping his adoptive mother in her laundry business, and bussing tables at local hotels. Lane played basketball and football in high school from 1945 to 1946.

His birth mother, Etta Mae King, resurfaced and they reconciled. He moved in with his mother in Council Bluffs, Iowa, where she and her partner operated a tavern. Lane played baseball with the Omaha Rockets, a minor league team affiliated with the Kansas City Monarchs. He played for a junior college team in 1947, followed by four years in the U.S. Army, still playing football. After his discharge, Lane worked at an aircraft plant. Impressed with his press clippings from the Fort Ord games and his tryout, the Los Angeles Rams signed Lane to a $4,500 salary contract. His rookie year, 1952, proved sensational. Playing cornerback for the first time, he corralled 14 interceptions and punished receivers ferociously over a 12-game season. Lane amassed 298 return yards by interception and took two interceptions to the "House" for touchdowns. Author Wayne Stewart documents the fear that Lane engendered every time he tackled an opponent.[42] Lane made the 1950s All-Decade team as the best cornerback. He entered the Hall of Fame in 1974 and was selected to the All-Time team in 1994. Lane mastered two deadly moves: the clothesline tackle and tackle around opponents' heads and necks, later banned by the NFL. Some experts contend that Lane invented the bump-and-run strategy to throw a receiver off his designated route.[43]

Over a 14-year career Dick Lane played in seven Pro-Bowl All-Star games. He spent two years with Los Angeles, six years with the Chicago Cardinals, and six with the Detroit Lions. Many of his younger teammates regarded Lane as a mentor and cornerback icon at 6'3" and 185 sculpted pounds. Lane was taller and faster than his rivals. Denied coaching opportunities, he served as special staff assistant on the Detroit Lions organizations for six years. So, one wonders, why the trades? There is no easy answer. Lane's life was no bed of roses. His three marriages failed. Lane's second wife, a jazz singer *extraordinaire*, died of a drug overdose, and perhaps he never overcame a traumatic childhood. Detroit's mayor, Coleman Young, appointed "Night Train" the first director of the Police Athletic League to help inner-city youths gain success through sports. Like many African American males, Lane developed diabetes and high blood pressure. Unable to earn more than $25,000 per year during his prime as an athlete and living on only a $200-per-month pension in retirement did not satisfy Dick Lane's basic needs. Attended by a personal care worker, Lane suffered a fatal heart attack on January 29, 2002, and laid his burden down.[44]

Wallace "Wally" Triplett also played both ways as linebacker and running back. As the first African American draftee to play for the NFL after the unofficial ban in 1934, Wally had a fascinating backstory like Dick Lane. He was born on April 18, 1926, in La Mott, Pennsylvania, a suburb of Philadelphia. Triplett's father was a postal worker, one of the most desirable jobs for African Americans in pursuit of a middle-class lifestyle at that time. The fifth of six male children born to

Mahlon and Estelle Triplett, Wally grew up as a fine student-athlete who excelled in football and baseball at Cheltenham High School.[45] As a graduating high school senior, he received a scholarship offer from the University of Miami, embedded in the Deep South. Initially delighted, the skeptical student replied that he was Black. Miami rescinded the offer. So Wally Triplett chose Penn State University (PSU) on a state-funded senatorial scholarship along with friend and teammate Dennie Hoggard. Playing halfback, Wally became the first African American to start as a PSU varsity player.[46] Before his death in 2018, Triplett seemed to have slipped under our cultural radar. Why? Author Terrence F. Ross points to the brevity of Triplett's pro career and his desire to avoid the limelight as possible reasons.[47] A 5'10" 170-pound speedster with "smarts," Triplett crested as halfback and kick returner. In 1947, he averaged 4.0 yards per carry and 28.2 yards per reception with two touchdowns, and sparkled on defense, leading PSU to a 9–0–1 record. As a senior in 1948, Triplett had 424 yards rushing, 90 yards in receptions, three interceptions for 62 yards, and 13.4 yards on five punt returns. Against West Virginia University, Wally returned a punt for an 85-yard touchdown.

Off the field, he also proved to be a profile in courage. When local barbers refused to cut his hair, he protested effectively to provide space for a Black barber. And when one of his college professors engaged in racial profiling through his grades, Wally had him suspended after he secured an African American PhD student to write a paper for him, as a litmus test, which the professor failed. Another opportunity for revenge occurred in 1946 when a game pitted Miami University against PSU. Miami refused to play if Blacks participated. In solidarity with their dynamic Black duo, the white PSU players voted unanimously to stay home. One year later, another racial challenge surfaced, this time at the Cotton Bowl in Dallas versus Southern Methodist (SMU) led by Doak Walker. Officials advised Penn State to leave their Black stars at home. PSU Captain Steve Suhey negated that that unsolicited suggestion, without a vote but with a now famous chant: "We are Penn State, there will be no meetings." In a major step forward, SMU Coach Matty Bell agreed to play the game, minus racial barriers, claiming: "After all, we're supposed to live in a democracy."[48]

Because of the prevalence of racism in Dallas, PSU players and staff had to stay together 14 miles away at a naval airbase, thus providing a lesson on the evil of segregation to its white players. A hotly contested game on January 1, 1948, ended in a 13–13 tie when Wally Triplett scored a touchdown on a pass for the final score. After he graduated from PSU with a degree in physical education, Wally earned another first when the Detroit Lions selected him in the 19th round of the NFL draft in 1949. Triplett's NFL record of 294 return yards in a single game lasted for 44 years. His 73.5-yard kickoff return average, however, remains a single-game record in the NFL. After the 1950 season, he served in the U.S. Army during the Korean War, fighting for the 594th Field Artillery Battalion. After two years in the military, Triplett returned to play one year with the Chicago Cardinals before retirement.[49] Subsequently, Triplett became a teacher and worked in the insurance field and for the Chrysler Corporation in Detroit. Although his pro football career was short, Wallace Triplett enjoyed a good long life, a marriage that lasted 66 years until his wife

Leonore died, four children, six grandchildren, and five great-grandchildren.[50] His song ended on November 8, 2018, but his memory and legacy should linger on.

Author William C. Rhoden captured that legacy, perfectly:[51]

> Triplett helped build the path that became a road that is now a superhighway, sometimes abused, for black athletes.... But Triplett's most enduring achievement took place in college when he inspired a program and a university that chose principle over expediency.

Born on August 31, 1918, Kenny Washington was raised by his grandmother and uncle because his father, Edgar "Blue" Washington, a Negro League baseball player, was "not around much anymore" after Kenny arrived. An outstanding athlete in baseball as well as football, he led Abraham Lincoln High School to city championships in both sports. Uncle Rocky Washington, Los Angeles's highest-ranking Black police officer, mentored his nephew. Kenny rose to prominence at UCLA. In 1937, Washington teamed up with another halfback/end, Woodie Strode, for two years, followed by the 1939 addition to this dynamic duo of a four-letter man named Jackie Robinson and his Pasadena friend, Rae "Red" Bartlett, who played end on that undefeated team that went 9–0–1. Although Washington had more total yards than any other college player that year, he only made the All-American second team.[52] Despite his outstanding credentials and excellent play against the NFL champion Green Bay Packers in the annual College All-Star game, Kenny Washington, unable to break racial barriers in 1940, went undrafted, though his fame transferred deftly to the silver screen. That year, he appeared in two films, *Crooked Money* and *While Thousands Cheered*. In the latter, Kenny starred as the football hero, surrounded by an all-Black cast featuring comic foil Mantan Moreland, Jeni Le Gon, and Florence O'Brien, among other talented but underutilized actors.[53]

So he and Woody Strode also brought marquee value to the Hollywood Bears, a kind of minor or semi-pro league football team in the Pacific Coast League (PCL). They were paid a fixed salary per game and could gain additional money from a proportion of gate receipts contingent on the number of paid attendees. From 1940 to 1945, Washington earned side money while he worked full-time. Strode served in the U.S. Army Air Corps unloading ordinance in the Marianas and in Guam. He also played football on an army team in California. Unable to serve in the war effort because of knee problems, Washington continued playing football on "bum" knees for the Hollywood Bears and San Francisco Clippers (three of four with the Bears). He also worked for the LAPD, assisted by Uncle Rocky Washington. Strode got a job with the district attorney, escorting prisoners.[54] After Woody married Princess Luana Kalaeloa—and thus into Hawaiian royalty—this mixed-race marriage became a political issue for Strode's boss, District Attorney Burron Fitts, who lost his bid for reelection. And Woody lost his job; now, except for some bit parts in Hollywood movies that projected the usual stereotypes, football became his primary source of income.[55]

Woody Strode, born on July 25, 1914, in Los Angeles of Black Cherokee and Black Creek lineage, met Kenny Washington in 1931, and they became fast friends. More aggressive than his younger buddy, Strode would not tolerate racial slurs, and he often retaliated in kind or with fists. He protected Kenny. Together, they succeeded at UCLA and waited for a chance to play for an NFL team. Blocked until the steel door opened a bit, they played for the Hollywood Bears. Then the door suddenly opened after Jackie Robinson and Branch Rickey signed that watershed contract on October 23, 1945. Several months later, on March 21, 1946, the Los Angeles Rams signed Kenny Washington to play pro football in the NFL. To lower the pressure on Kenny, who had undergone his third knee operation, the Rams purchased the contract of his buddy, Woody Strode, from the Hollywood Bears. Was this a paternalistic move by Rams management to secure a Black roommate for their new hire, as Strode surmised? Whatever the reason, Washington insisted and the deal was done.[56]

Both did double duty, playing defense and offense. Strode's tenure with the Rams was brief. More successful in Canada, Woody helped the Calgary Stampeders to win the Grey Cup in 1948. Recurring injuries, however, forced him to retire in 1949. Shed no tears for the resilient Woody. He found a safer as well as more lucrative career in film and on television. As Draba, the martyred rebel in *Spartacus,* he won critical acclaim. Director John Ford cast him in several adult westerns. When the legendary director lay dying, Woody Strode served as caretaker. He even went abroad to act in "spaghetti westerns," showing broad range in multiple roles as a "macho man" with a sensitive soul.[57]

Plagued by recurrent knee problems, Washington's debut with the Rams was delayed. He played sparingly, attempting only 23 rushes for 114 yards attempted, scoring one touchdown. Strode caught only four passes for 37 yards. A saving grace was their appeal in boosting attendance at their Rams Colosseum home games. In 1947, Washington radiated a glimmer of his old glory days at UCLA by scoring on a 92-yard touchdown run and leading the NFL in yards per carry, but five knee operations prevented a reemergence of Kenny Washington, vintage 1939. Nevertheless, Washington in 27 games managed to score eight touchdowns and rush for 859 yards in three injury-plagued years, averaging 6.14 yards per carry, the best in Los Angeles Rams history.[58]

After retirement, unable to match the cinematic success of buddy Woody Strode, Washington had small roles in the Hollywood films *Rope of Sand* and *Pinky* (1949). The latter movie was a tepid attempt to deal with miscegenation, in which the white actress Jeanne Crain played the lead role of a black woman who "passed" but ultimately retrieved her identity by refusing to marry her white fiancé. Kenny's final role, fittingly, was in *The Jackie Robinson Story*, playing a Negro League manager. Washington resumed his LAPD position coupled with forays into business ventures. He even scouted for the Los Angeles Dodgers briefly. As author Charles K. Ross laments, neither Washington nor Strode received adequate recognition or compensation for their noble efforts as barrier breakers. He firmly believes that "they are truly two forgotten pioneers whose contribution to the NFL cannot be measured by statistics but must be recognized for their sacrifices."[59]

Among his awards, Washington won the Douglas Fairbanks Trophy in 1939 as the top collegiate player and entered the College Football Hall of Fame in 1956. Clearly, both Kenny Washington and Woody played vital symbolic as well as substantive roles in football, breaking barriers in order to make a more perfect union.

As tired warriors beset by age and injury, they opened doors for other outliers to follow, including the first active NFL player to come out as gay, Carl Nassib.[60]

Arguably, the catalyst for significant reintegration in football issued from a combustion of competitive forces in post–World War II America. On the foreign front, our country had to demonstrate that capitalist democracy was a better solution to contemporary problems than what Soviet Russia and its communist satellites had to offer. Both "Worlds" sought favor and influence among "Third World" countries recently liberated from colonial status. Prior to World War II, Nazi propagandists referred to Black athletes like Jesse Owens as "Black Auxiliaries" in order to demean the role of African American athletes who excelled in the Berlin Olympics. These so-called auxiliaries continued—indeed expanded—their prominence in world competition. Again our principal foreign opponent, the USSR pointed to the racial divide in our country that kept African Americans in subordinate status and, worse, under threat of lynching. A more perfect union at home required purposeful change on several fronts, including in civil rights as well as in civil liberties. A disconnect between the American possibility or dream and the American reality required repair.[61] Marxist critics feasted on America's monopolies. Major league sports teemed with monopolies, including the NFL. Attempts to break this situation started in 1946 with the All-American Conference (AAC). To compete with the NFL, AAC owners tried to draft premier college players and tempt them with higher salaries. When this failed, they probed HBCUs for raw talent. Although the rival league failed to survive beyond 1949, most of the gifted Black players made a transition to the NFL after the merger.

Unable to purchase a majority interest with the Chicago Cardinals or an expansion franchise, Texan Lamar Hunt, son of oil baron H.L. Hunt, decided to corral "Bud" Adams and six other tycoons and convince them to create new league with at least two teams from Texas. Largely thanks to his efforts, a new league, the American Football League, was founded in 1960. It lasted as a separate entity until, like the AAC, its prior incarnation, it merged with the NFL in 1966. Highly innovative and with lucrative TV contracts with ABC and NBC, the new league flourished. It started with eight teams, extended later to 10 teams. In vivid contrast to the staid NFL teams, the AFL put a premium on offense with a premium on the passing game, recruited Black players, shared TV revenue among all owners, put names as well as numbers on the backs of jerseys, employed large field clocks, introduced hand-held field cameras to get closer to the action and capture sounds of bodies clashing, and permitted the two-point option following a touchdown. All these new moves contributed to spectator involvement. Clearly, according to author Charles K. Ross, two components of the AFL success story led to a transformation of pro football: the 1962 championship double-overtime game in which the underdog Dallas Texans defeated the favored Houston Oilers 20–17 and the drafting of Buck Buchanan in 1963. In stark contrast to his draft by the NFL in the 19th round, Buck Buchanan was selected in the first round of the AFL draft as the first African American from a historically Black school. That was a big deal![62]

Junious "Buck" Buchanan was born in Gainesville, Alabama, on September 10, 1940. He attended all-Black schools from elementary education to college. At Parker

High School, he played baseball as well as football. Legendary Coach Eddie Robinson offered Buck a scholarship to Grambling College, where he played both offense and defense in the line. As a freshman he was 6'6" and 225 pounds. In this senior year, Buck grew one inch, but added 20 pounds. Despite his hefty build, Buchanan ran the 40-yard dash in 4.9 second and the 100-yard dash in 10.2 seconds. He could use his length to bat down passes and his strength to overpower opposing centers. Early in his career, he played defensive end, switching to tackle in 1964. A true iron-man, Buchanan missed only one game in his 13-year career. Eager to prove that a player from a small Black college could make it in the pros, Buck played with fierce intensity as the core lineman. Joined by Bobby Bell (from Minnesota University), also a 1963 draft pick, and Willie Lanier, picked in 1967 from Grambling, the Kansas City Chiefs built a formidable defense. Buchanan advanced Kansas City prospects on the road to a Super Bowl win in 1970.[63]

A pivotal moment occurred over the AFL All-Star game slated for New Orleans on January 16, 1965, at Tulane Stadium. Racial discrimination, however, spoiled the party. Taxi drivers were not willing to take Black players from the airport to their lodgings at first when they arrived in New Orleans the week before the game. After some drivers did accommodate the irate players, they refused to taxi the same players around town while white players enjoyed full service. Kansas City linebacker Bobby Bell and Buffalo fullback Cookie Gilchrist both were repeatedly denied access to taxi service, and several Black players were subjected to overt discrimination at clubs and restaurants in the city. Consequently, San Diego Charger defensive end Earl Faison refused to play in the All-Star game. A meeting was called at the Roosevelt Hotel, where the players for the West team were staying. All the Black players assembled along with white players Ron Mix, a San Diego Charger tackle, and quarterback Jack Kemp, who had recently been traded from the Chargers to Buffalo. The Black players cited the recently passed 1964 Civil Rights Act that forbade such outrageous discrimination. Gilchrist summoned a vote of the 21 players punctuated by a threat issued by Gilchrist to kick the ass of any dissenter. Fearful or not, the voters unanimously supported the boycott, including the white players. Executives, including Ernest Morial, the New Orleans president of the NAACP, attempted to dissuade the players. After protracted discussion, AFL Commissioner Joe Foss, a highly decorated war hero, agreed to switch the venue to Houston, Texas, on the originally scheduled date of January 16.

This was first time that a protest by professional athletes resulted in a transfer of a game. To be sure, New Orleans paid a huge price in lost revenue. And two alleged ringleaders of this unprecedented action, Cookie Gilchrist and Kansas City Chiefs running back Abner Haynes, were traded to the weakest team in the AFL at that time, the Denver Broncos, shortly after the successful boycott. Delighted Black sportswriter Sam Lacey, who had shepherded Jackie Robinson through his neophyte seasons in the major leagues, roared: "When these young football players packed their gear and quit New Orleans in protest against local bigotry, the action was so totally unexpected that it rocked the entire sports words. And I for one, just loved it."[64]

The players mentioned in this chapter did not receive full recognition, nor did they get compensation comparable to that of their professional counterparts today. Many flew under our current radar. Nevertheless, they invite respect, gratitude, and remembrance. These heroic athletes rose above the injustice of their times and blazed across our firmament briefly, bringing illumination, life lessons, purpose, and joy. As poet Stephen Spender wrote in admiration of the truly great, they "left the vivid air signed with their honour."

5

Fritz Pollard
and Paul Robeson

Football provided another avenue for social mobility and positive identity in a war against the caste system. Moreover, this often-brutal sport permitted violence across racial lines. We begin this section with Fritz Pollard and Paul Robeson. The reasons stem from personal experience and the need to restore the great athlete, actor, singer, linguist, and activist to his rightful place in the American pantheon. Because he embodied the dualism that Dr. DuBois expertly delineated, my childhood icon Paul Robeson invites renewed study. Although athleticism was only part of his heroic lifestyle, which crossed so many different pursuits, I reasoned that since sports brought Paul his first national acclaim, it would provide a touchstone to the larger story.

Basically, aristocrats by nature if not nurture, heroes experience mercurial careers in democratic societies. They flash into fame and fade into obscurity in a single generation. "The sun also rises…." One day they are the people's choice, the next, society's discard. Each year sports authorities create lists of outstanding athletes. Most of my students in sports history classes failed to recognize anyone prior to the Michael Jordan era. Their apparent amnesia signifies a deeper malaise. The glaring indifference to history coupled with a minuscule span of attention issues no doubt from excessive exposure to cable television and digital devices. It is therefore categorically imperative to recapture figures like Robeson whose political persuasion pushed him into purgatory. Lest we forget, this brilliant scholar-athlete, in the best Socratic sense, blazed a path to glory for many Black athletes who excelled in football, baseball, basketball, track, tennis, and golf.

Jackie Robinson's mantra rings true: "A life is not important except in the impact it has on other lives." It applies to football as well as baseball. On the gridiron, Blacks had more margin to maneuver. Earning distinction as the first national football figure, Bill Lewis entered Amherst College in 1888. He played center for a fine team. After graduation, Lewis studied law at Harvard, where—unfettered by current NCAA rules—he continued his outstanding football play. One hundred seventy-five pounds of tempered steel, Lewis, agile and fast, played both defense and offense. Walter Camp dubbed him an All-American, the first Black to be so honored. As a great student of the game, he subsequently became a coach. Success went beyond the football arena. Bill Lewis also rose to prominence in the field of legal battle. He became the first Black to serve as U.S. assistant attorney general.[1]

Until a recent article in the *New York Times*, few readers (including this writer) knew about the tragedy that befell Jack Trice, the first Black football player at Iowa State University. In only his second game on the varsity team as a 6-foot 200-pound tackle, Trice suffered a shoulder injury, later diagnosed as a broken collarbone, in the first quarter. Playing without a facemask in a sport of sanctioned violence with few restrictions, Trice drove at the legs of a Minnesota blocker to impede the runner on a roll-block, now banned. He landed on his back in the third quarter and was crushed under a rush of cleats. Trice died two days later. Whether accidental or intentional, Trice's death was one of 18 in football in 1923. In the context of endemic racism exacerbated by the resurgence of the Ku Klux Klan, particularly in the Midwest, in the so-called "Roaring Twenties," Black players were evidently more vulnerable than their white counterparts. Future stars in Iowa football, Ozzie Simmons at Iowa University and Johnny Bright of Drake University, suffered similar if not fatal attacks inspired by racial hatred. Thus, African American gridiron participants had to steel themselves against foul play.[2]

A quick study in self-protection, and a halfback with blazing speed, Fritz Pollard played for Brown University. In 1916 he led Brown to victories over favored Yale and Harvard in successive weeks. Before graduating, he turned pro, earning admiration from opponents as well as from teammates. As other scholars have observed, heroes have flaws. In my prior publications, I pointed out that many sports heroes encounter a short shelf life. Some slide into anti-heroic mode. Frederick "Fritz" Pollard serves as an avatar of this prototype. Throughout his long life of 94 years, he oscillated from acceptance to aggression and back to acceptance. Like his Black predecessors in sports who incurred verbal abuse from white fans, Fritz had to overcome bigotry on the road to gridiron fame.[3]

Born in 1894 to a middle-class family that prized education, Pollard grew up in Rogers Park, Illinois. His father was a barber, the second most popular profession for African Americans according to the 1890 census.[4] Fritz's older brother was a high school football star at Northwestern University in the 1890s. Another brother, Hughes, also displayed athletic skills. When Fritz entered high school, he was 4'11" and only 98 pounds. Cocky and assertive, Fritz was inspired by his older brother Leslie, who played briefly for Dartmouth College, leading his Ivy League team to a 10–6 win over rival Princeton. Fritz admired his older brother, who dropped out for a career in music. Fritz also admired Jack Johnson.[5] At Lane Technical High School, the younger Pollard ran indoor and outdoor track, played both baseball and the trombone in the school band. Football, however, gained primacy. As a student, he maintained a C+ average despite his busy schedule.[6] After graduation, he became an athletic nomad, enrolling or attempting to enroll in several schools: Northwestern, Dartmouth, Harvard, Bates, and Brown, on a second try, starting at age 20.[7] On the gridiron, Fritz received racial insults and incurred physical injuries. Nevertheless, he led Brown to a record of 5–3–1 including an upset of mighty Yale. In that pivotal game, the Elis led at halftime 6 to 0. Pollard took control in the second half, running wild and deftly catching passes. Brown pulled ahead of Yale 7 to 6. Brown fans cheered as Fritz collared a punt on his 40-yard line, started right, sidestepped left, and raced into the end zone for 60-yard touchdown, hiking the score to 14 to 6. Another drive led to a third Brown touchdown, with Pollard doing most of the damage in the 21–6 victory.

Facing a favored Harvard 11 a week later, Brown pulled off an upset as 33,000 fans watched. Pollard scored the first touchdown. On defense, he made two touchdown-saving tackles. On offense he ran 46 yards to pay dirt, upping Brown's lead to 14–0. He set up a third score with a catch and run of 42 yards. When Brown's coach removed Fritz from the game, 8,000 Brown fans offered their star a standing ovation. These two upset victories probably prompted an invite to Pasadena's 1915 Rose Bowl. On a rain-soaked afternoon, Brown lost to Washington University 14–0 as the fleet-footed Fritz could not gain traction on the muddy field. Almost drowned after a pile-up, he was sidelined in the second half.[8]

Earlier that season, Pollard faced Paul Robeson of Rutgers on October 28. With Fritz scoring two touchdowns, Brown won 21–3. Despite their adversarial roles, the two stars formed a lifelong friendship during summers at a Rhode Island hotel. A quadruple threat, Pollard ran, passed, kicked, and played safety on defense, expertly. Walter Camp named Pollard to his All-American team, describing him "as the most elusive back of the year."[9] Walter Camp's honor bestowed on Pollard generated a long if hot-and-cold relationship with a Brown alumnus and donor named John D. Rockefeller, II.

When war fever struck America in 1917, Pollard joined the war effort with a brief stint as a director of physical education in military training. He also ran track. Exposed to raw racial violence in the "Red Summer" that followed in 1919, the previously accommodationist Pollard assumed a more militant outlook.[10] He joined the Akron Indians pro football team. In his first game, a 13–6 loss, Pollard scored his team's only points. In 1920, he joined ranks with Paul Robeson. As Fritz recalled, Robeson played tackle and end while he played halfback.[11] They went undefeated with a record of eight wins and three ties. Pollard became player-coach of the Akron Pros in 1921. At 6'2", the 220-pound Robeson, a giant among men, contributed on offense and defense. According to author Pollard, "Robeson played because of his love for the game, the considerable money involved, and the status it represented in the African American community." It also helped to finance his tuition at Columbia University Law School.[12] Injuries, however, plagued both athletes due no doubt to the rigors of 60 minutes of play each game. The Akron Pros finished with an 8–3–1 record in 1921.

Following his college pattern, Pollard switched affiliations with several professional teams in his eight years as player/coach. From Akron, he and Robeson went to Milwaukee. Minus Robeson who pursued a different career path, he went to Hammons, then to Providence, and finally back to Akron in 1926.[13] Though past his prime at age 32, he played in Pennsylvania's coal region. In 1928, Fritz formed the Chicago Blackhawks, which marked the first all-Black pro-football team. In 1935, he coached the Brown Bombers in New York City, a team that enabled Blacks banned from the NFL since 1934 to continue their football careers.

The best summation of Fritz Pollard's important legacy can be found in Carroll's biography of this football pioneer. Athletics, Carroll cogently argues, is one area where Black athletes "could be judged on merit."[14] Pro football failed to honor Pollard—and Robeson—with the kind of press coverage that Jackie Robinson enjoyed later to be sure, but they did ultimately emerge as folk heroes. Unlike Robeson, who pursued greatness on other stages, Pollard used sports as a personal "vehicle for success, fame, and fortune." An avatar of what sociologist E. Franklin Frazier disdainfully labeled the "Black Bourgeoisie," Fritz Pollard carefully navigated the road to success.[15] Thus, when he dabbled in politics, Pollard supported Republican candidates in local as well as national elections, especially in 1940 and 1952. In 1958, he actively campaigned for Nelson Rockefeller for New York's governorship.[16]

Out of touch, perhaps, with most Black voters, who veered towards the Democratic Party, he was, by self-definition, an elitist who curried status and sought money. He learned to survive in a white-dominated social order. Although primarily motivated by self-interest, Pollard "cared deeply about civil rights issues and worked for the betterment of his race," his daughter Leslie observed.[17] His son, Fritz Pollard, Jr., who won a bronze medal in the racially charged Berlin Olympics in 1936, placed his famous father at the cutting edge of careers in sports, finance, journalism, and entertainment. Finally inducted into the Pro Football Hall of Fame posthumously in 2005, Fritz Pollard was the first important Black in professional football, the first Black head coach, the first Black quarterback, and the first great running back.[18] Despite his faults, a not uncommon trait among many heroes, Pollard deserves a high perch in our pantheon.

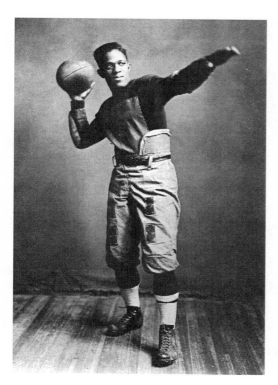

Frederick Douglass "Fritz" Pollard, 1919, in his Brown University uniform. As a quarterback and All-American halfback, he would lead Brown to its only Rose Bowl appearance in 1916. Three years later, he became one of the earliest African American players in pro football, and later the first head coach in NFL history. In 1954 he became the first African American inducted into the College Football Hall of Fame; Pro Football Hall of Fame membership followed in 2005 (Brown Digital Repository, John Hay Library, Brown University).

So does his friend and contemporary, Paul Robeson. Despite their diametrically different positions on the political spectrum, Robeson and Pollard remained lifelong friends. If any single scholar-athlete could dispel the racist stereotypes that dominated nineteenth-century thought, it was Paul Robeson. April 9, 1998, marked the 100th birthday of this complex, brilliant Renaissance man. Athlete, singer, actor, activist, Robeson transcended his first national arena, the football field. Growing up in a segregated society, Robeson enjoyed a spectacular career as an athlete. Most studies of this genius pay tribute to his sporting life and quickly move to other facets of his career. Nevertheless, it is important to remember that Paul Robeson became a national figure though his athletic prowess. Clearly, events in the sporting arena mirror American society. And it was through sports that African Americans entered the mainstream of our culture. I had the distinct honor to organize a celebration of Robeson's life at Long Island University's Brooklyn campus on February 28, 1998.

According to biographer Lloyd Brown, sports came naturally to young Paul. Born in Princeton, the youngest of four surviving children, Robeson was orphaned in 1904 when his mother, Maria Louisa, died as a result of an accidental fire. Robeson rarely referred to his mother. Perhaps he repressed painful memories. Yet one of his favorite spirituals spoke to this loss: "Sometimes I Feel Like a Motherless Child."

The family moved to Somerville, New Jersey, in 1910. Attending the town's "colored school," Paul attracted attention on the baseball field. While still in grade school, he was drafted as a "ringer" to play shortstop for the integrated high school. When Robeson entered Somerville High School legally, he was one of 250 students, and one of three Blacks and only one of eight enrolled in college preparatory work. Encouraged by his venerable father, William Drew Robeson, a runaway slave whom he affectionately called "Pops," young Paul excelled at Somerville High School. His model for athletic performance was older brother Ben "who most inspired"—he recalled—his "interest in sports." Ben had the ability to make it as an All-American in football or as a professional baseball player, although he ultimately became the pastor of the Zion African Methodist Episcopal Church in Harlem, New York.[19]

The younger Robeson played forward on the basketball team and hurled the javelin and threw the discus in track and field. In baseball he played shortstop and catcher. During inter-city games Paul experienced racism. In one encounter Paul whacked a tremendous triple. The High Bridge principal stormed out on the field and thundered: "That coon did not touch second!" A major rhubarb, to echo the signature phrase of broadcaster Walter "Red" Barber, was prevented when Robeson's teammates protected him from a possible physical confrontation instigated by the incendiary principal.[20]

In high school football Paul played fullback. On this field, too, he became the target of opposing players. In battling Somerville's archrival Bound Brook, Paul broke his collarbone. But he held his ground, winning approval from all with his courage, tenacity, and talent. His teammate, Doug Brown, later dean and provost at Princeton University, remembered Paul as the heart, at least 9/10 of it, of the football squad. Although sports brought young Robeson his public acclaim, he also excelled in debating, singing, and scholarship.[21]

As a result of a statewide exam, Rutgers opened its doors to this highly qualified scholar-athlete in the autumn of 1915. A private school then, Rutgers had only 500 students. Paul was only the third Black to attend Rutgers since its inception in 1766. While trying out for the football team, this 6'2", 190-pound marvel incurred injury and endured pain. In the very first scrimmage, he sustained a broken nose, a smashed hand, and a dislocated shoulder. Robeson's father, William, and brother

Ben did not let him quit, and after 10 days of recuperation, Robeson was back on the field. Robeson recalled his ordeal by fire in an interview with *New York Times* critic Robert Van Gelder.[22] He admitted to rage—a rage to kill. Lifting a tough running back named Kelly above his head for a bone-crushing tackle, he was deterred by Coach Sanford who blew the whistle to prevent serious injury. Robeson had made the team.

Former teammates differ on whether Paul was deliberately subjected to a brutal hazing during scrimmages. Biographer Martin Duberman, in an effort at objectivity, presents both sides. I tend to believe that Paul's reconstruction of this traumatic event gets closer to what actually happened. One mate, Robert Nash, recalled that Robeson "took a terrific beating."[23] Perhaps the "*Rashomon*ian" truth is no less elusive today than it was more than a century ago.

Robeson's skill as a football player, however, is beyond doubt. Contemporary reporters, cited by Lloyd Brown, extolled Paul's versatility and excellence. He played many positions on both offense and defense, brilliantly. Paul Robeson, Jr., informed me that his famous father established a pattern for contemporary players on offense as well as on defense. He developed into the prototypical tight end who could block proficiently and turn short passes into long yardage while bowling over would-be tacklers. As a roving defender, Paul Sr. inaugurated the role of middle linebacker. Contemporary observers marveled at Robeson's brilliance. The only places he was excluded were in segregated facilities such as the Rutgers dormitories and the year-end dinners. The young athlete affected an insouciant manner while engaged in a myriad of activities. He harbored hurts against the town of Princeton for the treatment accorded his father, brother, and fellow Blacks. He wanted to meet and beat Princeton on the playing fields as a channel for his pent-up anger.

Coach George Foster Sanford, whom Robeson adored, taught him how to protect himself with a well-placed elbow and how to play offense.[24] As a freshman, Robeson remained a substitute tackle until November 20, when he earned a start against Stevens Tech. Rutgers won 39 to 3. Stardom loomed in 1916 as Robeson played in six of seven games at guard and tackle. The only game that Robeson missed resulted from a demand issued by Washington and Lee to bench the n----r. Shamefully, Rutgers capitulated. Coach Sanford rationalized this as a move to protect Robeson from the hostile Southerners. It was not the finest hour for the Scarlet Knights. Without their star player, they could only manage a 13–13 tie.[25] When Robeson returned to his tackle position, *The Newark Evening News* reported, the whole line improved.[26]

In 1917 Paul gained fame as an offensive end, defensive end, and tackle. Robeson wrote about this year in detail. Reprinted in Philip Foner's excellent collection, *Paul Robeson Speaks*, the retrospective offers a solid analysis of Rutgers' banner year. More importantly, it provides a clue to his character. Published in the *Rutgers Alumni Quarterly*, January 1918, he begins with a bang.[27]

The season of 1917 is over, but the memories thereof will fire the hearts of Rutgers men as long as football is football. For the team fighting as only a Rutgers team can fight and inspired by the indomitable spirit of that greatest of football mentors, George Foster Sanford, rose to the greatest heights, and stands not only as one of the best teams of the year but as one of the greatest of all times.

Robeson mentions that only three veterans returned to the team: Rendell, Feitner, and himself (to whom he refers in the third person). In the first game, the Scarlet Knights defeated Ursinus 25–0. The next game was rout of Fort Wadsworth: 90–0. The third game was played in Syracuse. The home team capitalized on miscues to beat Rutgers 14–10. Shouldering the blame for the defeat, Robeson exonerated Coach Sanford.[28]

Redemption came against Lafayette one week later as the Scarlet Knights whipped the men of Easton 33–6. In the big game against a highly touted Fordham team led by future baseball star Frankie Frisch, the Scarlet Knights crested, and Robeson excelled. You would not know this from Robeson's narrative, but the *New York Times* provided ample evidence.[29] In the 28–0 rout, the paper reported that Robeson made two important catches of 35 and 24 yards to set up two touchdowns. As a blocker at left end, he knocked three Rams out of the game. The headline read: "Fordham Crushed by Rutgers Power: Robeson, the sturdy Negro End of the Visiting Eleven, Plays a Stellar Role in the Aerial Attack." No less graphically, Charles A. Taylor wrote: "A dark cloud upset the hopes of the Fordham eleven yesterday."[30] No silver lining appeared as Paul Robeson—evidently the "dark cloud"— was all over the field.[31] Threats against Robeson sullied the next game opposite Greasy Neale's team from West Virginia University. Crudely, Coach Neale warned that his Southern boys would try to murder Paul. To his credit, Coach Sanford refused to knuckle under to racist blackmail. Entering the contest, West Virginia was heavily favored. On the first play from scrimmage, an opposing player threatened Robeson: "If you touch me, you black dog, I'll cut your heart out." Roused to fury, Robeson clipped him and "nearly busted him in two," Paul remembered. He taunted the redneck: "I touched you that time. How did you like it?"[32] The target of enemy cleats and forearms, Robeson absorbed tremendous punishment. Nevertheless, he made a game-saving tackle on the two-yard line during the final period. Even the biased coach had to concede that Robeson showed a lot of "guts." Rutgers dominated the first half, but their opponents recovered a blocked punt on the 12-yard line from where they punched in a touchdown in two plays. The game ended in a 7–7 tie.[33]

Disappointed, the Scarlet Knights vented against Springfield College with a 61–0 drubbing. They bested the U.S. Marines from Philadelphia, despite a lackluster performance, 27–0. The season's climax occurred in Brooklyn's Ebbets Field on November 24. A team of navy reservists composed of All-Americans under the baton of Cupid Rogers invaded Brooklyn. Robeson enumerates the opponents: Barrett of Cornell, Black and Callahan of Yale, Schlacter of Syracuse, Gerrish of Dartmouth. Having trounced Colgate and Dartmouth, these gridiron Goliaths faced the Davids of Rutgers. Led by Robeson, the underdogs triumphed 14–0. The young star conferred praise on Coach Sanford. Again, the press pointed in another direction—his. For example, sports reporter Louis Lee Arms of the *New York Sunday Tribune* wrote, "A tall tapering Negro … dominated Ebbets Field." He cited the gaping holes that Robeson opened in enemy lines, lifting little Rutgers to victory.[34] Writing for *The New York World* on November 28, 1917, George Daley called the Negro star "a football genius." Significantly, Robeson earned kudos for brains as well as brawn. The young Knight scored one touchdown and starred on defense. The victory brought a season's best record: 7–1–1.

How did the one loss occur? Robeson, as writer rather than player, explained. Football, he argued, "is method and not men.... Rutgers has the best methods taught by the greatest of football coaches, George Foster Sanford." He goes on to sing the praise of this marvelous coach, as "advocate of clean play in life as on the field." He lauds the man as an adviser, guardian, and molder of characters. Above all, Robeson pinpoints teamwork and team spirit as the stuff of greatness. He analyzes every player and his contribution but his own. Foreshadowing his evolving political philosophy, young Paul Robeson put the group above the self. This uncommon man celebrated the common cause. Such selflessness is unique among athletes of today.[35]

In a questionable expression of patriotism, Walter Camp and other sports authorities refused to name an official All-American team. Evidently, the war to make the world safe for democracy, not to mention communism, precluded football honors. Camp hailed Robeson, however, as worthy of that temporarily suspended honor: All-American. The same applied to the 1918 season, which resulted in a 5–2 record for the Scarlet Knights of the Raritan.[36] Strangely, there is far less coverage of Robeson at Rutgers during the final year of World War I. As his illustrious collegiate career drew to a close, more attention was paid to his intellectual prowess including the coveted Phi Beta Kappa key and prizes for oratory.[37] Nevertheless, Robeson continued to excel in the sports arena. In June 1919, a campus paper reported that Robeson hurled the javelin 137' 5" against Swarthmore College, 12 feet better than his nearest competitor.[38] He also finally led the Rutgers lion to a victory over the hated Princeton tiger in baseball. On June 10, 1919, after delivering the valedictory address at his graduation ceremony (in which he exhorted his classmates to achieve justice, democracy, and equality for all in "The New Idealism"), he donned "the tools of ignorance" (his catcher's gear) and boosted his baseball team to victory over Princeton, 5–1. By his own admission, observes biographer Lloyd Brown, this last game for Robeson at Rutgers, in which the longtime nemesis was defeated for the first time, represented, arguably, his finest hour.[39]

A final chapter in the Robeson-at-Rutgers saga can be found in the Rutgers yearbook. Describing Paul's spectacular performance against Navy, the author writes[40]:

> And as a thorn in her flesh, the tall, towering Robeson commanded Rutgers' secondary, dived under and spilled her wide oblique angle runs, turned back line plunges and carried the burden of defense so splendidly that in 44 minutes those Ex-All-American backs ... made precisely two first downs.

Veteran journalist Lester Rodney interviewed a participant in that game. In 1953, Rodney, then writing for the *Daily Worker*, a radical newspaper that had helped Jackie Robinson break into Major League Baseball, encountered Jimmy Conzelman at Ebbets Field. Coach of the championship Chicago Cardinals pro football team in 1948, Conzelman played quarterback on the great naval team that, though heavily favored, lost to Rutgers in a major upset. Recollecting the game in tranquility, his "eyes lit up." Rodney quotes the former player/coach:[41]

How good was he? Great, that's how good, one of the greatest ever.... He was a tremendous offensive end. Did everything, blocked, caught passes, on defense he was a linebacker up, tremendous. They'd move him around to tackle to clear the way for ball carriers sometimes.... A fine fellow too. We played together later as pros at Milwaukee. And a wonderful singer, a real artist, and you know, he was Phi Beta Kappa, you know how smart you had to be to be Phi Beta?

After college, Robeson's "smarts" carried him into Columbia Law School. To pay his tuition, Paul assisted Fritz Pollard as coach at Lincoln University. He also joined Alpha Phi Alpha, the first Black fraternity in America. While studying law, he played professional football with both Pollard and Conzelman before a ban was imposed on Blacks in 1934. His first professional venue was Hammond, Indiana, in 1920. He switched to the Akron Pros that year and stayed until 1921. He finished his football career with the Milwaukee Badgers in 1922. He earned anywhere from $50 to $200 per game.[42] Largely ignored, professional football did not keep records, so it is difficult at best to judge Robeson's postgraduate performance. We do know, however, that Paul Robeson and Fritz Pollard led an all-Black team to victory over an all-white all-star team 6–0 at Schoolings Park on December 10, 1922. And by 1922, Albert Britt wrote, this "Dusky Rover" and "Football Othello" towered above his contemporaries in the sports pantheon.[43]

Did Paul Robeson make a difference as a sports hero? In assessing his athletic career, sociologist and baseball administrator Harry Edwards observed that Paul won respect from opposing coaches with his fierce play. His coach called him "the greatest player of all time." One coach, oblivious to the explicit racism in his praise, dubbed him "a white man in black skin." Yet, on road trips, Robeson had to sleep in segregated facilities and often took meals on the team bus. There is no evidence that Paul protested publicly. In short, he was compelled to adapt a posture of either acceptance or avoidance. On the field, however, he could—and did—act aggressively. Thus, Robeson developed a bi-polar stance against a bi-polar world.

Author Murray Kempton, in a less than generous appraisal, invidiously compared Paul Robeson to Blues singer Bessie Smith and union leaders Thomas Patterson and A. Philip Randolph. Kempton claimed that the great baritone escaped from the horrors of racism inflicted upon American Blacks. An expatriate's life in Europe constituted an "avoidance" adaptation. Lionized in London, Robeson did not shoulder the awful burden of race in America. Even the judgmental Murray the K had to concede that the young Robeson was also victimized on the gridiron, as rival football players were accustomed to reminding him that he was a Negro with concentrated violence. But his conduct on these occasions was a model for any sportsman. It was generally agreed that he knew his place. Only in 1950—so much later—would Paul Robeson remember his football days and report with dreadful satisfaction that there had been moments when he used his fist in the pileups.[44]

Kempton was wrong on at least one count. Robeson mentioned his aggressive behavior on the football field earlier than 1950. Moreover, his point about gentlemanly conduct articulates a superficial truth. Indeed, football was—and is—a sport of sanctioned violence. Robeson's game, unlike that of his brilliant Black contemporary Fritz Pollard, relied on awesome power and keen intellect rather than blinding speed. But Kempton deserves credit for describing the ambivalence that marked Robeson's persona.[45]

If ambivalence represented one "mark of" oppression, athletic achievement served as a counterforce. In persistence and perseverance, Paul became a forerunner, as he acknowledged: "Sports was an important part of my life in those days."[46] Professor Lamont Yeakey forcefully argues that Paul Robeson, as athlete and scholar, smashed the myth of white supremacy.[47] In his graduate thesis, Professor Yeakey made a powerful case for reexamining the early life of Paul Robeson. I believe that his innovative study sheds new light on "The Great Forerunner" and his subsequent career.[48]

It is imperative to recall the historical context during Robeson's collegiate years. *The Crisis* reported that 224 people were lynched in 1917. One Rutgers student, a white male, was in fact stripped, dipped (in molasses), feathered, and thrust out of town by classmates. Samuel Chovenson, the victim, had refused to give a speech in support of Liberty Loans in class. In this hate-filled era, Robeson demonstrated grace under pressure, the hallmark of a Hemingway hero. He also displayed a marked superiority to white players. Moreover, he did not fear whites.[49] In his successful pursuit of athletic glory, Robeson debunked the widely held belief that Blacks were inferior. In the process, Yeakey contends, Paul broadened the humanity of whites.[50]

Paul Robeson, photographed in 1942 by Gordon Parks, was an outstanding athlete, singer, actor, linguist, and social justice activist before the Red Scare made him a pariah. A two-time All-American defensive tackle at Rutgers, he also played in the nascent National Football League to pay his way through Columbia University Law School. Unjustly marginalized, Robeson was finally inducted into the College Football Hall of Fame in 1995 and fêted with a Grammy Lifetime Achievement Award in 1998 (Library of Congress).

Professor Yeakey takes many eminent historians to task for omitting Robeson from their tomes or neglecting his impact. He chides John Hope Franklin for ignoring this African American hero. A quick glance at the latest edition of his highly regarded *From Slavery to Freedom* confirms the critique offered in 1971. The Cold War campaign to destroy Paul Robeson, waged primarily through the media, permeated the historian's craft, lamentably. Public figures also attacked Robeson. He slipped into obscurity.

Unintentionally, the Scarlet Knight may have contributed to this underestimation. When the press lauded his talents and rued his graduation, Paul responded curiously. "Negro prejudice has two sides. When people hate you, they go a little crazy. But when they like you they go a little crazy too. In football days, I got more praise than I deserved."[51] Although he was offered thousands of dollars to engage in professional sports—boxing as well as football—Robeson spurned both as corrupting and alien.[52]

In 1954 Rutgers University published a list of its 65 greatest football players. Conspicuously and absurdly absent: Paul Bustill Robeson. Sports Information Director William McKenzie called it "a conspiracy of silence." Because his alma mater refused to sponsor him, the rejection of Robeson spilled over to the National Football Hall of Fame housed at Rutgers.[53] A reversal of fortune began in 1970 when a committee of sports cognoscenti and Rutgers personnel, including Coach John Bateman, put his name in nomination. Rejected until August 25, 1995, the great athlete at long last entered his Alma Mater's Hall of Fame.[54] For Robeson, the union with football's elite came too little, too late. For the faithful, however, this delayed honor proved author Leo Tolstoy correct in his profound observation that "God sees the truth—but waits."

In the final analysis, when football functioned as the moral equivalent of war, what did this noble warrior accomplish along the banks of the Raritan River? True, segregation did not vanish during his glory years. Nor could Robeson strike a fatal blow against segregation away from the battlefields of sports. Thanks to his enormous presence, however, Black participation in a once totally white intercollegiate environment measurably improved. And public appreciation of Black talent also increased, markedly.

As Professor Jeffrey Stewart astutely observes, Robeson's body became the subject of riveting attention, his intellectual accomplishments the object of awe. In a cache of photographs recently discovered, the portrayal of Robeson in the nude may have contributed to a profound insight issuing from the Harlem Renaissance in which Paul Robeson played an integral part, namely, that Black is beautiful, and this extraordinary athletic Apollo was the epitome of Black beauty.[55]

There is, alas, also one disturbing afterthought. Robeson's account of his football experience is almost too sweet in self-denial. He must have harbored deep rage within which, when unleashed, caused the fire in his soul to burn incessantly. The oxygen of such other atmospheres as the Soviet Union and Eastern Europe, where he was lionized, admired, and loved, fed it. Because of his "service to the state," we must not extenuate or distort the injustice visited on this great man. We must also remember that Paul Robeson's heroic entry into the deep river of American life coincided with his immersion—let's call it baptism—in sports.

Fritz Pollard and Paul Robeson met at a hotel in Rhode Island. They became lifelong friends though they differed in their politics. Pollard, a staunch Republican, identified with capitalism, while Robeson veered to the radical left in his ideological trajectory. Fritz Pollard served as one of twelve pallbearers at Robeson's Harlem funeral in 1976. Both fell into relative obscurity in their later years, only to be rediscovered by Black studies proponents, sports aficionados, political activists, and younger academics in 1970s. Moreover, the end of Cold War generated "Red Scare" tactics helped the cause of Robeson's rehabilitation. Jackie Robinson's apologia to Robeson in his revised 1972 autobiography, *I Never Had It Made*, paved the way.[56] Three documentary films restored Robeson to center stage. One of these, a 30-minute film that Sidney Poitier narrated in 1979, won an Oscar for Best Documentary Short Subject.[57] In 1995, Robeson, finally recognized by Rutgers administrators, was inducted into the College Football Hall of Fame.

Robeson experienced a major revival in 1998, the year of his 100th birthday, celebrated in major academic events at his alma mater, Rutgers University, Columbia College in Chicago, and at Long Island University in Brooklyn, where I headed a memorable conference. Today, Robeson is hailed as a hero. At Rutgers and other places of residence, he is lionized with awards, exhibits, archives, streets, and boulevards bearing his name. In a singular honor, bestowed posthumously, the Grammys conferred a Lifetime Achievement Award on the great baritone-bass artist at Radio City Music Hall on February 25, 1998.[58]

Yes indeed, F. Scott Fitzgerald was wrong and Leo Tolstoy was right. There are second acts in America, and God sees the truth but waits.

6

Jim Brown
and Black Quarterbacks

Following the Pollard-Robeson era, Blacks experienced segregation, especially after 1934. A breakthrough occurred after World War II. Marion Motley and Bill Willis joined the Cleveland Browns in the nascent American Football Conference in 1946. Likewise, Kenny Washington and Woody Strode reintegrated the NFL with the Los Angeles (formerly Cleveland) Rams that same year. Shortly thereafter, others joined the pro ranks: Claude "Buddy" Young with the New York Yankees football team in the AFC along with George Taliaferro with the Los Angeles Dons, Horace Gillom with the Cleveland Browns, Wally Triplett with the Detroit Lions, Emlen Tunnell with the New York Giants.[1]

Jim Brown

Preceded by Fritz Pollard, Paul Robeson, Marion Motley, and Joe Perry among other Black football stars, Jim Brown looms as the quintessential sports hero. His excellence in multiple sports—football, lacrosse, basketball, baseball, and track—was evident in high school. Though he was regarded as the best lacrosse player in America, Jim Brown gained iconic status in football. Born on February 17, 1936, on St. Simons, a coastal island near Georgia, he endured a difficult childhood. Abandoned by his father at birth and his mother at age two, he lived with an aunt until age seven, and later with a grandmother. Reunited with his mother, a domestic worker on Long Island, he still felt neglected. As a teenager, he often walked local streets rather than return home, where his mother entertained "gentleman callers." Author Dave Zirin suggests that Brown's anger toward women, mostly women of color, can be traced to abandonment by his mother.[2]

Befriended by Manhasset High School athletic director Ed Walsh, young Jim learned survival skills. Other white benefactors included Roy Simmons and Ken Molloy. The latter, a lawyer, took an abiding interest in Brown. A loyal alumnus of Syracuse University, he orchestrated admission to his alma mater and helped to finance Jim's education when the university failed to honor a full scholarship offer. As a freshman in 1953, Brown, the only African American on the football team, felt isolated as coaches ignored him partly because he refused to become a receiver.

Brown was housed with freshmen non-athletes, denied nutritious food, and advised not to date white girls. Frustrated, he considered a transfer to Ohio State. In his junior year, however, he emerged from fifth man on the running charts to starter in football, and also enjoyed success in lacrosse, baseball, and basketball.[3] Biographer Mike Freeman succinctly describes the paradox that is Jim Brown, a man who "walked the planet with supreme arrogance."[4] Blessed with brains and biceps, Jim Brown proved dominant on and off the field "with an 18" neck, 45" chest, broad shoulders, plus large thighs ... [he] ran head held high, legs pumping and broad arms swiping away tacklers." Smashing stereotypes, he redefined multiple roles: running back, movie stardom, sex symbol, civil rights leader, economic and social activist. His overwhelming concern was to be the baddest, smartest, longest lasting man ever.[5]

Unwilling to cry in public or hug his children, Brown favored young girls, around 19 years of age. His powerful libido led to broken relationships, one paternity suit, and several violent assaults on Black women. Before Brown's breakthrough to film stardom in the late sixties, Black men were desexualized in Hollywood. Witness Sidney Poitier as a non-threatening emasculated Black man in many films. Jim Brown reversed that trend in 1969's *100 Rifles*, in which he engaged in voracious sex with Raquel Welch.[6] Brown's macho demeanor was on full display in football. Drafted in the first round by the Cleveland Browns, he became an instant star in his rookie year. Possibly the greatest runner in football history, he led the NFL in yardage gained during seven productive seasons, listed in descending order: 1,863 (1963 season), 1,544 (1965), 1,527 (1958), 1,446 (1964), 1,408 (1961), 1,329 (1959), and 1,257 (1960). One hastens to recall a famously worded detraction of statistical analysis per se, popularized by and wrongly attributed to Mark Twain as "lies, damned lies, and statistics." A better way to describe Brown's skill is biographer Mike Freeman's description of an event on October 13, 1963, at Yankee Stadium. A New York Giants football defender applied dirty tactics aimed at Jim Brown's poorly guarded face when he was tackled and falling down. Gouged in his left eye, Brown suffered blurred vision. At halftime, the Giants led the Browns 17 to 14. In the second half, anger eclipsed fear. On a secret pass from quarterback Frank Ryan, Brown ran a 72-yard touchdown. He scored again on a subsequent series, shedding tacklers en route to another touchdown and a 35–24 win. Like Jackie Robinson, given the green light, Jim Brown eventually retaliated against abusive opponents like New York Giants linebacker Tom Scott, who used his meathooks to rearrange Brown's face under the mask. Brown responded with a well-aimed forehand, bloodying Scott's mouth in a *quid pro quo*.[7] On another occasion, after a defensive end, Joe Robb of the St. Louis Cardinals, threw a flagrant elbow to his head, Brown instructed his offensive tackle to allow Robb to penetrate the line, whereupon Jim leveled Joe with a mighty forearm and then added injury to insult by kicking him in the stomach. Both were ejected from a crucial final game of the season, which Cleveland won 27–24, on December 19, 1965.[8] Jim Brown identified with earlier heroes in sports like Jack Johnson and Paul Robeson and in racial politics with Stokely Carmichael and Eldridge Cleaver. Justifiably paranoid, he charged the FBI, CIA, and local police with collusion and repression. A former FBI agent corroborated Brown's suspicions with the confession that his organization regarded strong African American sports heroes as threats and subjected them to continued "observation." Cinematic inter-racial love scenes evidently infuriated FBI personnel. They targeted Jim Brown's business ventures, claiming—falsely—that he was a communist earlier and a rad-ical Muslim later. Nevertheless, Brown was able to secure monetary loans for his Negro Industrial Economic Union, as a bona fide capitalist, to help Blacks succeed in business. Perhaps Brown's political endorsement of Richard Nixon, who advocated Black Capitalism in his presidential bid in 1968, facilitated that loan. Finally, the FBI declassified Brown's file in 2003.[9]

Brown deserves mention as a successful entrepreneur. He secured a $40 mil-lion grant from Coca-Cola to produce African American films, but the mercurial Richard Pryor, plagued with drug addiction, screwed up. Having helped Pryor in his rehabilitation as Pryor famously related in his comeback performance, *Live at the Sunset Strip*, Brown felt betrayed. Resilient, Jim formed the Negro Industrial and Economic Union in 1966, garnering support from fellow gridiron stars like Brig Owens, Irv Cross, Erich Barnes, and Leroy Kelly (his replacement as featured Browns running-back).[10] The Ford Foundation forked over $1 million to feed Jim Brown's Black Economic Union (BEU), designed to promote Black capitalism. The BEU adopted Mississippi's Marshall County in a three-pronged offensive. Food came first, followed by tapping into government programs for medicine, small busi-ness, and farm ventures along with food. Thirdly, other counties like Boulder, Colo-rado, would be adopted. Jim Brown also tried to help young Black males, especially ex-convicts, to find work.[11]

In 1966, at age 30, Jim Brown announced his retirement from football. He desired to go out on top and did so with a bang, not a whimper.[12] He was inducted into several Halls of Fame honoring his feats in lacrosse as well as football, both col-lege and professional. Brown remains an enigmatic figure, defying facile analysis. Is he hero, antihero, or both? Citing sports psychologist David Belkin, biographer Mike Freeman weighs each side of this binary. "All heroes," he maintains, "seem to have tragic flaws; some are obvious and others are yet to be exposed." He goes on: "A hero is hero because he [or she, I add in this enlightened age] represents an ideal, the best of something in humankind.... The hero often falls short in other areas, because he [or she] is tragically human." Does Jim Brown fail to qualify because of his bouts of domestic violence?[13] Heroic on the gridiron and in the fight for causes he believed in, Brown's character flaws elsewhere "may have tarnished his personal relations." Opting for a Shakespearian definition, Freeman argues that Jim Brown is certainly scarred but with larger than life power, like Macbeth, Hamlet, and Othello. And like these tragic figures, he was heroic in combatting racially charged double stan-dards in his athletic as well as acting careers.[14] Brown has fought racism along with mistreatment of poor Blacks for decades. Freeman concludes that Jim Brown is the most significant Black athlete in American sports.[15] He lauds his subject for turning gang leaders into social activists, thugs into religious men, the uneducated into col-lege students. Brown has saved many lives. Now more communicative and pleasant, Brown has mellowed, according to Freeman.[16]

Jim Brown remains a paradox, argues another biographer, Dave Zirin. In 1968,

Brown could converse with Huey Newton yet endorse Richard Nixon. Earlier, in 1967, he had joined the "Ali Summit" with the great boxer, Bill Russell, and Kareem Abdul-Jabbar to express resistance to and disdain for the Vietnam War. Brown defended Ali and urged the restoration of his heavyweight crown. In a recent op-ed, "Football Has Forgotten the Men Who Made It Great,"[17] Brown requested better pensions for retired players from his era who

In a nine-year pro career, Jim Brown led the NFL in rushing eight times and won three MVP Awards. A social activist both during and after his playing career, Brown is shown here at the 2014 Civil Rights Summit sponsored by the LBJ Foundation (courtesy LBJ Presidential Library).

receive a paltry $365 each month. These older players retired before the current pension plans were put into place (thanks to two strikes in 1982 and 1987), and they deserve better. Fortunately, Brown built a comfortable nest egg in subsequent careers in film and in business. Nevertheless, he continues to forcefully champion the less fortunate. On the final ledger, if Saint Peter still patrols the pearly gates, his largesse must be measured against his violent relations with women. Filmmaker Oliver Stone, no stranger to controversy himself, likened Jim Brown to a Nietzschean *Übermensch* or Superman. Brown's former Syracuse teammate turned scholar Don McPherson refers to him as "a bad motherfucker."[18] Jim Brown personified sex, violence, and power. And that combination remains troubling.

Author Dave Zirin catalogues Jim Brown's misogyny and traces it to his mother.[19] Brown preferred young women. At age 53, he was dating a 19-year-old. In the 1970s, he participated in "creative orgies," as he put it. O.J.'s lawyer Johnnie Cochran also defended Brown against rape and assault charges. The prosecutor dropped charges brought by 33-year-old alleged victim Margot Tiff against Brown, then 49. Brown also eluded punishment for allegedly tossing a young girlfriend, Eva Marie Bohn-Chin, from a second-floor condo balcony.[20] After vandalizing his 25-year-old second wife Monique's car in 1999, he was fined $1,800 and jailed for misdemeanor vandalism when he refused to put in 400 hours of community service and to undergo domestic violence counseling for one year. Defiantly, Brown refusing to comply with Judge Dale Fischer; at age 66, he chose prison. While confined, he went on a much-publicized hunger strike that lasted 28 days. He called it a "spiritual cleansing."[21] He and his wife reconciled and are still married with two children, who reportedly receive more affection than the children from marriage number one.

When Brown turned 80 on February 17, 2016, the Cleveland Browns honored

him with a statue in front of their stadium. Despite the opposition of one
reporter, Bill Livingston, who compared Jim to O.J. Simpson and Aaron
Hernandez, most folks approved of
the honor bestowed on the hero who
brought Cleveland its last championship in 1964 until LeBron James broke
the *shneid*. Jim Brown is mellower
now and looms large as an elder states-
man.[22] Like Walt Whitman, he contains multitudes.

Black Quarterbacks

One of the last manifestations of
residual racism in football concerned
the quarterback position. Pigskin pundits almost invariably select a quarterback as Super Bowl MVP. One of the
canards plaguing pro football until
recently was the assertion that Blacks
lacked either the leadership skill or the
brainpower for that pivotal position.
Today, however, the best young quarterbacks are African American. As
indicated above, Fritz Pollard qualifies

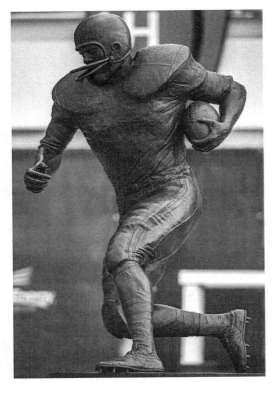

Standing outside of FirstEnergy Stadium in Cleveland, this statue of Hall of Famer Jim Brown was created by David L. Deming and unveiled on September 18, 2016 (courtesy Erik Drost).

as the first Black professional quarterback (QB hereafter) as a player/coach with the
Hammond Pros in 1923. Joe Hammond played QB for the Chicago Cardinals in 1932.
Then, in 1934, pro football lowered the boom on Black payers and turned lily-white
in 1934, remaining so until 1946. George Taliaferro, a star at Indiana University,
played several positions including QB for the Los Angeles Dons in the fledgling All
American Conference (AAC) in 1949. In 1953, after a merger joining the NFL with
the AAC, the Chicago Bears signed Willie Thrower, who had played QB at Michigan
State University.[23] Like others who preceded and followed, the aptly named Thrower
did not last long at QB. Charlie Brackins, a Negro college graduate, was out after
one game with the Green Bay Packers; Sandy Stephens, a Minnesota grad, played
one game for the Cleveland Browns but had a longer stint in the Canadian Football
League.[24] Some Black quarterbacks in college realized that they faced a bleak future
in pro football and requested a change. Stanford's outstanding sophomore QB, Gene
Washington, voluntarily switched to split end and had a successful career catching
passes for the San Francisco 49ers.[25] Drafted by the Denver Broncos in 1968, Marlin
Briscoe, a prototype of our current running quarterbacks, played only five games at
QB. Subsequently, he shifted to wide receiver with the Buffalo Bills, Miami Dolphins,

San Diego Chargers, and New England Patriots. Drafted in the first round, Eldridge Dickey was switched to wide receiver by the Oakland Raiders.[26]

At Grambling College, legendary coach Eddie Robinson recruited and mentored future NFL QBs such as James Harris. Born July 20, 1947, Harris grew to 6'4" and 210 pounds when he starred as Grambling State's premier quarterback for 1965 to 1968.[27] Drafted by the Buffalo Bills in 1969, he became the first Black QB to start in the NFL. Joined by O.J. Simpson before the tragic events that clouded his post-football career, Harris and O.J. made history together. Ironically, Harris threw several completions to former Black quarterback Marlin Briscoe, now a pass-catching split end or slot-back. After that first game, Jack Kemp—who ran unsuccessfully for vice president in 1996—replaced him. Thereafter, Big Jim made only two starts with the Bills and signed with the Los Angeles Rams as a free agent in 1972. Not until 1974 did Harris have a chance to show his mettle as a first-string QB. That year, he led the Rams to a playoff victory over the Washington Redskins, but lost the NFC title to the Minnesota Vikings. When needed, he could run as well as pass—a significant advantage but a dangerous option for Black quarterbacks. In the Pro Bowl, Harris won the MVP Award.[28] The Rams repeated in 1975 thanks in large measure to the strong right arm of James Harris. An injury in game 13, however, curtailed his effectiveness, and he was replaced by Ron "Jaws" Jaworski. A second shoulder injury put him on the shelf again, though his 89.6 efficiency rating tied him for first place in the NFC. Traded to the San Diego Chargers in 1977 despite posting the best completion average of 55.5 percent in Rams history, he contemplated retirement. After leaving as an active player, James "Shack" Harris had several administrative posts with the Baltimore Ravens, Jacksonville Jaguars, and Detroit Lions from 1997 to 2015.[29]

James Harris's successor, Doug Williams, also graduated from Grambling. Born on August 9, 1955, in Zachary, Louisiana, and comparable in size at 6'4" and 220 pounds, Williams cut an impressive figure. Mentored by his older brother, who was a Grambling alum, Doug began to play QB in the seventh grade. Actually, Doug preferred baseball and basketball to football, but his brother forced the issue: "Play football or fight me!"[30] In his senior in high school, he passed for 1,180 yards and 22 touchdowns. As an eighth grader, Doug was a scrawny 5'4". One year later, he grew two inches but still weighed close to nothing.[31] In high school, rival player Terry Robiskie ran right over him. Also a QB initially, Robiskie, like so many other Black QBs, was later switched to running back at LSU in 1973.

Doug Williams was recruited by only two Black colleges, Southern and Grambling. He chose the latter. Another growth spurt helped Williams gain leverage pursuant to a starting role. Legendary coach Eddie Robinson insisted that Doug concentrate on football and leave other sports behind. Grambling was the African American equivalent to Notre Dame as a football power. Acquiescent, Williams agreed. In his second year, he went from third string to starter. Dubbed "The Grambling Rifle," Williams led his teams to a 39–8 record with 93 touchdowns. Named All-American by the Associated Press, Doug finished fourth in the Heisman Trophy quest.[32]

Drafted by the Tampa Bay Buccaneers in 1978, Doug Williams impressed. In that rookie year, he tossed 18 touchdown passes and made the All-Rookie team. As a rookie in 1979, he led the team to a 10–6 record and its first Central Division title. The Bucs made the playoffs twice in the next three years. Doug won admirers. Even Black opponents on the Cleveland Browns rooted for him to succeed.[33] Tragedy, however, struck in 1983. His first wife, Janice, his college sweetheart, succumbed to a brain tumor leaving behind a three-month-old daughter.[34] Then, his father suffered the amputation of a leg. Like other underpaid stars, Doug Williams joined the fledgling football league USFL as the quarterback of the Oklahoma Outlaws for three seasons. When the league folded, the Washington Redskins signed him. Williams moved into the starting quarterback slot in 1987 after Jay Schroeder was injured. Doug drove his team to Super Bowl XXII. In a spectacular display of firepower, Williams threw four touchdown passes during the second quarter in a romp over the Denver Broncos, 42–10. He completed 18 of 29 passes for 340 yards. Williams made history as the first African American to win a coveted double: a Super Bowl victory plus an MVP award and a trip to Disneyland.[35] He played two more injury-plagued years. No team wanted to pay a backup quarterback $1 million, hence his termination as a Redskin. Williams also reasoned that racism contributed to his retirement after 100 passing touchdowns in 88 NFL games. Doug Williams scored 15 rushing touchdowns. After his playing days on the gridiron ended, he found employment as a high school coach, and then a college coach at Morehouse College and at his alma mater, Grambling State, succeeding his legendary mentor Eddie Robinson. He also worked as a scout for his first pro team, the Tampa Bay Bucs, and returned to the Washington Redskins as senior vice president of player personnel in 2020. Quite a career! Significantly, Doug Williams paved the way for future Black quarterbacks who can pass, run, and think.[36]

Drafted by the Pittsburgh Steelers in 1972, Joe Gilliam played four seasons as a backup to Terry Bradshaw. In 1974, he actually outplayed the injured Bradshaw during the regular season but yielded the starter's slot to the white quarterback in the playoffs on the road to their first Super Bowl victory.[37] Other potential quarterback stars in the NFL opted for a career in the Canadian Football League (CFL). Sandy Stephens, who had led Minnesota to a Rose Bowl victory, fled to Canada rather than switch positions, as requested, in both the AFL and NFL drafts in 1962. Warren Moon also went to Canada 16 years later, leading the Edmonton Eskimos to the Grey Cup championship in five consecutive years. Having proved his mettle, Moon was signed by the Houston Oilers, where he started a Hall of Fame career, including nine years as Pro Bowl player.

As proven "commodities," subsequent black quarterbacks did not have to go far north to establish their star value. Randall Cunningham electrified fans with his prolific running skills to complement his superb passing game, primarily with the Philadelphia Eagles, 1985–1995, and later with the Minnesota Vikings from 1997 to 1999. He ended his career with brief stopovers with Dallas and Baltimore from 2000 to 2001. Recipient of the Bert Bell Award for the NFL's best player in 1988, 1990, and 1998, he drove New York Giants fans like this writer crazy with his spectacular performances. Over his productive career spanning 17 years, this 6'4" 215-pound marvel amassed an excellent touchdown to interception ratio, and he gained a total of

29,979 yards with a spectacular rushing yard total of 4,928, including 35 rushing touchdowns. Regarded by many fans, including this writer, as markedly underrated, Randall, the younger brother of football star Sam "the Bam" Cunningham and the father of champion high jumper Vashti Cunningham, is part of a remarkable family. After his gridiron career ended he returned to finish his college degree at University of Nevada, Las Vegas and became an ordained minister. He also coached high school football and became active in the gospel music business. Recently, he was appointed team chaplain of the Las Vegas Raiders, the latest incarnation of the franchise originally known as the Oakland Raiders.[38]

In 1999 multiple Black quarterbacks were chosen in the NFL's first round, starting with Donovan McNabb (second) who replaced Cunningham in Philadelphia, Akili Smith (third), and Daunte Culpepper (11th). The following year, Michael Vick became the first Black quarterback to be the number-one pick. A star at Virginia Tech, Vick became the prototype of the modern quarterback because he ran the 40-yard dash in 4.33 seconds and had a strong left-handed passing arm, which he used accurately on the run. He signed a record-breaking 10-year contract for $139 million with the Falcons. McNabb's Eagles faced off against Vick's Falcons in 2005 for the NFC Championship. Unfortunately, Vick's brilliant career stalled with his conviction and prison sentence of 18 months for his role in illegal dog fights. His comeback with the Eagles fell short. Another tragic figure, Steve McNair, became the first Black quarterback to win the NFL MVP, an honor he shared with Peyton Manning. A Canadian League transfer to the NFL Houston Texans, Warren Moon was inducted in Canton, Ohio's Football Hall of Fame. In 2014, Russell Wilson became the second African American quarterback to win a Super Bowl.[39] Because of a questionable pass in the waning seconds of the 2015 Super Bowl, Wilson's Seahawks were denied a second consecutive title.

Cam Newton seemed to be on the verge of football immortality when he led the Carolina Panthers to a 15–1 record in 2015, only to lose to the Denver Broncos in the title game 24–10. Subsequent seasons were marred by injuries incurred mainly by Newton's predilection for running. In a stunning move, the Panther organization dropped Newton from their roster despite his Hall of Fame credentials in passing as well as running. At 6'5" and 248 pounds of blended speed and muscle, before injury, he appeared ready to leap over all his peers, past and present. Can Newton, most recently with the Patriots, match prior performances and gain redemption in a new football home? Stay tuned. Clearly, the premier pro quarterbacks are African American. Lamar Jackson, Dak Prescott, Deshaun Watson, Russell Wilson, Jameis Winston, Jacoby Brissett, Tyrod Taylor, and Kyler Murray played vital roles in the NFL's recent history. Patrick Mahomes II's spectacular season in 2019–20 elevated him to the highest paid NFL player in history.[40] Only Colin Kaepernick is on the sidelines now, awaiting his possible return to glory.[41] Yet he too has acquired recent support for his off-the-field activities if no contract to return to the gridiron.

Colin Kaepernick has game without a team. Ever since he took a knee to show his displeasure with police brutality and to assert "Black Lives Matter" in San Francisco 49ers preseason football games of 2017, he has been blacklisted. That display of protest triggered a nasty response from then president Donald Trump. When other football players joined in his silent protest, Trump blew his ersatz top and called them SOBs. Timid owners along with terrified tycoons threatened to suspend rebellious players like Eric Reid. Now, it appears that the tide has turned as even the NFL commissioner has apologized to the quarterback with a mission.[42] In 2003, ESPN fired Rush Limbaugh for claiming that Donovan McNabb was overrated because the Eagles quarterback was Black. Limbaugh refused to apologize.[43]

The subject of this to-do about the taboo, Colin Kaepernick was born to a white mother, Heidi Russo, and an absent Ghanaian father. Ms. Russo gave up her mixed-race infant to adoptive parents Rich and Teresa Kaepernick, a couple who had two older children: Kyle, a son, and Devon, a daughter. Two other children succumbed to congenital heart defects. His family moved to California when Colin was four. He started his football career at age eight. One year later, Colin threw his first long touchdown pass. In addition to excellent athletic skills, Kaepernick also excelled in academics. He graduated with a perfect GPA from John Pitman High School in Turlock, California, where he played baseball, basketball, and football. In a basketball playoff game, Kaepernick scored 34 points in a losing cause.

He continued to shine in both sports and studies at the University of Nevada at Reno, starting in 2007 as backup quarterback. Soon elevated to a starting slot, Colin (CK hereafter) threw for 2,175 yards, at a 53.8 percent completion rate, and 19 touchdowns. He also ran for six touchdowns coupled with 593 rushing yards. As a sophomore, CK upped his record with 22 touchdown passes, seven interceptions, with 2,849 yards through the air, plus 17 rushing touchdowns and 1,130 rushing yards. In 2009, the Chicago Cubs baseball team drafted him, but he preferred football. So, in his junior year, he racked up 2,053 passing yards, 20 touchdowns through the air, 16 touchdowns rushing, and only six interceptions. He led his team to an 8–5 record and an upset win over league powerhouse Boise State 34 to 31, snapping their 26-game win streak. In his last year at Nevada, CK passed for 3,022 yards, threw 21 touchdown passes, rushed for 20 touchdowns and 1,206 rushing yards with only eight interceptions.[44] All this and academic heaven, too, with a 4.00 GPA.

Coach Jim Harbaugh's San Francisco 49ers drafted CK with the 13th pick in the second round, 45th overall. In 2012, he started as a backup to quarterback Alex Smith. When Smith was injured, CK stepped up to become 49ers starting quarterback, finishing the season with a 11–4–1 record. In the playoff, San Francisco defeated the Green Bay Packers 45–31, in which he ran for a record-breaking 181 yards. Colin ran for two touchdowns and passed for two touchdowns against a tough defense. Success continued as Niners defeated Atlanta for the NFC title, 28–24. The season ended with a loss to the Baltimore Ravens 31–34 for the NFL championship. In the 2013 season opener, CK threw for 412 yards and three touchdowns. San Francisco finished the season with a 12–4 record. Again, they beat the Packers in the opening playoff series, 23–20. Next, they beat the Carolina Panthers 23–10, but in the NFC final, the 49ers fell to the Seattle Seahawks, led by the brilliant Black quarterback Russell Wilson, 17–23.[45]

Rewarded with a lucrative six-year $126 million contract extension, Kaepernick seemed on the verge of a Hall of Fame future. Then, things slowly started to fall apart. CK was fined for mouthing "bad language" and again for wearing the wrong headphones, in defiance of NFL sponsorship by Bose. San Francisco's season ended in a mediocre record of eight wins, eight losses. To make matters worse for Colin, his chief support, Coach Jim Harbaugh, decided to return to college coaching at his alma mater, the University of Michigan. In 2015, CK lost his starting job at quarterback after a loss 17 to 6. In 2016, when all hell broke loose, Kaepernick, beset with injuries that required surgeries, alienated new coach Kyle Shanahan. The probable source of CK's departure stemmed from two preseason games in 2016, when Kaepernick sat down in protest during the traditional honor America ceremony, prompted by the national anthem. A second display occurred during the fourth preseason game, when CK knelt along with teammate Eric Reid during the anthem, which he explained as a protest against "police shootings and rogue cops." Other players joined in this silent protest, shades of Smith and Carlos at the 1968 Olympiad, which also generated a storm of controversy.[46] WNBA's entire Indian Fever team knelt; so did soccer star Megan Rapinoe. At that time, President Barack Obama defended CK on September 5, 2016.[47] When several Miami Dolphins football players knelt prior to a game in October 2018, President Trump urged owners to suspend these and other players. A strident Dallas Cowboys owner agreed, but protests continued.[48]

Kaepernick, reporter Jeré Longman argued cogently 50 years after "the silent protest" of 1968, "is a direct activist descendant of Smith and Carlos, unyielding in his conviction. Fully understanding of risk and sacrifice and the power and dignity of silent gesture."[49] In fact, Carlos, speaking at Notre Dame, called Kaepernick his hero. The blackballed runner went on to predict that Kaepernick would be elevated to equal status with Dr. King, Malcolm X, and Rosa Parks.[50]

Released, he became a free agent on March 9, 2017. Evidently blacklisted, Colin filed a grievance against the NFL on October 15, 2017, accusing all 32 team owners of collusion. After two years of litigation and negotiation, Colin Kaepernick and his fellow protestor, Eric Reid, on behalf of "Black Lives Matter" reached a confidential settlement. Kaepernick insisted that he wanted to play football. Several tryouts were scheduled. A workout on December 11, 2019, produced no contract, while far less talented quarterbacks got jobs as backups. More players and coaches are joining Kaepernick's calls for justice. Even Commissioner Roger Goodell has seen the light and apologized to Kaepernick for the blacklist. In an NBA game on July 31, 2020, the only player standing during the anthem was John Isaac, and he is an African American. Colin Kaepernick, however, remains firmly grounded in his convictions. He started a nonprofit group, Know Your Rights Camp, which supports what he calls "freedom fighters," in protest. Quoted in the *New York Times*, he wrote[51]:

> When civility leads to death, revolting is the only logical reaction. The cries for peace will rain down, and when they do, and they fall on deaf ears, because your violence has brought this resistance. We have the right to fight back!

Recently, Colin Kaepernick negotiated a deal with the Walt Disney Company to produce stories that explore race, social injustice, and the quest for equity on Disney's platforms, including ESPN. A documentary series, already in production, will trace Colin's trajectory from pariah to freedom fighter. He has begun a publishing company, a memoir, and a Netflix series directed by Ava DuVernay covering his teenage years. Thus, Colin Kaepernick has heeded the call of Congressman John Lewis to stir up "good trouble, necessary trouble."[52] Unable to promote kneeling before salutes as a wedge issue in the 2020 election, Donald Trump may have yielded the last laugh to Colin Kaepernick.[53]

SECTION FOUR

BASEBALL

7

Black Players in Baseball
Before Integration

This author's passion for baseball and basketball is evident in the next two sections. Baseball, sports mavens maintain, is a pastoral sport, harking back to Thomas Jefferson's vision of America peopled by yeoman farmers. His rival, Alexander Hamilton, harbored a different view of America's future, grounded in urbanization, dominated by a business elite that proved more prescient. Baseball, we contend, serves as a bridge between these two blueprints. The object of what was once called the "national pastime" is to circle the bases and come home in victory. Time in baseball plays little or no role in the outcome. Thus, parents and their kids can bond at the stadium munching on peanuts (which I used to sell at Yankee Stadium in the 1950s), awful cotton candy, and overpriced beer and ice cream.

Bathed in nostalgia, unburdened by the industrialized clock, spectators could bask in the sun (before night games intruded for the purpose of profit) and share stories. Since baseball players were neither football behemoths nor basketball giants, fans could identify with them as well as fantasize about playing the game too. The pastoral myth in baseball, which puts a premium on harmony, tradition, simplicity, and style, enables the urban spectator to temporarily put aside the quickening industrial pace of Charlie Chaplin's *Modern Times* in favor of an Edenic return to green pastures.[1]

Professor Jacques Barzun—whom I met while attending Columbia University—famously declared: "Whoever would know the mind and heart of America had better learn baseball." Former commissioner of baseball and Renaissance scholar A. Bartlett Giamatti, who combined an Italian sensibility with a tragic sense of life, added a poignant comment about baseball[2]:

> It breaks your heart. It is designed to break your heart. The game begins in spring, when everything else begins again, and it blossoms in the summer, filling the afternoons and the evenings, and then as the chill rains come, it stops and leaves you to face the fall alone. You count on it, rely on it to buffer the passage of time, to keep the memory of sunshine and high skies alive, and then, just when the days are all twilight, when you need it most, it stops.

Because so many broken hearts prevailed among outstanding Black baseball players before the heroic advent of Jackie Robinson, I have divided this section into three segments: the Negro Leagues coupled with Hispanics whose dark skin precluded their entry to Major League Baseball, Jackie Robinson and his contemporaries, and those who followed along with Black Hispanics who crossed the "Color Line" after Jackie Robinson. Aware that my approach may elicit potential criticism of personal preference in the selection of these heroes, I plead guilty with an explanation. Not only were the following athletes heroic in their performance on the field, but they also served as pioneers and role models off the field.

They too had overcome the stacking quota, discussed in our football section. The central positions in baseball are pitcher, catcher, shortstop, second, and third base, all overwhelmingly white according to data collected in 1983, 36 years after Jackie Robinson's arrival. Take a look.[3]

Position	White %	Black %	Latino %
Catcher	93	0	7
Pitcher	86	7	7
Third Base	82	5	13
Shortstop	73	11	16
Second base	65	21	14
First base	55	38	7
Outfield	45	46	9

Since Charles Johnson in 2005, no African American has been a starting catcher in MLB. The above statistics might explain why only two Black managers, Dusty Baker of the Houston Astros and Dave Roberts of the Los Angeles Dodgers, serve as managers today. Culled mainly from the ranks of central thinking positions, former Black players have little opportunity to rise to managerial rank. Thus, even as doors opened for players of color, their rise to positions of authority was impeded. "It is now," James Diamond wrote, "exclusively the domain of white and Latino players."[4] Black players number eight percent of the MLB population, while Latinos from the Dominican Republic and Venezuela have zoomed to approximately 30 percent. More than one third of MLB managers are, like Joe Girardi, former catchers. And catchers are avatars of leadership and communication, rendering them Bernard Malamud "naturals" for managerial posts. As Black numbers in MLB decline along with the stacking paradigm, the Black catcher *cum* manager will become a vanished species unless a reversal of fortune comes quickly.[5]

A Hidden Heritage

"We cannot escape history!" This memorable phrase, coined by President Lincoln, echoed by Dr. King, and experienced by Long Island University students on my final exams for 52 years, serves as the guiding light of our odyssey through Black baseball. A colleague, Don Swift, embarked on a major study of the African American experience in our national pastime. This chapter was designed as an introduction, or burnt offering, to the unfinished (like Schubert's last symphony) Swiftian project, which was predicated on the belief that knowing the past anchors our present and charts our future. When a heritage lies hidden or obscured, the current generation remains shortchanged. We believe that it is imperative to recapture the glory of forgotten players cast adrift by a segregated society. We also feel obligated to trace the roots of those players who crossed over from the Negro (the designation then) Leagues to the major leagues. Thanks to the indefatigable efforts of John Holway, James Riley, Donn Rogosin, Lawrence Hogan, Leslie Heaphy, Larry Lester, Robert Peterson, Michael Lomax, Don Swift, and other historians, the saga of players, coaches, and entrepreneurs is becoming more accessible to all Americans. Someday soon, we predicted, an African American candidate will rise on merit and in triumph to national office. Barack Obama and Kamala Harris brought that hope to fruition. And the prescient authors can proudly point to the paths of glory paved by the pioneers we honor in this study.

Happily and belatedly, Major League Baseball elevated seven of the Black professional baseball leagues in operation from 1920 to 1948 to equal status with MLB. Commissioner Rob Manfred's edict added about 3,400 players to official records books and statistics. Some purists will no doubt question the accuracy of these records. Lawrence D. Hogan, Larry Lester, and Scott Simkus have worked tirelessly with distinguished colleagues to comb box scores from newspapers and archival material, separating official Negro League games from exhibitions and barnstorming tours. In addition, the Elias Sports Bureau will contribute to the arduous process. MLB's official historian, John Thorn, said approvingly: "Granting MLB status to the Negro Leagues a century after their founding is profoundly gratifying."[6]

My involvement in this project started with a conference, April 3–5, 1997, at Long Island University where scholars, fans, journalists, players (including Hall of Fame baseball gods), politicians, writers, and Rachel Robinson gathered to honor the trailblazer, the great second-baseman in the sky, number 42 in Brooklyn Dodgers Blue: Jackie Roosevelt Robinson. Boning up on his illustrious history, I stumbled upon a neglected treasure, the Negro Leagues. Plagued by an acute sense of guilt issuing no doubt from a deep Semitic sensibility, I plunged into the deep rivers of African American culture and read every available book on Black baseball. With each morsel of knowledge, I became convinced that the conventional wisdom on this neglected subject invited revision and reevaluation.[7]

One major point of contention, for example, is the wrong-headed notion recently advanced by authors John Hoberman and Jon Entine. Based on prior studies, including the work of Arthur Ashe and Harry Edwards, they argue that excessive devotion to athletic activity diverts young African Americans from education.[1] We concede that an inordinate number of Black youths spend too much time and expend excessive energy on the playing fields and too little of both in libraries, but we believe that success in sports, especially in baseball, proved salutary at a critical period in African American history.

This route out of the wilderness began "long ago and far away." Contrary to myth, baseball originated in New York City, not in Cooperstown. During the post–Civil War period, a few Black men—namely, Bud Fowler, Frank Grant, Bob Higgins, and brothers Fleet and Weldy Walker—played with white professional teams. Whites were less than hospitable. As early as 1871, a national association of professional baseball players banned Blacks. Several circumvented this rule. One was John

"Bud" Fowler. Born in Cooperstown in 1854, he played for a variety of teams active in Pennsylvania and Minnesota. We don't have too much data on his performance other than press items, which indicate that he excelled. Nevertheless, he was spurned on the grounds of race.

Record keeping improved as industrialization advanced. When Frank Grant entered swinging, he compiled a .325 batting average for Meriden in 33 games in 1886. That was the year of the Haymarket Riot in Chicago, Illinois, and the onset of a deep economic depression nationally. Class warfare added to the American mix, which would soon include racial confrontation. In this milieu, then, Grant continued his baseball career, hitting .340 for a team in Buffalo where his white teammates refused to pose for a team photograph. To ward off deliberate spiking, he invented shin-guards for self-protection as a catcher. For safety's sake, he eventually moved to the outfield.

Perhaps the most intriguing of the early African American players was Moses Walker. Dubbed "Fleet" or "Fleetwood," Walker played for a major league franchise in Toledo, Ohio, in 1884. He hit .251. A son of a physician and a teacher, and a graduate of Oberlin College in Ohio, he too was a catcher. "Fleet" became a target for the verbal and physical abuse of players and spectators alike. But he continued to play until 1889. After baseball, he essayed several vocations including a stint as a newspaper editor. He engaged in a barroom brawl with a white adversary, whom he killed. On trial for his life, Walker won acquittal. But he was repelled by the lack of justice in America. He wrote a book. In its angry summation, he exhorted Blacks to return to Africa. Only there would they find peace.[8]

With the advent of pervasive Jim Crow laws in the 1890s, Blacks were banned. Segregation found sanction from the top down. In an infamous 8-to-1 decision, the United States Supreme Court ruled that apartheid was constitutional. *Plessy v. Ferguson* (1896) legitimized a host of local ordinances that established impenetrable barriers between Blacks and whites. When Cap Anson refused to play on the same field with Blacks in 1887, he inaugurated baseball segregation. George Stovey, ace pitcher for the Newark Little Giants, was slated to pitch against Chicago's entry in the National League, the White Stockings (later Cubs). Their star player, Cap Anson, refused to play if Stovey pitched. The Newark manager submitted to this "blackmail." The era of fair play was over. Fortified with Booker T. Washington's acquiescence speech at the Atlanta Exposition in 1895, America proceeded to chart two paths, clearly separate and patently unequal. Was Anson merely reflecting the prevailing zeitgeist in America or does he deserve banishment from our baseball Valhalla? On merit, buttressed by batting average statistics, Cap belongs. Perhaps we ought to establish a parallel Hall of Shame and offer all segregationists a place of dishonor starting with the Chicago first-sacker. We could thrust all other bigots—Ty Cobb, Judge Landis, Jake Powell, and Ben Chapman—into this abode.

Clearly, unable to compete on a level playing field and abandoned by so-called race leaders, Blacks had to form leagues of their own. The earliest Black team on record was the Thompson Nine, which hailed from Babylon Long Island. Headwaiter at the Argyle Hotel, Frank Thompson summoned fellow waiters to the baseball diamond. Under the ownership of Walter Cook, the team moved to Trenton,

New Jersey, where new stars, dubbed the Cuban Giants, were born. They pretended to be Hispanic to conceal their true color. They spoke a Spanish-sounding gibberish to foster that illusion. Other less inventive Black teams followed. But they could not penetrate the recently erected race barriers.

When Cap Anson issued his infamous threat, the reputed grandfather of Black baseball, Sol White, was 19 years of age. When Jackie Robinson reintegrated the national pastime, White was 79 with only one year left to live. In that 60-year period, the scholarly White made significant contributions to the game, as player and as chronicler. He played for and managed a host of teams. In 1887, one year before the great blizzard, Sol White, a hot hitter, pounded the horsehide at a .381 clip. He later played for the Cuban Giants with other Black stars including Frank Grant. After 11 years of club hopping and barnstorming, he was elevated to manager of the Philadelphia Giants. His baseball career was long, spanning the years 1887 to 1926. He retired as a player in 1912. A fair-minded man, he established a basic salary schedule for his players from $60 to $90 per month. When he lost the World Series to a superior Chicago nine, he promptly lured their best players—Rube Foster and Chappie Johnson—to Philadelphia. Thus, a pattern was set in motion, which dictated that "greener" pastures meant more money and less loyalty to a specific city or team. John Holway documents this process in his excellent study.[9] While in retirement, White wrote a column for the *Amsterdam News*. His vast knowledge of baseball can be found in his book *Sol White's History of Colored Baseball*—the publication of which, coming as it did in 1907, made White perhaps the first historian of Black baseball.[10]

White's prowess was matched by other Black stars and pricked the interest of white managers. When John J. McGraw left the Baltimore Orioles to pilot the New York Giants, he tried to sign a Black second baseman named Charlie "Tokohama" Grant, passing him off as a Cherokee Indian. Yielding to peer pressure, McGraw dropped the ball on this issue.[11] In 1905, the Giants manager tried to circumvent segregation by signing two outstanding pitchers, Rube Foster and José Méndez, a Cuban. Again, the white owners turned

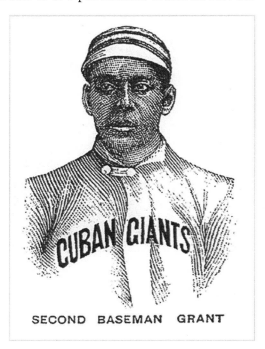

Hall of Famer Ulysses Frank Grant, shown here in a line drawing from 1889, began his International League career at age 20 in 1886. He led the Buffalo Bisons in batting each of his three years in the league, despite being targeted by white players who slid into the second baseman with spikes high. (He withstood the attacks by donning improvised shin guards.) He would go on to star for top clubs such as the Cuban Giants and Philadelphia Giants (author collection).

thumbs down. Thereafter, iron-man McGraw became a "paper tiger" as an ardent supporter of Jim Crow baseball presumably operating on the premise that if you can't sign them for your team, ban them from all others.

Blacks took another path. They challenged white teams. Initially, the white teams prevailed. The Chicago Cubs beat the Chicago American Giants in three close games while the Philadelphia A's beat the Cuban X-Giants in 1908. Fortunes shifted during a Cuban tour. An all-Black Cuban team defeated the Cincinnati Reds 1–0 in three consecutive games. Ty Cobb's Detroit Tigers fared no better. Although Cobb hit at .371 clip (Pop Lloyd hit .500), he was caught stealing four times in this brief encounter. Two other Black players, Grant Johnson and Bruce Petway, outhit Cobb.[12] Embarrassed, the Tigers were clawed by the Cubans eight games to four according to Bruce Chadwick (though Robert Peterson claims that the Tigers won seven, lost four, and tied one). Whatever the outcome of this particular series, both authors agree that Black teams played white major league teams evenly from 1908 to 1911.[13]

One last attempt at breaking the color barrier occurred in 1911 when the Cincinnati Reds tried to sign two Cubans, Rafael Almeida and Armando Marsans. Both were light-skinned and therefore acceptable. In harmonic vibration with the later hit song "*Abre la puerta, Ricardo!*" it was hoped that the door would swing open for all. Lamentably, it did not. Darker *compadres* could not gain entry. Major League Baseball drew the color line in the proverbial sand. *No pasarán. No pasarán!!*

The Negro Leagues, argues G.E. White, provided an antithesis of Major League Baseball with barnstorming, contract jumping with impunity, trick plays, and the presence—perhaps prevalence—of racketeer owners.[14] Once the realization hit home that as players they could not join major league teams, for the most part they did not bemoan their loss. Prior to World War I, that Wilsonian "war to make the world safe for democracy," the vast majority of African Americans lived in the South. Opportunity forged in wartime spurred the Great Migration. Menial labor, however, prevailed in both sections after the war. Thus, baseball offered both adventure and remuneration. Ballplayers could net $50 to $250 per month all year with a barnstorm season in Latin America. High status, fun, and fame: all beckoned. Most, issuing from the South, felt privileged.[15]

Thus, Blacks had to build their own baseball establishment. Several African American players found employment

Grant "Home Run" Johnson was an early star of Black baseball and one of the greatest players, regardless of color, of the late nineteenth and early twentieth century. A hard-hitting shortstop and second baseman, Johnson was also a born leader, serving as captain or manager on several of the greatest teams of his day (author collection).

in New York. One experiment involved the creation of the Brooklyn Royal Giants by Black entrepreneur John W. Conner. From his perch as owner of the Royal Café and Palm Garden in Bedford-Stuyvesant, he wanted to promote his business through baseball. Rooted in Brooklyn with star players Grant Johnson and Bruce Petway, the team became a great favorite until the late 1930s. Manhattan also provided a home for the Lincoln Giants with pitcher Smokey Joe Williams as its stellar attraction. If baseball loomed large in New York, it was gigantic in Chicago, "the city of the big shoulders" and hog butchers. Here, the principal architect of this structure, Rube Foster, reached for the stars well before Wernher von Braun hit London. Meteoric and mercurial, Rube Foster was a native of Texas. As a player, he pitched, starting in 1902. His field artillery featured a fastball, screwball, and curveball. Initially, he barnstormed with the Texas Yellow Jackets. Later, he pitched for the Chicago-based Leland Giants, the Philadelphia Giants, and the Cuban Giants. In the 1905 Black World Series, Foster led his team to four victories. He returned to Chicago in 1906 and continued his mastery on the mound. Gradually, he moved up to management (he doubled as player-manager in 1910) in preparation for the launch of a two-division Negro League. Ultimately, Foster would schedule games for a 40-percent slice of ownership. He established a precedent for years to come. Players and management shared the gate, each getting 50 percent of proceeds.[16]

With the help of John Schorling, Charlie Comiskey's brother-in-law, Foster crafted a new team and drafted a new league. He leased a park, which contained 9,000 seats. In fact, the Leland Giants outdrew the Cubs and the Sox on one Sunday. For 50 cents, a spectator entered the park with a free ice water. In 1911, Foster's team amassed an amazing 123–6 record. After the Great War, Foster hatched a plan, which in effect entitled him to be remembered as the "Father of Negro Baseball." Other moguls vied for supremacy. Nat Strong owned the Brooklyn Royal Giants. Ed Bolden founded Pennsylvania's Hilldale Daisies. A Negro National League emerged from a meeting in Kansas City on February 13, 1920. Each team anted $500. They agreed to bylaws and established an emergency fund. Four teams had permanent roots. They included the Chicago Giants, Cincinnati Cuban Stars, Dayton Marcos, St. Louis Giants, the Kansas City Monarchs, and Chicago American Giants. One team, the Indianapolis ABCs, was strictly for the road.

The bold experiment, which began formally on May 2, 1920, experienced mixed results. Three teams in Chicago, Kansas City, and Indianapolis drew an average of 8,000 fans. But problems plagued the fledgling league. Dayton folded and moved to Columbus as the Buckeyes. Games between the Negro Leaguers and white semi-professionals outdrew regular games. Moreover, the schedules lacked consistency. In 1921, for example, the American Giants (of Chicago) played 62 league games, Kansas City 81 games, and Chicago's Giants only 42. Despite the evident weaknesses, Foster felt compelled to defend his "baby." He pointed to the jobs and salaries ($430,000) generated. In addition, $165,000 was spent on ballparks and $130,000 on transportation. Foster could have cited other benefits: community pride, individual self-esteem, and economic self-interest.

Starting with the Cuban Giants, Black baseball introduced a new dimension to baseball: to wit, comedy. Stephen Fox quotes an awestruck James Weldon

Johnson, who marveled at the players' comic pantomime. Catcher and pitcher engaged in continual banter to the delight of spectators. It served a vital purpose in defusing racial tensions when Black teams usually defeated their white opponents. Unfortunately, there was a downside to this comedy. It reinforced the minstrel show stereotype and set a precedent of happy Blacks, loud in laughter, posing no threat to white folk.[17] Six teams formed a rival Eastern Black League in 1922. Each of the owners served as commissioners. To get first-rate performers, they raided the Negro National League. The Brooklyn Royal Giants, Atlantic City Bacharach Giants, New York Lincoln Giants, Baltimore Black Sox, Cuban All-Stars, and Hilldale Daisies constituted a formidable rival for Rube Foster's NNL. To prevent further carnage, Foster called for a truce in September 1924.

Andrew "Rube" Foster in his Chicago Lelands uniform, 1909. A 6'4" giant of a man, he was a top-flight pitcher before spearheading the foundation of the Negro National League in 1920. A tireless worker, his duties as manager, owner, and league president eventually caught up to him when, in 1926, he was institutionalized after a nervous breakdown. He died four years later, still hospitalized (author collection).

Manifesting bipolar behavior that would ruin his twilight years, Foster lashed out at fellow owners and administrators for their deficiencies in business savvy and baseball knowledge. A control freak on and off the pitcher's mound, he lamented the loss of mastery on vital matters, as managers curried favor with owners and deferred to the demands of star players.[18] His plan, G.E. White observes, was modeled after Major League Baseball. Stability and competitive balance would lead to success. He therefore insisted that teams had to secure a ballpark before entering the NNL. He wanted to limit trades to maintain balance and eliminate the influence of booking agents by giving owners a percentage of the gate. Non-salaried himself, Commissioner Foster took five percent of league gate receipts.

Two teams—the Toledo Tigers and the Milwaukee Bears—dropped out before the season ended. Attendance averaged 1,650 fans per game or 402,436 for an entire season. Total gate proceeds amounted to $197,218; players' salary amounted to $101,000; rail fare, $25,212; meals and streetcar fare, $9,136; baseballs, $7,965; umpires, $7,448; advertising and miscellaneous, $11,664. The net profit, according to G.E White, was $34,793 split among club owners with Foster taking a larger share of approximately $10,000.[19]

Foster could not control events. He tried to mollify malcontents on his own

team with bonuses and performance incentives. In this activity, the rotund inno-
vator invites credit. No doubt a great manager, Foster was a flawed individual.
Though purporting to champion sound principles, he was stridently authoritarian
and excessively disciplinarian.[20] Once he bopped Jelly Gardner in the head with a
pipe because, instead of bunting, the insubordinate player hit a triple. On another
occasion, recollected by Ted "Double Duty" Radcliffe as a young batboy, he fined a
pitcher for ignoring an order to issue an intentional walk to Oscar Charleston and
yielding a home run to the award-winning Oscar.[21]

Contrary to the power game of Babe Ruth, Foster favored speed. The bunt, the
steal, and the element of surprise became part of his team's arsenal. A chess master, he faced an 18 to 0 deficit on July 4, 1921. He ordered 11 batters in a row to bunt.
Unnerved, opposing pitchers served up two grand slams and suddenly the score was
tied 18 to 18. Always seeking an edge, he altered fields to accommodate bunters and
played mind games with opponents.

Dependence on major league parks proved problematic. This condition fostered irregular schedules and uneven distribution of games. Advertising in general
and advanced publicity for specific contests were uneven at best. At worst, certain
teams dominated and weaker teams folded. For example, the Kansas City Monarchs
were 55–22 in 1924 while the Cleveland Barons were 15–34. In the Eastern Colored
League (ECL), the dominant Hilldales were 47–22, while the weakling Washington
Potomacs were 21–37.[22] This was a recipe for disaster. Unable to establish balance and
order on the field of play, Foster slipped into despondency. Unable to control his own
demons, he cracked in 1926 and died on December 9, 1930. He was only 51. According to Rick Roberts, Rube Foster died a martyr.[23] Foster's breakdown was not unique
to the decade of "ballyhoo" and its ripple effects. Other prominent Americans suffered. Witness F. Scott Fitzgerald, whose sobering lament for the "Roaring Twenties"
and the dissipation of his own talent was titled, aptly, "The Crack-Up."

Just as James Agee and Walker Evans paid homage to the silent Americans in
the 1930s, "let us now praise famous men." Negro players in the formative years
deserve recognition, indeed admiration, especially the pitchers: "Smokey" Joe Williams, Dick "Cannonball" Redding, John Donaldson, José Méndez, Wilbur "Bullet"
Rogan, Martín Dihigo (who, like many others in the Negro Leagues, played several
positions), and Rube Foster. Among the other outstanding players, we hail Oscar
Charleston, William "Judy" Johnson, John Henry "Pop" Lloyd, Dave Malarcher,
George "Chappie" Johnson, Bruce Petway, Grant "Home Run" Johnson, "Cool Papa"
Bell, and Charlie Grant. Some of these superb athletes played well into subsequent
decades.

Speed, a salient characteristic of Black baseball, transformed the national game.
As Fox writes, it was "faster, rougher, more daring and exuberant."[24] It was almost
as if the players, having suffered long, tedious road trips, anxious over inaccessi-
ble food and lodging, took their pent-up frustration out to the ball field where they
enjoyed—to borrow a title from novelist Philip Roth—letting go. The result was a
game on eight cylinders, chock full of fun. Rube Foster's imprint marked each game
with constant motion: bunting, stealing, running. Almost everyone could run like
the wind. Pitchers fretted and fielders fidgeted as holes opened for cunning hitters.

The Hilldale Nine in the 1920s had four men of mercurial speed: Judy Johnson, Frank Warfield, Clint Thomas, and George Carr.[25] In addition, sluggers like Josh Gibson and Oscar Charleston could "tear up the pea patch." Looming above the rest, Cool Papa Bell exemplified the best of Black ball on defense as well as in offense. He played a shallower center field than Tris Speaker did. Legends of his dazzling speed provoked hyperbole. As Satchel Paige observed, Bell could turn out the light and get into bed before the room got dark. He circled the bases in 12 seconds. Thus, in stark contrast to the brute force of Babe Ruth, Black baseball evoked Machiavellian strategy, coupling the lion and the fox, speed as well as power.

Americans faced a new era with the advent in 1929 of the Great Depression. Emerging from the ashes of economic disaster, Negro baseball found renewed life in Pittsburgh, Pennsylvania. Here, Cumberland Posey and Gus Greenlee—or "Big Red," as his partners in crime dubbed him—vied for supremacy in gambling and in baseball. Despite a middle-class background (both of his parents were professionals) and a college education (he dropped out of Penn State University in 1913), Cum Posey preferred an easy life predicated on bending, if not beating, the system. This light-skinned, blue-eyed marvel loved sports. As a semi-pro, he played baseball and basketball.[26] He became manager of the Homestead Grays in 1917, remaining in this capacity and as part-owner well into the 1940s. The team rented Forbes Field from the Pirates but were barred from using the locker rooms. Evidently, the owners feared "racial contamination." Undaunted, Posey managed to corral 75 percent of the gate. In October 1926, the Grays played a team of major league all-stars, winning three of four. In 1927, major leaguers gained a reversal of fortune, winning four straight. In 1928, it was the Grays' turn to crow when they copped two straight games.[27]

Although Cum Posey was king of the (sugar) hill, he encountered fierce competition from Gus Greenlee during the Great Depression. A fight promoter with criminal connections, Gus established a rivalry with his Pittsburgh Crawfords. His first coup was inking Satchel Paige to a contract in 1932 after the Cleveland Stars folded their franchise. In that same year, which witnessed the triumph of Roosevelt over Hoover, Posey forged a new deal in Pittsburgh by raiding the Grays for the services of Oscar Charleston and Josh Gibson. The Grays beat the Crawfords in a mano-a-mano challenge series in September 1932 to retain the bragging rights in Steel City. Hooking up with Rufus Jackson, a notorious local racketeer, in 1935, Cum was ready for entry into the Negro National League (NNL). Numbers men began their control of this and other franchises throughout the 1930s and 1940s. Greenlee moved from hijacking liquor to restaurant and nightclub ownership laundering dirty money through the NNL.[28]

Before we leap to value judgments from a high moral perch, however, let us give the *goniff* (crook) his due. Moribund since Rube Foster's death in 1930, the NNL owed its renaissance to Gus Greenlee and Cum Posey. The Grays remained in business until 1947. As a laundry for unclean money, the teams' fortunes remind one of Mel Brooks's scenario for his comic film *The Producers*, in which the con-men earned money only if they lost money as theatrical angels. Thanks to "The Producers"—Pittsburgh style—baseball fans were introduced to an All-Star game, annually from 1933 on. They witnessed greatness in flannel till 1947 thanks to these "shady" entrepreneurs. In 1937, G.E. White astutely observes, the Crawfords and Grays of Pittsburgh, the Black Yankees of New York, the Elite Giants of Washington (later Baltimore), the Stars of Philadelphia, and the Eagles of Newark flew high under the "crooked" aegis of numbers operators.[29]

The *Pittsburgh Courier* waged a vigorous campaign to promote the annual All-Star game. Editorial writers saw it as a vehicle to show off Negro talent on a national scale. The first encounter, held on September 10, 1933, at Chicago's Comiskey Park, was a high-scoring affair before 8,000 who saw the West best the East 11–7.[30] The *Courier* (September 1, 1934) reported that 25,000 attended the 1934 classic thanks to improved weather. This impressive number encompassed many beautiful women, celebrities, government officials, and, significantly, almost 5,000 white fans. The latter's presence sparked hopes for integrated baseball. Throughout the 1930s, attendance at these major events drew more than 20,000 spectators regularly. White offers a cogent explanation.

Society turned out for these annual galas. It had become a social affair featuring celebrities and the "beautiful people." Moreover, it was a major source of profit for Black businessmen. It provided an escrow fund for both players and owners for "rainy days" ahead. Although booking agents like Gus Greenlee (10 percent) and Abe Saperstein (5 percent) and the Comiskeys (25 percent) skimmed profits like cream from the top (or crop), there was enough to feed the coffers as most of the money wound up in the African American community. Unfortunately, until 1942, the players received nothing for this game.

Robert Leroy "Satchel" Paige spearheaded a move to rectify this wrong. In 1942, players received $50 plus expenses. Dissatisfied, Paige upped the ante for himself with a percentage of the gate. In 1943, the Negro ace earned $600 while winning East players received $200 and the defeated West players got $100. White indicates that, in 1945, managers and coaches received $300, owners $3,500, and players $100 plus expenses.[31] By comparison to major league standards, this represented "peanuts." Comparisons, however, in a caste-dominated society elude facile formulation. Perhaps a closer look at outstanding players and successful teams will yield a clearer portrait of this era, once shrouded in ignorance and mired in myth.

In 1937 the Monarchs of Kansas City entered the newly recreated Negro American League. For a decade, they reigned supreme. One of few whites in Negro baseball, J. L. Wilkinson, an honorable man, built a powerful franchise, which, from 1942 to 1945, averaged an annual profit of $25,000. During its first nine years, the team captured five pennants. So many fine players donned the Monarchs uniform from Satchel Paige to Jackie Robinson to Ernie Banks. One major innovation issued from Kansas City: night baseball in 1930. Wilkinson invested $100,000 to activate the system of two parallel poles vaulting 50 feet up, five feet apart, in support of six floodlights. Powered by a generator in center field, the system was cumbersome, noisy, and expensive, but it was portable. Ideal for travel, it served the teams who were compelled to barnstorm for economic survival. Night baseball enabled day workers to enjoy baseball for the first time. In 1934, the Monarchs played a series of games against the Dean brothers' All-Stars. Charging 75 cents a ticket, the games drew from 14,000 to 20,000 fans.[32] Night baseball gave the Monarchs an edge, which they honed effectively.

Success, White asserts, hastened the decline of Negro League baseball. White entrepreneurs noticed the large crowds gravitating to All-Star games and to barn-storming series. Bill Veeck—as in wreck—threatened to purchase the Philadelphia Phillies franchise and stock this disastrous National League team with Black play-ers. Major league owners colluded to thwart the best-laid plans of maverick Veeck. Nevertheless, after a successful war against fascism, they could not hold back the tide initiated by progressive minded Americans.

Before we trace the integration process, we must assess the pre-1947 experience, a hard road to glory. According to John B. Holway, players learned their craft in Sun-belt semi-pro ball. Several future stars were discovered on the barnstorming treks.[33] When he was discovered in 1932, Buck Leonard was playing for the Portsmouth, Vir-ginia, Firefighters. He joined the Baltimore Stars en route to a Hall of Fame career. The mercury-footed Cool Papa Bell switched from the East St. Louis Cubs to the St. Louis Stars before you could say Jackie Robinson. There was a marked differ-ence between southern and northern players. The latter tended to be more sophis-ticated, while the southerners exemplified country and a certain clownish quality that, allegedly, went wild with the bonanza of $150 per month. On a higher plane, southern Black colleges provided a pool of baseball talent that streamed into the Texas Negro League or Southern Negro League. Here too a salutary difference is dis-cernible. There was less racial tension in Texas than in the Deep South.[34] Texas teams also enjoyed fields, operated by the Texas League, of superior quality. Out of this milieu Smokey Joe Williams and Biz Mackey surfaced.

Another rich source of Black talent sprang from Cuba. Matinee idol handsome, Martín Dihigo originated there. This multitalented versatile pitcher-outfielder was joined by a host of outstanding Cubans, including Luis Tiant, Sr. In the Mexican League, the great Dihigo amassed a 119–57 pitching record with an impressive 2.84 earned run average. As a hitter, he compiled a .317 batting average. First to pitch a no-hitter and get six hits for six at bats, south of the border, down Mexico way, he started with the New York Cubans in 1923. Eventually, he played all nine positions.

Life in the Negro League was no bed of roses. For economic reasons, rosters ranged from 14 to 19 players. Two hundred positions were jealously guarded and zealously defended. Outstanding players had long careers. Cool Papa Bell hit .373 in 1945. He was 42 years old! John Henry Lloyd, the "Black Honus Wagner," did not hang up his spikes until age 47. Buck Leonard and Oscar Charleston retired at 48. Afraid of the Wally Pipp syndrome, i.e., permanent replacement by the Black equivalent of Lou Gehrig, most played despite injury. Larry Brown earned the nick-name "Iron man" by catching 234 games in a single season. When Willie Mays was beaned while playing for the Birmingham Black Barons in 1950, he lay groaning on the ground. His manager, Piper Davis, asked if he could see first base. "Yes," the "Say-Hey" kid replied. The tough-minded manager bellowed: "Then, get on it!"[35]

Versatility gained primacy. Smokey Joe Williams played the outfield when not on the mound. Relief pitching and platooning à la Casey Stengel did not exist. Wil-liams learned to hit, as his .345 lifetime batting average attests. Ted Radcliffe, who lived to the age of 103 (but who's counting?), won his sobriquet "Double Duty" the hard way. In double headers, he often pitched the first game and caught the second. Joe Rogan batted cleanup when he wasn't pitching. Pitcher Dave Barnhill opted for first base on his "off" days.

Salaries varied. About $230 per month in the 1920s, they actually declined in the 1930s to a monthly average of $170. Stars of course commanded more money. Satchel Paige earned $350 per month in 1937. In the early 40s, the immortal Josh Gibson made $1,000 per month. So Black players earned good money—12 months each year. This salary differential explains the relative absence of malice among players. Their vocation provided money, self-respect, prestige, and public esteem when all were too often denied to other members of their race. For Ted Page, it was better than washing windows and sweeping floors. For Roy Campanella, it represented "a way to beat that [slums] and move on to something better."[36] Negro baseball players did not achieve nirvana. Venerable journalist Sam Lacy complained that they ignored the fundamentals. Both Roy Campanella and Buck Leonard echoed this criticism. There was little coaching. Trial and error supplanted extra batting practice and spring training. By comparison to the major leagues, there was a paucity of star players at all positions, according to Buck Leonard. Perhaps he was needlessly tough on his colleagues when he asserted that most teams would have ranked as competent for Triple A competition. Forced to travel, they slept in fleabag hotels and rode in segregated trains and broken-down buses. Buck Leonard remembered bedbugs and the use of newspapers between mattress and sheets.[37] His team covered 30,000 miles in a single summer. Unable to eat in most restaurants, they had to share food, purchased in a grocery, either on a bus or in a stuffed car.

There was another discordant note. Baseball players fell into a crack between honest working-class denizens and "sportin' life" *demimonde*. Many "cool cats" descended from the baseball field to the recreations of nightclubs, gin mills, gambling dens, and houses of commercial affection. Black entertainers, Stephen Fox observes in his brilliant book *Big Leagues*, attended Negro League games.[38] Some, like Louis "Satchmo" Armstrong and Bill "Bojangles" Robinson, owned ballclubs. Lured into the fast lane, Negro players found trouble with women and the law. In 1925 two stars of the Lincoln Giants were charged with murder in separate cases. In 1926 an irate woman—shades of the Fred Lane tragedy—shot her beau, Monarchs shortstop Dobie Moore, thereby aborting a promising career. Another Monarch, pitcher Dimps Miller, was shot in the arm—his pitching arm. Author Stephen Fox cites brawls, murders, maiming, and mayhem, with names attached to each.[39]

Press coverage also suffered a double standard. With so much travel, even the Negro press could not adequately report on local teams. One egregious example, cited by G.E. White, provides a case in point.[40] Perhaps the best Black franchise ever, the Monarchs called Kansas City their home base. The Monarchs earned less ink than the Blues, an all-white minor league club with a mediocre record. Black fans as well as white fans, albeit in segregated quarters, turned out for both clubs. *The Kansas City Star*, however, offered only partial reportage of the team and gave no information about the Negro National League. In the eyes of white owners, Blacks remained invisible. How this played out with Black fans is illustrated by the admission of Art

Rust, Jr., writer and broadcaster: He rooted for the St. Louis Cardinals rather than the Monarchs despite having been the target of racist remarks by pitcher Clyde Shoun. A notion of inferiority of Black teams had taken hold.[41]

Mark Ribowsky expresses outrage at the clownish antics of certain teams. He points to the Indianapolis Clowns franchise, which lasted until the 1980s with more whites than Blacks in its twilight years. Did clowning desecrate a noble tradition? Was this a vile extension of minstrelsy as Ribowsky contends?[42] Not without coincidence, Clowns owner Abe Saperstein also owned the Harlem Globetrotters. Working on a sure-fire format, both operated at a profit; both featured Goose Tatum. Later, under new owner Ed Hammond, the Clowns hired a midget and a giant and featured a dentist routine in the seventh inning. Sleight of hand, behind the back tosses, shadow ball: all became staples of this traveling circus. Bruce Chadwick describes the routines minus the rancor that marks Ribowsky's critique. He argues that the quality of baseball remained high and the clowning pleased crowds.[43]

Another redeeming feature in the Clowns' approach to baseball was the employment of Toni Stone, the first woman in professional baseball. She hit .267 for Indianapolis in 1953. She also played for the Monarchs. Two more women joined the Clowns.[44]

Black baseball nonetheless had its problems, of course. Contracts could be abrogated at the drop of a hat or bat, for instance. And if owners reneged on agreements, players did, too, jumping contracts to join new teams, which meant abandoning their old ones. Add these indignities to the prevalence of Jim Crow laws and a clearer picture of black baseball emerges. Defenders of segregation pointed to the criminal subculture to justify their fixed views. Most whites, however, seemed oblivious to Black baseball whose players remained—in the apt descriptive of Ralph Ellison—invisible men.

One player proved an exception to the above rule. Highly visible, Leroy "Satchel" Paige became a legend in his own time. Like Babe Ruth, he dominated his milieu. Robert Peterson persuasively notes the similarities. Both were awesomely talented and highly charismatic.[45] Both drew huge crowds to their games. Paige's amazing record can be traced in two monumental studies: one by James A. Riley, the other a collaboration between Larry Lester and Dick Clark. But cold statistics or raw facts do not convey the vast folklore generated by the great Black pitcher. "Just the sight of [Satchel] strolling languorously towards the mound—an improbable figure high on pencil-thin legs [like Ruth's]—was enough to send waves of excitement coursing through the ballpark," writes Robert Peterson.[46]

Up from poverty, Paige was the seventh of 11 children born in Mobile, Alabama. As a boy of seven, he toted satchels to the train station in his hometown: hence his nickname. Petty larceny at age 12 landed young Leroy in a reform school for five years. There he learned the rudiments of reading and writing and grew to 6'4" on a 140-pound frame. Starting as a pitcher for a local semi-pro team 1924–25, he learned his craft. Soon, as the Beatles would later sing, he was "here, there, and everywhere." By 1930, his blazing fastball, radar control, and colorful personality put him into southern folklore.[47]

Paige gathered huge crowds wherever he went. Pitching for Gus Greenlee's

Pittsburgh Crawfords, 1932–38, Paige racked up sensational feats on the mound. In barnstorming sessions, he consistently outpitched the great Jerome "Dizzy" Dean and baffled the greatest hitters in the national game including Joe DiMaggio and Charlie Gehringer.[48] Extant records indicate that Paige's All-Stars won two out of every three games from Dean's All-Star teams.

After years of overuse, Satchel suffered a sore arm. Was it dead? Fans wondered. Paige fretted. Suddenly, as if he had visited Lourdes for a miracle cure, the fastball regained its zip. From 1939 to 1947, the ancient mariner-fireballer returned to form. He pitched for the pennant-winning Monarchs of Kansas City and for semi-pro teams on "lend lease." He mirrored Alan Ladd's breakout film of 1942. Pointing to his right arm, one could hail: "This gun for hire." How did the Negro League spell relief in the 1940s? S-A-T-C-H-E-L. He saved Black baseball. Folklorist Tristram Porter Coffin remembers a game played in Newark, Ohio, as quoted in Benjamin Rader's *Baseball: A History of America's Game.*[49]

> Between innings, Paige sat in a rocking chair and sipped from a black bottle. He used all his eccentric pitches, throwing overhand, sidearm, underhand; showed the batters the hesitation pitch, the two-hump blooper, the fastballs Long Tom and Little Tom…. He joked and hammed around, played first base, and even got a hit. It was a minstrel show transferred to the ball field—a show Paige had acted out a thousand times before and which had kept body and soul together for close to half a century.

By 1940, he made the mainstream journals: *Time, Life,* and *The Saturday Evening Post.* Engaging copy, he personified some of the most glaring stereotypes. He played pool, he pursued women, he drove fancy cars, and he dressed to the nines—a veritable Jim Dandy up from minstrelsy. He disregarded schedules, violated contracts, responded to his own urges, ignored team rules, flouted convention, broke the rules. On the mound, he was blessed with divine gifts. Joe DiMaggio named him the hardest pitcher he ever faced. Dizzy Dean called Satch the best hurler in baseball.[50] In a word, Paige represented the ambiguities in the American pastime.

In the last analysis, Albert B. "Happy" Chandler described Black baseball with sage words: "They had magic hands, feet that literally flew, muscles of steel, the eyes of eagles, hair trigger savvy—and black skin."[51] Following the late baseball commissioner, author John Holway cited specific contributions. Bill Monroe introduced shin guards; Willie Wells, the batting helmet; J. L. Wilkinson, games at night; Rube Foster, the hit-and-run. More significantly, we hasten to add, Black baseball gave us Jackie Robinson, Larry Doby, Roy Campanella, Don Newcombe, Satchel Paige, Willie Mays, Hank Aaron, Elston Howard, Monte Irvin, Ernie Banks, and the recently departed Joe Black, to name only the first of our major league Black baseball gods. The "Say Hey" kid, Willie Mays, hailed his Negro League ancestors: "You were pioneers…. You were the ones who made it possible for us."[52]

And they were good. In the 436 interracial games played between 1900 and 1950, Blacks won 268 to only 168 for the lily-whites. After Jackie Robinson came the flood of African American talent, which transformed the national pastime. The sudden dominance of National Leaguers in All-Star competition is undoubtedly the result of the predominance of Blacks in the senior circuit. Only the Yankee hegemony in World Series contests obscured the impact of integration. Then, like

Humpty-Dumpty, the Yankees had a great fall. Only the king's (read George Steinbrenner) horses and only the king's (Clyde King?) men plus the infusion of Reggie Jackson, Roy White, Chris Chambliss, Willie Randolph, Mickey Rivers (1977 to 1978), and later Bernie Williams, Derek Jeter, Tim Raines, Darryl Strawberry, Dwight Gooden, and Cecil Fielder pumped vital blood (1996–1999) into America's team: the New York Yankees.

Black baseball clearly played an important part in the drama that is African American history, as Bob Ruck's evocative book *Sandlot Seasons* demonstrates. Summoning testimony from those who played the game and cheered the players, Ruck demonstrates how local teams built community and a sense of belonging. While Steel City declined in the 1920s and 1930s, Blacks arrived in large numbers, reaching more than 100,000 in 1960, the year a great Pirates team upset the favored Yankees in the World Series. Throughout the preceding years, Black baseball energized African American consciousness, group pride, and self-esteem. Some of the greatest players performed in Pittsburgh like Josh Gibson, Buck Leonard, and Satchel Paige. For novelist John E. Wideman, sports were a masculine rite where a man could exert some control absent from other areas in society. He remembered the older men who populate the plays of August Wilson discussing sports—not the stock market. Exclusion from society's big house served as the spur for a room—indeed an arena—of their own. That room was filled with outstanding athletes.[53] Even the owners were Black, and Pittsburgh had two Black teams. The Pittsburgh Crawfords, Monte Irvin remembers, were equal to the 1927 Yankees. They had Oscar Charleston and Smokey Joe Williams. They stirred dreams that were fulfilled when Branch Rickey enlisted Jackie Robinson to start "the great experiment."

Negro League baseball also opened doors for women. In her illuminating article on this important if neglected subject, historian Leslie Heaphy cites three female pioneers: Mamie Johnson, Connie Morgan, and Toni Stone. More than novelty figures to attract larger crowds, they were highly competent players. Only 5'3", Johnson earned the epithet of "Peanut" but gained accolades for her 33–8 pitching record. She also had a .273 batting average with the Indianapolis Clowns. Toni Stone, who hit .254 with the Kansas City Monarchs, reached Satchel Paige for a single, and made the All-Star team as a second basewoman in 1954.[54]

Mr. Robinson changed America. "The fate of a race," observed Jesse Jackson, "rode on his swing." Dick Gregory added, "It was the first time a black man shook a stick at a white man and 50,000 white people cheered."[55] Helped by men of conscience, Jackie advanced in and out of baseball. To Harry Edwards, Jackie was a hero. He was also good for business, though his impact on the bottom line is still doubted by revisionist writers. Mrs. Rachel Robinson urges us to regard him as a man, not a saint, who taught an unforgettable lesson, namely "that an individual can make a difference."[56]

Lest we forget, Jackie had Black antecedents. Negro Leaguers harbored a sense of responsibility. They functioned as role models. In dress, manners, and style, they strove for professionalism. Thus, they never sank into Ellisonian invisibility. They played a superior—though controlled when contesting white pros—brand of baseball. Indeed, as Lipsyte and Levine affirm in their excellent book, "The Negro

Leagues were a parallel world, almost a twilight zone of baseball." The great Black players had white counterparts. Lipsyte and Levine cite Buck O'Neil rather than Buck Leonard, who is the more appropriate symbol, I think, of "a shadow identity." Regardless of mistaken identity, Black players "hustled for a buck" at a game they loved. In their careers, they fulfilled the tri-part criteria spelled out by James Michener in his book *Sport in America*, namely, the promotion of health, joy, and entertainment.[57] In their storied careers, they served as symbols of competence and achievement at a critical period. In purveying joy and excitement, they enriched their culture at a time when these qualities shored up a community alongside of other vital Black institutions: churches, colleges, music, theater, and film.[58]

A scientific game based on the art of bunting, stealing, and running, Black baseball posed no direct threat to Jim Crow America. Cresting in 1946, the year of Jackie

Robinson's advent, future Hall of Famers Larry Doby and Monte Irvin led the Eagles of Newark to victory over the Monarchs of Kansas City. Exuding stamina—often playing three games in a single day—and finesse, these players taught by example. Black baseball provided 400 jobs, which generated money, fame, attention, adventure, and dignity. Negro Leaguers gained status and married upward, even embracing schoolteachers as desired mates. And they were surprisingly free of self-pity or race hatred.[59]

The absence of malice is the most striking feature of oral testimony issuing from veterans of Negro baseball. For readers raised in the era of civil rights agitation and affirmative action implementation, this tone of passive resignation is hard to fathom. One seeks clues to this mysterious response to oppression. Before Ken Burns's documentary *Baseball*, few knew the marvelous octogenarian, spinner of verbal magic, the first black to coach in Major League Baseball: John "Buck" O'Neil. Now, thanks to this magisterial retrospective of baseball—Black as well as white—we know this heroic survivor of segregation and grizzled griot of baseball, Mr. O'Neil. Listen to his pithy words[60]:

Buck O'Neil was a slick-fielding, line-drive hitting first baseman who played all but one season of his 10-year Negro League career for the Kansas City Monarchs. (He began with a brief stint with the Memphis Red Sox in 1937.) He was also a Negro League manager, a scout for the Chicago Cubs, and, after starring in Ken Burns's *Baseball*, perhaps the most beloved baseball ambassador of his time. He is shown here at Long Island University's 1997 conference honoring Jackie Robinson (author collection).

There is nothing greater for a human being to get his body to react to all things one does on a ballfield. It's as good as sex; it's as good as music. It fills you up. Waste no tears for me. I didn't come along too early—I was right on time.

As Donn Rogosin points out, "accommodation without acquiescence" marked the African American response to segregation. A frontal assault on the citadel of "Jim Crow" was fraught with danger and, prior to World War II, carried little hope of duplicating Joshua's triumph at Jericho, as celebrated in song by Paul Robeson, "...and the walls came tumbling down." During the grim years, Negro League baseball provided escape, entertainment, economic opportunities, and emotional satisfaction and proved that Blacks were equal, if not superior, to whites. They became heroes in the eyes of common men and women. Rogosin quotes Quincy Trouppe:

> Baseball opened doors for me. When I felt low and disgusted it gave me a lift. When I was riding high and the wind of glory was caressing my ears,
>   it brought me down to earth. Because of this great National game, I have lived a life comparable to the wealthiest man in the United States.[61]

On February 13, 2020, scholars and fans marked the 100th anniversary of Negro League history, launched in Kansas City. Negro League veterans who never got the opportunity to join major league teams deserve recognition and respect along with those like Jackie Robinson, Roy Campanella, Don Newcombe, Joe Black, Junior Gilliam, Larry Doby, Al Smith, Dave Pope, Dave Hoskins, Monte Irvin, Willie Mays, Hank Thompson, Reuben Gomez, Ernie Banks, Gene Baker, Henry Aaron, Luke Easter, Minnie Miñoso, and Satchel Paige. Their departure may have caused the demise of Negro League baseball, but they provided opportunities for those who followed. Indeed, to echo the words of poet Langston Hughes, they made America America again.

8

Jackie Robinson

The Jackie Robinson saga, biographer Jules Tygiel insisted before his untimely death in 2008, was comparable to an Easter/Passover service that invites public recollection every year because "it must be told to every generation so that we never forget."[1] Indeed, we must never forget what our country once represented and what it became thanks to the heroic life of Jack Roosevelt Robinson. Nobel laureate Ernest Hemingway defined a hero as one who demonstrates "grace under pressure." Our concept of heroism with a thousand faces has changed dramatically from the ancient Greeks to contemporary America. Once the realm of aristocratic warriors, our pantheon is now peopled by women as well as men who rise from humble roots in a democratic society. Witness Jack Roosevelt Robinson. Ironically, a democratic society seems uneasy in the presence of heroes because, aristocratically, they loom larger than life. Thus, throughout our nation's history, Americans have shown a propensity to elevate the extraordinary individual only to topple him or her from the pedestal. In short, we are prone to smash icons. Some heroes, however, may go into temporary eclipse, but their accomplishments and their traits resist our throwaway culture.

"A life is not important except in the impact it has on other lives," wrote Jackie Roosevelt Robinson shortly before his death in 1972. His was a short life by modern standards, but what a life! It calls to mind Stephen Spender, who in one of his most famous poems, "The Truly Great," recalls those "who, from the womb, remembered the soul's history":

> Born of the sun, they travelled a short while toward the sun
> And left the vivid air signed with their honour.[2]

Born in Cairo, Georgia, on January 31, 1919, Jackie would now be 103 years old. The youngest child of Mallie and Jerry Robinson, sharecroppers, he was an infant when his father, burdened by debt, abandoned his family. Undaunted, Mallie moved her children to Pasadena, California, where her brother had moved in quest for a better life. Mallie did double duty as a domestic and laundress. With meager savings, she bought a house in a predominantly white neighborhood, a source of conflict and confrontation with local racists.

Joining the Pepper Street Gang, Jackie was incarcerated and humiliated after an incident provoked by a racial slur. Burning with a fierce anger that would smolder and erupt in later encounters, Jackie became a fierce competitor. As an athlete in public school, junior college, and at UCLA, he proved superior in every sport:

track, football, basketball, tennis, and baseball, possibly his weakest sport. He also excelled in golf and ping-pong. In his junior year at UCLA, Jackie and future pro stars Kenny Washington and Woody Strode dominated Pacific Coast College football. With his blazing speed and brilliant athleticism (he won four letters in four different sports, the first UCLA athlete to accomplish this Herculean task), Jackie won national attention.[3]

Yet, several credits short of a college degree, he dropped out. Facing a bleak future, unable to secure a position in a major professional sport, Robinson drifted until the U.S. Army called. Eager to enter officer training, Jackie encountered rejection. Persistent, he asked heavyweight champ Joe Louis for help. The "Brown Bomber" contacted an influential person in Washington, D.C., and before you could say "Jackie Robinson stole second base," he was indeed an officer as well as a gentleman.[4]

Then "Old Man Trouble" arrived at Fort Riley, Kansas. Lieutenant Robinson, as morale officer, protested the constraints placed on Black soldiers' access to the post exchange. This led to a volatile verbal confrontation. His commander wanted Robinson to play football. Initially compliant, Robinson balked when he was sent on furlough while the fort's football team played the all-white University of Missouri. When Robinson returned from California, he resigned from the team. Unable to play baseball and plagued by a recurrent ankle injury, Jack receded from sports competition in the military in response to his commander's edict: "Coloreds don't mix with whites on the baseball field." Then, because JR refused, he was sent to Fort Hood. One day, when Robinson was riding on a military bus on the base, the driver ordered him to move from his seat—next to a light-skinned Black woman married to a fellow officer—to the back. Knowing his rights, Lieutenant Robinson naturally balked. The "cracker" bus driver pulled over and had him arrested. Refusing to play an Uncle Tom, Robinson insisted on respect and his rights. He reprimanded a racist secretary and spoke mockingly to a subordinate military police sergeant. The reward for such resistance was a court martial. Fortunately, a first-rate lawyer and Robinson's athletic fame coupled with support from NAACP leaders led to a favorable verdict.[5]

Acquitted, Robinson was offered a chance to lead a segregated force into battle abroad. Declining this dubious honor, he opted for a discharge. The newly appointed president of an all-Black Methodist college in Texas, Karl Downs, recruited the recently discharged officer to coach the basketball team. The college had only 300 students, only 36 of whom were male. Despite a small pool of male athletes, Robinson performed admirably. During a brief stint as basketball coach, Jackie tried out for the Kansas City Monarchs, once the elite team of Negro League baseball. Who recruited Robinson remains unclear. Monarchs player-coach Newt Allen evaluated the raw recruit as "fast, heady, could hit a little, was a fine bunter and showed a good glove." But his weak arm prompted Allen to advise Monarchs owner J. L. Wilkinson, the only white owner in that era, to use Robinson as a utility player.[6] Subject to an oral contract and/or a written contract (as Larry Lester documented at our 1997 Long Island University Conference), Robinson was offered a salary of $400 per month—a substantial salary by Negro League standards.

When the regular Monarchs shortstop, Jesse Williams, developed a sore arm, he switched to second base, allowing Robinson to play short. In this position, Robinson received lots of favorable coverage from the *Chicago Defender*.[7] Robinson started his short Negro League career on Sunday, April 1, 1945, in Houston, Texas against a team of minor league stars. In a 14 inning 4–4 tie, rookie Robinson exhibited a good field, no hit performance. One week later, however, he banged out two hits and stole one base against the Birmingham Black Barons.

Soon, the *Pittsburgh Courier* began covering every Robinson exploit. Ace reporter Wendell Smith even followed Jackie Robinson to Boston with Marvin Williams and Sam Jethroe in tow for an alleged tryout at Fenway Park on April 16, 1945. Arranged by city councilman Isadore Mushnick, who threatened to reinstate Boston's Blue Laws regarding Sunday baseball unless Blacks were given a chance to play for the Red Sox, this pseudo tryout proved that Boston's baseball brass were opposed to integration as they turned a blind eye to Robinson's splendid hitting and the talents of Jethroe and Williams.[8]

Disappointed but undefeated, Robinson returned to Negro League play. Eager to learn, Jackie was a quick study. He had to hone baseball skills after a long hiatus from UCLA baseball, his least effective sport in college. Sponge-like, Jackie rapidly absorbed the essence of Negro baseball: speed coupled with power. Conversely, he experienced acute dissatisfaction with the league's constant travel and poor conditions on and off the field, due to lack of training. While he admired their baseball skills, Jackie disliked the behavior of his teammates and kept his distance from their bibulous carousing. They in turn found Robinson quick to anger and quite distant.[9] During one road trip through Oklahoma, Jackie ordered a white gas station owner to stop pumping gas after he and teammates were refused admission to a "whites only" bathroom because the one consigned to "blacks" was out of order. Monarchs roommate Hilton Smith observed Jackie's courageous stand and informed John "Buck" O'Neil. Another teammate, Othello Renfroe, remembered Robinson's anger in similar confrontations with gas station attendants in Mississippi.[10]

On the field, Robinson's offensive skills exceeded those on defense. Due to football injuries, his arm from deep short did not always find its mark accurately. In one double-header against the Homestead Grays, he banged out seven consecutive hits, but poor fielding contributed to twin losses. Against a Navy All-Star team in Boston on Braves Field, in mid–August, Robinson got two hits and stole three bases, including a theft of home in leading the Monarchs to an 11–1 victory.[11]

In that abbreviated but stellar season, according to pioneer historian Robert Peterson, in 41 official games, Robinson hit a team-leading .345 with 10 doubles, four triples, and five home runs. Stout and Johnson claim a higher batting average at a robust .387. Biographer Arnold Rampersad notes that the Monarchs played 62 official games and about 20 games off the record with 32 wins.[12] Whatever the precise numbers, Robinson drew attention from one major league scout, Clyde Sukeforth of the Brooklyn Dodgers, an emissary of that "ferocious gentleman" Wesley Branch Rickey. Fortified by City Council and New York State legislation (Quinn-Ives Law, 1945), Rickey determined to sign a player of color. Summoned to 215 Montague Street in Brooklyn (one block from St. Francis College), Robinson engaged in an historic exchange with Rickey. Rickey laid out the ground rules for a "noble experiment" to break the racial barrier in baseball. JR complied with Rickey's Christ-like turn-the-other-cheek terms, for starters.

Rickey chose Jackie Robinson for the right reasons. As a former army officer and a current gentleman, he was mature. Having lettered in four varsity sports at UCLA, Robinson was an outstanding athlete. In resisting Jim Crow constraints in the army leading to a court martial, he demonstrated courage; in the elegant words of Ernest Hemingway, Robinson personified "grace under pressure." No doubt, Branch Rickey also appreciated that Robinson had attended college, that he was well spoken, and that he was engaged to be married to Rachel Isum. Finally, Robinson neither smoked tobacco nor drank alcohol.

Organized baseball came to Montréal in 1898. Jackie Robinson arrived in 1946. Canada, historically, had been a terminal point for the Underground Railroad, bringing escaped slaves to final liberation, including recapture by slave catchers south of the Canadian border. Prime Minister Trudeau's grandfather joined two partners in taking control of the local baseball club in 1931. Montréal formed part of the Triple A International League along with Toronto, Syracuse, Jersey City, Newark, Rochester, Baltimore, and Buffalo. Affiliated with the Brooklyn Dodgers, the Royals of Montréal won the pennant in 1935 and served as a source of Dodgers talent. It proved an excellent starting point for Jack Roosevelt Robinson.[13] An agreement reached in August but consummated and publicized on October 23, 1945, sent Robinson to Montréal's Triple A Dodger farm team for the 1946 season.

Problems rooted in race, however, surfaced when the Royals traveled south in mid–March.

During spring training in Florida, the "noble experiment" in racial integration ran into trouble. Robinson became the target of opposing players, egged on by hate-driven fans, verbally as well as physically. In an era when Jim Crow still ruled the South, Jackie Robinson—in concert with Dodgers general manager and part owner Branch Rickey—did nothing in retaliation. Four thousand spectators, including 1,000 African Americans, showed up for the first game in Daytona Beach on March 17, making history by breaking racial barriers. Subsequent games, however, were cancelled because of local segregation laws, starting on March 21 when Jacksonville authorities demanded that Robinson and Black teammate John Wright not play, forcing a cancellation. Additional cancellations occurred on March 28 and April 5. On April 7, in Sanford, Florida, where Trayvon Martin was later murdered by vigilante George Zimmerman, the chief of police stopped the game between two Dodgers farm teams from Montréal and St. Paul.[14]

North of the Mason-Dixon Line, conditions improved measurably, culminating on opening day in Jersey City on April 18, 1946, before a crowd of 25,000 spectators. Though he grounded out in his first at bat, Robinson received thunderous applause. With two men on in his second effort, Robinson blasted the first pitch for a 340-foot home run as the crowd roared even louder. His teammates—some with southern accents—cheered too. He garnered three more hits on two perfectly placed bunts, and a line drive into right field. According to reporter Wendell Smith, he ran wild on the basepaths, stealing two bases, scoring four runs, two of them by balks induced by Jackie's signature dances on the basepaths, leading the Royals to a romp over the

Jersey City Giants. After the game, it took five minutes for Robinson to reach a joyous locker room, as fans gathered around him.[15]

That year, Jackie Robinson "tore up the pea patch" (in the words of peerless broadcaster Red Barber), leading the International League in hitting at a .349 clip, scoring 113 runs, stealing 40 bases (second only to teammate Marv Rackley, "the rabbit"), fielding his second base position brilliantly, and sparking his team with timely hits and expert defense to a come-from-behind Junior World Series victory over the Louisville Colonels, a rabidly racist top Red Sox farm team. Jackie faced hurdles to be sure, but he survived and triumphed, though scars remained. Syracuse players taunted Jackie, mercilessly. One threw a black cat onto the field, bellowing, "Hey, Jackie, here's your cousin." Typically, Jackie retaliated with performance. He doubled after the cat's appearance. Subsequently, he scored a run and shouted, "I guess my cat is happy now."[16] On the verge of a nervous breakdown, Jackie suffered great pain. Though his doctor advised rest, Robinson found baseball therapeutic and ultimately rewarding. As the southern-most city in the International League, Baltimore was a hotbed of racism. Nevertheless, the city's Black population comprised 50 percent of attendees when Robinson played. So, he had a support group. Even white fans there began to cheer for him in response to his stellar play.[17]

At the first game at home on May 1, 1946, Maurice "the Rocket" Richard was among the 16,000 fans who turned out to cheer for Robinson and the Royals. After winning the game, 12–9, the Royals went on to win 16 of the next 20 games, on the royal road to copping the league championship by 19.5 games. In August, Jackie hit over .370.[18]

On September 11, 1946, the playoffs began as the Royals of Montréal faced the Bears of Newark. In game one, Robinson got three hits and three runs batted in in a 7–5 win. After the Royals lost the next two, they won game five, 2–1. On September 18, Robinson hit two doubles. Trailing 3–4, Royal Les Burge hit a home run to tie the score, 4–4. The winning run was scored as Newark catcher Yogi Berra fumed, as he did in the first game of the 1955 World Series, when Jackie Robinson stole home plate. Royals catcher Herman Franks doubled home the winning run in a bang-bang play. Next came Syracuse. The Royals lost game one but won the next four, the league title, and a chance to face the Louisville Colonels (a top Red Sox farm team) for the Triple-A Championship.[19]

In the first game in Louisville, Robinson was subjected to verbal abuse from 13,000 fans. African Americans were assigned to a small, segregated section while thousands of Black fans milled around Parkway Field, unable to get in. The Royals won 7–5 as Jackie went hitless. Hitless again in game two, Robinson slumped as the Colonels won, 3–0. They repeated in game three, routing the Royals 15–6. Returning to Montréal, Robinson now heard loud cheers instead of incessant boos, thanks to angry Montréal sportswriters who covered the Junior World Series. The Colonels now became the target of boos and catcalls. Losing 5–3 entering the ninth inning, the Royals rallied, as Colonels pitchers lost the strike zone. Robinson scored the tying run on a wild throw. In the 10th inning, the Royals loaded the bases. Robinson—"Mr. Clutch"—drove in the winning run with a single, knotting the series 2–2. Robinson starred in game five with a key triple in the seventh inning and scored the lead run. In the ninth inning, Robinson executed his forte, a squeeze bunt, which sent Al Campanis home with the winning run. The Royals won game six and the title, 2–0, as Jackie contributed two hits and several excellent fielding plays, and Curt Davis hurled a shutout.[20]

Jubilant fans chased Jackie Robinson, their hero, after the game. They refused to leave. Singing "*il a gagné ses épaulettes*" (he won his spurs), they urged Robinson to come out of the clubhouse and join them. "When he emerged," Jules Tygiel wrote, "they gathered around him, hugging and kissing him, and tearing at his street clothes. As they lifted Robinson to their shoulders, tears appeared in his eyes."[21]

A close friend of Jackie and Rachel Robinson, Sam Maltin, writing for the *Pittsburg Courier* and the *Montreal Herald*, famously wrote the following tribute:

> He's strictly Brooklyn. He never belonged in this league, despite his Class AAA rating since the first month of play. To the large group of Louisville fans who came here with their team, it may be a lesson of good will among men. It's the man, not race, color, or creed. They couldn't fail to tell others down South of the riots, the chasing of a Negro—not because of hate, but because of love.[22]

In the spring of 1947, Robinson joined the Brooklyn Dodgers. Again "with grace under pressure," he met every challenge—opponents' slurs, spikes, taunts, and attempted "bean balls"—with unflagging determination. Despite external enemies (the Phillies, Cubs, and Cardinals threatened boycotts) and opposition within the team (Dixie Walker, Eddie Stanky, Bobby Bragan, and Kirby Higbe), he excelled. He hit .297, scored 113 runs, stole 29 bases, and earned Rookie of the Year honors. During that turbulent first season, Robinson earned the support of several teammates, namely, Ralph Branca, Duke Snider, George Shuba, Gene Hermanski, and Pee Wee Reese. In the '47 World Series, he drove Yankee catchers crazy with his base-running antics. Although the Bronx Bombers won the seventh deciding game, 5–2, Robinson's narrative dominated. He was voted America's second most popular personality, second only to crooner Bing Crosby.[23]

Robinson's subsequent career, spanning 10 years, produced high achievement: a .311 lifetime batting average, six pennants (two more were lost on the final day), a World Series win— Brooklyn's only one—in 1955. Voted National League MVP in 1949—a first for African American players—JR hit a league-leading .342, knocked in 124 runs, scored 122, and stole 37 bases. He smashed barriers on and off the baseball diamond. In 1953, he also broke the color barrier in St. Louis's Chase Hotel just as he paved the way for desegregation in southern stadiums (one incident in New Orleans invites mention), civil rights legislation, and judicial decisions favorable to integration. Moreover, Robinson opened doors for future athletes of color and gender: brown, yellow, and Black.[24]

In business, he established positive precedents in corporate America, banking, insurance, construction, broadcasting, and politics. In sum, JR eschewed accommodation, deplored avoidance as he aggressively pursued social justice. He vigorously denounced Malcolm X's anti–Semitism. Jews, he argued, are the allies of Blacks in their common struggle for equal rights. His first post-baseball employer, William

Black (né Schwartz); his lawyer; his young correspondent Ron Rabinowitz; his first neighbors in Brooklyn and his last ones in Stamford, Connecticut (singer Carly Simon's family), were all Jewish. In addition, the Robinson family's favorite place for R & R, Grossinger's Hotel, had a Jewish ambience. Indeed, it can be argued that Brooklyn provided the best environment for the Rickey-Robinson "noble experiment" because of the ethnic mix and working-class composition of its heterogeneous populace, largely immigrant: Irish, Italian, Scandinavian, Polish, and Jewish.[25]

Jackie spurned accommodation, chiding the NAACP for its inability to march swiftly and appeal to more militant youth. Thus, he opted for an aggressive strategy: marching with Dr. King and raising funds for the Southern Christian Leadership Conference and other civil rights organizations that promoted progress through education—in short, leading by example. Black militants, however, tired of waiting for major change in the socioeconomic structure, veered left and away from Robinson's moderate Republicanism. Yet, his reputation as an angry rebel post 1948 when Branch Rickey liberated Jackie from top-down restraints alienated the baseball establishment. Involvement in a multitude of business ventures from Chock Full o' Nuts to banking, insurance, and construction dimmed Robinson's once luminous persona.

The struggles that JR faced—the victories on and off the field of dreams—brought tragedy along with triumph. A *Sports Illustrated* article, citing Roy Campanella and Bill Talbert, claimed that Jackie Robinson also pioneered play at age 30 with insulin-treated diabetes.[26] He lost his first child and namesake, first to drug addiction, then to death in an auto wreck on the Merritt Parkway at age 26 in 1971, which triggered guilt and heartache to this "Lion at Dusk" in the poetic words of author Roger Kahn. Illness—diabetes and heart trouble—plagued Jackie in his post-baseball life. Jackie Robinson and a select few athletic heroes defy the debunkers and compel us to contemplate their cultural roots and historical branches. With amazing grace under enormous pressure, Jackie changed the game, bringing Negro League style—speed coupled with power, daring with panache—to the center of American baseball. Not only did Jackie change the game, but he also transformed the nation. In 10 years as a Dodger, he led his team to six pennants and one World Series triumph (1955). His on-base percentage of .411 ranks historically among the best 25. That he accomplished so much with diabetes makes his achievements even more amazing,

After a dispiriting seventh game loss to those "Damned Yankees" in 1956, Robinson retired with a hefty lifetime batting average of .311. As Mark Twain once warned, however, statistics convey only half-truths. Jackie's contributions transcend quantification. Unwilling to be bartered to the Giants, #42 hung up his spikes. Robinson went on to break barriers in business, banking, broadcasting, construction, the baseball dugout, and the executive suite. Our nation's premier athlete—the only UCLA Bruin to letter in four sports: track, football, basketball and baseball—he fulfilled the American dream, rising from rags to riches. Rookie of the Year in 1947, Most Valuable Player in 1949, Hall of Fame in 1962: Robinson seemed to have it all.

It was an American success story scripted from vintage Horatio Alger just in time for the confrontation with the USSR, almost too good to be true. And it was. The truth was more complex, more disturbing. Racism did not vanish. African Americans did not zip up to that elusive room at the top. Jackie became a pawn in the Cold War. Persuaded to testify before the infamous House Un-American Activities Committee, he refuted Paul Robeson's contention that Black soldiers would not fight against the Soviet Union. Set up by his "baseball father" Branch Rickey, an arch Republican, and Urban League Director Lester Granger, he denounced "the siren song in bass"—a reference to Robeson's brilliant voice. Warmly hailed by the establishment press and mildly criticized by the Black press, Jackie urged legislators to remove the shackles of Jim Crow. That progressive message was downplayed in favor of his strong patriotic pitch. Years later, shortly before he died, Jackie apologized for his cruel criticism of Robeson but not for his staunch defense of America. Here, culled from his autobiography, are his reflections[27]:

> That statement was made over twenty years ago, and I have never regretted it. But I have grown wiser and closer to painful truths about America's destructiveness. And I do have an increased respect for Paul Robeson who, over the span of those twenty years, sacrificed himself, his career, and the wealth and comfort he once enjoyed because, I believe, he was sincerely trying to help his people. He realized, after all, towards the end of his monumental life and his painfully honest book that he "was a black man in a white world. I never had it made."[28]

The great Jackie Robinson in 1950, fresh off a season that saw him win the National League MVP Award with a .342 average, .432 on-base percentage, 16 home runs, and 37 stolen bases. Entering his fourth season in the integrated major leagues, Robinson had established himself as not only courageous in the face of prejudice but outstanding as an all-around player (National Archives).

To be sure Robinson opened doors, but disparities between rich and poor, white and Black, urban and suburban grew wider. The turbulent 1960s—featuring the new gods of relevance, pleasure, and celebrity—cast aside old heroes befitting a throwaway culture, Jackie Robinson among them. Even his alleged Dodgers adversary Dixie Walker expressed the belief that Jackie Robinson did not receive sufficient credit for his contributions to Black advances in American life. This erstwhile "People's Choice" in a 1981 interview called Robinson the most "outstanding athlete.... [he] ever saw." "He had the instinct to always do the right thing on the field," he said.[29]

Robinson did not manage or coach. Some labeled him a troublemaker, and the label stuck. Youngsters cited his conservative politics and his support of Richard Milhous Nixon. Robinson did not fit the radical chic or the new sexuality. As a devoted family man, business executive, and Rockefeller Republican, he must have seemed the ultimate square. Obscured by the high-salaried celebrities and targeted for low blows from mindless militants, Jackie went into temporary eclipse. The major 1965 study *The Negro American*, edited by preeminent scholars Talcott Parsons and Kenneth Clark, contains no mention of Jackie Robinson! Other tomes demonstrated a strange indifference to this noble giant in Dodgers uniform. An inane remark by a contemporary player coupled ignorance with amnesia. And this failure of memory was shared by many.

A reappraisal started in the 1970s with the advent of Roger Kahn's brilliant *The Boys of Summer* and continued in the 1980s with Jules Tygiel's magisterial *Baseball's Great Experiment: Jackie Robinson and His Legacy*. Maury Allen, Peter Golenbock, Bob Lipsyte, Arnold Rampersad, and Carl Prince added to this impressive genre. These books demonstrate the danger, courage, and cost of this noble experiment. Martin Luther King, Jr., confided in Dodgers pitching great Don Newcombe that Jackie Robinson was indispensable. In effect, he confessed: no Robinson, no King—a statement substantiated by the Reverend Wyatt Tee Walker, a close associate. Quoting the civil rights leader, he said: "Jackie Robinson made it possible for me in the first place. Without him, I would never have been able to do what I did."[30]

Indeed, crossing the color line in baseball, the national pastime, in 1947 was more dangerous than Neil Armstrong's first footfalls on the silvery moon in 1969. While the astronaut had the support of all Americans, Jackie Robinson—with the exception of mentor Branch Rickey, beloved wife Rachel, and a few crusading journalists—basically ran alone. He had enemies, a fifth column on his own team. He had to overcome the stereotypes of Sambo, Amos 'n' Andy, Aunt Jemima, and Uncle Ben. Media-forged manacles had captured the soul of Black folks and had beamed a benighted image of the docile Negro.[31] Throughout the sports arenas, before Robinson, Black athletes projected personas of brute force like Jack Johnson and Joe Louis or gifted clowns like the Harlem Globetrotters. Even the enormously popular Joe Louis was not an adept speaker. Then came Jackie: daring, daunting, dignified. With the solid stroke of his bat, a spectacular snatch of line drive heading over second base, and a sensational steal of home, Robinson vaulted into our national psyche. Off the field, his high-pitched tenor voice spoke cadenced sentences that parsed and imparted incisive commentary. Not only did Jackie redefine baseball culture by bringing a new combination of speed, power, and style to the national game, but he also destroyed the way Blacks were perceived. Italian, Irish, and Jewish kids (I was almost 11 when Robinson joined the Dodgers) rooted for Robinson and our erstwhile Bums. We began to see our Brooklyn neighbors and Negro classmates differently: once through a glass darkly, now through a lens brightly. A pioneer on the frontier of race, ethnic, and ultimately gender relations, Jackie Robinson brought us closer to that holy grail of peace, justice, and the American way. Bill "Bojangles" Robinson called Jackie "Ty Cobb in Technicolor."[32]

Our landscape is graffitied with celebrities instead of heroes. Historian Daniel Boorstin inferred that a democratic society bears an intrinsic bias against individual heroes. Earlier, our nation's heroes arose from common origins like Jackie Robinson, powered by merit. Today, however, the celebrity—often devoid of talent—occupies center stage in both sports and entertainment. Character and achievement often play second string. These celebrities blur the boundaries between heroes and antiheroes. As one conference presenter put it, Robinson brought a revolutionary style to American baseball culture. As a fighter against his times, he also provided a model of heroism in an age of antiheroism.[33] Shortly before—nine days, to be precise—his death at age 53, Jackie appeared at a World Series game in 1972 to celebratory recognition of the 25th anniversary of his historic entry into Major League Baseball. He spoke briefly. Robinson thanked Captain Pee Wee Reese for his leadership and support, then pleaded for a Black manager in the dugout and a Black coach peering from a third base perch to advance racial integration to a higher level.

Cincinnati Reds second baseman Joe Morgan (later a color commentator on a weekly baseball telecast), who proudly wore a uniform with his hero's number 42, thanked him. Sportswriter Jim Murray, suffering from failing eyesight, greeted the now legally blind Mr. Robinson with these poignant words: "Jackie, it's me, Jim Murray." Robinson responded: "Jim, I wish that I could see you." "Oh, Jackie, I too wish that I could see you again!" Keynote speaker and author Roger Rosenblatt said it best with these concluding words: "Who would not?"[34]

Nine days later Jackie died of a massive heart attack. Many fans came out to Riverside Church to see the body of Jackie Robinson lying in state. A young preacher, Jesse Jackson, delivered the eulogy. The salient words culled from his tombstone 1919–1972[35]:

> On that dash is where we live. And for everyone there is a dash of possibility, to choose the high road or the low road, to make things better or worse. On that dash, he snapped the barbed wire of prejudice. His feet danced on the base paths! But it was more than a game. He was the black knight. In his last dash, he stole home and Jackie is safe. His enemies can rest assured of that!
>
> Call me nigger, call me black boy! I don't care…. No grave can hold this body down because it belongs to the ages; and all of us are better off because that man with that body, that soul and mission passed this way.
>
> On that dash, 1919–1972, Jackie changed history.

To be sure, Robinson served as both liberator and catalyst. However salutary for race relations and Major League Baseball, his historic breakthrough ultimately led to the demise of Negro League baseball and that rich, vibrant culture from which it grew and in turn nurtured. Critics lamented the downside of this Robinson-Rickey "noble experiment." Poet Amiri Baraka labeled (or libeled?) Robinson a "race traitor." He equated baseball integration with white theft and expropriation. Author Nelson George, in less vituperative language, echoed these sentiments. These assertions are examined in Brian Carroll's excellent article recently published in *Black Ball*. Carroll examines the complicity of the Black press in covering the integration saga at the expense of Negro League baseball. While lamenting the demise of the latter, Carroll does not conceal the shame and degradation that attended segregated baseball. Nor—in a "fair and balanced" perspective—does he conceal the feeble attempts to keep Negro Baseball alive through clownish antics and novelty acts— shades of minstrel traditions. In the final analysis, as Carroll perceptively points out, "double consciousness" was in play here too, as Dr. Dubois so presciently and accurately observed in 1903. Clearly, the zeitgeist demanded integration into America's mainstream, swimming as it were behind Jack Roosevelt Robinson.[36]

Thus, we return to poet Stephen Spender, who guides us through the urban wilderness. Robinson "signed the vivid air with his honor."[37] Forever fixed in the mystic chords of memory, he summons what Abraham Lincoln also called the "better angels of our nature."

9

Don Newcombe
and Roy Campanella,
Monte Irvin and Larry Doby

The arguments raised by Jon Entine, Harry Edwards, and Arthur Ashe, regarding the significant role that African American athletes play at an exorbitant price in terms of identity, invite rebuttal when we assess the heroic lives of African American pioneers in sports who followed Jackie Robinson. As Jackie famously wrote, "a life is not important except in the impact it has on other lives." That statement, inscribed on his tombstone, applies to Roy Campanella, Don Newcombe, Monte Irvin, and Larry Doby.

Campy and Newk

At our Long Island University celebration of Jackie Robinson in April 1997, one of our presenters, Lester Rodney, learned that Roy Campanella's granddaughter Akua was in the audience. He asked me, as co-director of the conference, to introduce him to her, which I did, gladly. In an extremely sensitive exchange, Lester Rodney, who had vigorously campaigned for integration of Major League Baseball as sports editor of the *Daily Worker*, wanted to reassure Akua that her grandfather and Jackie Robinson were not enemies as some sportswriters claimed. As recorded in his book, as told to Irwin Silber, he told her:

> I thought you might like to know that I was a sportswriter and I knew your grandfather very well. I wrote about him and Jackie Robinson a lot. I know you may have heard that your grandfather was just a ball-player, as opposed to Jackie Robinson. That he wasn't a strong advocate of correcting injustices. Well, let me tell you, in his own quiet way, he knew as much as Robinson. He just projected himself in a different way. I thought you might like to know that. You could tell she was glad to hear that. And she cried a little.[1]

They disagreed, Rodney insisted, on means perhaps, but were on the same page as to the goals of racial integration. They actually admired each other's talent and work ethic. Campanella acknowledged Jackie Robinson's sacrifices and said: "Jackie made things easy for us."[2] Satisfied with this effort at reconciliation, we returned to our seats surrounded by famous ballplayers, ardent fans, eager students, prolific authors, and elected officials to honor Jackie Robinson 50 years after his historic transformation of modern baseball.

A vital performer in the Brooklyn Dodgers success story, Roy Campanella was born on November 21, 1921, the youngest of four children to Ida, an African American mother, and an Italian-American father named John Campanella. In his autobiography, *It's Good to Be Alive*, Roy remembered his parents as warm, loving, and supportive. His white father was wonderful, and his Black mother was the disciplinarian.[3] To supplement family income Roy helped his dad with selling vegetables out of a truck, shined shoes, sold newspapers, and helped his older brother Larry on a milk route.

At the age of 15, Roy played semi-pro baseball for an all-Black team for $35 per week with his mother's permission, on the condition that he attend church on Sunday, prior to games.[4] He attended integrated public schools, which he left at age 16 to play baseball, first as a semi-pro with the Bacharach Giants, later with the Baltimore Elite Giants as a full-fledged pro in the Negro Leagues. He replaced injured player/manager Biz Mackey as the starting catcher in 1939 and was named MVP of the Negro League All-Star game in 1941. Because he was already married with two daughters with a draft status of 3-A when Congress declared war in 1941, Campanella did not go on active duty but worked in war-related industry. Although a salary dispute with the Elite Giants propelled Campanella into Mexican League baseball from 1942 to 1943, he returned to Baltimore in 1944 and played through 1945. During a five-game exhibition series at Ebbets Field, Dodgers coach Charlie Dressen scouted and recommended him to general manager and part-owner Branch Rickey. Believing that he was offered a contract to an all-Black team, the Brooklyn Brown Dodgers, Roy initially refused to sign a contract with the Dodgers. A chance meeting with Jackie Robinson in Manhattan, however, revealed the true intent of Mr. Rickey, and Campy decided to join the Dodgers organization.[5]

Originally, Rickey wanted Campanella to join a recent addition, Don Newcombe, to play in the Three-I League in the Midwest. When that league rejected Black players, Rickey changed directions. He sent his two future Black stars to Nashua in the Class B New England League.[6] Campanella took a pay cut from $600 per month in Baltimore to $185 per month in Nashua. But it paid off as Campanella won the league's MVP award with a .290 batting average, 13 home runs, 96 runs batted in, and superb fielding.[7] He also proved an ability to defend himself. When Sal Yvars, future New York Giants third-string catcher and participant in the illegal sign-stealing scheme in 1951 that propelled the Giants over the Dodgers in the pennant race, threw dirt in Campy's face, the usually unflappable catcher threw down his mask and warned the malefactor: "Try that again and I'll beat you to a pulp." Yvars complied.[8] The muscular 5'9" 190-pound Campanella had fought in the Golden Glove.[9] Hitting home runs proved a boon to John and Ida, Roy's parents. A local farmer offered 100 chickens for every homer hit in Nashua's spacious park. After adding a homer in the playoffs, Roy sent 1,400 chickens to his parents, enabling them to start a farming business of their very own outside of Philadelphia.[10]

In 1947, Campanella went to spring training in Havana on the Montréal roster.

Along with other Black players, he encountered racism in Cuba, if somewhat less virulent than in the southern states, rife with segregation. Like his predecessor Robinson, Roy Campanella set the International League on fire early in the season, but cooled off to hit .273 with 13 homers and 75 runs batted in, good enough to win the league MVP.[11] Up to his old tricks, Rickey wanted to hide Campanella on the roster in the minor leagues. Campanella and Durocher balked at this maneuver, but Rickey insisted. Campanella was sent down to St. Paul's Triple-A club, where he tore up Red Barber's "pea patch" with 13 homers and a .325 batting average. Thanks to Campy's performance after his recall, the deadbeat Dodgers picked up their game. Before jumping to the New York Giants, Durocher moved second-string catcher Gil Hodges to first base and slid Campanella behind the plate as popular first-stringer Bruce Edwards tailed off due to injury. But they were unable to catch the Boston Braves, who—with "Spahn and Sain and two days of rain"—ran away with the National League pennant.

The Dodgers' fortunes dramatically improved in 1949. So did Campanella's, as he upped his batting average to .287 with 22 homers and 82 runs batted in plus superb work behind the plate. He was named to his first All-Star game, played at Ebbets Field. With rookie Don Newcombe anchoring a formidable pitching staff, the Dodgers won the pennant on the season's last day. Again as Dodgers fans lamented, God proved a Yankees fan as the Bronx Bombers beat Brooklyn in the World Series four games to one. The best National League team could not defeat those "damn" Yankees. In 1950, a notorious blunder on the base paths was all that stood between the Dodgers and the Series. In the ninth inning of the last game of the regular season, with the score tied, Duke Snider singled—but Cal Abrams, who had been on second base, was thrown out at the plate by the weak-armed Philly center fielder Richie Ashburn. If Abrams had held up at third base, leaving the bases loaded with Jackie Robinson up next to bat, the Brooklyns might well have won. Who knows? So, Philadelphia's "whiz kids" went to the Word Series, where the Yankees swept them in four straight games. That year Roy continued his great ascent with 31 home runs with a .281 batting average.[12]

The year 1951 enabled Roy Campanella to win his first of three MVPs with a monumental year, batting .325 (a career best), 33 home runs, and 108 runs batted in. A leg injury forced Campy to miss two crucial playoff games against the "cheating" Giants. Bobby Thomson's "blast heard round the world" ended Dodger hopes in a 5–4 defeat. So, the Dodgers answered the annual cry of "Wait 'til next year!" with a pennant win in 1952, helped by a new Black pitching ace, Joe Black, as both starter and relief. Ahead of the Yankees, three games to two, the Dodgers again managed to snatch defeat from the jaws of victory in a seven-game thriller. Plagued by a recurrence of injuries, Campanella had a sub-par year.

A revitalized Roy had a banner year in 1953. With a league-leading 142 runs batted in coupled with a .312 batting average and 41 home runs, Campanella won his second MVP. Ready to lead his team to their first World Series victory, Campy was hit by an Allie Reynolds fastball that reduced his batting and catching prowess. An unlikely Yankees hero, Billy Martin led his team to a World Series title. Another injury to his left wrist in a meaningless spring training game in 1954 resulted in

Campy's worst year with a career-low .207 batting average and a relatively easy pennant run for their archenemies from Manhattan, the New York Giants.

Injuries continued to plague the unlucky catcher in 1955, that year for Dodgers fans to remember and savor. The Dodgers had the best battery of catcher-pitchers in baseball. Although he missed 30 games due to injury, Campanella won his third MVP with a .318 batting average, 32 home runs, and 107 runs batted in. He led the team in hitting as the Dodgers finished with a 98–55 record, 13.5 games ahead of the Milwaukee Braves in second place. Don Newcombe led the pitching staff with a sparkling 20–5 record and a 3.20 earned run average. Finally, the Dodgers got off the *shneid* with their only World Series title in Brooklyn as Johnny Podres emerged as the pitching star, winning two games in their victory over the Yankees. Campy contributed two home runs. Brooklyn fans celebrated in the streets minus police intervention. In 1956, however, a reversal of fortunes put the Yankees in Red Barber's "catbird seat" with a four games to three victory. Injury-plagued Campy slumped, while Don Newcombe had a spectacular year during the regular season, winning 27 games, losing only seven, posting five shutouts, and sporting a .306 earned run average. Unfortunately, he suffered a dismal Word Series in two appearances.

In 1957, minus Jackie Robinson, who had retired after a deplorable trade to the rival New York Giants, the Dodgers slumped to 84–70 and a third place finish in the National League. Both Campanella and Newcombe had sub-par years. When the Dodgers abandoned Brooklyn for the big bucks that beckoned for Walter O'Malley—still considered in our borough as the epitome of evil by authors Jack Newfield and Pete Hamill, slightly behind Hitler and Stalin—a 10-year fixture behind the plate for Brooklyn, Roy Campanella, planned to play in Los Angeles.[13]

Fate, however, dictated otherwise. Driving home in a rented Chevrolet (his regular Cadillac was in a repair shop) from his Harlem liquor store on January 28, 1958, Campanella, minus a seat belt, slid on a patch of ice five miles from his home. The car slid into a telephone pole and turned upside down, pushing Roy into the steering wheel, his head whiplashed, resulting in a broken neck and a spinal cord injury. Surgery saved his life. Rehab in the NYU's Rusk Institute followed to help Campanella, now a quadriplegic, cope with a diminished life. Despite excruciating pain, a broken marriage, the death of his adopted son David in a drug overdose, and vulnerability to a host of illnesses, Campy persevered.

Thanks to intensive physical therapy, Campanella was able to regain use of his arms and hands.[14] Talk show hosting on radio's "Campy's Corner" also provided mental stimulation. As a part-time Dodgers coach during spring training at the now abandoned Vero Beach facility and radio announcer for Dodgers home games, Campy reconnected with a life in baseball. Voted into the Baseball Hall of Fame in 1969, Campy also worked for the Los Angeles Dodgers in community relations under his former battery mate, Don Newcombe. He died of a heart attack on June 26, 1996, to the disbelief of author Dave Anderson, who claimed that Campy had the biggest and strongest heart in baseball.[15] Baseball's statistical expert Bill James cited Roy Campanella as the third best defensive catcher in history behind Yogi Berra and Johnny Bench.[16] This once avid Yankees fan disagrees. With the best caught stealing percentage—57 percent—in baseball history coupled with his agility behind the plate, Campy belongs at the top. Ty Cobb said it best: "Campanella will be remembered longer than any catcher in baseball history."[17]

Roy Campanella was not only a hero on the field as a baseball pioneer, but he also earned that honor in his second career in coping with disability. Unlike Jackie Robinson, he spoke softly and carried a big stick. As Don Newcombe recalled: "Jack would blow his top, and Campy would calm him down. We were all going through so much back then, we needed Campy as our stabilizing influence." Like the biblical Job, he survived. Hall of Fame broadcaster Vin Scully famously stated: "Although he was a remarkable ballplayer I think he'll be remembered more for his 35 years in a wheelchair."[18]

Don Newcombe was a Hall of Fame pitcher who did not get in. Richard Goldstein's obituary in the *New York Times*[19] explains why. At 6'4" and 225 pounds, he cut an imposing figure. Blessed with a blazing fastball and a wicked curve, he was the National League Rookie of the Year in 1949. In 1956, after his spectacular year in the regular season, he was named league MVP and Cy Young winner in both leagues as the best pitcher in baseball, a rare distinction. In addition, he was considered the "second coming" of Babe Ruth because of his exceptional hitting with a lifetime batting average of .271 and 15 home runs. As the first Black pitcher to start a World Series game, he deserves consideration. Aye, and there's the rub: his fall from grace in crunch time at that annual event. The "undeserved reputation" of his failure to win key games or control alcoholism, insufficient playing time due to military service during his peak years (1952–1954), and his delayed entry (1949) into the major leagues all contributed to his omission from baseball's Valhalla.[20]

Born on June 14, 1926, in

Willie Mays places an arm around Roy Campanella in 1961. Both men had started off in the Negro Leagues, Mays with the Birmingham Black Barons and Campanella primarily with the Baltimore Elite Giants. The photograph was taken two years after Campanella's career was cut short by a late-night car accident. Still in his mid-thirties at the time, Campanella had already won three MVPs in 10 years with the Dodgers (Library of Congress, *World Telegram & Sun* photograph by William C. Greene).

Madison, New Jersey, to Roland and Sadie Newcombe, Don had three older brothers and one sister. His father worked as a chauffeur, which led to frequent moves in conjunction with Ronald's boss during the Great Depression. Finally settled in Elizabeth, New Jersey, Don attended Jefferson High School and played semi-pro baseball on the side. At age 8, he started to drink beer, leading to a lifelong challenge.[21] A high school dropout at age 17, and unable to join the U.S. Army when war broke out in 1941, he hooked up with the Negro League's Newark Eagles. Owner Effa Manley needed ballplayers to replace those who left for the war effort. He signed for $170 per month. In two years with the Eagles, Newk won four games and lost seven according to baseball-reference.com. Another (perhaps more reliable) reference, James A. Riley, maintains that Newk incurred three losses minus any wins in 1944 but sported an 8–3 record in 1945.[22] Thirdly, *Pittsburgh Courier* reporter Wendell Smith as cited by Jules Tygiel has Newcombe having a 14–4 record in 1945.[23] Yet, in a fourth observation, inviting comparison to a Japanese classic film *Rashomon*, Newcombe told Peter Golenbock that, though wild, he managed to win seven games in his first season with Newark. Newk also mentioned that his manager, Mule Suttles, ordered him to throw at future teammate Roy Campanella's head. Reluctantly, he threw it hard and high, but Campy knocked it out of Ruppert Stadium, where the Eagles played their home games.[24] Dodgers scout Clyde Sukeforth spotted him in an exhibition series and recommended him to the mahatma, Branch Rickey.

Dodgers general manager Rickey had at one time considered Newcombe along with Campanella to break the color barrier together, but political pressure and Newcombe's youth, lack of education, and military service may have pointed to Jack Roosevelt Robinson instead. Farmed out to Nashua with Campanella, a former rival, Newcombe pitched a shutout in his first game. He also became a proficient hitter, inviting comparisons with the "Babe." Newcombe finished a 14–4 record and an earned run average of 2.21.With this dynamic duo leading the way, Nashua made the playoffs and ultimately copped the New England title.

Invited to spring training in Havana in 1947 to ease Jackie Robinson's transition into Major League Baseball, the Black players were excluded from Havana's plush Hotel Nacional and consigned to a third-rate facility, also used for military training. The Black players had to eat in cheap restaurants. Newcombe threw up after spotting a cockroach emerging from his plate of soup.[25]

He lost a lot of weight and spent another summer of discontent in New Hampshire. Again he excelled with a 19–6 record and a 2.91 earned run average while battery mate Roy Campanella was moved up to Montreal and Triple-A competition. Expecting to be promoted like Campanella in 1948, Newk suffered another disappointment. Like the "Good Soldier Schweik" in a German film, he obeyed orders. There, he displayed great stuff as he completed 16 games, compiling three shutouts and 144 strikeouts with a 17–8 record and a .317 earned run average. Newk added a slider to his repertoire of fastball and curve and pitched his only no-hitter. In the playoffs, a steady Newcombe won key games as the Royals bested their other Dodgers Triple-A team, the St. Paul Saints, in five games. Naturally, Newcombe expected a promotion in 1949. It did not come easily. On the spurious grounds that he had not matured sufficiently, he was dispatched to Montréal, where he tossed two shutouts and lost two games by one run. Evidently, he had alienated the crusty old Dodgers manager who could not tolerate Newcombe's rebellious spirit.

Slumping, the Dodgers called up Newk on May 20, 1949. In his second appearance—this time as a starter—he tossed a shutout. Rapidly gaining confidence and garnering victories, Newcombe was named to the National League All-Star team. In that memorable rookie year, big Don Newcombe went 17–8, tossed five league-leading shutouts, and completed 19 games with a .317 earned run average. Facing the Yankees, who had also won their pennant on the season's final day in game one, he pitched brilliantly for eight shutout innings with 11 strikeouts. Yankee ace Allie Reynolds yielded only two Dodgers hits. Unfortunately, the first batter up, first baseman Tommy Henrich, hit a line drive home run to end the game. They did not call Henrich "Old Reliable" for nothing. Each of the five games was competitive until the last one, resulting in a Yankees win, 10–6.[26]

Despite this unhappy ending to his season, Don Newcombe was named Rookie of the Year. The Dodgers tried to repeat in 1950. On the final day of the season the Dodgers trailed the surprising Phillies by one game. Newcombe was seeking his 20th win against the Phillie ace Robinson Roberts, also seeking his 20th win. With the game tied, as mentioned above, the Dodgers ran themselves out of a sure victory with a running blunder. Foolishly, a tied Newcombe pitched the 10th inning and yielded a three-run opposite home run to Dick Sisler, losing the game, 4–1.[27] Charlie Dressen replaced Burt Shotton as Dodgers manager.

In 1951, Dodgers fortunes looked bright. They led the second place Giants by 13.5 games on August 11. Based on Joshua Prager's research, we now know how the Giants caught up with the "Bums" from Brooklyn entering the season's final day. As author Joshua Prager proved beyond a shadow of a doubt, they cheated![28] They set the table for another cheating scandal involving the Houston Astros in recent years. The Dodgers' final game was a seesaw affair that saw the Phillies build a lead 4–0 before stretching it to 6–2. Then the Dodgers rallied with three runs; Robinson knocked one in and scored one, narrowing the lead to 6–5. The Phillies tacked on two runs. Now, trailing 8–5 in the eighth inning, the Dodgers rallied again. Hits by Hodges, Cox, Walker, and Furillo knotted the score 8–8. Dressen called on Newcombe in relief. He pitched five scoreless innings, the last one a nail-biter. Tired, Newk loaded the bases with two outs and Eddie Waitkus at bat. The Phillies first sacker lined a shot headed for center field, which Jackie Robinson, diving to his right, speared, saving the game and season. Two innings later Robinson, facing Robin Roberts in relief, hit an upper-deck home run to win the game as Dodgers reliever Bud Podbielan held the Phillies scoreless in the bottom of the 14th inning.[29] Since both teams—Dodgers and Giants—had won games in their last games, they squared off for a three-game playoff series.

In the first game, Ralph Branca started for the Dodgers, Jim Hearn for the Giants. Andy Pafko's homer gave a temporary lead to the Dodgers, 1–0. Home runs by Bobby Thomson, a Dodgers nemesis throughout the season after he switched from outfielder to third-baseman, hit a two-run bomb in the third inning, followed by a Monte Irvin solo home run for a 3–1 win. In game two, Clem Labine, normally a relief pitcher, hurled a shutout in a 10–0 rout, setting up a winner-take-all third game, pitting Don Newcombe against Sal "the Barber" Maglie. Entering the ninth inning of this critical game, the Dodgers led 4 to 1. Alvin Dark led off with a single off Gil Hodge's glove. In a questionable move, Hodges held Dark close to first base, leaving a gaping hole through which Don Mueller, called "Mandrake the Magician" for his batting skill, drilled a single, putting runners on the corner bases. Newcombe induced Monte Irvin to foul out to Hodges. Batting next, Whitey Lockman lined a double down the left line. Sliding into third base, Mueller broke his ankle and was replaced by pinch runner Clint Hartung, a pitcher by trade. Evidently "pooped," Newcombe was given the "hook." In the bullpen, two Dodgers pitchers were warming up: Carl Erskine with a devastating curve ball and Ralph Branca, who had lost five consecutive games since midseason, when he had a competent record of 13 wins and only six losses. Bullpen coach Clyde Sukeforth recommended Branca because Erskine's curve was bouncing short. So Branca, number 13, came into pitch. The Giants had been stealing signs since midseason. Branca threw a high strike. Unluckily, he hit the same spot, which Thomson tomahawked into the left field stands. As Giants announcer Russ Hodges chanted infamously: "The Giants win the pennant! The Giants win the pennant! The Giants win the pennant!"[30] *Ad infinitum, ad nauseam.* Jackie Robinson, hands on hips, watched carefully to make sure that Thomson touched all the bases as his former manager Leo Durocher and former teammate Eddie Stanky embraced.

The next year arrived minus Don Newcombe. He was drafted into the U.S. Army during the Korean War and missed two baseball seasons in his prime. I recall seeing him at a football game during that strange interlude in civilian garb: a blue coat and grey fedora hat towering above us all below. Returning in 1954 to another year of Giants domination, Newcombe looked rusty while eking out a 9–8 record with an elevated earned run average of .455. Despite drinking heavily, he had an excellent comeback year in 1955, winning 20 games while losing only five with 17 complete games and an earned run average of 3.20. Although he got roughed up by Yankees hitters in game one and did not pitch afterward due to a sore arm, presumably, the Dodgers found a new hero in southpaw Johnny Podres, who defeated the Yankees in game three and game seven, the latter a shutout, crowning the Brooklyn Dodgers with their only world title in history.[31] Ironically, Newcombe's best year as a Dodgers ace followed in 1956, during which he won 27 games and lost only 7 with an earned run average of 3.06 including 18 complete games and five shutouts. He even pitched two ends of a doubleheader, a unique performance in Major League Baseball.

A roller coaster ride followed in 1957, the last year of Dodgers baseball on the East Coast. Drinking heavily, Newcombe slid to a record of 11–12 and rose in earned run average to 3.49. He had been imbibing lots of beer from 1949 to 1955. After buying a liquor store in 1956, Newcombe began drinking "the hard stuff" mixed with grapefruit or grape juice. As a functioning alcoholic, he could still pitch, but with big hangovers.[32] His first wife, Freddie, with whom he adopted two children, had become an alcoholic, which led to a divorce in 1959. Clearly, excessive booze affected his career.[33] In 1958, he joined the Los Angeles Dodgers and lost six games in a row. Traded to the Cincinnati Reds, Newk experienced something of a revival. He won seven games and lost seven. In 1959, he improved to 13–8 with 2 shutouts and a solid earned run average of 3.16 plus 17 complete games. Mediocrity marked the next three years, two in Cincinnati and one in Cleveland. Newcombe played his last season in Spokane in the Pacific Coast League with a 9–8 record before departing for Japan for a final year in organized baseball. Playing for the Chinuchi Dragons in 1962, primarily as a first baseman and outfielder—he pitched only one game—Newk hit .262, 12 homers, and knocked in 43 runs. Larry Doby also played for this Japanese team.

In 1966, Newcombe quit drinking cold turkey when his second wife, Billie Roberts, whom he married in 1960, and his three children, suitcases packed, were prepared to leave him as he lay sleeping off a "bender" on the floor. As he recalled that pivotal moment: "I took a vow on the head of my son, Don, to my wife and God that I would never drink again if they would stay."[34] Newcombe's post-baseball and drinking life belies novelist F. Scott Fitzgerald's pronouncement that "there are no second acts in American lives." After his fall from grace, Newcombe rose to advocate for sobriety and reform. He established a personal services company to help victims of alcohol and substance abuse. He helped Maury Wills among others who struggled with drug problems. In 1970 he started a long relationship with the Los Angeles Dodgers as director of community relations until 2017. After divorcing for a second time in 1994, he married his third wife, Karen. Several weeks before his assassination, Dr. King came to Newcombe's house in 1968 and told him, "I would never have made it as successfully as I have in civil rights if it were not for what you men did on the baseball field."[35] Forty-two years later, President Barack Obama offered a comparable compliment to "Newk" when he said: "I would not be here if it were not for Jackie and if it were not for Don Newcombe." Dodgers president Stan Kasten commented: "He was a constant presence at Dodger Stadium and players always gravitated to him for his endless advice and leadership. The Dodgers meant everything to him and we are all fortunate that he was a part of our lives."[36] Don Newcombe's life ended on Tuesday, February 19, 2019, but his song of redemption lingers on.

Monte Irvin and Larry Doby

Munford Merrill (his given name) "Monte" Irvin, the seventh of 10 children—six boys, four girls—was born in Haleburg, Alabama, on February 2, 1919, to Cupid Alexander and Mary Eliza Irvin. That halcyon year also brought a formal end to World War I, the birth of Jackie Robinson, and a surge of race riots in a number of American cities. A victim of the sharecropping system in Alabama, Monte's father confronted his landlord over money. In dire straits, Cupid had to flee first to Georgia and later to New Jersey. Since two older children had moved to the "Garden State," Cupid followed with his wife and children in tow. They eventually settled in Orange, a suburb. There, Monte attended East Orange High School, an integrated institution where he excelled in athletics. But the restaurants were segregated and movie theaters confined Blacks to the balcony only.[37] Sports provided the principal passport to success in America.

Earning letters in football, track, basketball, and baseball (like Paul Robeson),

Irvin, at 6'1" and 190 pounds, gained a reputation as his high school's greatest ath-lete. On graduation night, however, Monte and his date, along with two other Black couples, could not eat at a local restaurant near the school because of their color. Depressed, these youngsters left. A scout from the University of Michigan offered Monte a football scholarship. Unfortunately, he lacked the funds to reach Ann Arbor. Thus, he lost a splendid opportunity to play in the same backfield with Tommy Har-mon and Forest Evashevski. He settled on Lincoln University, an all-Black school in Pennsylvania where he formed a lifelong friendship with future Eagles teammate Max Manning. Less than two years later, Monte left to play baseball with the Newark Eagles. Starting in high school, Monte used the pseudonym Jimmy Nelson in order to maintain his amateur status. As soon as he dropped out of college, he reverted to his real name.[38] After he learned to pull the ball by watching Joe DiMaggio, Irvin became one of the dominant hitters in the Negro League. While statistics are not always available or reliable, it is clear that Monte could match skills with the best white ball players. As an Eagle of Newark, Monte flew to the top of the league as a hitter with hefty averages of .403 in 1939, .377 in 1940, and .400 in 1941. Whether perched at third base, shortstop, or center field, Irvin became a wizard on defense as well. He honed his skills and learned some painful truths while on tour. In 1941 he and teammate Max Manning were driving through Daytona Beach, Florida, when a policeman stopped them.

"Where are you goin'?" he barked.

"Home," a nervous Manning replied. "Home!"

"Don't you know how to say, sir?" Manning froze in anger.

"Yes, sir," Irvin volunteered quickly.

"What's wrong with your buddy? Can't he say it?"

As the young redneck began to unbuckle his billy club, Irvin explained that they were learning to play baseball. They wanted no trouble. This traumatic inci-dent, recalled nearly 60 years after it happened, revealed the survival skills of Monte Irvin. He realized that uttering the magic words, stuck in the throat of Max Man-ning, saved them from a beating or worse.

This is how one dealt with racism in 1941. Irvin dismissed it : "No problem.... I know the son of a bitch is ignorant ... and no skin off my teeth to say sir. It's not going to make me a lesser man." In retrospect, Irvin may have rationalized his stance of accommodation. Taking the less evil route, Irvin survived this ordeal but not without enormous psychic pain. Unable to wrest a salary increase from tight-fisted Eagles owner Effa Manley, Monte "jumped" to the Mexican League to join the Vera Cruz team. He led the league with a .397 average, 20 home runs, and 79 runs batted in and captured the MVP award.[39]

Monte went off to war in 1943. He experienced segregation over there—Europe—as well as over here. For example, a company commander warned Monte and his Black buddies to spurn social invitations and to avoid contact with white women. These absurd orders made a person feel "like you were nothing." The war left Monte with shattered nerves. Based on his pre-war baseball performance, Monte Irvin—not Jackie Robinson—should have been the designated pioneer to break the color barrier. According to one source—his daughter Pamela—Monte's wife intercepted a letter from Branch Rickey soliciting Monte's service for the Brooklyn Dodgers. Mrs. Irvin realized that Monte could not at that time shoulder the Herculean labors.[40] Rickey persisted until Eagles owner Effa Manley demanded monetary compensation for Monte's contract.[41]

Thus, when he returned to civilian life, he opted for more seasoning in the Negro League and in Latin American winter ball. In 1946, he, Leon Day, Larry Doby, and Max Manning led the Newark Eagles to victory over Satchel Paige's Kansas City Monarchs in the Negro League World Series. Irvin hit three homers and batted .462 against a team with two future Hall of Famers in Paige and Hilton Smith.[42] While the team traveled in Mississippi in an air-conditioned bus, white farmers jeered at the "jigaboos." Irvin sensed the incongruity of the hooting crackers broiling in the southern heat while the Eagles rode in comfort. Laughter eclipsed anger.[32] When Monte finally reached the major leagues as a New York Giant, he proved his mettle. A fine career curtailed by injury and late entry propelled Irvin into the Hall of Fame belatedly in 1973. Over eight years, he hit .293 during the regular season and .394 in two World Series (1951 and 1954). His finest hour came in the "miracle year" of 1951 when he hit .312, 24 home runs, and league-leading 121 runs batted in. With Hank Thompson in left and Willie Mays in center, Monte formed the first all-Black outfield. In the World Series, he stole home in game one and proceeded to pulverize Yankees pitching at an amazing .458 clip with a then record-setting 11 hits in 24 at bats. The Giants lost to the Yankees in six games. Irvin claimed that his theft of home against Yankees pitching ace Allie Reynolds ranked as his "biggest thrill in baseball."[43]

After retirement, Irvin worked for Rheingold Beer in promotions and public relations. From 1968 to 1984 he worked as a special assistant to Baseball Commissioner Bowie Kuhn during a turbulent era sparked by free agency and other volatile issues. As the only Black administrator in the commissioner's office, Irvin worked quietly behind the scenes to secure justice for his fellow Negro Leaguers. He served as go-between between Commissioner Bowie Kuhn and Curt Flood during the latter's litigation. Author Brad Snyder considered Monte "a company man, not a boat rocker."[44] Even if Snyder's assessment is accurate, as an insider Monte Irvin worked behind the scenes to honor his fellow Negro Leaguers after his own induction into the Baseball Hall of Fame on August 6, 1973. He steered Ray Dandridge, Martín Dihigo, Rube Foster, Judy Johnson, and John Henry Lloyd through the portals of baseball immortals. A survivor, despite ill health in his later years, Irvin lived to just one month short of his 97th birthday. Unlike Robeson and Robinson, two aggressive Black heroes, Monte followed a course of least or—more accurately—lesser resistance. One should remember there are many roads to glory. Mr. Irvin took the one more traveled by and that has made all the difference.[45]

Ever in Robinson's shadow, the soft-spoken Larry Doby deserves to be hailed as a hero as well. Born and raised in Camden, South Carolina, from 1923 to 1938, young Lawrence was left fatherless at age eight. Looking back in anger, he recalled his early years when whites would come to the Black neighborhood and throw coins at small Black children. They would also rub the children's heads in search of good luck. Larry's mother warned him against taking gifts from strangers. He listened.[46] At

15, he arrived in Patterson, New Jersey, where he set the high school athletic world on fire with sterling performances in baseball, football, basketball, and track. He too adapted an alias—Larry Walker—to preserve his amateur status while playing professional baseball, like Irvin, for the Newark Eagles. Admitted to Long Island University on a basketball scholarship because he admired Coach Clair Bee, Doby stayed briefly before transferring to Virginia Union. His college career was cut short by service in the U.S. Navy starting in 1943. Segregation in the navy shocked him after relative integration in northeast New Jersey, though it prepared Doby for the challenges ahead.[47]

When he returned, the svelte slugger reunited with Monte Irvin on the championship Newark Eagles, for whom he played second base opposite Irvin at shortstop before their military service during World War II. This dynamic duo arguably constituted the best hitting keystone combination in baseball history, but they were converted to outfielders in the post-war period. Before entering Major League Baseball, Doby led the Negro National League with a whopping .415 batting average and 14 home runs. In only 42 games, he whacked 16 doubles, knocked in 35 runs, and scored 35. Cleveland Indians owner Bill Veeck (as in wreck) was watching. This marvelous maverick had wanted to integrate baseball in the 1940s with the purchase of the hapless Philadelphia Phillies but was thwarted by then Commissioner Landis.[48] In 1947 things had changed, dramatically.

Branch Rickey beat Bill Veeck to the races with the historic signing of Jackie Robinson. On July 5, 1947, as Jackie launched his majestic career, Veeck inked Doby to a contract and advised him how to behave. Unlike the parsimonious Branch Rickey, Veeck paid Effa Manley $15,000 for Doby's contract. Acting as a father figure, Veeck cautioned Doby with many avoidance mechanisms. "Don't argue with umpires" and "no dissertations with opposing players, either of those might lead to a race riot. No associating with female Caucasians." Doby listened. Veeck watched. When he entered the Indians locker room for the very first time, several unnamed players refused to shake his hand. Former Yankees star Joe "Flash" Gordon broke the ice. He played catch with the Negro newcomer, as did manager Lou Boudreau.[49] Jackie Robinson called him with encouraging words about hotels and food in order to prepare Doby for the challenges he would face. Quiet and self-effacing, Doby did not receive the adulation and publicity meted out to Jackie, but, on the other hand, he avoided many of Robinson's gut-wrenching encounters with white bigots and black cats.

In his debut, Doby struck out. The young slugger was converted into an outfielder. One day, he misjudged a fly ball with the bases loaded. It resulted in a loss of face—the ball hit Doby in the head—and the loss of a game.[50] Answering a challenge posed by Coach Bill McKechnie, Doby hit a home run the very next day to win a game. Player-manager Lou Boudreau helped Doby adjust along with Joe Gordon. Later, others tried to befriend the shy slugger. Doby withdrew into silence. He experienced abuse. Opponents spit in his face. Vile epithets hounded him. He took his aggression out on the field. In 1948, his first full year in the majors, Doby hit .301 with 14 home runs and 66 runs batted in.[51]

Larry played 13 stellar years with the Indians and the White Sox. Overshadowed by his peers—Mays, Mantle, Snider—Doby did not get the benefit of larger market venues. Yet he too could—and did—hit tape-measure home runs: a 470-foot clout to dead center in Yankee Stadium and a 500-foot blast at Griffith Stadium in Washington. Statistically, his best year was 1950, when "Larrupin' Larry" (as Mel Allen called him) hit .326, smashed 32 home runs, and knocked in 126 to lead the American League in the latter two categories. When he finally hung up his spikes, he had amassed 253 round trippers to go with a .283 lifetime batting average.[52]

As a player, Doby also made history in 1957. According to biographer Joseph Moore, an incident merits consideration as a turning point in baseball history. Yankees pitcher Art Ditmar aimed a ball at Doby's head. Dusted, Doby charged the mound and sent a solid left hook to the jaw of Ditmar. Never before had a Negro player thrown the first punch at a white player in a baseball brawl. *Washington Post* writer Shirley Povich hailed the incident as a milestone. It signaled the full acceptance of Blacks into baseball. The placid Doby seemed to be the least likely player to punch the face that launched a thousand stories.[53]

In 1978, Bill Veeck tabbed him again to serve as trailblazer. He appointed him manager of the Chicago White Sox. Again, he played second fiddle to a Robinson—this time to Frank, the manager of his former team in Cleveland. Despite his historic role in breaking barriers, it is evident that Doby lacked the fiery temperament of either Paul Robeson or Jackie Robinson. More like the even-tempered Irvin, he avoided confrontations. He seemed content with "loner" status. Initially, Jackie Robinson also had to keep his mouth shut. This repression, so contrary to his nature, engendered a series of ailments: high blood pressure, diabetes, arthritis, and blindness. Doby did not fully escape. He developed an ulcer.[54]

So often linked in the great chain of baseball and social history, Doby and Robinson invite different reactions. The talented if erratic poet Amiri Baraka preferred Doby as an authentic Negro.[55] "Buck" O'Neil, wise old man, loved all: Larry Doby, Jackie Robinson, and Satchel Paige. "I loved Jackie as a person, I love Satchel as a friend, and I love Larry as a son."[56] Doby was more typical of Black athletes. "We couldn't appear uppity and we couldn't allow our intelligence or knowledge to show."

Larry Doby, shown here in 2000, played baseball for the Newark Eagles before and after serving in World War II, and he helped his team win the Negro League championship in 1946. One year later he broke the color barrier in the American League, joining the Cleveland Indians. He was elected to the National Baseball Hall of Fame in 1998 (author collection).

After his "release" from managerial duties, Larry Doby left baseball in 1979. Don Newcombe regards that departure as a shame and a loss. Despite the shameful rebuff, Doby switched sports. He moved into pro basketball, serving as director of community relations for the New Jersey Nets.[57] After all those dues, he deserved a better fate. Doby is different. He did not disarm an adversary as Satchel Paige did with humor, Jackie Robinson with a verbal attack, Monte Irvin with sweetness, Paul Robeson with eloquence.

What do Irvin and Doby share with Robinson in the last analysis besides the color of their skin and the content of their character? All three grew up in adversity. Robinson lost his father as an infant; Doby lost his at eight. Irvin had two strong parents to be sure, but like the other two he had to battle bigotry and confront bias. Though they chose separate paths in their common quest, they kept their eyes on the same prize: social justice and fair play. Robeson battled the status quo openly. Doby avoided conflict by withdrawing into discreet silence. Irvin, a nice guy to the last, worked within the system. Despite apparent differences, they gave—and continue to give—us something to cheer about.

10

Willie Mays, Ed Charles, Henry Aaron, Frank Robinson, and Ernie Banks

Jackie Robinson's legacy is apparent in every sport. In baseball, author Steve Jacobson, longtime reporter at Long Island's *Newsday*, has written a beautifully crafted book, *Carrying Jackie's Torch*, that sheds additional light on Robinson's legacy. Much of what follows stems from Jacobson's research and writing. He establishes the historical context in the opening pages. For example, he writes that the year after Willie Mays—who recently celebrated his 91st birthday—won his MVP in 1954, Emmett Till was brutally murdered for allegedly whistling at a white woman. The photograph of his battered body lying in an open casket at the behest of his keening mother horrified a nation. In 1964, when Bob Gibson won the World Series MVP, three civil rights workers—James Chaney, Mickey Schwerner, and Andy Goodman—were also murdered in Mississippi ("God damn" in Nina Simone's heart-breaking song). Many years later, 2005 to be precise, justice was finally served when a Klansman, only one of several perpetrators, was tried and found guilty. Back in 1947, the year of Robinson's historic debut in Major League Baseball, four Black World War II servicemen were lynched in the South. When the U.S. Senate passed a law making lynching a federal crime, 15 Republican senators refused to sign it in 2009.[1] In "Strange Fruit," Abel Meeropol, a teacher, wrote and Billie Holiday sang of "Black bodies swinging in the southern breeze / Strange fruit hanging from the poplar trees."

Jacobson recalls one of Robinson's greatest moments in 1951. On the final day of the season, the Dodgers of Brooklyn needed to beat the Phillies to stay alive in the pennant race to tie the Giants, who it was later learned had employed illegal means to get this far. Earlier that day, the New York Giants defeated the Boston Braves. In a seesaw battle in Philadelphia that ended in an 8–8 tie, Jackie Robinson saved the Dodgers. After the Phillies loaded the bases with two outs, Eddie Waitkus came to bat against Don Newcombe in the 12th inning. The left-handed first baseman hit a line drive between first and second, which the Dodgers announcer Connie Desmond mistakenly called a base hit, which would have won the game. Jackie Robinson made a sparkling catch, saving game and pennant. Desmond reversed his call: "NOO! Robinson's Got it!"[2] Knocked unconscious in making the catch, Robinson had to be revived with smelling salts. Two innings later, a resilient Robinson stepped to the plate in the 14th inning against Phillies ace Robin Roberts and hit a long home run into the upper left-field deck, leading to a Dodgers win 9–8. Jacobson concludes: "What he showed every day of his career, talented black players could make their teams better."[3] White fans identified with and emulated Jackie Robinson. Both he and the Dodgers made history turn.[4]

Willie Mays

Robinson's closest rival as the most electrifying player, Willie Mays, was born on May 6, 1931, in a working-class suburb of Birmingham, Alabama. His parents were 18 when they married. They separated when Willie was three years old. Thereafter, he lived with his father and two older orphan girls who helped raise him. Willie Sr., worked as a porter and in the steel mills.[5] His father also played baseball with the Birmingham Black Barons in the Negro League. When Willie Jr. reached age 16, he joined Willie Sr. in the Barons outfield. In high school, Junior played quarterback in football and starred in basketball. Willie left high school education and sports for a life in professional baseball, a game he loved as much as eating ice cream. In 1948, he played in the last Negro League World Series.

A Boston Braves scout touted his skill, but Boston, one of the last cities to sign a Black baseball player, dropped the ball on Willie Mays. New York Giants scout Eddie Montague picked up the ball with a supremely confident boast that Mays was the best prospect he had ever seen. The Giants signed this young phenom on June 20, 1950. Playing for the Trenton Class B club, Mays hit .353. He leapfrogged to the Millers of Minneapolis in Class Triple-A, where he hit .477 in 35 games. Called up to the parent club in 1951, he slumped, going one for his first 25 at bats. Manager Leo Durocher—"Mr. Leo" to the deferential rookie—encouraged him, and Mays upped his average to .274 with 20 home runs. Due to the tainted "miracle of Coogan's bluff," the Giants defeated the Dodgers in a three-game playoff series, punctuated by Bobby Thomson's three-run homer off reliever Ralph Branca with one out in the ninth inning with Willie Mays waiting on deck. Against the New York Yankees in the '51 World Series, Monte Irvin assumed star status in leading the Giants to a 2–1 lead in the series. God, arguably a loyal Yankees fan, caused rain to cancel the fourth game, allowing the "Old Professor" Casey Stengel to pick his ace, Allie "Wahoo" Reynolds, for a win that turned the momentum back to the "Bronx Bombers" who won three consecutive games to take the title four games to two. Willie Mays had an abbreviated '52 season because Uncle Sam wanted him to serve in the U.S. Army during the Korean War. The following year and a half found Willie Mays in a khaki uniform instead of a baseball one, which probably aborted his chances to bypass Babe Ruth's all-time home run record.

Returning to the National League in 1954, Mays upped his batting average to a league-leading .345 with 41 home runs, 119 runs scored, 110 runs batted in, and a Most Valuable Player award. To crown this glorious season, the Giants upset the Cleveland Indians in four consecutive games. In that memorable and pivotal first game, the score was tied 2–2 in the eighth inning with two Indians runners, Larry Doby and Al Rosen, on base. Vic Wertz hit a booming drive off reliever Don Liddle to cavernous centerfield in the Polo Grounds. At the crack of Wertz's bat, Mays turned, darted rapidly towards the bleachers without looking back, and made a spectacular catch. He swirled and threw an accurate peg to cutoff man, shortstop Alvin Dark, to hold the runners. Considered by many the greatest catch in World Series history, the throw that he made after stopping abruptly and whirling 180 degrees to hold the runner was equally magical. The Giants won the game in the 10th inning when reserve "Dusty" Rhodes's pinch-hitting for Monte Irvin smacked what was then called a "Chinese" home run that just made the right field seats, driving in three runs, in a 4–1 win. Mays hit .286, going four for 14 in the four-game sweep of the Indians, who boasted the highest winning percentage—.721—in American League history up to 1954. Rhodes went four for seven with timely pinch hits and two home runs. Mays's brilliant catch and throw, however, proved pivotal.

A five-tool player, Mays could hit, hit with power, run, field, and throw. Author Howard Bryant succinctly summarizes his gifts: Willie had the power of Babe Ruth, the speed of Jackie Robinson, and could hit for average like Joe DiMaggio. And Mays did everything with flair.[6] He was a hero in his early years as a New York Giant when he played stickball in Harlem, captured in iconic photos as "a man-child in the promised land." In 1955, he hit .319, smacked 51 home runs, knocked in 127 runs, and was credited with 23 assists. In 1956, he stole 40 bases, leading the National League in that category, affirming a Negro League trademark that combined speed with power. In 1957, he belted 20 triples while compiling a .333 batting average and blasting 35 home runs. When the Giants moved to San Francisco in 1958, Mays hit .347. Continuing his prolific output coupled with peerless defensive play, he had to share glory with Orlando Cepeda, Willie McCovey, and the Alou brothers, younger stars who matured in the "golden" state rather than New York City, proving how fickle is fandom and the fate of aging if not fading stars. In 1962, Mays helped the Giants to win the National League pennant with 49 home runs and 141 runs batted in. That year, he finally won the hearts of San Francisco fans.[7] To get to the World Series the Giants had to play the Los Angeles Dodgers in a strange history redux in a different city and state with the same outcome. The Giants won game one 8–0 as Billy Pierce bested Sandy Koufax. The Dodgers rebounded to take game two 8–7 after trailing 5–0. Even though the Giants outhit the Dodgers, their relief pitchers faltered until former Yankees pitcher Don Larsen closed the door in game three. The Giants scored four runs in the ninth to overcome a 4–2 Dodgers lead, shades of 1951, four to two. Aided by porous Dodgers defense and weak relievers, the Giants rallied. Matty Alou got a pinch-hit single to start the ninth inning. After Harvey Kuenn grounded into a force-out, Willie McCovey walked, and Felipe Alou walked to load the bases. "Say Hey" Willie Mays greeted Dodgers reliever Ed Roebuck with a line-drive single to the mound, scoring Kuenn with a run. Orlando Cepeda hit a sacrifice fly off reliever Stan Williams, knotting the score 4–4. With men on second and third, true to the sac fly and wild pitch, Ed Bailey was intentionally walked to load the bases. Jim Davenport walked, forcing in run five. On second sacker Larry Burright's error, Mays scored the sixth run to ice the game as starter-turned-reliever Billy Pierce closed out the Dodgers. History repeated in the World Series too.

Facing the Yankees as they did in 1951, the Giants split the first two games at home, losing game one 6–2 and winning game two 2–0. At Yankee Stadium, they split the two games with the Yanks again winning the opener at the stadium that Ruth built, 3–2, and the Giants taking game four (which I witnessed from the bleachers on Yom Kippur) 7–3 as Hiller and Haller homered. Game five went to the Yankees 5–3. A five-day rain delay gave pitchers sufficient rest to recharge their batteries with the Giants taking game six 5–3, knotting the series 3–3 and requiring a seventh game tiebreaker. The seventh game turned out to be a nail-biter, with excellent pitching from both starters, Ralph Terry and Jack Sanford. The Yanks scored the only run in the fifth inning when Tony Kubek grounded into a double play scoring Bill Skowron from third. In the ninth inning, the Giants pinch-hitter Matty Alou bunted (a lost art, currently) for a lead-off single. Yankees ace Ralph Terry, eventually voted series MVP, struck out the next two batters. Willie Mays stepped to the plate and banged a double to the opposite field in the right corner. Only the strong-armed right fielder Roger Maris prevented the tie run from scoring. As I watched this mano-a-mano encounter between Terry and McCovey with Cepeda in the on-deck circle, I sipped a beer at the West End Cafe on Broadway opposite Columbia University, my stamping grounds. As McCovey smashed a line drive between first and second, I closed my eyes for a second, but not too long to see second baseman Bobby Richardson snatch victory from the jaws of defeat with a game-ending catch. Mays only hit .250, seven for 28 but he was always capable in the clutch as his ninth inning double attested. He still regrets that with two outs Matty Alou did not try to score on his double.[8] Later, Mays led his team to a National League playoff at the age of 40 in 1971.

Unable to reach the World Series again until his twilight years with the New York Mets in 1973, Willie persisted in outstanding play on offense as well as defense. In 1964 and 1965, Mays hit 47 and 52 home runs, respectively, and won the MVP award in the latter year. On April 30, 1961, he hit four home runs in a single game. Traded to New York, fittingly according to Mets owner Joan Whitney Payson, Willie returned for two years, 1972–73. Facing the Oakland Athletics, the "Amazin'" Mets called on Mays to deliver in game two. After misplaying two fly balls in the sun, Mays singled in the 12th inning to knock in the lead run in a 10–7 victory. He also announced his retirement following the game.[9] Ever competitive, Willie recalls a missed opportunity in game seven of that series, which the Mets once led three games to two. Facing the final out on an Athletics error, the Mets put a runner on. Mays wanted to pinch-hit righty against left-handed pitcher Darold Knowles. Instead, manager Yogi Berra let Wayne Garrett hit, and he popped out. "I kick myself," Mays writes in his book. "I've got to pinch hit, man." Willie passively, in accommodation mode, said nothing. Willie avoided controversy on other occasions, drawing the ire of Jackie Robinson, who felt that Mays "could have done more for civil rights."[10] Nevertheless, former U.S. presidents Clinton and Bush II said that as youngsters they wanted to be like Willie. President Obama anointed Mays with the Presidential Medal in 2015 and flew with Mays on Air Force One to the 2009 All-Star game.[11] Fêted at Shea Stadium, Mays ended his career in the third person,

"Say goodbye to America, Willie." Over his magnificent career, he manufactured 3,283 hits and played in 24 All-Star games with 660 home runs and lifetime batting average of .302. In All-Star competition, facing the best American League pitchers, he hit .307. But statistics are often deceptive. If you shave Mays's nine last plate appearances during his over-the-hill years, when he went hitless, his All-Star batting average rises to .358.[12] As Ted Williams, with a .304 batting average in 18 All-Star contests, quipped: "They invented the All-Star game for Willie Mays."[13] After 24 years it was time to say goodbye and remember when we are all young and everything was possible, including a game of stickball with Willie Mays on the streets of Harlem.

Bill Rhoden offers the best summary of Willie's impact. Mays personified "Black Style." That style, Rhoden adds, is Willie Mays's basket catch, a trumpet solo in jazz, and Jackie Robinson dancing off the bases.[14] He points out that Mays was 20 as a rookie whereas Robinson was 28. Thus, Mays represents the first African American superstar in sports, symbolizing youth, vitality, and style that redefined baseball. Both body and soul, "there was something magnetic about Mays, [his] body language." His undersized cap, which regularly flew off, and his basket catch, which angered traditionalists—Rhoden argues—incorporated jazz, rhythm and blues. While Robinson had to apply restraint initially, Mays was free to be creative.[15] Indeed, Mays was cool, detached, resigned, yet—joyful. He put soul into play, paving the way for other Black athletes. Yet, on social issues, as Jackie Robinson complained, he was silent. Was that part of a Faustian bargain that plagued others who followed? They took separate roads to glory. And that has made, as the poet Robert Frost wrote, "all the difference."[16] Robinson died in 1972. As of 2022, Mays is alive— still walking, still talking.[17]

Ed Charles

Ed Charles was 13 years old when Jackie Robinson debuted in Daytona Beach, Florida. He cut school to watch the exhibition game through a fence. As he recalled the electrifying experience to prolific author Peter Golenbock, Charles beamed[18]:

> Jackie coming down to Daytona made a definite impact on the lives of the blacks in my community. I was just a kid, and I was awed by it all, and I prayed for him. I would say, Please God, let him show the whites what we can do and that we can do what they can.

After he moved to St. Petersburg, Florida, Ed and his friends did not have to play hooky on a Sunday in St. Petersburg, Florida, to watch Jackie and the Brooklyn Dodgers play the New York Yankees. An overflow crowd saw Jackie field flawlessly, bang out two hits, and thrill the crowd with exciting moves on the base paths. Charles remembered that he and his friends went to the railroad station to wave goodbye to Jackie, their hero. One version of that experience is conveyed in the film *42*, with Ed putting his ears to the tracks after the train departed from view, to hear the echoes of history transformed.[19]

Edwin Douglas Charles was born on April 29, 1933, in segregated Florida.

One of nine children, Ed witnessed brutality in his home, where his father beat his mother and the local police beat his father, enlarging the circle of violence. Ed learned about racism through his grandpa's razor strap after a brawl with white kids who had stolen a toy. In rural Florida, such encounters could and did result in lynching.[20] Indeed, one Black man, Lee Snell, was lynched in Daytona when Ed was five years old. Charles dropped out of school in the eighth grade.[21] Jackie Robinson came to town and changed everything.

Ed Charles moved to St. Petersburg to live with older siblings and to reenter school. At Gibbs High School, he played football as well as baseball. He captained the latter team and quarterbacked his team to the Class A state championship. Scouted by the Braves organization, he signed in 1952. As a young player, Charles played minor league baseball for eight years, starting with the Braves Class C League farm system, starting in the far north. Tutored by manager George McQuinn, former Brown and Yankee, Ed finally enjoyed life north of the Mason-Dixon Line, up in Québec, where he encountered good white people. His landlords, both teachers, treated him well.[22] His teammates included Vic Power, Bob Trice, Ray Brown, and Silvio Garcia, who once was Branch Rickey's choice to break the color line. But when Rickey learned that Garcia reportedly dodged the military draft in Cuba, he backed off.[23] As a rookie, Charles hit .317 and led the league in triples with 11. Teammate Humberto Robinson, a Panamanian, would be the only other player to make "The Bigs."[24] Thereafter, Charles labored mostly in the South, steeped in segregation. He encountered bigotry anew in Fort Lauderdale during the 1953 season. Quota systems propelled competent Black players out in favor of mediocre white players. Though being flanked by three other Black players and managed by Pepper Martin, who valued merit over skin pigmentation, helped ease discomfort. After almost two years in military service, Charles returned to racial taunts in Macon, Georgia, and Knoxville, Tennessee. In the latter city, Ed recalled a painful example of southern "gentility." After a great day in the field and at bat, Charles was leaving the stadium when a man approached, saying: "By golly, nigger, you are one hell of a ballplayer." Charles, trained in accommodation, did not reply. He just shook his head and walked on by. From this negative, reflected in retrospect, he derived a positive, namely, that excellent play could ultimately "lift the cloud of ignorance."[25]

Mired in the minor leagues despite commendable hitting states of .284, .270, .252, and .305, Charles fretted. Unable to move up to the parent club in Milwaukee because Eddie Mathews was anchored there at third base, Red Schoendienst was added to play second base, and Félix Mantilla, a minor league teammate of Charles, was kept as a utility infielder, Charles was finally traded to the Kansas City Athletics before the 1962 season. As a 29-year-old rookie that year, he hit .288 with 17 homers and a .454 slugging average. These impressive figures merited recognition as he finished second to Yankee Tom Tresh for Rookie of the Year honors. The eccentric A's owner, comparable to the innovative Bill Veeck but lacking his wit and wisdom, rewarded Charles with a $3,000 bonus over his minimum rookie wage of $7,000 but reneged on a raise, as promised, to $15,000. Steady of not spectacular, Ed Charles came to lead the Kansas City A's in games played and total bases. Second in runs scored, hits, and runs batted in, he never made the American League

All-Star team.[26] He was expendable with the rise of Sal Bando. So, Ed Charles was traded to the New York Mets for a nondescript player and $50,000 in 1967. His batting average dipped to .238 and his slugging average to .319. In 1968, Ed had to make the roster the hard way under a minor league contract, in spring training. Newly appointed manager Gil Hodges drove the Mets with renewed purpose. Charles won the third base position on merit and held it over 1,117 games with a .276 batting average and a team-leading home run total of 17 in "the Year of the Pitcher." As a team, the Mets hit a league low of .228. Because of his fluidity afield, he was dubbed "The Glider" by pitcher Jerry Koosman. Charles served as a bridge between the old-timers on the team, Ed Kranepool and Ron Swoboda, and youngsters like Tom Seaver and the self-doubting Cleon Jones. Charles even tried to train Amos Otis, an excellent outfielder, to take over his position at the "Hot Corner." Otis rejected that offer and would soon be dealt to Kansas City in a lopsided exchange for Joey Foy. Soon, Charles began to platoon at third base with Wayne Garrett.

At 34 years old, Ed Charles emerged as a father figure to the younger players, particularly his African American teammates from Alabama: Cleon Jones, Tommie Agee, and Amos Otis. His hitting came alive after Memorial Day with a three-run homer off spitballer Gaylord Perry and a runs batted in single to ice the game 4–2 en route to an 11-game winning streak. On June 2, he helped the Mets win 2–1 with a go-ahead run. Jerry Koosman capped a happy ending with a poetic quip: "Never throw a slider to the Glider."[27] The two platoon system worked at first base with the acquisition of Donn Clendenon at first as well as at third base. Batting woes for Ed returned in July and August, though the Mets continued to amaze, passing Leo Durocher's Cubs. One win away from clinching their first division title, they faced Steve Carlton's Cardinals. Bud Harrelson started the rally with a single, followed by an Agee walk. Cleon Jones struck out, but Donn Clendenon smacked a three-run homer. Ron Swoboda walked, and Ed Charles glided to the plate and smashed a home run to the opposite field, his last major league four-bagger. The Mets won 6–0. The Mets swept the Braves, Charles's original team, in three games.

Heavily favored, the Baltimore Orioles took game one in the World Series as Mike Cuellar outdueled Tom Seaver. Charles went hitless in four trips. Game two featured a matchup between crafty southpaws Dave McNally and Jerry Koosman. The game was tied 1–1 going into the ninth inning. Charles, who doubled earlier, now singled with two out. On a hit and run, Charles reached third base on Jerry Grote's base hit to left. Charles scored the lead run after weak-hitting Al Weis singled. In the bottom of the ninth, Koosman got the first two batters but lost his edge walking two batters in a row. In came Ron Taylor, a medical student between baseball seasons, entered in relief. Taylor ran the count full on Brooks Robinson. The great fielding third baseman hit a smash towards third base where Ed Charles made a diving stop. Unable to get a force-out, he threw low to first base. Thanks to a splendid scoop by Clendenon, the series was now tied 1–1. Charles's flawless fielding eclipsed his anemic hitting in importance. After game five's final out, Ed Charles beamed, triumphantly. In the joyful locker room, Charles said: "We're number one in the world and you just can't get any bigger than this."[28]

After retirement, Charles failed to obtain a position, as promised, in the Mets promotion department. He tried several business ventures that did not pan out. In 1972, however, while seeking a loan from the Small Business Administration, he met his idol, Jackie Robinson, the object of his veneration evoked in a poignant poem quoted below. That poem gave this writer an opportunity to befriend Ed Charles. While planning a major conference to honor Jackie Robinson at Long Island University Brooklyn in 1997, I was urged to devote one session to poetry. Aware that Charles had written poetry, I contacted him. He immediately agreed to my invitation.

Ed Charles, one of baseball's poets laureate, at the 2015 Queens Baseball Conference. He was presented that day with the Gil Hodges Unforgettable Fire Award, given annually to a person who "brings together the best elements of sportsmanship and humanity." Charles enjoyed a fine eight-year major league career that was capped by a championship with the '69 Mets (courtesy Flickr user slgckgc).

To promote the conference, I participated in televised interviews and radio broadcasts. Public Radio WNYC's host Leonard Lopate invited Ed Charles and me to discuss the upcoming event in conjunction with Stan Isaacs, *Newsday* reporter. We had a heady exchange discoursing on Jackie Robinson's immense impact on America as well as baseball. Charles stated the case for Robinson's role: "Hope, hope, hope, hope is what [he] brought to all of us, Black and white. … I looked upon him as being some sort of Messiah because of what he was trying to accomplish."[29] Charles accomplished much as a social worker working with troubled youths needing guidance in New York City's Department of Juvenile Justice and in the Bronx with Youth Options Unlimited, offering hope and guidance.[30] Years later, I was invited to the John Henry "Pop" Lloyd Conference to reinforce the legacy of Jackie Robinson at Rowan University. On that panel, I sat with writer Frank Deford, Monte Irwin, and Ed Charles. Always eager to entertain as well as inform, I reenacted Jackie Robinson's great catch of Eddie Waitkus's line drive off Don Newcombe in 1951, playing all three characters: pitcher, hitter, and fielder. To the delight of attendees, including panel members, I slid across the stage in emulation of the immortal Robinson.[31] Laughing, Ed Charles picked me off the hardwood floor. It was one of several memorable hours. Later, Ed Charles reprised his ode to Jackie, which he had presented on April 5, 1997, at Long Island University.

> He accepted the challenge and played the game
> With a passion that few men possess
> He stood tall in the face of society's shame
> With a talent that God had blessed
>
> He banged out hits and aroused the fans
> with his daring base-running skill.

This great great player and proud black man
Many bigots did threat to kill

Yes, he made his mark for all to see
As he struggled determinately for dignity
And the word is grateful for the legacy
That he left for all eternity.

Thanks, Jackie, wherever you are
You will always be our first "super star."
For history shall record and eternal proclaim
Your great deeds in its halls of fame.

So, go now and rest for awhile
For again you shall come a "spirit aflame"
In the bosom of another black child
That God and destiny shall name.

After Mr. Charles finished his poem that memorable Saturday, I felt tears rolling down my cheeks. Many other attendees cried too. Poet laureate of baseball Ed Charles died on May 15, 2018, today, as I write, four years ago. Inspired like so many others by Jackie Robinson, Ed Charles celebrated his hero in poetry. So, now we pay tribute to the ball player *cum* poet, echoing his teammate Tom Seaver: "He was a pro's pro…. Everybody loved him."[32]

Henry Aaron

An American Dilemma, so profoundly delineated by Gunnar Myrdal in his classic study, postulated a disconnect between our core values and the treatment of Negroes in American society. Witnessing Jackie Robinson's heroic career and the gates that he opened for African Americans provided hope for future African American athletes, many cheered in kumbaya exaltations. Unfortunately, as we watched in horror, a Minneapolis policeman, foot on the neck of a Black man, killed George Floyd. While less violent, the hate mail sent to Hank Aaron as he neared his possible dream indicated that racism was very much alive as well as insidious in modern America. Inundated with hate mail, including many death threats against the usually stoic slugger, Hammerin' Hank Aaron was driven to the brink of a breakdown.

Born near Mobile, Alabama, on February 4, 1934, Henry was third child of Herbert and Estella Aaron's eight children. He weighed 12¼ pounds. His sister, Stella, was born first. Herbert Jr. arrived in 1930. Though poor and illiterate, his parents provided a solid family core. They moved frequently. His father, Herbert, the oldest of 12 children, built his own house in 1942 in Toulminville, Alabama. Henry, Herbert Jr., and Tommy Aaron slept in the same bed. Ownership provided some safety in an area where the KKK marched and lynching was a constant threat. A race riot erupted in 1943.[33] All the children pitched in. Hank, for example, picked cotton and did odd jobs. Unable to afford baseball gear, young Henry used broomsticks to whack bottle caps.[34] Hank gravitated to baseball at an early age, hitting right-handed but with his left hand overlapping his right hand in a highly unorthodox way. Biographer Howard Bryant describes Hank as a mediocre but natural hitter at the time.[35]

In 1948 Hank entered high school. One of his pivotal moments was a meeting with his idol, Jackie Robinson. Aaron cut school that day in 1948 to hear Robinson speak at a corner drug store. During spring training, Robinson enjoyed talking to youngsters, advising them to benefit from education. As Aaron remembered it for his autobiography[36]:

> I was in the back, but I felt like I was hugging him you know? Holding his hand, I saw a concerned citizen. He was something like, 'Hey, just give yourself a chance. If I can make it all of you can make it.'

Robinson prioritized. Work hard in school first and then concentrate on being a great baseball ballplayer. Hank heeded the second part of Jackie's exhortation. He would indeed become a great ball player, but initially his father was doubtful. When Hank told his dad that he wanted to become a pilot, his father replied: "Ain't no colored pilots." To which Hank retorted: "Okay, then I'll be a ballplayer." His dad said: "Ain't no colored ball players." That changed, however, when father and son watched Jackie Robinson in Hartwell Field in the colored section.[37]

Life in pre–civil rights Alabama was no picnic in the park. Drumbeats outside the Aaron home signaled the KKK nearby. Hank's mom, Estella, woke her children and made them hide under the bed until the danger passed.[38] In his first two years in Central High School, Aaron played football and baseball; later, while enrolled in a private high school, he played semi-pro baseball, earning $3 per game as a third baseman and outfielder. He tried out for the Dodgers at 15, but his cross-handed batting stance hurt his chances. Two years later, he joined the Indianapolis Clowns in the Negro American League, upping his earnings to $200 per month, mostly at shortstop. In 26 games, Aaron hit for a .366 batting average with five home runs, 23 runs batted in, and nine stolen bases. Scouted by several teams, he signed with the Braves because they offered $50 more per month.[39] While playing in Washington, D.C., Aaron's team breakfasted at a local restaurant near Griffith Stadium. After they finished eating, he and his teammates heard the clatter of broken dishes, which were "defiled" by the mouths of African Americans.[40] The Boston Braves bought Aaron's contract for a bargain price of $10,000. Assigned to their Class C team in Eau Claire, Wisconsin, in 1952, Hank learned to hit properly, right hand over left. Playing as an infielder, Hank batted .336 over 87 games and was named Northern League Rookie of the Year. Even north of the Mason-Dixon line, he elicited racial taunts, which Hank Aaron handled with "external detachment."[41]

In 1953, Aaron returned to the South, still plagued with overt racism, to play for the Jacksonville Tars, where he befriended future Major Leaguers, also Black, who broke the color line in the Sally League. Heroically, Hammerin' Hank Aaron won friends and influenced fans with his league-leading batting average of .362 along with 208 hits, 36 doubles, and 135 runs batted in. Voted the league MVP, Aaron, according to one observer, "led the league in everything except hotel accommodations."[42] He also met a woman named Barbara Lewis who became his first wife. That winter, Aaron played winter ball in Puerto Rico under manager Mickey Owen, who helped him to play the outfield and to hit to all fields, expertly.

Aaron faced several hurdles in order to make the Braves roster with Bobby

Thomson in left field, Billy Bruton in centerfield, and Andy Pafko in right field, with Jim Pendleton, a recent recruit from the Negro League, as a reserve. A fortuitous accident, however, to Braves left fielder Bobby Thomson, Giants hero of the tainted 1951 season, broke his ankle in an exhibition game on March 13, 1954, which opened the door for young Henry. Trying to break up a double-play grounder at second base Thomson suffered a triple fracture of his right ankle.[43] The following day, Aaron replaced Thomson in left field and hit the first of his many home runs in a Major League uniform. During the regular season, Aaron's first hit and first home run came against former Yankee ace Vic Raschi, now with the St. Louis Cardinals. Ironically, Aaron's successful rookie season, in which he hit .280 and banged out 13 home runs, ended on September 5, when he too suffered a fractured ankle.[44]

Aaron won the National League batting title with a .328 average in 1956. The 1957 season proved to be Hank's breakout year, serving notice that the best was yet to come. He belted 44 home runs, sported a .322 batting average with 132 runs batted in, hitting cleanup behind Eddie Mathews in the third slot. In the World Series against those "damned Yankees," Aaron hit .393 with three homers and led the Braves to a World Series title, abetted by pitchers Lew Burdette, an ex-Yankee farmhand, and the peerless leftie Warren Spahn in a seven-game thriller. Not only was Hank Aaron voted National League MVP, but he also became a father in 1957. His two sons, Hank Jr. and Larry, were born, like "Irish twins," nine months apart.[45] In 1958, Aaron spearheaded the Braves' return to the Word Series, but this time the Yankees, down three games to one, rallied to take the seventh and final game thanks to timely fielding by Elston Howard, hitting by Hank Bauer, and pitching by Bob Turley. Hank Aaron led all hitters with a .333 batting average in a losing cause.

Despite Hank's heroic play, his white teammates resented Aaron's smooth style. Fearing the loss of their own jobs, biographer Howard Bryant opined, they mocked Aaron's slow movement on quick legs. Manager Charlie "Jolly" Grimm called Hank "Snowshoes," claiming that he was "sleepwalking a la Stepin Fetchit." When that "son of the south," first baseman Joe Adcock, called him "Slow Motion Henry" because of the way he shuffled on and off the field, Aaron just laughed. But the young slugger knew where Adcock stood in his use and abuse of the "N" word. Unlike Leo Durocher, who aggressively defended Jackie Robinson before he was suspended in 1947, and Willie Mays when he managed the New York Giants in 1951, manager Grimm encouraged hazing of the brilliant rookie.[46] Somewhat of a buffoon, Grimm had earned the nickname "Jolly Cholly."

Serious and intense, Aaron could really hit that ball, according to no less an expert than Ted Williams, who marveled at the sound of Aaron's bat as he crunched pitched balls. In 1959, Aaron realized that home run hitters make more money than high average hitters, a variation of a theme first struck by Hank Greenberg in advice to Ralph Kiner in 1947: while singles hitters drive Chevrolets, home run hitters drive Cadillacs. After participating in a TV program called *Home Run Derby*, he altered his swing to echo a Duke Ellington favorite, "It don't mean a thing, if it ain't got that swing." In 1963, he demonstrated speed along with power when he stole 31 bases and hit 44 homers. He lost the triple crown by .007 to Brooklyn-bred star Tommy Davis.

When the Braves ownership decided to move the team to Atlanta, Aaron had reservations about returning to the South. In his early years in professional baseball, Hank witnessed bigotry in housing, dining, and socializing. When he played for Jacksonville, the mayor warned him to suffer racial taunts quietly in 1953. Aaron and other Black players received death threats. Fans threw black cats onto the field. Umpires warned Aaron and Felix Mantilla not to socialize with white fans or opponents.[47] Although Milwaukee was more congenial than Jacksonville, northern racism, more subtle, persisted. Aaron's teammates lacked sensitivity. Joe Adcock peppered Hank with repeated vulgarities. During the Montgomery Bus Boycott, Warren Spahn asked Aaron, "What do you people want?" Such attitudes were commonplace, even among his mates.[48] Despite progress made in the legislative arena, southern racism was embedded in mores that superseded and circumvented laws. Ever the good soldier, Aaron returned as an Atlanta Brave. In his first game, the scoreboard flashed an ugly sign, "April 12, 1861, First Shots Fired on Ft. Sumter, April 12, 1966, the South Rises Again!" Shouts of the "N" word roiled Aaron's return, motivating him to win them over with his baseball prowess.[49] Braves executives joined by then governor Jimmy Carter embraced Aaron and assured him of their support. "The times," as Bobby Dylan sang, were "a-changin'."

In the summer of 1965, I went to Atlanta with a group of academics and clerics to bend the arc of history. Working under the umbrella of Dr. King and the Southern Christian Leadership Conference, we engaged in a voter registration drive. Racial conflict, rising from the steamy Georgia atmosphere, was apparent everywhere following the Freedom Summer of 1964, when three civil rights workers (two from my interracial summer camp), were brutally murdered in Mississippi. Asked to introduce ourselves at our first meeting by Chairman Bayard Rustin, I took the mic and said: "My name is Joe Dorinson, I teach history. Someday, I plan to write history. I have come to Atlanta to make history!" Rustin graciously praised my oratory as the crowd, including civil rights leaders Hosea Williams and Andrew Young, cheered. Our efforts in 1965 eventually bore "familiar" fruit in the 2020 Georgia senatorial races, with the election of the Reverend Raphael Warnock, Georgia's first Black senator, and Jon Ossoff, the state's first Jewish senator.

One rainy Georgia night in 1965, a group of us went to a club, and violence erupted. In retrospect, I can appreciate Hank Aaron's trepidation about a return to the South one year later. Nevertheless, thanks to Aaron's contributions on the playing field and Dr. King's organized efforts everywhere, salutary if imperfect change accrued. When I returned to Atlanta in 1992 to attend the annual American Historical Association conference as chairman of Long Island University Brooklyn's History Department, I witnessed a major transformation as a result of civil rights legislation powered by the expansion of voting rights, our singular contribution in 1965. Andrew Young, the future mayor of Atlanta who managed that voter registration campaign, and Dr. King, an avid baseball fan, both encouraged Aaron, who felt somewhat guilty that he did not take a more active role in the movement. They reassured the svelte slugger that his job was to belt baseballs to help their common cause.[50]

In his first year in Atlanta, Hank slugged his 400th home run. He continued to thrive in a Braves uniform, accumulating accolades with his mounting number of home runs. As a lean six-foot, 180-pound home run hitter, his power derived from excellent hand-eye coordination plus extraordinarily strong wrists.[51] In his best single year slamming balls over the fences, Aaron hit 47 at the age of 37. He also hit .327 that year. Closing in on Babe Ruth's home run record proved traumatic. Hate mail exploded; many messages carried death threats mired in hate speech. And fear came along for the ride challenging pride in that quest. On April 4, 1973, Aaron tied Ruth at 714 against Cincinnati hurler Jack Billingham. Four days later, facing Dodgers pitcher Al Downing, former Yankee, Aaron blasted homer number 715. Listen to Dodgers announcer Vin Scully[52]:

> It is over, and for the first time in a long time that poker face of Aaron shows tremendous relief…. What a marvelous moment for Atlanta and the state of Georgia. What a marvelous moment for the country and the world. A Black man is getting a standing ovation in the Deep South for breaking a record of an all-time baseball idol. And it is a great moment for all of us, and particularly for Henry Aaron. He was met at home plate by not only every member of the Braves, but by his father and mother. He threw his arms around his father, and as he left the home plate area, his mother came running across the grass, threw her arms around his neck.

Hate-filled letters had poisoned Aaron's path to this pivotal moment. Some of the more venomous items are now housed in the Hall of Fame in a special exhibit, "Hank Aaron: Chasing the Dream," which my son Robert and his father-in-law, Eric Yonenson, and I visited in October 2019. We were happy to note the many supportive letters that followed, also in this precious exhibit. Strangely, Aarons's reward for this monumental achievement was a trade back to Milwaukee, where Hank finished his career with 755 home runs, 3,771 hits, and 2,297 runs batted in. Life's wheel had come full circle twice: from Milwaukee to Atlanta, back to Milwaukee, and a return to Atlanta.

In 1976, Henry Aaron rejoined the Braves in an executive position. Six years later, he was voted into the Hall of Fame with almost 98 percent of the vote on his first year of eligibility. As the Atlanta Braves senior vice president of player development starting in 1980, he burnished his heroic status and signaled the readiness of African Americans to take their rightful place in the executive suite. Aaron also served in media as corporate vice president of community relations for Turner Broadcasting Systems. Aaron ventured into the business world, owning several successful car dealerships. Among his many awards, two presidential medals loom largest. Shortly before leaving office, President Bill Clinton presented Hank Aaron with the Presidential Citizens Medal on January 6, 2001. Clinton's successor, President George W. Bush, conferred the nation's highest civilian honor, the Presidential Medal of Freedom, proving that heroism transcends political boundaries and can bridge that growing divide between Blue and Red states.

Bill Johnson's excellent biographical sketch in sabr.org ends appropriately:[53]

> Dignity. Pride. Courage. Those are words often reserved for describing heroes.
> They also describe Henry Aaron's character as well. Perhaps, that is not a coincidence.

Hank Aaron's heroic life ended on January 22, 2021, as a nation mourned. The jeers had turned to cheers—and tears.

Frank Robinson

America's first Black Major League Baseball manager, Frank Robinson, was born in Beaumont, Texas, on August 31, 1935, the youngest of Frank and Ruth Shaw's 10 children. His parents divorced when he was young. His mother moved the family to Alameda, California, and later to West Oakland. Attracted to baseball at an early age, Frank was discouraged by his surly father, who predicted that his son would not make it as a ballplayer. Frank grew up in an ethnically diverse tenement. Sports proved an outlet for youths raised in poverty. Frank loved three major sports: baseball, football, and basketball. He grew up near future star athletes Bill Russell (with whom he played basketball in high school), Vada Pinson, and Curt Flood. Coach George Powles, a frequent presence in this book, became mentor when Robinson, at age 14, met him. Powles encouraged the extremely shy youth. At McClymonds High School, he became a star athlete, winning a local American Legion tournament in 1950 with a timely triple.[54] After graduation in 1953, Frank signed with the Cincinnati Reds for $3,500.

Robinson began his pro career in Class C in Ogden, Utah, at age 17. He entered a religious environment in which the Mormons, at that time, considered Black people unworthy of equality and entrance into their churches or tabernacles. Black patrons were banned from theaters and restaurants. Despite this hostile environment, Robinson hit .348 and mustered 83 runs batted in before being promoted to Class A stops in the South, ending in Columbia, South Carolina. Though subjected to racial catcalls and segregated housing, Robinson continued his hot hitting with a .336 batting average and 25 home runs. Called up to the majors by the Reds, he joined a powerful team that went 91–63 and blasted 221 home runs, with Robinson contributing 38 as a rookie left fielder. Hitting .290 and knocking in 83 runs, he made the All-Star team and earned Rookie of the Year laurels. In 1957 Robinson upped his batting average to .332 but slumped in 1958 to .269. A return to stardom in 1959 witnessed a resurgent Robinson with 36 home runs, 125 runs batted in, and a .311 batting average.

Success at the plate came with a price. Because Robinson leaned over the plate to cover outside pitches, he was often hit by opposing pitchers—118 times in 10 years while with the Reds. In 1961, as National League MVP, Frank spearheaded the "Big Red Machine" into the World Series with 37 home runs, 124 runs batted in, and a 323 batting average. Despite his heroics, the Reds won only one game (which I attended in the Yankee Stadium bleachers) as the Mantle-Maris Yankees took four out of five for the title. After 10 outstanding years as a Red, minus a House Un-American Activities Committee inquiry, Robinson was traded to the Baltimore Orioles for three under-performing players, including pitcher Milt Pappas. Responsible for this blunder, Reds owner Bill DeWitt should have been dubbed "DeWittless" for labeling Robinson as "an old 30."[55] Orioles manager Hank Bauer, "The Man of the Hour" in broadcaster Mel Allen's dulcet words during their victorious Yankees years, welcomed Robinson with open arms. Finding a new home, however, proved difficult as whites refused to rent or sell to non-whites in Baltimore. One seller, a university professor no less, withdrew his house after learning that Frank not Brooks Robinson was the applicant. The Robinsons had to settle for a flytrap apartment.[56]

As with his Reds debut, Frank Robinson got off to a flying start. In a game with their chief rival the Cleveland Indians for the American League pennant, Robinson hit a home run off Cleveland ace Luis Tiant out of Memorial Stadium on a 540-foot journey that tied the Indians for the league lead.[57] He won the triple crown that year, hitting .316, smacking 49 home runs, and knocking in 125 runs batted in en route to a pennant and a World Series victory over the Los Angeles (feh!) Dodgers in four straight games. Rewarded with two MVPs, one for an unprecedented two different leagues and one as the World Series MVP with two home runs, a .286 batting average, and 3 runs batted in. Always hustling, Robinson tried to break up a double play against the White Sox; he slid hard into second base, where his head made contact with shortstop Al Weis's knee, causing a concussion, which may have adversely affected his hitting.[58] During the off-season, Robinson managed in the Puerto Rican Winter League.

In 1969, after leading the Orioles to a 109-win season, Robinson faced the weak-hitting, excellent-pitching "Miracle" Mets from New York City. It was one of baseball's greatest upsets and strangely comparable to the Baltimore Colts' loss to the New York Jets in Super Bowl III, when the Jets beat their heavily favored opponents. In that short span of time, the New York Knicks won the NBA Championship several months later. On June 26, 1970, Robinson hit two grand slams in a single game. After the 1971 season, the Orioles traded Robinson to the Los Angeles Dodgers, who then turned him over to their cross-town rival, the California Angels. He wound up as playing manager of the Cleveland Indians in 1975. In his first at bat, in his first game as the first African American manager in Major League Baseball, Frank Robinson, as a designated hitter, dramatically hit a home run on a 0–2 count to help the Indians defeat the Yankees 5–3 as 56,204 fans in Cleveland's Municipal Stadium cheered triumphantly. Subsequently he had managing stints with the San Francisco Giants, the Baltimore Orioles, the Montréal Expos, and the Washington Nationals. He also held administrative posts under Bud Selig and Rob Manfred in the baseball commissioner's office.[59] Voted into the Baseball Hall of Fame in 1982 in his first try along with Hank Aaron, Robinson gave a humorous speech praising his mentors George Powles and Earl Weaver. He also paid tribute to Curt Flood and the owner of his Puerto Rican team who permitted Robinson, pioneer manager, to hone his skills in Santurce. As the only player to win MVP Awards in both leagues and as the first African American to manage in Major League Baseball, he made history.

In 1997, aided by my late colleague, Joram Warmund, I organized a conference to honor Jackie Robinson's heroic breakthrough 50 years prior on April 15. To this major event, we invited former players (a veritable Who's Who), current fans, journalists, and academics. Andrew Parton, vice president of Chase Bank, secured a sponsorship of $20,000 for our conference. In addition, Trans World Airlines (may the company rest in peace) offered to fly in baseball luminaries at no cost if they travelled in the economy class. All accepted this generous offer except for Frank Robinson, who insisted that he always travelled first-class. Unwilling to lose such an important person, we agreed. At lunch-time on April 4, 1997, we provided food for the baseball luminaries from local Brooklyn bistros including Junior's with America's favorite cheesecake and Gage & Tollner, a luxurious restaurant harking back to the so-called gay nineties. So, I asked Mr. Robinson, what would he like to eat? To our surprise, he replied, "McDonald's is one of my favorites," proving that he was truly a man of the people.

Earl Weaver wrote that "he had great baseball instincts and tremendous physical attributes that allowed him to do everything right on a ball field…. He never griped and he was always able to counsel any younger players who sought his advice."[60] Robinson was "the best player I ever saw," said Orioles pitcher Jim Palmer. "He made us all better." Duane Kuiper cited him as "the best manager [he] ever played for."[61] At Frank Robinson's Hall of Fame induction ceremony, Rachel Robinson, whose husband had implored Major League Baseball to hire a Black manager nine days before his death at age 53, said of the great players who followed her heroic husband: "they represent the epitome of what Jackie wanted: excellence."[62]

Ernie Banks

Born January 31, 1931, in Dallas, Texas, Ernie Banks was the second oldest child of Eddie and Essie Banks. For eight years, Ernie's father played baseball as a catcher for the Dallas Black Giants, a travel team, and worked as a porter in a warehouse after he retired. Eddie gave Ernie his first glove and ball when his son was eight years old. To entice him to play, he would nickel-and-dime him with incentives or bribes. Consequently, Ernie broke many windows.[63] Ernie attended Booker T. Washington High School and played football and basketball, but not baseball. So, Ernie took up softball. A keen observer, Bill Blair advised him to try baseball with a travelling team like his father. His parents reluctantly agreed. As a member of the Detroit Colts, Banks travelled across the Southwest and learned a lot from his older teammates. He played shortstop. It was much more fun than picking cotton. In his second year with the Colts, Banks impressed legendary Negro Leaguer "Cool Papa" Bell, then managing the Kansas City Stars.[64]

Bell recommended Banks to Kansas City Monarchs manager John "Buck" O'Neil. When Monarchs shortstop Gene Baker was signed by the Chicago Cubs organization, Banks filled a vacuum at shortstop at $300 per month. No longer reluctant, Banks's parents encouraged the move. He hit only .250 in 1950, but he fielded expertly. After the season, Ernie had the good fortune to barnstorm with the Jackie Robinson All-Stars. Playing with and against Campanella, Newcombe, and Doby, Banks picked up valuable lessons and $400 to boot. Jackie Robinson prepped Banks on turning double plays safely. After a two-year stint in the army during the Korean War, Banks returned to civilian life in 1953. Although Brooklyn and Cleveland expressed interest in Banks, he returned to Kansas City. In September, the Monarchs sent Banks to the Chicago Cubs for $20,000. As a newly minted Cub, Banks now earned $800 per month.[65] Banks debuted on September 17, 1953. Three days later, Gene Baker, who had opened the door for Banks in Kansas City, was called up as his roommate and moved to second base, forming a Kansas City Monarchs keystone combo. Later, their former manager Buck O'Neil joined the Cubs as the first African American to occupy that position in Major League Baseball, thereby creating a Kansas City trifecta in Chicago.

In 1955, during his second full season, Ernie Banks became a star with a .295 batting average, 117 runs batted in, and a league-leading .972 fielding average. He made the National League All-Star team, the first of 10 more to come. Moreover, on September 20, 1955, he hit a record fifth grand slam home run. At 6'1" tall on a 180-pound frame, he was not built like a slugger. More like Hank Aaron, Banks used strong wrists and a light bat, weighing 31 ounces, to generate power.[66] Ernie Banks was named the National League MVP in two consecutive years, 1958 and 1959. In '58, Banks led the league in homers and had the most runs batted in the following year. His fielding improved measurably with only 12 errors and .985 fielding average, setting Major League Baseball records in both categories for shortstops. Banks had another banner year in 1960 with 41 home runs and 117 runs batted in. To make room for a "Bonus Baby," unable to gain minor league experience, Ernie Banks moved to another position at the request of Cubs management. Always eager to please, Banks volunteered to patrol left field. There, he banged up his left knee, which reduced his mobility. He became a regular first baseman in 1962. Though he smacked 37 homers that year, his hitting tailed off. Banks suffered through a plethora of coaches and managers plus an awful trade that sent soon-to-be great Lou Brock to the Cardinals for a sore-armed pitcher Ernie Broglio, who pitched only two mediocre years.

Dissatisfied with mediocrity, the Cubs hired Leo Durocher as their manager. Although Leo "the Lip" pontificated that "nice guys finish last," Ernie Banks, the ultimate nice guy, welcomed him. Banks, in his 14th year as a Cub, wanted to finish first, finally. A jealous Durocher did not reciprocate warm feelings for Banks according to longtime Cubs broadcaster Jack Brickhouse. They feuded incessantly according to several Cubs teammates. Leo tried to push him aside with other prospects at first base that never worked out.[67] Banks became player-coach in 1967, a position he occupied until 1971, the year that he retired as a player. After two third-place finishes in '67 and '68, the Cubs seemed ready to end their *shneid* in 1969. They had a fine pitching staff anchored by aces Ferguson Jenkins and Bill Hands, plus solid players in Ron Santo and Billy Williams. Late in August, the Cubs held a four and a half game lead over the surprising New York Mets. The Cubs slumped to a 8–12 record while the "Amazin'" Mets posted a splendid 18–5 record to run away with the pennant in their division. The year of 1970 proved equally frustrating as the Cubs faded behind the Pirates in late September. While Pittsburgh crested, Chicago played like the pirates of Penzance. Relegated to substitute player status, Ernie Banks retired after the 1971 season. In his splendid 19-year career, he played excellent defense at shortstop and first base. With 2,583 hits, 512 home runs, 1,636 runs batted in, and a .274 lifetime batting average, Banks entered the Hall of Fame in 1977, his first eligible year. Banks coached first base for his alma mater from 1973 to 1974. His mantra, succinctly stated in 1969 on a hot summer day, was "It's a beautiful day, let's play two."[68]

President Barack Obama conferred the Presidential Medal of Freedom on Banks in 2013. Unlike Jackie Robinson, Banks did not get involved in politics or racial issues. Was that a mistake? His three marriages ended in divorce; he had twin sons and a daughter with wife number two. Wife number three, who separated from Ernie before his death, sued his estate and the caregiver who received the bulk of his estate in a questionable later alteration of his will as he slid into senility. Unlucky in marriage, Banks, a staunch Republican, became a successful businessman. He remains a beloved Chicago icon as his jersey bearing number 14 wafts over Wrigley Field's left field flagpole deep in the heart of the Windy City.

11

Bill White
and Curt Flood

Bill White

In his provocatively titled autobiography, *Uppity*, Bill White writes, "I didn't love baseball. Because I knew that baseball would never love me back." He goes on to explain the consequence of these seemingly incongruous thoughts.

> That approach occasionally caused me trouble with owners and front office types. Some of them thought I was cold and arrogant; I was told that on occasion that word uppity was used, although never to my face.[1]

Subsequently, White explains his ambivalence as a defense mechanism against the emotional highs and lows of a baseball career. Being emotionally detached and analytical, he argues, made him a better ball player—if not a better person. His family wanted the highly intelligent young man to become a doctor. Perhaps guilt was central to his ambivalence about a career that propelled him—a proud Black man—to new professional heights as player, broadcaster, and president of the National League.

William Dekova White was born on January 24, 1934, in Paxton, Florida, in the panhandle section. Essentially fatherless, White was raised by his grandmother Tamar Young and his mother, Edna Mae Young.[2] In Florida, he lived in a shack minus electricity. His mother took Bill to Warren, Ohio, when he was three years old, as part of the Great Migration. Work was available in the steel industry. Bill and family lived in segregated public housing. His mother left domestic service to attend secretarial school, which led to a government job. While she travelled as required by her employer, the U.S. Air Force, Bill stayed in Warren with his grandma. He encountered racism in school. Because the prom queen was white, the school principal voided a tradition in which the queen danced with the student-body president because the popular White had been elected president. After graduating from Warren G. Harding High School, where he starred as a student-athlete, White headed for college. A multitalented athlete with no expertise in anything by his own admission, Bill played football, basketball, and baseball. Eager to study medicine, he attended, Hiram College on an academic scholarship, a rarity among baseball players of that era. Bill also played baseball.

A New York Giants scout watched a crucial game in Crosley Field in Cincinnati in which Bill hit two home runs. At a subsequent workout, Giants manager Leo Durocher agreed to a $2,500 bonus plus a new pair of spikes to finish college.[3] At the Giants spring training site in Phoenix, Arizona, Bill White could not get into a movie theater due to his race. Blacks were consigned to the balcony, but this theater had no balcony. His experience as a Giants farmhand down South intensified his anger, where "some red-necked tobacco-chewing Carolina cracker with a fourth-grade education was calling me a nigger?" Unable to "kick ass," he had to take it. White painfully recalls an incident in Wichita, Kansas. Watching from a bus window as his teammates ate at a segregated restaurant, unable to join them, he did something, he declares, that he never repeated: "I held my face in my hands and cried."[4] Monte Irvin advised him to be patient, to go along to get along, hoping for change in the future.[5] In the minor leagues, White encountered racism as the second African American to play for a Carolina League team, the Danville Leafs. As the only Black player on the team, he took a lot of verbal abuse. After suffering unrelenting hostility, White raised his middle finger in defiance. A near riot ensued. His white teammates provided a cordon of raised bats as they ran to their bus, ready to carry all to safety.[6]

Sent north the following year to Sioux City in the Class A Western League, White continued his solid hitting with 30 home runs and running, stealing 40 bases. He returned to the South in Double A Dallas, where he hit 20 homers and decided to drop out of college and play winter ball. Called up from the AAA Minneapolis Millers, White became a full-fledged Giant in May. In his first game, he hit a home run. In describing that baptismal moment, White displays verbal eloquence to match his powerful bat:[7]

> There's a physical sensation when you connect with a ball in just the right way, a kinetic charge that travels through the bat and into your arms and then all the way down to your spikes. As you complete your swing, you know that ball is going out of the park.

On the last day of the season, he homered twice off Phillies "ace" pitcher Robin Roberts, finishing with 22 round-trippers in 1956. White lived in Harlem Heights, attended the Red Rooster and Small's Paradise for food, music, and companionship. Willie Mays became a mentor to White, who regarded the "Say Hey Kid" as the greatest player among the greats. Mays could have been a great manager, according to White, and, lamentably, "he was never given a chance."[8]

After the baseball season, Uncle Sam came calling for the U.S. Army. When he was refused service in a local Kentucky restaurant without any support from his white teammates, he quit the Fort Knox baseball team. Upon returning to the Giants, now "stationed" in San Francisco, he discovered that a young Orlando Cepeda had replaced him as a starting first baseman. With Willie McCovey, also a first baseman, heating up in Triple A, a rebellious White asked for a trade. Although the indignant Giants vice president Chub Feeney disdained such demands, he sent White and infielder Ray Jablonski to St. Louis for two pitchers, including Sam "toothpick" Jones, a strikeout artist. Reluctant to join a club that had two competent players and one aging star, Stan "the Man" Musial at 38, listed at first baseman, the trade proved beneficial to White. Playing outfield in 1959, White would eventually become the premier fielding first sacker in the senior league, winning seven Gold Gloves and hitting for average plus power.[9]

Bill White made his most important contribution to civil rights in spring training. As late as 1961, St. Petersburg, where the Cardinals trained, was still segregated. Wendell Smith, who had championed and chaperoned Jackie Robinson through segregated cities before, took up the cudgels against a deplorable incident in his newspaper column. Bill White was the only Cardinal not invited to the St. Petersburg Chamber of Commerce's annual "Salute to Baseball" breakfast. After Smith wrote his cogent column, other newspapers picked up the story. Angry protestors called for a boycott of Budweiser and Busch beverages. So, in 1962, August Busch bought two motels to house all Cardinal players including major Cardinal stars Ken Boyer and Stan Musial. Boyer manned the barbecue grills and White's wife, Mildred, taught classes for the Cardinals children. Black and white kids and their parents broke precedent by swimming in the same pool! Togetherness in the spring led to success in the summer.[10]

When Johnny Keane replaced Solly Hemus as manager, Cardinals fortunes improved as Bill White enjoyed the best years of his baseball life. In 1962, White hit .324. In 1963, as the Cardinals inched closer to the National League pennant, White manufactured 200 hits, scored 106 runs, smacked 27 homers, and knocked in 109 runs. With a terrific infield quartet—Boyer at third, Javier at second, Groat at short, and White at first—the Cardinals almost caught the first-place Dodgers. Finally, the Cards hit pay dirt on the last day of the 1964 season, and Bill White played a major role. Against the pesky if still not ready for primetime Mets, White singled in the fifth inning and later scored the lead run. In the next inning, White hit a two-run homer to seal the deal. He finished the season with a solid .303 complemented by excellent defense. White's clutch hitting carried over into the seventh game against the favored New York Yankees. Although he hit a paltry .111 in that pivotal series, he regained his stroke with two hits and scored a run to defeat those "Damned Yankees."[11]

After a subpar season in 1965 after their well-liked manager left to manage the equally hapless Yankees, Cardinals general manager Howser unloaded three top infielders—Boyer, Groat, and White—in trades, the latter two to the Phillies. Howser added fuel to White's simmering fury when he claimed that Bill White was 37 years old, not 31, and that he had lied about his age in an interview the general manager conducted with the *St. Louis Globe Dispatch*. Apprised of this lie, White stormed into Howser's office and screamed "Bullshit!" Cowed, Howser promised not to continue this base deceit.[12]

In 1966, White had a decent year with 22 home runs, 103 runs batted in, and a .276 batting average, plus the last of his seven Gold Gloves as a fielder. I witnessed one of his line drive home runs against the Mets in Shea Stadium that helped the Phillies win the game. Gene Mauch, however, proved to be a control freak and turned White off. Bill's stint with the Phillies lasted three years; he was subject like his teammates to scorn from the local fans and media.[13] A torn Achilles tendon sent his career plummeting. Traded back to the Cardinals in 1969, he retired after 16 seasons in the sun.

Gradually, White worked himself into a successful career in broadcasting. He became a sports anchor on Philadelphia's WFIL-TV. Encouraged by Harry Caray and Howard Cosell, he took voice lessons. Cosell recommended White to the New York Yankees to do their play-by-play broadcasts with Frank Messer and Phil Rizzuto.[14] Thus, White became the first Black full-time announcer in major league history. Messer played it straight while Rizzuto and White bantered in between plays. Little Phil touted birthdays of friends and his favorite restaurants, especially those who favored him with free cannoli. He yacked about Scooter, his son, and Ann, Scooter's wife, ignoring his three daughters. White and Messer provided some gravitas, and Rizzuto remained a goofy child in arrested development. Rizzuto often departed from games early to beat the traffic back to New Jersey. They became partners and friends. Scooter Rizzuto had welcomed Larry Doby and Elston Howard into the big leagues unlike so many other white ballplayers during their transition from the Negro Leagues.[15] When the former Yankee shortstop sank into senility, White visited him in a rehab facility in 2006, one year before he died. Unable to speak, Rizzuto held White's hand for 45 minutes. White wrote of that incident: "Two old men, old baseball players, holding hands in a sunbeam. I didn't know whether to laugh or cry—but I'm pretty sure Phil would have wanted me to laugh." Fighting back tears, Bill White said, "I loved Phil Rizzuto."[16]

After 18 years in the broadcasting booth, White decided to retire at age 55. Perhaps his inability to tolerate the bully who owned the Yankees had something to do with his departure. White reveals that the "Boss" cheated in a meaningless basketball game when Bill White was playing basketball, and the "Fat Man"—Rick Cerone's bitter caricature of dishonest George—actually pulled at White's jersey from the bench as White was dribbling down the sidelines. Unapologetic, Steinbrenner related the story to his victim many years later at Mama Leone's restaurant. He actually seemed proud of his misdeed. Later "The Boss" offered White the job as Yankees general manager. Knowing that he could never work for Steinbrenner, he rejected the offer from a man he correctly considered a control freak.[17]

Al Campanis and Jimmy "the Greek'" Snyder made racially charged statements on national television in 1987 regarding the superiority of Black athletes based on pseudoscience. Adding to their inane analysis, they both questioned the ability of Blacks in positions of leadership.[18] Therefore, when the opportunity arose, baseball moguls were eager to hire a Black president for the National League. Pressured by his good friend and former teammate Bob Gibson, Bill White reluctantly accepted. He became the first Black national executive in baseball and the first former player to achieve that role that Joe Cronin had initiated in the American League. White faced several challenges. Among them was Cincinnati Reds owner Marge Schott, given to praise for Hitler and racist rants fueled by alcohol. Pete Rose's penchant for gambling and lying about his addiction posed another problem.[19]

He had trouble with some rowdy players and angry umpires like Joe West and Richie Phillips. True, he paved a smooth road for expansion teams in Colorado and Florida, which led to conflict with then baseball commissioner Fay Vincent. White grew disenchanted with his role when promises to hire Black executives failed to materialize in the Colorado Rockies organizations. White's rocky relationship with the press diminished his clout, and his surprising silence on social issues earned a rebuke from Frank Robinson. Ultimately, White conceded that minorities made few advances during his limited tenure on top. Though he differed with Fay Vincent on key issues, he opposed his ouster in 1992 in favor of Milwaukee Brewers owner Bud Selig. White preferred Colin Powell as Vincent's replacement, an offer that General Powell could and did refuse.[20] Thus, this last angry man in baseball resigned in disgust in 1994. He refused a dinner in his honor that his African American successor, Leonard Coleman, wished to organize. Former baseball commissioner Fay Vincent shared Bill White's self-analysis in a quote: "Bill once told me: 'I have a terrible problem with authority. I've never been able to get along with anyone in authority.' I think that explains a lot."[21]

In retirement, White continues to play golf, fish for halibut in Alaska, and move around in his motor home with Nancy McKee, a "lady friend." He has abandoned "the rat race."[22] He refuses to watch baseball on television or at stadiums. He dislikes the politics of baseball and found the owners as well as Commissioner Vincent disappointing. What comes across in his searing autobiography are racial incidents in Southern venues that plagued White and other Black players in the 1950s and 1960s. I am no psychoanalyst or psychotherapist, though exposed to both at "shrink" times, but I venture to suggest that Bill White regrets that he did not become a doctor as his mother and grandmother had wished. Carrying this mother lode of guilt, despite his many achievements on the field of dreams, Bill White remains an angry man, perhaps the last angry man in baseball.

Curt Flood

A close friend and Cardinals teammate of Bill White, Curt Flood was an outstanding ball player and a man plagued by demons. The youngest of four children born to Herman and Laura Flood, Curt was born in Houston, Texas, on January 18, 1938. He was two years old when his family, frequently on the move, departed for Oakland, California, where he grew up. Curt's mother had resided in the pre–World War II South, rife with racial subjugation, and Oakland proved far more hospitable, while his father found work during the war on the docks and in military installations.[23] Herman "taught his children to love art and music." Curt loved to draw and learned to play piano by ear. While their neighborhood, a working-class Black community, was relatively more comfortable than what the Flood family left behind in Texas, crime beckoned to vulnerable youngsters like Curt's brother Carl. Curt was saved by George Powles. A teacher with heart, a coach with compassion, Powles served in World War II, including the Battle of the Bulge. After the war, he tried various jobs before finding his niche as a high school teacher and athletic coach at McClymonds, a school for predominantly Black youngsters. As the summer playground director at Poplar Park, Powles "took a shining to Flood" at a time when Curt was drifting into petty crime.[24] Baseball would prove Curt's salvation. After sustaining an injury while catching, Curt shifted to the outfield. Living nearby, Powles and his wife entertained and mentored youngsters in their home.

Powles had also rescued a 12-year-old orphan named Bill Russell, who was the 16th man on the JV basketball team in 1947, the same year that Jackie Robinson's barrier-breaking baseball entry "symbolized hope." Robinson became a role model in the Flood family. Powles groomed two other future baseball all-stars in Frank Robinson and Vada Pinson. In 1949, at age 11 and weighing only 105 pounds, Curt worked for a local furniture company. Lettering signs, moving furniture owned by E. Bercovich & Sons, setting up window displays, all with an artistic flair, young Curt made pocket money. His employers sponsored youth baseball teams. Flood moved to Oakland Technical High School in order to play in Bill Erwin American Legion Baseball. Seventy-five percent of the student population at his new high school was white. To qualify for entry, Curt moved in with his older sister Barbara, the estranged wife of pro football running back John Henry Johnson. On an American Legion team in southern California, the diminutive Flood outhit his teammate Frank Robinson, .429 to .424.[25]

In 1955, Flood helped his team to cop the American Legion state championship, hitting a robust .620 with 12 doubles, five triples, and nine home runs.[26] Only 5'9" tall and 165 pounds after graduation, Curt attracted only a few pro scouts. One happy exception to this indifference, Cincinnati scout Bobby Mattick, sensed Flood's enormous potential. Inspired by hero Jackie Robinson and eager to join high school teammate Frank, the other Robinson, Curt signed for $4,000. Unable to live with white teammates in segregated Florida, where most major league teams trained, he found quarters in a Black boarding house with Frank Robinson and Chuck Harmon, a condition that had fueled Jackie Robinson's fiery anger. At one time, Curt had to stay in a garage.[27] Flood's ire simmered on a lower burner. Hecklers' invective-laced bromides elicited a flood of tears. To honor Jackie Robinson, Curt wore #42 on his uniform.[28]

Flood learned to duck and dodge, as beanballs often targeted his head. After one beaning, Flood stole second and third base. As further retaliation, he also hit a home run. Performing in the Deep South proved dangerous. White violence could flare up at any time, as Nat King Cole learned on April 10, 1956, when six racist brutes assaulted the great singer as part of an insidious conspiracy of 100 bigots to kill him. That year, Flood won the Carolina Class B League batting title with a batting average of .340 with 190 hits, 133 runs scored, 29 home runs, and 19 stolen bases. In addition, Curt's stellar defense earned him a player-of-the-year award.

Traded to the St. Louis Cardinals for three forgettable pitchers, Flood suffered under player-manager Solly Hemus, who rarely used him for two and a half years. Cardinal executives replaced Hemus in 1961 with Johnny Kean, under whom Flood began to flourish along with Black teammates Bob Gibson and Bill White. He hit .322 in 1960. Curt Flood joined Bill White to lead the fight for integrated housing and dining. They alerted AP reporter Joe Reichler (who in turn contacted Cardinals owner Gussie Busch) that a local St. Petersburg yacht club hosted a breakfast only for white Cardinals.[29] Thanks to their initiative, the Cardinals' integrated spring training at St. Petersburg Skyline Motel included 137 people, counting family members. Coach Howie Pollet made salad while Ken Boyer and Larry Jackson manned the grill. A weekly fried chicken dinner created unity among the Redbirds.

Also politically active, Flood was one of the first active players to join the civil rights movement, unlike Frank Robinson and Willie Mays. Curt went to Jackson, Mississippi, with Floyd Paterson, Archie Moore, and Marguerite Belafonte, Harry's ex, to advance the cause at NAACP's Southeast Regional Conference. Three thousand folks gathered at the Masonic temple. The iconic Jackie Robinson served as emcee, training the celebrities who came. Flood came at the behest of Robinson, his hero, because "he wanted to show his solidarity with Southern blacks fighting for freedom. Civil Rights was embedded in Flood's soul."[30]

In 1964, Flood hit .311 with 211 hits and won a second Golden Glove. Indeed, he won that coveted award for defensive excellence seven times. His superb fielding and timely hitting contributed to Cardinals success in the 1960s as they won two World Series in 1964 and 1967. They might have won a third, but Flood made a rare unlucky miscue in game seven, inning seven of the World Series, misjudging and stumbling after a two-run triple hit by Tigers outfielder Jim Northrup. The Tigers won, 4–1.[31] In the late 1960s Cardinals management decided to rebuild. So, on October 7, 1969, they traded Curt Flood to the Philadelphia Phillies along with Tim McCarver, Byron Browne, and Joe Hoerner in exchange for Dick Allen, Cookie Rojas, and Jerry Johnson. Egged on by his then girlfriend, Maria, he decided to sue. He first consulted with the Major League Baseball Players Association, seeking the union's financial as well as moral support. His Cardinals teammates were shocked, but they tried to dissuade Flood from litigation even though they regarded him as a friend. Given the circumstances, they felt it was a losing effort. Union leader Marvin Miller, however, offered support but was equally skeptical about the outcome, pointing to prior lawsuits proffered by Danny Gardella and George Toolson. Both lawsuits failed to reverse the reserve clause, in force, thanks to an injudicious Supreme Court decision, when the high court then, as now, was dominated by archconservatives. Appearing before his peers and appealing for their backing, Flood insisted that his action was not about money. It was about justice and dignity.[32]

Aware of the risk, Marvin Miller backed Curt Flood. He pleaded for the best counsel to nullify a bad law. Dodgers rep Tom Haller expressed concern about the lawsuit as a "black thing." "No," Flood replied. The reserve clause, he argued, affected all players, regardless of color.[33] Convinced, the player reps gave Miller and Flood the green light. Then Cardinals rep Joe Torre led the charge; Flood agreed to return legal fees if he won damages. The reps voted 25–0 in favor of Flood.

Former Supreme Court justice Arthur Goldberg took the case. Earlier, he had litigated for George Mikan on that same issue, the reserve clause. Goldberg and Flood drafted a letter and sent it on December 24, 1969, to Baseball Commissioner Bowie Kuhn. It read[34]:

> Dear Mr. Kuhn:
>
> After twelve years in the Major Leagues, I do not feel that I am a piece of property to be bought and sold irrespective of my wishes. I believe that any system which produces that result violates my basic rights as a citizen and is inconsistent with the laws of the United States and the several States. It is my desire to play in 1970, and I am capable of playing. I have received a contract from the Philadelphia Club, but I believe that I have the right to consider offers from other clubs before making any decisions. I, therefore, request that you make

known to all the Major League Clubs my feelings in this matter and advise them of my avail-
ability for the 1970 season.

Sincerely yours, Curt Flood

Author Bill Rhoden points out that Curt Flood was "the first person to use the plantation metaphor in connection with professional athletes" in 1969.[35] An All-Star center fielder like Willie Mays, Flood glided effortlessly to snare would-be hits. In 1949
Judge Jerome Frank opined in the Danny Gardella case, ultimately settled in a paltry cash payout, that the reserve clause "results in something resembling peonage
of the baseball players that was comparable to 'involuntary servitude,' in violation
of Amendment 13.I."[36] Outside of baseball, basketball forward Chet Walker, football rebel Dave Meggyesy, and National Hockey League (NHL) great "Red" Ber-
enson, president of the NHL Players Association, shared Curt Flood's disdain for
the "hallowed" reserve clause.[37] Most of the sportswriters denigrated Flood, with
Dick Young's poison pen particularly venomous. Most of the St. Louis beat writers
unleashed a fusillade of Flood bashing.[38]

Ignoring Marvin Miller's advice, Curt opted to skip the 1970 season and reject
the $100,000 salary offered. Most of his peers were afraid to follow his lead. Bob Gib-
son and Jackie Robinson, however, stepped up to the plate for him.[39] In fact, Jackie
Robinson told him: "You can't be out there by yourself and I would be remiss if I
did not share these burdens with you." As Bill Rhoden, who provided this important quote, also wrote: "Robinson understood history—he was history."[40] The case
reached the Supreme Court in 1972. Initially Justices Burger, Douglas, Brennan, and
Powell seemed to favor Flood, with Stewart, White (who had played pro football),
Blackmun, and Rehnquist in favor of the baseball establishment. Because he owned
880 shares of Anheuser-Busch stock, the parent company of the St. Louis Cardinals,
Powell recused himself. Blackmun, an avid baseball fan, caught up in his pipe dream
that baseball was a sport, not a business, was chosen to write the majority opinion.
After a slow waffle, Blackmun penned a 27-page ode to baseball.[41] In a 5–3 decision,
Flood lost his case. Reversing his earlier decision in the Toolson Case, Justice Douglas wrote a blistering dissent. Thurgood Marshall and William Brennan joined in
dissent.[42] Later, standing up for outsiders, Justice Blackmun, a moderate Republican
from Minnesota, became more liberal on cases dealing with abortion and the death
penalty.[43]

Subsequently, Flood sank deeper into alcohol, as did his son Curt Jr. Consequently, his marriage and liaisons collapsed. Richard Reeves profiled Flood for a
March 1978 *Esquire* article, "The Last Angry Man: A Search for Heroes." He paid
Flood $750 for the interview, the only time he ever paid a source. "The saddest man
I ever met," Reeves noted as Curt drank straight vodka all night.[44] Flood felt like a
failed father and admitted to deficiencies as a husband. His art business, in which
he sold "authentic" paintings as his own, proved fraudulent. Rootless, he went into
voluntary exile, to Denmark in 1970 and Spain in 1971. Homesick, unable to control
his drinking, Flood returned. In an abortive comeback attempt, he played briefly
for the Washington Senators after taking two years off. In that hiatus, Flood seemed
to have aged 10 years. His manager, Ted Williams, treated him disdainfully. During

Flood's litigation, the once great hitter and now inept manager joined a group of former players, writers, and magazines who supported the owners and applauded the Supreme Court decision. They included Joe DiMaggio, Dick Young, and the *Sporting News*.[45] No active players offered support at this time, no doubt fearful of reprisals. "House-man" Joe Garagiola testified for the owners but later apologized. In 1973, the owners agreed to federal arbitration. Two years later, Dave McNally and Andy Messersmith sued and won. Flood regretted that two white players succeeded where he had failed. On the other hand, Howard Cosell, who had come to the defense of Ali in 1967, befriended Flood, treated him to New York visits, and remained a staunch advocate to the bitter end. Red Smith also championed Flood. So did most major newspapers in editorials critical of the U.S. Supreme Court.[46]

With the help of Karen Brecker, his partner for six years, he entered rehab in 1980 at a Berkeley, California medical center. Gaining sobriety, he headed a youth baseball league in West Oakland. Joe Morgan contributed $4,000 and Reggie Jackson coughed up $2,000 for this worthy cause. Flood regained stature as a local hero, contrary to F. Scott Fitzgerald's dictum that "there are no second acts in American lives." The local NAACP honored him on March 8, 1980, with a banquet. Oakland public schools celebrated Flood: March 24–29, 1980 was "Curt Flood Week."[47] Though still blacklisted by Major League Baseball, Flood traveled to Cooperstown to witness the inauguration of his high school teammate Frank Robinson into the Hall of Fame in 1982. At the ceremony, Robinson urged his old buddy to stand up. Robinson went on to praise Curt for his free agency fight, one that Frank had avoided. Robinson "stayed in the game by keeping his mouth shut," observed a judgmental Brad Snyder, from whose work much of this chapter was shaped.[48] In his acceptance speech, Robinson suggested that Flood's fight was also worthy of Hall of Fame induction.

That same year, 1982, Flood relapsed following a Cutty Sark advertisement plug. He left his lady friend Karen the following year. Another female savior appeared in the person of Judy Pace, giving Curt a chance for a third act. Recognized by modern players for paving the way for higher salaries and improved conditions, Flood was honored at various events. He won friends and influenced people, including Joe Garagiola. Even conservative columnist George Will became a friend. When baseball players went on strike in 1994, Curt invited them to join a new league of their own, which did not come to fruition. Nevertheless, 80 players gave him a standing ovation when he met with them in Atlanta on December 6.[49] Flood was welcomed at fantasy camps, All-Star games, and by filmmakers Ken Burns and Spike Lee. Flood graced Ken Burns's magisterial baseball documentary with pertinent commentary on his contributions to the "national pastime." At the film's debut in Washington, D.C., Curt and his wife Judy attended, as a photograph vividly indicates, in concert with President Bill Clinton and his wife, future presidential candidate in her own right, Hillary Clinton.

Alcoholism finally overcome was superseded by throat cancer as Flood's last challenge. Diagnosed in 1995, Curt received favorable odds for recovery because he had quit smoking in 1979 and drinking in 1986.[50] Radiation, chemotherapy, and surgery provided hope, and financial support from the MLB Players Association and the Baseball Assistance Team founded by Joe Garagiola and Ralph Branca helped pay his medical expenses. When he lost his voice due to surgery, National League president—and Flood's close friend—Bill White quietly provided a computer that could transcribe Curt's written words into vocal messages. He used that computer to communicate with Spike Lee for a 15-minute segment, read by wife Judy, on HBO's *Real Sports*.[51] Flood lingered for 19 months. He died on Martin Luther King Day, January 20, 1997. A memorial service at the First African Methodist Episcopal Church, aptly named "Curt's Ninth Inning," in downtown Los Angeles brought out 300 mourners. Not a single active baseball player attended, but the roster of former players included pallbearers, Joe Black, Bob Gibson, Orlando Cepeda, Bob Gibson, Earl Robinson, Bill White, and Maury Wills, while Lou Brock, Don Newcombe, Lou Johnson, and John Roseboro served as honorary pallbearers.[52] Bob Gibson, who spoke at the funeral, remembered Flood as a friend of 40 years, a teammate for 10 who always made him smile while choking back tears. Conservative author George Will compared Flood's fight for free agency to Dred Scott's quest for freedom in 1857, and Jesse Jackson concluded the service with these trenchant words:

> Don't cry for long. Curt is the winner. The courts lost. Curt won. Baseball is better. And people are better. America is better. Because. God sent an instrument his way. Let him rest. Fought the good fight. Finish his race. He kept the faith…. Thank God that Curt came this way. We love you Curt. You are a winner.[53]

Thus, an imperfect man in an imperfect world became a perfect hero. According to a Jewish tradition in *tikkun olam*, good deeds are essential to change the world. By the standards set in Jesse Jackson's eulogy, Curt Flood personifies that moral imperative. He is an authentic American hero, warts and all. Flood paved the way for free agency, thereby liberating professional athletes from involuntary servitude.

12

Minnie Miñoso, Vic Power, and Roberto Clemente

At our 1997 Jackie Robinson Conference mentioned above, a young scholar delivered an excellent paper, "Jackie Robinson and the Emancipation of Latin American Baseball Players," that eventually became the template of a powerful book, *Viva Baseball!* That author, Samuel Regalado, the nephew of Cleveland Indians star Rudy Regalado, points out that, prior to 1947, few Latino-Americans made it into Major League Baseball, especially men of color. When Rafael Almeida and Armando Marsans were signed by the Cincinnati Reds in 1911, they had to provide documentary proof of "whiteness." A journalist affirmed their racial purity by describing them "as two of the purest bars of soap ... ever floated to these shores."[1] Washington Senators owner Clark Griffith, no friend of racial integration, hired a few light-skinned Hispanics, but, like other baseball tycoons, drew the color line on African-Latino players. Ironically, the Homestead Grays rented Griffith Stadium grounds when the Senators played on the road, and because of their superior brand of baseball they occasionally outdrew the all-white Senators and made a lot of money for their landlord, the racist owner Clark Griffith.[2]

From 1911 to 1947, of the 54 Latinos who played Major League Baseball, 45 were from Cuba and considered all right because they were all white. Several became legitimate stars. One, pitcher Adolfo Luque, compiled an impressive record over a 21-year career with a record of 194 wins, a .324 earned run average, 1,130 strikeouts, and one World Series victory as a New York Giants relief pitcher in 1933. Contributing to an ethnic stereotype, Luque, while pitching for the Reds, is remembered for his hot-tempered explosion in response to racial slurs from the New York Giants bench and thrashing Casey Stengel, sitting next to the real perpetrator, Bill Cunningham.[3] Another early pioneer, Mike Gonzalez, was also born near Havana, Cuba, on September 24, 1890, like his compatriot Dolf Luque. Gonzalez started his major league career with the Boston Braves, interrupted by three years in Negro baseball, but ended it in St. Louis with the Cardinals for whom he played in three different shifts—1915–18, 1924–25, and 1931–32—plus two shifts as interim manager and as coach from 1934 to 1946. A tall (6'1"), gaunt catcher who hit only .253, 13 home runs, and 263 runs batted in, he epitomized a phrase that he had coined as a scout: "Good field, no hit." In his last hurrah, Mike Gonzalez as Cardinals coach in the 1946 World Series waved Enos Slaughter—starting from first base—home with the winning run after Harry Walker singled. Red Sox center fielder Doc Cramer—subbing for the injured Dom DiMaggio—and shortstop Johnny Pesky botched the relay to home plate, yielding the winning run that climaxed a dramatic seven-game series. While managing in the Cuban Winter League, Mike Gonzalez hired banished pitcher Fred Martin, a "Mexican jumper." Under duress, Gonzalez resigned as Cardinals coach and protested the unjust ban by Baseball Commissioner A. B. "unhappy" Chandler, thus ending his Major League Baseball tenure. Author Donn Rogosin claims that Gonzalez was a light-skinned Black who "passed."[4]

Unable to gain entry, the darker-hued stars could only shine in the Negro Leagues.[5] José Méndez, dubbed "El Diamanté Negro," pitched brilliantly in the early twentieth century, compiling an overall 138–60, .697, with 26 shutouts. He also played shortstop. In 17 years in the Negro Leagues, he posted a 76–26, .731 win-loss record with an ERA of 3.16.[6] He was voted into the Cuban Hall of Fame in 1939, 11 years after his death at age 41. In 2006, he joined fellow Cuban star Cristóbal Torriente in U.S.A. baseball's Valhalla. Skeptic Peter C. Bjarkman questioned whether Méndez's credentials warranted Hall of Fame induction. After all, he argues, his "dead arm" limited him to only a few outstanding seasons. Yet, Bjarkman concedes that he had three undefeated seasons in 1908, 1910, and 1913–14 and was 15–5 in his comeback year in 1923 with a Negro League best earned run average of 1.89 for the Kansas City Monarchs.[7] Author John Holway offers a radically different assessment of José Méndez. Holway wrote that Méndez "threw a fast ball that looked like a pea" and "a curveball that looked like it was falling off a pool table." At age 36, he beat the Hilldale Club to win the 10th game of a marathon series to claim the first Colored World Series on October 20, 1924. Philadelphia Athletics catcher Ira Thomas, who had faced Méndez on a tour of Havana, ranked him "with the best of the game, … just below Walter Johnson … and if he were [was] a white man would command a good position on an any Major League club in the circuit."[8] Bjarkman rests his dubious argument on the scarcity of reliable information, including the precise dates of his early death due to poverty-induced tuberculosis.

Cristóbal Torriente entered the Hall of Fame the same year as his fellow Cuban fortified with a better-documented résumé. He was dubbed the "Black Babe Ruth," largely as a result of a nine-game exhibition series in which he outhomered Babe Ruth who was playing for the New York Giants. Torriente's team, the Almendares, took the series five games to four, largely due to the Cuban slugger's bat at home plate and glove in center field. Torriente brought both tools to the United States, supplemented by speed, arm, and power to play for the Cuban All-Stars. Five years later, he helped his new team, the Chicago American Giants, to win three consecutive Negro National League pennants, 1920–22. He also claimed two batting titles in 1920 and 1923. In subsequent years, he played for six other clubs, including the Kansas City Monarchs. A left-handed bad-ball power hitter, prefiguring Yogi Berra, Cristóbal could hit to all fields, steal a base when needed, cover a lot of turf in center field, and throw like a cannon. He also loved the night life, surrounded by pretty women and fueled by excess libation. He was light-skinned, but his kinky hair precluded a crossover entry into the major leagues. He was voted into the Cuban Hall of Fame in

1939, one year after his death due to acute alcoholism and tuberculosis. Only 44 or 45 years old, Torriente was buried in his native land with the Cuban flag draped over his coffin. Cristóbal Torriente batted .347 and slugged .520 over a 17-year career.[9] His complete baseball career spanned 1912–1932 with an overall lifetime batting average of .331. In two of his best seasons, he hit .411 and .412. Sabermetrics pioneer Bill James ranked Cristóbal Torriente as the 67th greatest player.[10]

An earlier Hall of Fame inductee, fellow Cuban Martín Dihigo, emulated Babe Ruth as an excellent pitcher with a 252–132 record and a .307 batting average and 130 home runs. Sporting matinee idol looks, he was inducted into the Hall of Fame in 1977. Dodgers general manager Al Campanis identified Dihigo as "the most complete player he had ever seen."[11] Dihigo played all nine positions. Hollywood tall and handsome but too dark to crack the color bar into Major League Baseball, Dihigo was born on May 25, 1906. His baseball debut occurred in 1922 at age 16. One year later, he joined the Cuban Stars as a second baseman, the first of his multiple positions. Like many other Cuban stars, Martin played all year: summers in the United States, winters in the Caribbean. A terrific fastball hitter, he applied a rigorous work ethic to master the roles of both pitcher and hitter. At third base, later at shortstop, he flashed a strong arm that proved quite useful when he shifted to the outfield. As a pitcher he excelled, throwing the first no-hitter in Mexican League baseball, while batting over .300 in 1938.

Still climbing, Dihigo became player/manager in the Dominican Republic, where a large number of stars are now groomed. Playing for Dihigo's team, "Big Cat" Johnny Mize called him the greatest player he had ever seen. Subsequently, longtime Dodgers executive and one-time TV "boob" Al Campanis echoed Mize's evaluation. At age 41, Dihigo retired. His claim to immortality is manifest in his enshrinement into the Halls of Fame of Cuba, Mexico, Dominican Republic, Venezuela, and the United States. In a stellar career, Martín Dihigo compiled a 252–132, .676 pitching record coupled with a .302 lifetime time batting average with 130 home runs (absent 11 unrecorded seasons). After Fidel Castro ousted Batista from power, Dihigo returned from exile. Appointed Minister of Sports, Dihigo spearheaded programs in which he also taught amateur athletics. His success in this capacity was evident in the large number of Olympic medals that this small island country garnered in boxing, track and field, and baseball. Author Lawrence Hogan has chronicled and documented Dihigo's Negro League career records: batting .307, slugging .511, 431 hits, 64 homers, 61 doubles, 17 triples, 227 runs batted in, 292 runs, 41 stolen bases, pitching 26–19, earned run average 2.92, 176 strikeouts, and 80 base on balls over 354 innings.[12]

Minnie Miñoso

As stated earlier, Jackie Robinson's arrival changed almost everything. Prior to his advent, racial purists had trouble drawing the color line accurately because miscegenation in Latin America blurred boundaries. Moreover, the few Black Latinos who tried to pass as whites were "mocked for their broken English and toiled in obscure jobs." In 1951, I played on a softball team in a summer camp that sported two Hispanic dishwashers who had played baseball in the high minor leagues. I forget their names but recall that one played for the St. Paul Saints, a White Sox affiliate from 1936 to 1944 and a Brooklyn Dodgers affiliate from 1944 to 1960. In this particular game, he played left field and I played center field. Running at full speed to left center, I made a fine catch before hitting the fence. My *amigo* in left field gave me a thumbs-up sign and later, at a local bar, touted my efforts to his fellow workers. That night, I learned about his baseball credits, too late to profit from Jackie's breakthrough. Others, more fortunate, benefited.

The first beneficiary, Orestes "Minnie" Miñoso, was born near Havana on November 19, 1925, to Carlos Arrieta and Cecilia Armas.[13] He quit school to work in the sugarcane fields. Baseball's field of dreams beckoned and provided an escape from this poorly compensated hard labor. Starting as a catcher, Minnie, like Martín Dihigo, moved on to other positions, except for pitching; He signed as a third baseman with the Ambrosia Candy baseball team situated in Havana at $150 per month. He was either 16, 18, or older depending on what Minnie said at different times.[14]

In 1945, Miñoso signed a pro contract with Marianao, a Havana-based team with whom he won rookie of the year honors. He was spotted by Alex Pompez, numbers tycoon and owner of the Negro League's New York Cubans. One year later, he switched teams. Leading off and playing third base, this "Cuban Comet" became a fan favorite in New York. Miñoso earned $300 per month in his rookie year. After three years in New York, hitting .260 or .262 or .309 in 1946 (depending on the source), .294 or .277 in 1947, and .403 in 1948, he caught the attention of Abe Saperstein scouting for Bill Veeck, who lured Minnie to Cleveland in 1948.[15] Unlike Branch Rickey, who refused to pay Negro League owners, claiming that they were racketeers, Veeck paid a cash-needy Alex Pompez $15,000 for Miñoso's services. After a "cup of coffee" in Cleveland, where he managed only three hits in 20 at-bats, Miñoso was sent back to the Triple A San Diego farm team in the Pacific Coast League. There, he hit .339 with 70 extra base hits in 1950. Unable to unseat "hot corner" emerging star Al Rosen, Minnie was traded to the Chicago White Sox.

In his first at-bat with his new team, Orestes Minnie Miñoso socked a home run against archrival, perennial pennant winner the New York Yankees. That season, he hit .326 and led the league in stolen bases, triples, and hit-by-pitch balls. Yet, Yankee third baseman Gil McDougald, who hit .306, won Rookie of the Year honors. For the next 10 years, Miñoso hit .305, with .395 on base percentage, .471 slugging average, 200 runs, and 98 runs batted in per year. Add to these impressive numbers superb fielding and charming personality—Hall of Fame credentials, some would argue. Exuding joy and beloved by local fans, he was dubbed "Mr. Chicago" about the same time that cross-town star Ernie Banks earned the moniker "Mr. Cub."

He also suffered racial slurs from bigoted spectators and was forced to stay in segregated motels. Miñoso played 17 seasons, 12 with the White Sox. Miñoso's blazing speed earned him the nickname "the Cuban Comet."[16] Among his 1,963 hits were 186 home runs, 1,135 runs scored, and a .298 lifetime batting average. He also stole 205 bases. As the first Latin Black to break into Major League Baseball and having played in five different decades, the last game at age 53, making him the oldest player in MLB history, he certainly merits consideration as the first designated Black Latin hero. After all, he made the American All-Star team in 1952, 1953, 1954, and 1957. Another indicator of speed coupled with power is manifest in leading the league in triples in 1952 and 1953. A statue of Orestes Minnie Miñoso bestrides the White Sox stadium like a mini Cuban American colossus.

After his major league career ended, Miñoso continued to play ball at an advanced age in the Mexican League. With the Jarrisco nine as a first baseman, Orestes Miñoso hit .360, banging out 35 doubles and a league-leading runs scored at 106. He was 40 years old. Subsequently, he also played for other clubs, retiring in 1973 at age 48. As author Mark Stewart points out, citing researcher Scott Simkus, Miñoso compiled more than 4,000 hits during his long, stellar career. White Sox owner Bill Veeck recalled Minnie to Chicago in 1976 as player-coach, where he occasionally pinch-hit from 1978 and 1980, thereby appearing in five different decades. In 1993 and 2003, Miñoso appeared as a pinch-hitter as a St. Louis Saint. Evidently, he loved the game and the game loved him. At the age of 89 or 90 or 92, Miñoso died in his car on November 29, 2015.[17] Orestes "Minnie" Miñoso was inducted into the Hall of Fame on July 24, 2022.

Vic Power

Based on his minor league performance, Vic Power should have been the first Black star to put on a New York Yankees uniform. One of six children, Victor Pellot (a first grade teacher changed it to Pove, which was later changed to Power to avoid a derogatory term in French) was born in Puerto Rico on November 1, 1927, to Regino and Maximina Pellot. His father forced young Victor to work in the sugarcane fields with other family members and forbade baseball to interfere with work. After his father died, Victor, aged 13, could freely indulge in his passion for baseball. Former Negro League star Quincy Trouppe, acting as his surrogate father, mentored him and signed Pove to play in a local league at $100 per week. When that league folded, Trouppe took Pove to the Drummondville Cubs in the Provincial League in Québec, Canada where New York Yankees scout and former interim manager Johnny Neun, assigned by scout Tom Wade, watched Victor play the outfield in 1950 and signed him to a minor league contract in the Yankee organization. Power, his name newly minted, hit .334 in 105 games with Drummondville with 138 hits, 20 doubles, 10 triples, and 14 home runs.[18]

Starting out with the Syracuse Chiefs in the International League, Power had another fine season, hitting .294 with 22 doubles, five triples, and six homers. Moved to the Kansas City in the American Association, also in Triple A Division, Power upped his stats including his power numbers to 16 per year with hefty batting averages of .331 and a league-leading .349 over two seasons in 1952 and 1953. In addition, Power was an excellent fielder, mostly at first base. So, why did the Yankees brass ignore his *bona fides*? General Manager George Weiss offered one clue to this deplorable decision when he opined: "He's impudent and he goes for white women, Power is not the Yankee type. The truth us that our box seat customers from Westchester County don't want to sit with a lot of colored fans from Harlem."[19] Dan Topping, Yankee co-owner, offered a lame, indeed deceitful excuse, conceding that Power was a good hitter but claiming he was a poor fielder and lacked hustle. The real reason for his trade to the Philadelphia A's was Power's penchant for dating white women, his driving a Cadillac, and his outgoing personality. He revolutionized the way first base was played, catching one-handed and playing far from the bag. Proof of his superior fielding came from the first baseman called up in lieu of Power, none other than Bill "Moose" Skowron, who said, contrary to Yankee propaganda: "Power plays 15 feet farther back than me or anyone else and takes throws on the dead run. He can do it because his reflexes are so great and because he has the best glove in baseball."[20]

Cheekiness may have also impeded Power's ascent to the "Big Ball Orchard in the Bronx" (a phrase coined by Art Rust, Jr., a Black pioneer in sports media). Many stories, some perhaps apocryphal, indicate Power's aggressive wit. When a white waitress rebuffed his attempt to eat in her Jim Crow restaurant with the usual words of rejection to people of color—"We don't serve Negroes here"—Power responded: "That's cool. I don't eat Negroes; I only want rice and beans," anticipating a Dick Gregory routine by several years. In response to insistence by the manager of his Puerto Rican baseball team that he catch all balls with two hands, Power reluctantly acquiesced, but added: "If the guys who invented baseball wanted us to catch with two hands, they would have given us two gloves, and I had only one."[21] In defense of dating white women, he joked that he did not know white women were that bad. He also pointed out that a current Yankee, Billy Martin, was dating Black women.[22] He had a method to his wild batting stance. Unable to master the low inside fastball, he used to flail his bat in that vulnerable spot so that the opposing pitcher would throw one high and outside, his preferred spot. Cheeky to be sure, but Vic Power was blessed with a biting sense of humor. Years later, he reflected on the Yankee rejection: "I wish someone would have explained to me about the racial problem. They just let me find out for myself. I gained so much respect for Jackie Robinson, Willie Mays, and other blacks who came before me."[23]

Yankees executives used reporter Dan Parker to spread a rumor that Power lacked brainpower. Actually, Vic had sufficient brainpower, absent blazing speed, to steal home plate twice in one game.[24] Yankees brass preferred the more pliable Elston Howard to become the first African American to join their team. Was he a showboat, as some critics charged? Yes, in what author Bill Rhoden aptly called "the Black Style." In his rookie year in Philadelphia—he was dispatched there in a multiplayer deal, in 1954—he hit a meager .255, using a lighter bat at the behest of coach Wally Moses.[25] The next year, Power went back to his 36-ounce bat and hit .319 and fielded brilliantly according to manager Lou Boudreau. In 1956, he moved to second base to make room for lumbering Yankees castoff Eddie Robinson, a southern racist who gave Larry Doby a hard time in 1948. Power hit a robust .309. Traded to the Cleveland Indians, he went on a 22-game hitting streak while playing all infield positions with a .992 fielding average, winning the first of seven consecutive Golden Glove Awards. Contrary to Eddie Robinson, Joe Gordon, who had welcomed Larry Doby in 1948, loved Vic Power in 1959. In his 12-year major league career, Power managed a .284 batting average, 125 homers, and 658 runs batted in. Power and New York Giants pitcher Rubén Gómez emerged as the two best Puerto Ricans in the Major Leagues during the 1950s. Voted to six All-Star games, Power spent his post-Major League years in his native Guaynabo, Puerto Rico, where he was honored with a ballpark in his name. He groomed many future major leaguers in the Dominican Republic as well as in his native land. He tutored Roberto Alomar, José Oquendo, Jerry Morales, and Willie Montañez. He also influenced Roberto Clemente, to whom he passed the baseball baton before succumbing to cancer at age 78 in 2005.[26]

Roberto Clemente

Clearly the greatest dark-skinned Latino African American baseball player, Roberto Clemente was the youngest of seven children born to parents Luisa and Melchior in Puerto Rico on August 18, 1934. Because his family was poor, Roberto worked odd jobs, including milk delivery, to supplement limited family income earned by his father, a sugarcane laborer.[27] Like many other youngsters of his generation, he loved baseball, yet in high school he played softball as a shortstop. As biographer David Maraniss points out, "there were no legal or overt racial barriers separating the races. Years before they integrated the majors, American blacks ... played in the Puerto Rican Winter League."[28] Monte Irvin befriended young Roberto when Clemente carried his suit bag to the locker room and secured a free ticket to the game. Monte became Roberto's idol.[29] When he transitioned to baseball, scouts noticed. Dodgers scout Al Campanis offered Clemente a $10,000 signing bonus after he finished high school. Like his other idol, Clemente started his professional career in Montréal. When the Dodgers failed to list Clemente on their 1954 40-man roster, he was claimed in a supplemental draft by the wily former Dodgers boss Branch Rickey.

Like his forerunner, Jackie Robinson, Clemente-Walker (his original surname) faced discrimination as a Black man as well as a Latino. Because he came from multi-racial Puerto Rico, Clemente found segregation deeply disturbing. "I didn't know about the stuff when I got here," he said. "I don't believe in color. I believe in people."[30] During spring training, he resided with a Black family in Fort Myers because he could not live among white teammates for seven years. He could not attend the annual golf outing at the local country clubs. Unable to eat in roadside restaurants, Black players travelled in their own station wagon, an experience that Clemente likened to imprisonment.[31] Stereotypes dogged him throughout his illustrious career. He was called a "showboat," a "hot dog," a malingerer who feigned illness, and worse. Actually, a near fatal auto accident caused many of his neck and back health issues as columnist George Will revealed in a book review of David Maraniss's brilliant biography of Roberto Clemente.[32] His broken English—phonetically imparted in press accounts—produced fodder for reportorial fun at his expense. Longtime Pirates broadcaster Bob Prince insisted on calling him Bobby rather than his preferred Roberto. Through it all, Clemente persevered, winning friends, fans, and belated recognition. Like his idol Jackie Robinson, he had a great impact. In 1960, for example, there were only 49 Blacks in the National League and

15 in the American League, up from 28 Black regulars in 1955, Clemente's rookie year.[33] In 1971, Clemente's Pirates fielded nine Blacks and Latinos in the starting lineup when Doc Ellis pitched.[34] The charismatic Clemente, at 5'11", possessed sufficient power to hit timely home runs and exciting triples (a total of 166), which catcher/telecaster Tim McCarver—the first catcher to lead the Major Leagues in triples—regarded as better than sex.[35]

In the 1960 World Series upset win over those "Damned Yankees," minus the intervention of the Faustian devil, Clemente excelled at bat, on the bases, and with a rocket for a right arm. In the crucial seventh game, Clemente beat out an infield single that prolonged the winning rally after Tony Kubek suffered a bad-bounce hit to his Adam's apple. Though Clemente managed hits in all seven games at a .471 clip and fielded with his usual grace under pressure, Yankees second baseman Bobby Richardson, in a losing cause, won MVP honors.[36] Glory denied in 1960 was glory confirmed in 1971, a banner year for Clemente and the Pirates. In the playoffs against the San Francisco Giants, he hit .333. The World Series gave Roberto a larger stage to display his greatness when it came to crunch time, going two for four in game one, two for five in game two. At home in Pittsburgh, he manufactured hits in all three games, including a three for four in game four. In game six, Clemente hit a triple in a loss to Baltimore pitching ace Jim Palmer. Game seven featured a Clemente home run that gave his team a lead that they never surrendered. The underdog Pirates rallied to defeat the Orioles of Baltimore with Clemente amassing a .414 batting average, leading the way to victory. In the locker room, as the TV cameras beamed the joy of victory throughout the land, Roberto Clemente, the MVP (the first Latino to win this award), thanked his parents back in Carolina, Puerto Rico, in Spanish. The all Black-Latino Pirates lineup also sent a triumphant message to people of color that, at least in the baseball, they had arrived. *Arriba! Viva Beisbol!*[37]

In 1972 he mustered his 3,000th hit in the season's last game against Mets pitcher Jon Matlack. Earlier that month I attended a Mets-Pirates game at Shea Stadium as Clemente neared the 3000-hit mark and everyone in the stands seemed to be rooting for him. In his Hall of Fame career, he won four National League batting titles and two World Series rings. This fan has vivid memories of his signature basket catches; his long, nearly perfect pegs from right field; and his liquid grace on the base paths. Reckless to a fault in baseball, he took risks off the field of dreams as well. Visited by premonitions of early death, Clemente faced the future without fear. Truly philanthropic, Clemente established multiple charities. On an errand of mercy carrying supplies to victims of a massive earthquake in Nicaragua, Clemente, pilot, and supplies crashed on December 31, 1972, a date that will live in sympathy. Only 38, Clemente died in the crash. Posthumously, one year later, he was inducted into the Hall of Fame. In his definitive biography of Clemente, David Maraniss highlights his subject's saintly status in Nicaragua, where he was headed when his rickety plane crashed shortly after takeoff; Puerto Rico, where he was born; and Venezuela, where he was revered by Ozzie Guillén and so many other Hispanic baseball fans.[38] The coda belongs to David Maraniss who invested his biography with exhaustive research, deep insight, and elegant prose:

The mythic aspects of baseball usually draw on clichés of the innocent past, the nostalgia for how things were. Fields of green. Fathers and sons. But Clemente's myth arcs the other way, to the future, not the past, to what people hope they can become. His memory is kept alive as a symbol of action and passion, not of reflection and longing. He broke racial and language barriers and achieved greatness and died a hero ... the classic definition is of someone who gives his life in the service of others, and that is exactly what Clemente did.[39]

SECTION FIVE

TENNIS

13

Althea Gibson, Arthur Ashe, Venus and Serena Williams, and Naomi Osaka

Tennis derives from the twelfth-century cloisters in France as Jeu de Paume. Identified with European royalty, the game morphed into the lawn tennis of Great Britain, still linked to the social elite. It was imported to the United States in 1872, where it remained tied to the leisure or upper class. This connection also applies to golf and polo. A certain code of genteel behavior informed elite sports with emphasis on self-restraint and good manners. This code remained in force until the advent of Jimmy Connors, Ilie Năstase, and John McEnroe, Tennis clubs serve as training grounds for social mobility as well as the accumulation of social capital.[1]

Thanks to a fairly new website, *The Undefeated*, readers can discover salient information about African American athletes in all sports, including tennis. Until the arrival of Ora Washington, Althea Gibson, Zina Garrison, and Arthur Ashe, tennis in America was dominated by white elites. Nevertheless, as author Rhiannon Walker demonstrates, black participation in tennis goes back 110 years plus. Reverend W.W. Walker established the first interstate tennis tournament for Blacks, won by Lincoln University's aptly named player Thomas Jefferson.[2] The Reverend Walker went on to win the next two annual tournaments. Tennis clubs were formed in Chicago in 1912 and Harlem in 1915. On Thanksgiving Day, 1916, the American Tennis Association (ATA) was founded in our nation's capital. Los Angeles followed in 1917. That same year, Lucy Diggs became the first African American women's national champion in any sport. Scotch Plains, New Jersey, witnessed the first Black-owned country club in the United States. Attempts to integrate tennis failed in 1929, so Black tennis had to operate in a parallel universe until the advent of Althea Gibson.[3]

On February 15, 2021, *The New York Times* reprinted an obituary of Jimmie McDaniel, who integrated tennis on July 29, 1940, in Harlem. Before 2,000 spectators McDaniel challenged world champion Don Budge. A nervous neophyte, McDaniel lost, 6–1, 6–2, but history was made. Belatedly, he was posthumously inducted into the Black Tennis Hall of Fame. ATA's historian Art Carrington has labored to rescue McDaniel from obscurity because, as he wrote, "people should know that Althea Gibson and Arthur Ashe didn't just pop out of the sky.... Before them, there was Jimmie McDaniel."[4] Now we have Serena Williams and Naomi Osaka. At 39 and 23, they reflect the aging megastar and the future tennis queen. They admire each other's game.[5] To echo a variant of a patronizing, male chauvinistic slogan for a cigarette commercial: "You've come a long way, baby." As two of the highest earning professional athletes—male or female—they have indeed come a long way, bringing other Black female athletes along for the ride to fame and fortune.

Althea Gibson

On August 25, 1927, Althea Gibson was born in South Carolina, the first child of sharecropper parents, Daniel and Annie. At age one, she was sent to live with her mother's sister in New York. Later, she lived with a Philadelphia-based aunt. Althea eventually rejoined her nuclear family, including three younger sisters and one brother, in New York City, where her father worked as a garage attendant. Gibson played hooky, shot pool, engaged in petty theft and street fights. As a youngster she enjoyed movies, stickball, softball, bowling, and paddle tennis.[6] At 12, Althea won the New York City paddleball title. Her neighbors raised money for Althea to join the Sugar Hill Tennis Club. In 1941, Althea won the American Tennis Association championship. She repeated in 1945. After one loss in 1946, she copped 10 straight titles.

She left school early, dressed casually, and self-identified as a tomboy. Her autobiography subtly suggests repressed lesbian feelings, but masculine toughness enabled her to survive the mean streets. She was less successful in warding off her father's violence. Once, after staying away for several nights, she was punched in the face by her father. When she called the police and showed them welts on her body, she was rewarded with another beating. No stranger to violence in Harlem, Gibson recalled one incident with a class bully who called her a "pig-faced bitch." With one punch Althea knocked out her opponent. Sullen at times, she was prone to bouts of depression as well as violence. Fortunately, Althea found an escape through tennis.

At 5'10½" and blessed with a strong physique, she excelled in sports "as the wildest tomboy you ever saw." Both physically and psychologically abused, she ran away from home finally to escape her father's wrath. Yet, she blamed herself for bad behavior. Althea found temporary sanctuary in a children's shelter and greater stability in her late teens at the home of sponsor/mentor Doctor Hubert Eaton. Plagued with "issues" throughout life, probably a result of an unhappy childhood, she found solace in sport. She evoked Paul Dunbar's poetic mask minus the smile to hide "human guile." Indeed, because of a "torn and bleeding heart," Gibson rarely smiled except for winning moments of tennis.

At the Sugar Oil Cosmopolitan Club, Gibson gained respect and elicited smiles from supporters when she won the junior championship of the all-black American Tennis Association. Groomed by Doctor Johnson, she applied hard work coupled with natural talent to break a long-standing color barrier. Johnson teamed up with Doctor Eaton to prepare Althea Gibson for college. A diamond in the rough, she needed lots of polish plus instruction in Emily Post etiquette for entry into the genteel sport of tennis. Gibson gained entry to Florida A&M University on an athletic scholarship. While there, Brough won several ATA tennis titles. Thanks to support from tennis legend Alice Marble, who wrote a blistering editorial in a United States Lawn Tennis Association magazine, wherein she attacked bigotry then regnant in American Lawn Tennis, Althea Gibson was invited to play at the South Orange Tennis Club in New Jersey. There, she became a color-barrier breaking pioneer. Subsequently, she competed against Wimbledon singles champion Louise Brough at the Forest Hills West Side Tennis Club. Althea led her opponent in a tie-breaking set, 1–6, 6–3, 7–6 when a rain delay stopped play. That delay probably helped a tired Brough to rally and win 9–7. Nevertheless, history was made with another stumbling block to racial integration in a major tournament removed. In a stellar career, Gibson became the first African American to gain top world ranking in tennis. She also was the first to win a Grand Slam title in 1956.[7] Her first victory in the French Open paired her with Angela Buxton, a British Jewish woman who became a lifelong friend. They repeated their doubles triumph at Wimbledon, where Althea also triumphed in the singles competition. Other victories ensued at the French Open in

Up from poverty and physical abuse in Harlem during the Great Depression, Althea Gibson became the Jackie Robinson of women's tennis, the first African American to win a Grand Slam tennis title. Unable to earn much money as a professional, Gibson turned to golf in 1964, at which she excelled but again saw little financial reward. Felled by a heart attack, Althea Gibson died on September 28, 2003. She is shown here, photographed by Fred Palumbo of the *World Telegram & Sun*, in 1955 (Library of Congress).

1956, Wimbledon in 1957, and the U.S. Open 1957 and 1958. In sum, Gibson won 11 titles: five singles, five doubles, and one in mixed doubles.

Gibson's relationship with Buxton invites further study. Both were marginalized in the world of white privilege in the 1950s as a Black woman with roots in South Carolina and a Jewish woman with roots in czarist Russia. They met and bonded in a then "third world" country—India—in 1955. Angela's coach paired them in doubles competition one year later. In 1956, they won in Paris and made the finals at Wimbledon. After the traditional Wimbledon Ball was over, Buxton was scheduled to compete in both singles and doubles finals. With her mother Violet in tow, Angela Buxton showed up for tickets. Rejected, they were informed that a sell-out precluded their attendance. They left, sensing pervasive anti–Semitism at work, threatening to boycott the finals. To avoid a colossal blunder, tickets were found.[8] Angela Buxton realized that Althea Gibson had incurred comparable insults on her road to glory.

Althea Gibson benefited from Cold War politics. The U.S. State Department sponsored goodwill tours to boost American capitalist values in order to thwart Soviet propaganda regarding their charge of rampant racism in the United States accentuated by the brutal lynching of Emmett Till in 1955. Gibson went on a joyful tour of Asia on the government's dime prior to joining Angela Buxton for glory in England.[9] Yet, Althea declined to be a role model for her race. She deemed it a burden, an attitude that offended fans. Unwilling to emulate Jackie Robinson, she just wanted to be a regular tennis player. With these words, Althea explained her stand: "I do not beat the drums for any special cause, not even the cause of the Negro in the United States.… I try to stay clear of political involvements and make my way as Althea Gibson, private individual."[10] Thus, she opted for avoidance.

Billy Jean King likened her to Jackie Robinson, in that she never backed down. After her triumphant return from Wimbledon, Althea Gibson was greeted with a ticker-tape parade in 1957. One year later, she turned pro, adding new honors and titles, but little money. Multi-talented, she took up singing and cut a record in 1964. Too old for tennis, she turned to golf. Again, she excelled with little payoff. Now, too old for the grind of pro golf, she retired in 1978. Subsequent comeback attempts failed. In later years, she directed women's sports in New Jersey's Essex County. In 1976, Gibson was appointed New Jersey State Athletic Commissioner, the first African American in that distinguished role. She even tried politics when she ran for state senate but wound up second in the Democratic primary.

Ill health punctuated by cerebral hemorrhages in the 1980s and two strokes in 1992 brought her down physically and financially. In a letter to Angela Buxton in 1995 she considered suicide.[11] Fortunately, her old tennis buddy stepped up to raise $1 million for Gibson's sustenance. A heart attack in 2003 ended her life at age 76. Althea Gibson was buried near her first husband (she was married twice, divorced twice), Will Darken. She was mourned by many and praised by several sportswriters. She was honored in song ("Althea") by the Grateful Dead.

In a perceptive study, Mary Jo Festle vividly describes the hurdles that Althea Gibson had to overcome. The Black community frowned on masculine female athletes, for starters. That bias cut across class and geographic lines with middle-class opposition and rural women eager to participate. Coaches tried to impose a dress code on female athletes. Because Althea loved to play football and baseball, she was regarded as some kind of "freak." In tennis, she played a man's game, combining a powerful serve with an aggressive volley. Sportswriters like Paul Gallico demeaned female athletes including major stars like Mildred "Babe" Didrikson. Black female athletes fared no better, perhaps even worse. Plagued by such obstacles, Gibson found her better self in sports. True, she wore the mask fashioned by poet Paul Lawrence Dunbar to defend herself against the recurrent criticism by Black sportswriters. Thus, Gibson became a pioneer on two fronts: one as an African American, the other as a powerful Black female. Despite her failures in business and in marriage, she paved the way for the rise of Arthur Ashe and the Williams sisters.

Years after her death, thanks largely to the 20 years of lobbying efforts by Billie Jean King, the United States Lawn Tennis Association planned to unveil a statue honoring Althea Gibson. Just in time for day one of the U.S. Open in Forest Hills on September 5, 2019, it was unveiled. Sculptor Eric Goulder formed five granite blocks into a monumental tribute to Althea Gibson, whom Billy Jean King lauded as "our Jackie Robinson."[12] Doubles partner and loyal friend Angela Buxton, true to British lingo, declared, "It's about bloody time." She confided in Sally Jacobs, author of a forthcoming biography of Althea Gibson: "She [Althea] was completely isolated. I was too, because of being Jewish. So it was a good thing we found one another."[13]

Gibson's inscription reads: "I hope that I have accomplished just one thing: that I have been a credit to tennis and to my country." No mention of race adorns the impressive structure. Sculptor Eric Goulder opined: "Althea reoriented the world and changed our perception of what is possible. We are still struggling, but she broke the ground." Jimmy Cannon's paean to Joe Louis applies to Althea Gibson after all. She was indeed a credit to her race—the human race.

Arthur Ashe

Arthur Ashe's road to glory was paved with similar obstacles to the one trod by Althea Gibson. Born in a segregated city—Richmond, Virginia—on July 6, 1943, Ashe did grow up in a middle-class family. His mother, however, died when Arthur was six years old after giving birth to his brother, Johnnie. She was 27 years old. His father, Arthur Ashe, Sr., encouraged his two sons to study as well as to play. Because Arthur Jr. had a scrawny body, earning the moniker "Bones," he was an easy target for bullies until he discovered tennis. He confessed to being "too small for any sport but tennis." "My father would not let me play football because of my size," he said.[14] An aptly named Black tennis player, Ron Charity, tutored Ashe in the basics of tennis. Dr. Robert Johnson, who had also helped Althea Gibson, took Ashe under wing for seven years, from 1953 to 1960. Following a pattern of accommodation, Dr. Johnson infused his protégé with core values of sportsmanship, etiquette, and a "cool," "grace under pressure" demeanor. At the Richmond Racket Club, Ashe learned about race and class. Akin to Jackie Robinson's initial encounter with Branch Rickey in which he was urged to follow a Christ-like scenario of turning both cheeks,

Arthur Ashe wrote: "I was burning with resentment inside but Dr. Johnson had cautioned me not to show anger."[15] Ashe won his first title as the first Black youngster to play in the Maryland boys championship and stunned the tennis world by winning the national juniors championship in Michigan.[16]

Since Ashe could not compete against white players in Virginia, he moved to St. Louis under a new coach, Richard Handlin, who could arrange interracial matches in Missouri. Still slender at 6'1" as a high school senior, Ashe learned quickly to master a serve and volley strategy. In 1961, he began to compete against white players, which caught the attention of *Sports Illustrated* and UCLA after he won the national juniors indoor title in 1963. Granted a legitimate tennis scholarship to UCLA, Ashe picked up valuable pointers from tennis legend Pancho Gonzales and coach J. D. Morgan. During his UCLA years, Ashe enrolled in their ROTC program, thereby becoming an officer as well as a gentleman. Ashe seethed when he was forced to sit out one tournament that barred Blacks. Despite these racist roadblocks, he led UCLA to an NCAA title in 1965.

The first African American to be named to the U.S. Davis Cup team in 1963, Ashe garnered glory by winning the NCAA singles and doubles titles as an undergrad at UCLA. Although Roy Emerson defeated him in the Australian finals two years running, 1966 and 1967, in 1968 Ashe won both the U.S. Amateur title and the U.S. Open title, earning recognition as the first Black male to win that double crown. Ironically, because he was still an amateur, Ashe had to waive $14,000 in prize money and settle for a $20-per-day expense allowance. That same year, Ashe led the U.S. Davis Cup team to victory, avenging prior losses to the Aussies. After leading the United States to a third consecutive Davis Cub win, Ashe turned pro. In March 1971, he lost the Australian Open to Ken Rosewall. Ever resilient, he bounced back to take the French Open men's doubles. In the U.S. Open, Ashe lost to "nasty" Ilie Năstase after leading two sets to one. In the ceremony following the match, the gentle Ashe vented his long-suppressed anger by calling attention to Năstase's crude behavior, which evidently got under his skin during the match.

As a tennis administrator, Ashe led a boycott of Wimbledon, showing a long-suppressed rebellious side. After South Africa refused to permit him to play because of racial constraints, the organizers of the African Open rescinded the ban. Though Arthur lost the final to another "nasty"—Jimmy Connors—he won the doubles with Tom Okker, a Dutch Jew. Amid controversy over his decision to play in South Africa, Ashe's rationale for this reversal was designed to educate the apostles of apartheid. Responding to blowback from critics, Ashe rejoined the boycott movement. Controversy dogged Ashe when Connors sued him and the American Tennis Association, which Ashe headed as president.

Tennis gave Ashe, a "gentle militant," a "social platform." Author Damon Thomas added that golf and tennis were country club sports constituting a matrix of WASP elite culture, a concept deftly delineated in several studies by social historian E. Digby Baltzell.[17] Derived from the nineteenth-century Victorian era mores, real gentlemen exemplify self-restraint, strong character, and *noblesse oblige*. The set of values coupled with rigorous work ethic seemed to validate social Darwinism (the subject of a brilliant dissertation by Richard Hofstadter) and justify white supremacy. Evidently Ashe's mentor Dr. Johnson imparted these tenets—including deference to the power structure—to African American youth as a roadmap for success in a segregated society—in short, accommodation. Initially, Ashe embodied this formula to (double?) fault. It appears this subordinate posture caused deeply suppressed anger and stifled aggression. Therefore when the "Bad Boy" from Romania, Ilie Năstase, flouted convention with his boorish behavior and recurrent rudeness, it psyched out Ashe in the 1972 U.S. Open, resulting in a five-set loss. Ashe's stoic behavior stood in stark contrast to "bad boys" Jimmy Connors and John McEnroe.

A brewing confrontation between "good" and "evil" came to a head in the 1975 Wimbledon Open competition. In six prior confrontations, Ashe never won. Employing a unique strategy, featuring a change of speed, frequent lobs, and pinpoint drop shots, Ashe won the first two sets 6–0, 6–1. Connors rallied to win the third set, 7–6. Trailing 0–3 in the fourth set, Ashe rallied this time to win game, set, match 6–4. His chip and dunk shots invite comparison with Ali's "rope-a-dope" tactics in Zaire to reclaim the heavyweight crown. Ashe's upset victory evoked praise and sparked a brilliant study comparing Clark Graebner and Arthur Ashe in the semifinals match in 1968 in the U.S. Open.[18]

Originally averse to social protest, Ashe extolled the work ethic and deplored laziness. In sync with Booker T. Washington's advocacy of a bootstrap mentality,

Arthur Ashe flashes his signature backhand in this photograph from Rotterdam in 1975. That same year, he beat the heavily favored Jimmy Connors in the 1975 Wimbledon finals, achieving lasting fame. Ashe went on to write sports history, produce documentary films, and advocate for civil rights. After news broke that he had become infected with HIV during a blood transfusion, Ashe used his platform to address the need for improved healthcare. He was only 49 when he died. Photo by Rob Bogaerts (National Archives of the Netherlands, the Hague).

he played the game of life, safely. In his first autobiography in 1967, he questioned civil rights tactics. He confessed: "I am not a marcher. I am not a sign carrier."[19] At this stage, Ashe was compliant. His white admirers, including reporters, had been more comfortable with Arthur because of "his cool demeanor" in stark contrast to Ali, Carlos, and Smith.[20] What produced a change of heart in Ashe? Perhaps, Harry Edwards's effort to boycott the 1968 Olympics provided the spur. Clearly, the increased presence of African Americans in professional sports, especially in baseball, football, and basketball, had a dual effect. While many athletes of color slid into complacency, others, like John Carlos, Tommie Smith, and Lew Alcindor, adopted a different attitude. Arthur Ashe finally channeled stored-up aggression outward toward apartheid in South Africa. His 25-game winning streak gave him a public platform, because, as he understood, people "don't listen to losers." In 1968, Ashe angrily suggested that South Africa invited a nuclear attack, yet accepted Cliff Drysdale's offer to play tennis in a place that Alan Paton wrote about in *Cry, the Beloved Country*. Ashe's visa application to South Africa had been denied due to his race and previous remarks denouncing apartheid in concert with Muhammad Ali, Bill Russell, Jim Brown, Curt Flood, and Bill White. A staunch supporter of Nelson Mandela, Ashe was arrested outside the South African embassy in Washington, D.C., in 1985.

Finally, after three rejections, Ashe's effort to expel South Africa from the International Lawn Tennis Federation hit pay dirt, forcing dramatic changes in that country. Ashe was less successful in preserving his health. Because of heart trouble, a family trait, he retired from tennis in 1980 at age 37. During his career, Ashe garnered 33 singles victories and scored 818 wins. Undaunted, he moved on to other fields of endeavor as historian, writer, activist, and public intellectual. Insisting that Black youngsters should spend more time and effort in libraries advancing their education and less time and energy on playgrounds, Ashe wrote editorials in the *New York Times* and the *Washington Post*, winning adherents while generating debate. Significantly and ironically, he wrote books that highlighted African American heroes in sports. That mission inspired this writer to follow suit in that noble quest for that "hard road to glory." In a review of Ashe's several volumes of sports history, author David Halberstam conceded that Arthur Ashe, while not a professional historian, penned a positive assessment, deeming his work "nothing less than remarkable. His accomplishment is monumental."[21] *Nation* critic Nicholas Mills blamed disappointing book sales on "dreary prose" and, pointedly, "general disdain for sports history in both the academic world and the broader arena of public affairs." The haughty critic is wrong on both counts. Ashe's prose is far from dreary, and sports history has acquired cachet plus cash ever since Jim Bouton's *Ball Four* and Roger Kahn's *The Boys of Summer* became blockbuster hits. Today, sports history is, in one word, "hot." And, as author David Higgins points out, "Arthur Ashe accomplished a great many things in his short life," including his literary efforts.[22]

In 1979 Ashe suffered a heart attack that required two surgeries, one to repair his heart and another in 1983 to repair the damage caused by the first surgery. Unfortunately, the second surgery caused more, indeed fatal complications because it involved a tainted blood transfusion containing the AIDS virus. Stoically accepting his fate after the HIV diagnosis in 1985, Ashe went public on April 8, 1992, and remained active. For supporting Haitian refugees in a public protest, he was arrested. He chided Michael Jordan for his neutrality on social issues and lamented the lamb-like silence of other high-profile athletes who claimed to be quietly working for social change. Neither quietly nor gently, Ashe entered into that "good night" of Dylan Thomas on February 6, 1993, at age 49. Before he died, however, Ashe videotaped a message on AIDS for the Connecticut Forum on that subject, warning youngsters to avoid unsafe sex and promoting education of the public on this dread disease through the Arthur Ashe Foundation, that he had created. Ashe finished his memoir, *Days of Grace*, just one week before his death.[23]

Author Damian Thomas expertly analyzes the dilemma that faced Ashe and other African American athletes. Succinctly, he summarizes the paths taken by various trailblazers prior to Ashe and concludes that he belongs in that select company. A monument celebrating the life of Arthur Ashe was placed on Richmond's Monument Avenue, incongruous alongside Confederates who fought to maintain slavery, on July 10, 1997.

Venus Williams and Serena Williams

With the arrival of a new generation, the road to glory proved more accessible for African American athletes. The Williams sisters benefited from predecessors Althea Gibson and Arthur Ashe. Born on June 17, 1980, and September 16, 1981, respectively, Venus and Serena enjoyed a stable childhood with a premium on strict control. As their father, Richard, wrote,[24] "I was born in Shreveport, Louisiana. Wimbledon, with its white rule and its traditions and its royalty was the other side of the world." That realization powered his will to rise and to steer his gifted daughters on the correct course. He dubbed them "Ghetto Cinderellas," capturing their meteoric rise from humble roots. Authors R. Pierre Rodgers and Ellen B. Drogin Rodgers regard this formulation as a somewhat imaginative urban legend.[25] The sisters grew up in Compton, California, where they were homeschooled at one time and raised in their mother's faith as Jehovah's Witnesses. Richard served as their primary coach, which spectators would witness at their matches. Each daughter showed unusual talent when they both played in their first tournament at age four. Richard presciently predicted that Serena—who was meaner at age nine—would become better than Venus, age 10.[26]

The Williams family moved to Florida for improved training facilities. Evidently, the move succeeded, as the girls turned pro at age 14. Venus had won all 63 of her tennis matches on the junior circuit by the age of 12.[27] Though unseeded, Venus reached the U.S. Open finals in 1997. Richard, who incurred insinuations that he was a control freak, justified his behavior with these words: "I was not going to let my girls be swept into a culture of drugs and bad people. Too many young black girls in the ghetto got pregnant because they did not have parents to avoid it. ... I didn't let my girls play with dolls. ... I didn't want Venus or Serena to believe that motherhood was the end goal of their lives."[28] If somewhat overbearing, this strategy proved quite effective.

In 2000, Venus won her first Grand Slam event at Wimbledon, taking the singles title. Fifteen months younger, Serena beat Venus in the semis and went on to take the U.S. Open in 1999 with a victory over Martina Hingis. Together, the "Cinderella Sisters" won the Wimbledon doubles that same year. Between 2000 and 2016, Venus won five Wimbledon singles titles, Serena seven. Both sisters also won gold medals in the 2008 and the 2012 Olympics. Ranked at the top of women's tennis years, Serena explained her success vis-à-vis Venus this way:[29]

> I'm quicker. Like at the net I'm really quick. But Venus can hit any ball. Venus is the type of player that will stab at person, draw back and stab, and draw until they eventually die. I would shoot 'em and then go about my business.

Winning with a killer's deadly aim either way evoked criticism. The Williams sisters have been described as aloof and arrogant. In his role as commentator, John McEnroe claimed with unintentional irony that the sisters lacked respect, which equated to the proverbial pot calling the kettle black. Coming from the "Bad Boy of Tennis," of all people, that assessment combines incredulity with chutzpah. A more credible source, Martina Navratilova, rebuked Venus and Serena "for cheating the game and themselves." Martina also attacked their character and derided their lack of humility. Was this a just critique or animated by envy with a touch of racism? Indeed, subtle racism is still operative, along with the overt variety, as sports sociologist Stuart Hill cogently argues. The Williams sisters have experienced both forms.

The Rodgerses' article—from which derives much of what we know about racial undercurrents buffeting the Williams sisters—focuses on one significant event for illumination. It occurred during a tournament in March 2001. Because of tendonitis in her right knee, Venus had to drop out before facing her sister in the semifinals. Speculation spread that Richard Williams had orchestrated this departure in favor of Serena. Consequently, during the final, which Serena won, and after, the crowd booed, unleashing a stream of invective, laced with the "N" word, highly racist in content. For Mr. Williams, it was a wake-up call as he staunchly defended his daughters against charges of collusion. Serena's defeated opponent, Kim Clijsters, a Belgian teenager, gained crowd approval, rewarded with resounding cheers for every winning shot. At the winner's podium, Serena maintained her poise, gracefully: "I would like to just thank everybody who supported me and if you didn't, I love you anyway and I'll see you next time."[30]

Facing criticism from rivals like Martina Hingis, who spewed venom at the sisters more than once, the Williams sisters grounded their rhetoric, the Rodgerses contend, in racial rhetoric. They deftly employed a dismissive strategy deferring to their father for defense as they continued, until recently, to pile up victories on the courts of tennis if not in the arena of public opinion. Later Serena married Alex Ohanian, founder of Reddit, and gave birth to a daughter, taking a brief leave of absence from play to breastfeed Alexis Olympia Ohanian for six months.[31] After a slow start in regaining her once unbeatable game, Serena won the 2018 French Open in a grueling match, but victories have not come easily since. Regardless of where the future takes the Williams sisters, they have made their mark with avoidance off the courts and aggression on as the model responses to their roles as "marginal" heroes who gained gold and glory in their successful careers.

Overshadowed by her younger sister when Serena forged ahead to become *numera una* in tennis, Venus did not sulk. She acknowledged Serena's mastery "as the greatest player in the world." Then she explained her significance as a true hero in these words[32]:

> Being the big sister meant that, when I became world No. 1 in 2002, I wasn't just world No. 1. I was also the first black American woman to reach No. 1. And it meant that I had to carry with me the importance of what I had accomplished; And I was honored to do that.
>
> Being the big sister meant that when my little sister made her professional debut, I became a lot of new things to her—her colleague, her business partner, her doubles partner. But I was still, first and foremost, the one thing I had always been: her family. I was her protector—her first line of defense against outside forces. And I cherished that.

Venus Williams was also her father's daughter, who fulfilled his dreams and advanced his political agenda. Both sisters continue to play, Serena on a higher level. In 2017, at age 36, Serena became a wife and mother. *Times* reporter Karen Crouse marvels at Serena's career and multitasking ability, especially her advocacy of working mothers everywhere. At the Australian Open, Serena survived a grueling match with a 22-year-old Aryna Sabalenka, 6–4, 2–6, 6–4. One shy of Margaret Court's record of 24 major singles titles, Serena forges ahead for the love of the game with the support of her big sister, Venus, and husband, Alexis Ohanian.[33] And her beat

Serena Williams about to backhand the ball at Wimbledon in 2012. Sister Venus became the first African American woman to reach #1 in the Open Era, but Serena would soon establish herself as a dominant force in the sport and perhaps the greatest of all time (courtesy Katherine Shann).

goes on! After extolling her virtuosity, or *arete* as the ancient Greeks referred to excellence, Gerald Marzorati concludes his illuminating article on Serena with this insight: "A match or tournament, like life, is more than its outcome. Let's take our last measures of Serena in moments."[34]

Serena lost the Australian Open semifinal to Naomi Osaka 3–6, 4–6. Unlike their last encounter, Serena avoided a meltdown and graciously congratulated her rival. Still short of her goal to tie Margaret Court's 24 Grand Slams, she will soldier on. Jennifer Brady, who lost the final to Naomi Osaka, paid homage to Serena, the aging star, as the G.O.A.T, implying that Osaka is not there yet in these parting words: "But I don't think ... she's a God. I think Serena is. Maybe she'll [Naomi] get there, I don't know."[35]

Naomi Osaka

I had no intention to write about Naomi Osaka until I discovered her mixed racial heritage as well as her identification with "Black Lives Matter." The highest paid female athlete who earned $37.4 million in 2019 refused to play her scheduled semifinal match against Elise Mertens in the Cincinnati Western & Southern Open tournament on August 26, 2020. She forcefully explained her refusal in a Twitter message[36]:

> However, before I am an athlete, I am a black woman. And as a black woman I feel as though there are more important matters at hand that need immediate attention, rather than watching me play tennis ... but I can get a conversation started in a majority white sport I consider that a step in the right direction. Watching the continued genocide of Black people at the hand of the police is honestly making me sick to my stomach. I'm exhausted of having a new hashtag pop up every few days and I'm extremely tired of having this same conversation over and over again. When will it ever be enough? #JacobBlake, #BreonnaTaylor, #ElijahMcclain, #GeorgeFloyd.

Born to a Haitian father and a Japanese mother in Osaka, Japan, on October 17, 1997, Naomi and family moved to Valley Stream, Long Island to live with her father's parents. Leonard Francois, her dad, followed the pattern of Richard Williams in teaching his daughters after watching the French Open in 1999, when the Williams sisters, ages 18 and 17, won the doubles tennis title.[37] Osaka's parents used the Williamses' playbook to nurture future tennis stars. Rigorous tennis training during the day was supplemented by homeschooling at night. In order to secure better training facilities, the Francois-Osaka family moved to Florida in 2006. Much like the Williams sisters, Mari dominated their practice games until Naomi enjoyed a growth spurt and she vaulted ahead of her older sister. Carrying dual Japanese-American citizenship, Naomi now identifies as Black and Asian. Subsequently, the family opted to surrender American citizenship in order for Naomi to represent Japan in tournament play. Though the family denied a financial motive behind this decision, a large Japanese fan base and endorsements continue to fill family coffers. Like the Williams sisters, Naomi and Mari are extremely close and play doubles too.[38]

Winning the U.S. Open title in 2018 from her idol, Serena Williams, triggered mixed feelings: elation as well as sadness. Serena's meltdown proved embarrassing. Osaka captured the Australian Open in 2019, giving her two consecutive Grand Slam titles. When fans booed the winner at that event, Serena consoled Naomi. Their friendly rivalry continued. Even in the semifinal of the 2021 Australian Open, where Naomi's 6–3, 6–4 victory denied Serena her quest to tie Marjorie Court's record of 24 Grand Slam wins in tennis, marking perhaps the inevitable decline of a tennis great and the ascent of her successor, cordiality before and after this dramatic event prevailed. Prior to the match Serena said: "I think we both have had closure. And we have reached out to each other. I have definitely reached out, and ... she's a great competitor and she's a cool cat."[39]

During her drive for the U.S. Open title, Naomi Osaka wore seven masks, honoring the seven victims of racial injustice and police brutality for each match, inspired by Serena Williams. Given voice by the 39-year-old role model, Osaka offered her appreciation in these words: "Honestly, she's like a living icon. I would not be here without her."[40] So, the baton has been passed, although Serena, unwilling to retire, will pursue Margaret Court's record of 24 Grand Slam victories. Naomi, ascendant, beat Jennifer Brady 6–4, 6–3 for the title. She is now a perfect four for four in Grand Slam finals. She is ranked number two behind Australian Ashleigh Barty. Though Osaka does not expect to win all the time, she hopes for more ups than downs.[41] Based on her heroic efforts in Australia, it would be unwise to bet against her. Mental issues, however, have impeded Naomi's progress, calling attention to this recurring problem among athletes today.

PART SIX

BASKETBALL

14

The Harlem Renaissance Five

When James Naismith started the ball rolling in 1891 in response to the mission of "Muscular Christianity," he could not have imagined in his wildest dreams—assuming a missionary is permitted wild dreams—that his invention of peach-basket basketball would capture global attention. Basketball is the city game with universal appeal, second only to soccer in popularity. All that you need, Bill Bradley opined, is "a ball, a rim, and imagination."[1] Unlike all other sports in America, this one emerged from native soil. No myth hangs over its origins, though its creation, like Athena from the head of Zeus, sprang from the brain of Dr. Naismith, designed to impart core values: competition, teamwork, health, excellence, joy, and agility. One hundred thirty years later these values remain germane.

When religious and moral leaders feared the impact of urbanization and immigration on the social order, they turned to sports for relief. When minority groups—Catholics, Jews, and Blacks—wanted to prove their mettle, they joined YMCA, YWCA, CYO, and YMHA teams, respectively. When poor, inner-city youngsters needed a vehicle to channel their aggression and enter mainstream American culture, basketball became a driving force. In a land still rife with racism, basketball provided a proving ground as well as a refuge for Black athletes. Whether in Pittsburgh or New York City, these athletes carved out a community and built self-esteem as Professor Susan Rayl's excellent dissertation on the Harlem Renaissance Five attests.

Long Island University's quintet set an intercollegiate record of 43 consecutive wins over a two-year span and produced the first Black hoopster, William "Dolly" King, to integrate pro basketball with the Rochester Royals in the fledgling National Basketball League in 1946 and the Scranton Miners in 1948. King excelled in baseball and football too. LIU coach Clair Bee recalled that King played football at Ebbets Field on Thanksgiving Day, 1939 in the afternoon and rushed to Madison Square Garden for a basketball game that night.[2] After the two major basketball leagues merged in 1950, Chuck Cooper, Earl Lloyd, and Nat "Sweetwater" Clifton followed Dolly King's precedent when they signed pro contracts with Boston, Syracuse, and New York City franchises.

When scandal rocked the college basketball world in 1951, primarily in New York City, the center of hoopdom shifted to the South, the West, and to professional games. Black athletes played a pivotal role in that transformation and rehabilitation of "the City Game."

The Early Days

Basketball blossomed in urban America. Less expensive than other team sports, minimal costs went into shorts, tee shirts, sneakers, and a ball. Youngsters—especially the children of immigrants—gravitated to round ball. It was particularly popular among children living in densely populated spaces. In 1891, Doctor James Naismith invented this uniquely indigenous American game to bridge the fall football season and the spring/summer season of baseball. Naismith aimed to foster core Christian values and to offer a safe channel for aggression for youngsters during the winter months. Ironically, basketball attracted Jewish youth, who became obsessed with this nascent sport. When racial segregation pervaded all social-athletic networks, Blacks had to establish their counterculture of basketball before integration became the norm, buttressed by the law. They enjoyed the sport in local YMCAs and CYOs.

The first pro game on record, according to Susan Rayl, was played in Trenton, New Jersey, on November 7, 1896. Trenton's team defeated Brooklyn's YMCA club, 16 to 1. Each player earned $15. Spectators spent 25 cents to sit and 15 cents to stand.[3] According to author Robert Peterson, in *Cages to Jump Shots*, the National Basketball League formed in 1898 with a reserve clause, but with no salary cap.[4] Two Black teams participated, one in Pittsburgh owned by Cumberland Posey, the other in New York City run by Will Madden. Unlucky in hoops but successful in the numbers operation in Pittsburgh, where he starred in athletics and rose in business, Cum Posey became a baseball mogul in Negro League baseball with various teams situated in "Steel City."[5]

Fortunately, an immigrant from the British West Indies, Robert L. Douglas, developed the first successful Black basketball team, according to Professor Susan Rayl whose masterful study of the Harlem Renaissance Five provided my principal source of information. Born in St. Kitts in 1882, Bob Douglas came to New York City in 1902. Working as a messenger and porter, this elegant entrepreneur formed the Sports Field Club in 1908. Initially engaged in soccer and cricket, the club under the aegis of Douglas later branched out to track and basketball.[6] The Renaissance Casino, owned by Jews as well as Blacks, opened on January 8, 1923. Black v. white contests proved a popular trifecta as building business, entertainment, and pride with Leone Monte, Hy Monte, Zack Anderson, Clarence "Fats" Jenkins, and Frank Forbes (later, the first Black boxing judge).[7]

Douglas synthesized ballroom dancing with winning basketball at a venue called the Harlem Renaissance, which served as a fitting moniker—the Rens—for this pioneer team. On November 23, 1923, the Rens won their first game 28–22 over an all-white team called the Collegiate Five.[8] They continued to play local teams, the Visitations, Whirlwinds, SPHAS (South Philadelphia Hebrew Association), and the Original Celtics.[9]

Black basketball benefited from the Great Migration, which accelerated during World War I. Thanks to an innovative developer, Phil Payton, Harlem experienced a cultural renaissance featuring writers, actors, and musicians like Langston Hughes, Zora Neale Hurston, Paul Robeson, and Duke Ellington.[10] Sports added to the mix in dance halls. For 50 cents to one dollar one could buy an exciting combination on Saturday night. Basketball games began at 9 p.m., sandwiched between dances.

The Original Celtics, arguably the most popular and successful early quintet, had electrifying players led by Nat Holman and Joe Lapchick who gave the Rens their stiffest competition. Though bitter rivals on the court, they were friends off the court because "skin color," one player noted, "didn't matter."[11] Finally, the Rens defeated their rivals in their fifth try in December 1928, 37–30 as 5,000 attendees cheered while 1,000 other fans were unable to get in. Significantly, the Rens roster contained multi-talented athletes in other sports. In 1926, for example, Eyre Saitch won the ATA title in tennis. Many Rens also starred in baseball; Jenkins, Yancey, Holt, and Fiall played both sports in the 1920s, as did Wynn and John Isaacs in the 1930s. King and George Crowe repeated "double duty" in the 1940s. Operating on a handshake, rather than written contracts, Bob Douglas incurred problems with players who "jumped" franchises for higher salaries. He also demanded a rigorous standard of conduct from his players who, he insisted, had to serve as role models. Those who could or would not conform were fired. For breaking rules, Fiall departed in 1928.[12]

Celtics owner Jim Furey tried to steal several Rens, forcing Douglas to use written contracts. Facing the Great Depression, the Rens became a travelling team. They borrowed the Celtics' style with quick passing, floor work, accurate shooting, tough defense, and the employment of reserves against weaker opponents. As a well-conceived ploy for continuous business, they never ran up the winning scores. Rens star John Isaacs, who befriended this author in 2000, is cited in Dr. Rayl's article presented at a conference on "Basketball: The City Game," which I co-hosted at St. Francis College of Brooklyn in 2001, saying that the Rens never aimed to crush their opponents because they wanted a rematch. They needed a 10-point lead, however, to minimize referee bias.[13]

The Rens' "golden era" was built around 6'5" Willie Smith, who joined the team in 1932. Flanked by "Fats" Jenkins, James "Pappy" Ricks, Eyre Saitch, Bill Yancey, Johnny Holt, and Charles "Tarzan" Cooper, the Rens compiled a 473–49 record, including an 88-game winning streak in 1932–33 that still stands.[14] During the 1930s, the Rens often played in the Midwest while based in Chicago. To avoid humiliating encounters spurred by racial discrimination, they stayed in Negro sections during road trips. Bad weather often resulted in cancellations and loss of income. Despite occasional switches or "jumps" to other teams, most of the Rens proved loyal. Only 60 men wore the Rens uniform in a 26-year period.[15] To counter "hard times," the Rens played benefits, donating proceeds to worthy causes like the Boy Scouts of Harlem, highlighted by a Cab Calloway performance, the Scottsboro Defense Fund, the American Jewish Congress, and the Welfare Fund of Philadelphia Sports Writers, all in 1935.[16]

In 1933, the Rens departed on a dangerous journey. They travelled south, where they played Black college teams at Tuskegee Institute and Alabama State, drawing white as well as Black fans. Staying in Black college dorms, colored branches of the YMCA, or with Black families provided safety, but travel on the back roads in the segregated South invited trouble, which the Rens managed to avoid. The Rens travelled in southern comfort with the acquisition of an air-cooled bus called the Blue Goose. John "Wonder Boy" Isaacs joined the Rens in 1936 as a 6'3" guard. A major contributor to team success, he was praised by owner/coach Bob Douglas as having "the most natural ability of any man ever to play for me."[17] In 1938, they added pop and belligerence when Clarence "Pop" Gates, a graduate of Manhattan's Benjamin Franklin High School, joined the team. A great defender with a deadeye set shot who had an excellent drive to the basket, he and Isaacs served as outstanding guards on arguably the best basketball team in America.[18] During this era, another Black team began to challenge the Rens' supremacy. Abe Saperstein's Harlem Globetrotters—misnamed because they were based in Chicago—borrowed the Harlem rubric, but not their style of play. Saperstein's team stressed entertainment, resorting to stereotyped, indeed clownish behavior. Twelve teams were invited to the first annual professional tournament to determine which would be crowned number one in the country. In game one the Rens defeated the New York Yankees, then beat the Globetrotters in the second round, 27 to 23. The finals pitted the Oshkosh All-Stars against the Rens. By a score of 34 to 29, the Rens emerged as the number one team in America in 1939.[19]

The Globetrotters turned the tables on the Rens, 37–36, one year later in the quarterfinals. By defeating the Chicago Bruins 31 to 28 in the finals, they emerged as the number one team. They repeated their success in 1944, beating the Rens 37 to 29. Low scores were prevalent in the early days of professional basketball due to a number of conditions including the center jump after each basket until the 1938–39 season, the absence of a time constraint regarding shot-taking, and the desire to maintain a lead until time expired. The Globetrotters dominated serious games until the 1950s by recruiting superior talent, going on global jaunts, and engaging white fans with superb skills and entertaining antics, often to the detriment of dignity.[20]

During World War II, Bob Douglas and the Rens joined the war effort. Douglas served on the local draft board in Harlem while his players worked in war industries by day and played basketball at night. Following the Harlem Riots in 1943, "Douglas used sport as a vehicle for easing racial tensions" (Professor Rayl points out). The Rens' fortune ebbed in another national tournament in 1947, when they lost to George Mikan's Minneapolis Lakers, despite fine performances from Nat ""Sweetwater" Clifton, Dolly King, and Pop Gates, who joined the team that year. Douglas then yielded control to Eric Illidge and saw his former franchise join the National Basketball League, the first Black team admitted to a major league. They finished last. Basketball mogul Ned Irish spurned the Rens' effort to join the fledgling Basketball Association even though Knicks coach Joe Lapchick heartily supported the Rens' bid.[21]

Author Rayl cites a major contribution of the Rens, echoed later by hoopster turned author Kareem Abdul-Jabbar: the team sent two of the four first African American players into the newly formed National Basketball Association (NBA) in 1950, namely Nat Clifton and Hank DeZonie. Rayl concludes that they "were real Renaissance Men as agents of racial integration, thereby earning heroic status." Chuck Cooper and Earl Lloyd emerged as the other distinguished twosome. Former head of the NBA Alumni Association Zelda Spoelstra observed at a basketball conference that I co-hosted at St. Francis College of Brooklyn in November 2001 that the original African American professional hoopsters specialized in defense, particularly rebounding, rather than scoring. Offensive stars were waiting in the wings.[22]

Nat "Sweetwater" Clifton deserves praise as a transitionary hero. As a New York Knick at 6'6", he played against centers like George Mikan at 6'10" and 40 pounds heavier. Nevertheless, Clifton held his ground (and air) in all facets of the game: passing, running the floor, rebounding, defending, shooting from long distance when needed, and fighting. Fans as old as this author can recall how, given the green light by coach Joe Lapchick, Clifton scored a one-punch knockout of a Boston Celtics bully, Bob Harrison, favored by Celtics coach Arnold "Red" Auerbach.[23] As a former boxer among many athletic forays, Clifton inspired fear after another clash with Syracuse Nationals tormentors. Most Knicks shied away from physical confrontation in self-defense until the advent of "Sweetwater" followed by the arrival of Willis Reed 14 years later. Clifton played on a highly competitive Knicks team from 1950 to 1956 until Bill Russell appeared on the scene and changed everything.

Born in the segregated South—Little Rock, Arkansas, to be precise—as Clifton Nathaniel, he moved to Chicago, where his love for soda pop allegedly earned the sobriquet "Sweetwater." But hoopster *cum* academician Gus Alfieri discovered a different source. Nat's grandmother used snuff, and he imitated her by "putting cocoa between cheek and gum, then sucked in water over to achieve the same effect."[24] Powerfully built, Clifton boxed and played baseball in the Negro Leagues and later for a Cleveland Indians farm team. Though an outstanding hitter, Clifton was forced to concentrate on basketball when he joined the Harlem Globetrotters at the behest of owner Abe Saperstein. Blessed with enormous hands fortified with Stickum (provided by a Knicks ball-boy in a paper cup for each hand), he could catch and palm a round ball deftly with either hand. Probably older than his stated age of 28 in a Knicks press guide, he quickly became a fan favorite. Though extraordinarily successful as a Globetrotter, Nat no longer trusted Saperstein after he learned that not always honest Abe paid College All-Stars more money than he paid Nat's teammates. So, after NBA owners voted six to five to integrate pro basketball, Clifton signed with the Knicks, a decision heartily welcomed by Coach Lapchick.[25]

In the 1947 World Tournament, Clifton had helped the Chicago Rens to a near upset of the mighty Lakers of Minneapolis, scoring 24 points in a losing effort. Saperstein sold his contract to the Knicks for a reported $12,500, of which $2,500, or 20 percent, went to the Black star.[26] Later, Clinton inked a contract for $7,500. He was the first African American to sign but the third selected after Chuck Cooper went to the Celtics and Earl Lloyd went to the Washington Capitals.[27] Clifton's baptism under fire occurred in an exhibition game in Raleigh, North Carolina, where he was not allowed a room in the same hotel that housed his teammates. Experienced in an acceptance mode, Nat Clifton was no rebel like Nat Turner. He had learned to adjust during Globetrotters tours.[28] Nat remembered a rope separating Black spectators from white spectators. Shamefully, Knicks players made little or no effort to fight for their teammates, though some Knicks suggested other hotels in Baltimore and Indianapolis. Nat refused their offer.[29] According to Alfieri, Nat Clifton was the

NBA's ideal Black: "talented, reserved, and rarely complaining about racial slights." Clifton, however, fought back when targeted with the "N" word as mentioned above. After Clifton bamboozled Celtics rookie Harrison with his bag of Globetrotters tricks, Harrison put a sharp elbow into Clifton's gut and added insult to injury with the nefarious "N" word. Slam bam, alakazam, one-two left-right combo: Harrison went down for the count. A "sleeping tiger" had been roused. Nat sent a message to would-be bullies. Clifton preferred fair play to brawls. Harrison's puffed-up face cautioned others to beware.

Black pioneers in basketball were expected to play defense, set screens, rebound, and avoid showboating. That said, I recall a hotly contested game at Madison Square Garden BR (before Russell) when Clifton made key shots on drives to the basket, some of them of the non-look variety, and, when left unguarded, hit several long two-handed set shots. On one fast break, surrounded by defenders, he jumped back to the basket and flipped the ball gently off the backboard and into the basket as Marty Glickman spun his verbal magic on the radio, chanting "Good—like Nedicks." The crowd, including this writer, cheered in disbelief. Wow!

Clifton resented restriction on his style of play. Knicks rules, mirroring National Basketball Association norms, stifled his talent. In retrospect, he regarded this regimen as a form of prejudice. Black styling would have to wait. Like many of his contemporaries—white as well as Black—Nat had little money after retirement. Absent a pension plan until 1965 when NBA stars threatened a walkout of an All-Star game, the old timers were excluded until 1988. Unfortunately, Clifton drove a cab in Chicago to support his mother and daughter, and died in 1990. Had he lived longer, he would have earned $800 per month. Evidently, the more aggressive athletes of 1965 provided a path to financial security.[30]

15

Bill Russell
and Oscar Robertson

Bill Russell

A key player, Bill Russell made quite a difference. Standing on the shoulders of giants, Russell paved the way to glory road for future Black stars as a giant himself. William Felton Russell was born in 1934. West Monroe, Louisiana, his birthplace, was marked by segregation and racial oppression. Two incidents scarred his early years. One involved his father, the other his mother. When his father, Charles, stopped at a gas station, the white proprietor told him to wait until he served a white patron who had arrived after Charles Russell. Unwilling to wait and attempting to leave, Charles was forced to stay put by the white "boss," wielding a gun. The other incident involved a white policeman who stopped Bill's mother while she walked on a local street. The cop ordered her home to put on a different dress, one that did not resemble a white woman's outfit.[1]

Shortly thereafter during World War II, Bill's family moved to Oakland, California, as part of the ongoing "Black Migration" out of the South. Charles Russell worked as a janitor; later, he became a truck driver. The family, including older brother Charles Jr., mother Kate, and father Charles, lived in public housing. Bill's mother died in 1946, when he was 12 years old. "Mr. Charlie," as Bill called his stern father, "was long on self-reliance and encouragement but short on sympathy," as he recalled.[2] A motherless child, Bill became a loner, while his brother, later a prominent writer, blossomed. Mr. Charlie put heavy emphasis on education. He took both sons to a local library in Oakland. Jolted into a shock of recognition after reading a book about the American Revolution, in which the author argued that the Black slaves were treated better here than in Africa, an enraged Russell began to search for heroes elsewhere. He found one in Henri Christophe, a rebellious slave in the Haitian Revolution.[3] Like his indomitable mother, Kate, Christophe refused to remain a slave and provided a role model for young Russell.

At age 16, Bill secretly smoked and openly sought a driver's license. Father Charles derided the smoking habit and refused the latter request. Both Russells, stubborn and angry over Bill's request for money to buy new clothes, did not speak to each other for nine months until brother Charles brokered a peace. Mr. Charlie "showed ... only two soft emotions: laughter and pride."[4] Russell sought guidance elsewhere and found support in George Powles, a father figure to many young Black athletes in Oakland. Powles taught Russell the basics of basketball. As Russell's high school coach, Powles took a scrawny teenager at 6'2" and 120 pounds under wing and prepared him to fly higher than a junior varsity player. Powles noticed the neophyte's huge hands—10.5 inches from the wrists to the fingertips—and his skinny legs with plenty of spring. He had an eye for talent and a talent for coaching. Among his other protégés one can find Joe Morgan, Curt Flood, and Vada Pinson.[5] George Powles was the only white man Russell trusted because his coach encouraged and tutored him.

At first, Russell played sparingly. During his high school years, Russell grew to 6'5" and 150 pounds. As he gained height, weight, and experience, Russell's game improved. At McClymonds High School, players preferred "Negro basketball," which featured "high speed" and "jumping to the moon." Led by two Black youngsters, they won easily, including one game in which they outscored their opponents 144 to 41.[6] Originally, Russell had to be prodded into angry mode. Teammate Bobby Woods provided the push. After two centers graduated, a more aggressive Russell filled that slot. His love for basketball grew. A scholar of the game, Bill read every article and scouted players he expected to face. And college scouts noticed. One observed that Russell was a winner with excellent defense, jumping ability, hustle, and floor coverage—in short, a great player. Nonetheless, few colleges offered Bill Russell a scholarship. In his last high school game, big Bill scored 14 points, eight in a row at "crunch time" in the first half and six in a row in the second half. A University of San Francisco freshman alerted his basketball coach, Phil Woolpert, about this "string bean" who could really jump.

Once a football powerhouse, the University of San Francisco, a Jesuit school, dropped that sport in 1952, after their premier star, Ollie Matson, had graduated.[7] Unable to afford the rising costs of fielding a football team, USF prudently switched to basketball. "All you have," retired pro Ronny Turiaf commented, "is two hoops, twelve guys, twelve uniforms, and a basketball."[8] Basketball coach Phil Woolpert was old-school, favoring a horizontal game. He wanted his players to stay rooted to the ground, while Bill Russell, a vertical game avatar, wanted to leap and roam, not to stay stationary under the basket. Bill also preferred a fast-paced up-tempo game. Early in his USF career, Russell held his future Celtics teammate Tommy Heinsohn scoreless in a contest with Holy Cross. Russell jumped to his own drumbeat, rarely the recipient of praise from his coach. Russell and high school buddy K. C. Jones duplicated a hide-and-seek strategy based on their uncanny peripheral vision, allowing Jones to steal passes while Russell covered for him with his long arms and lively legs. Bill mastered shot blocking from behind an opponent, angling his body deftly to the side without incurring a foul.[9]

Because of Russell's dominance, the NCAA widened the three-second lane during his junior year. Starting three African Americans—K. C. Jones, Hal Perry, and Bill Russell—USF eclipsed a consecutive win record held by Long Island University since 1935–1936 with 55 straight wins from Russell's junior year until his graduation in 1956. It started after a loss to UCLA 47–40, featuring a future teammate, Willie Naulls.[10] Bill Russell's superior skills powered USF to their winning streak and two national NCAA titles. In a 1989 book, coach/telecaster Billy Packer ranked USF the fourth greatest team in history. Coach Red Auerbach, in disagreement, placed them higher. Packer had to concede that the University of San Francisco's "defensive machine ultimately changed the face of basketball."[11] During his stellar collegiate career, Russell averaged 20.7 points per game as well as 20.3 rebounds per game. In addition, he starred as a high jumper with a leap of 6' 9.5" in the West Coast Relays. Bill also competed in track with a time of 49.6 seconds in the 440-yard dash.[12]

Despite his extraordinary feats, Russell tasted the bitter fruit of segregation. In one incident, Russell and his Black teammates were denied access to residence in Oklahoma City during a trip to this city, teeming with racism. In order to prove his merit as a man as well as an athlete Russell opted to delay his professional career in order to compete in the Melbourne Olympics of 1956. He and longtime buddy K. C. Jones walloped the Russians for the gold medal, 89 to 53. Russell averaged 14.1 points per game while Jones contributed 10.9 points per game. Both played excellent defense.[13]

Courted by Abe Saperstein, Bill Russell spurned his offer to join the Harlem Globetrotters. The imperious Saperstein used an intermediary to lure the USF star, an offense to Russell's sense of dignity in addition to the clowning antics so prevalent in the Trotters' game plan.[14] At the same time, tipped off by Bill Reinhart, his former coach at George Washington University, Arnold "Red" Auerbach, realized that Russell was a diamond in the rough. Some pundits questioned Russell's ability to shoot. That said, player-coach Fred Scolari added, "He's only the greatest basketball player I ever saw!" So, the wily Auerbach engineered a brilliant trade sending "Easy" Ed McCauley and Cliff Hagan to St. Louis in exchange for draft rights to Bill Russell. When a Harvard basketball coach denigrated Russell at a weekly basketball luncheon, Red Auerbach remarked loudly to Sammy Cohen sitting next him: "He's full of shit!"[15]

In his first game as a Celtic, Russell hauled down 21 rebounds in 16 minutes. In his third game he limited high-scoring former NBA scoring champ Neil Johnston to zero field goals in 42 minutes. Russell blocked his hook shots, once deemed unstoppable. Jumping four feet above the ground with great hang time and high intelligence, Bill Russell transformed the game. Early in his career against the Knicks in the old Madison Square Garden on Eighth Avenue and 49th Street, he blocked a Connie Simmons hook shot, then collared the ball and started one of his many patented fast breaks after a Russell rebound. I was there to witness his magic. Thereafter, the Celtics dominated the Knicks, my favorite team, until 1969–70. Sportswriter Frank Deford cogently argued that Russell established the Black man's place in the game. Thus, he functioned as a catalyst on three levels: "defensively, offensively, and culturally."[16]

Statistically, Russell is the most successful athlete in history, winning 11 NBA titles in 13 seasons with the Boston Celtics. His mano-a-mano combat with Wilt Chamberlain constitutes the stuff of legend. While the taller and stronger Chamberlain—7'1", 260 pounds—outscored Russell (6'10", 225 or so pounds) in these contests, the Celtics won most of these crucial games 75 to 57.

In their first meeting in Boston, Wilt scored 30 points and collected 28 rebounds while Bill tallied 22 points and 35 rebounds as almost 14,000 fans watched in awe. Boston beat Philly 115 to 106. For icing on the cake of victory, Russell blocked one of Chamberlain's shots. Chamberlain concentrated on piling up statistics in points scored, rebounds garnered, and assists rendered. Obsessively and to the detriment of team effort, he took pride in his ability to avoid six personal fouls during every game. Wilt often played the entire game, to his credit, but placed his team at a disadvantage on defense. All Russell cared about was winning. Tony Kornheiser, a sports maven, took Russell's full measure by citing another expert journalist, Jim Murray, who wrote:

> Bill Russell is like Wellington to Waterloo
> Like Grant to Richmond
> Like the Russians to Stalingrad
> He is where the war ends.[17]

Author Bill Simmons recalls his youthful "crush" on the Celtics of Boston, where he grew up. He was particularly fond of the Black players, principally Bill Russell. Simmons confesses that he wanted to be Black with a Muslim name of Jabaal Abdul Simmons. He attributes Celtics success to superior teamwork. An ardent Celtics fan while growing up, the often snarky Simmons adores Russell as the supreme winner, yet he rates him number two GOAT, reluctantly, after Michael Jordan.[18] Baffled by Boston's failure to embrace their greatest hoopster, Simmons wonders why. Was it incipient racism? Or Russell's aloofness? To be sure, his hero Bill Russell was both "complex and stubborn." Moreover, Russell was unfriendly to fans, unwilling to sign autographs, shockingly outspoken about his color and plights. When a coffee shop in Lexington, Kentucky, refused to serve Black Celtics on their way to honor Frank Ramsay and Cliff Hagan, both alums of Adolph Rupp's Wildcat team, in an exhibition game, Bill Russell, Sam Jones, "Satch" Sanders, and K. C. Jones refused to play. In protest, they flew home to Boston. Neither Bob Cousy nor coach Auerbach protested, though owner Walter Brown apologized, as did "Couse" belatedly.[19] Significantly, "Russell cared only about being a superior teammate and a proud black man." No doubt, the degradation of his home with excremental deposits on his bed and on his walls by local bigots did much to fuel his anger. Yet, Russell refused to become, in his own words, a "Causist" and later failed to acknowledge, let alone accept, Bob Cousy's belated apology for not reaching out to Russell with empathy during their Celtics years from 1956 to 1963. Once in New York City they roomed together but did not get along. Cousy, Russell recalled, jabbered to his wife, Missy, in French on the phone. After games, they went their separate ways. Ironically, Russell's first wife, Rose, had a warmer relationship with Cousy's wife than their husbands did with each other.[20]

Although Russell's marriage ended by divorce in 1973, he and his wife had lived apart before that legal breakup. His extramarital affairs were related in several sources, including his own autobiography and later in Gary Pomerantz's book *The Last Pass*. His first passionate affair with a woman that he called Iodine almost proved fatal. She stabbed him in the shoulder during a playoff. They broke up in 1960. Next, Bill took up with a white stripper from New York City. Kitty Malone was older than Bill.

She encouraged him to read history and discuss politics. Kitty introduced Bill to the writings of Frantz Fanon, awakening his social conscience with the book *The Wretched of the Earth*.[21]

At the advice of his former wife, Rose, and friend William McSweeney, Russell attended a lecture at Columbia University, delivered by Dorothy Height, the head of the National Council of Negro Women. Inspired by what they heard, both men joined. For author McSweeney it marked a turning point wherein college-educated Black athletes like Bill Russell were now willing to speak out against social injustice. Hostile to most white folks at one time, Russell now found exceptions in Lenny Bruce, Mort Sahl, and Pete Seeger outside of basketball and Red Auerbach inside.[22] In 1966, Russell had a chance conversation on a flight from Philadelphia to Los Angeles with a Black Marine about the war in Vietnam. The officer argued that our mission was designed to stop communism. "Russian or Chinese?" Russell asked. "Chinese, of course," he replied. "Orientals have a low regard for human life." Unpersuaded, Russell insisted that Hiroshima and Nagasaki proved otherwise. The Marine, Bill concluded, "was looking at the world through eyes of a white empire builder." Therefore, he reasoned, "the underdog culture is subdued and invisible." Like Catholics in Northern Ireland and Indians in Paraguay.[23]

Once nonviolent, Russell promised a grieving Charles Evers to count on him after brother Medgar was murdered in Mississippi. One year later, after the triple murder of Chaney, Goodman, and Schwerner in that same infamous state, Charles Evers invited Bill Russell to come on down. Reluctantly, Bill went and offered basketball clinics in Jackson, providing, he wryly wrote, a tall target for KKK bigots. More inclined at that point towards Malcolm X's aggressive stance, he still defended moderates like Roy Wilkins. Self-aware, Russell confessed: "Like Kong, I am a misfit— and a triple threat at that.... I have quirks." He viewed his position as a paradox: a point of vision as well as a source of blindness.[24] In a 20-year span, Blacks went from the outhouse to the in-crowd.

Russell raged at whites, then married one. Paradoxically, King Kong killed and ate Black men yet fell in love with a white woman.[25] Run-ins with white cops in Boston fueled his anger. Though his fame saved him from more violent encounters, Russell seethed at the brutalization of less prestigious people of color. His continued refusal to sign autographs incurred the wrath of fans and Boston sportswriters. One beat writer from "Beantown" named Ryan conceded that "Boston was very tribal, very clannish. The [Blacks] were pretty much herded into a section called Roxbury." According to Tom Heinsohn, two Boston reporters refused to vote for Russell as the National Basketball Association's most valuable player because of race.[26] White neighbors had protested when the Russell family purchased a house in their neighborhood. A proud man, Russell called himself Black, rather than Negro. In 1963, he joined the March on Washington, openly supported Ali in his anti-war stance, and became the NBA's first African American head coach.[27]

Russell had a warm relationship with coach Red Auerbach, a fiery Jew, son of Russian immigrants. As he aged, Russell requested less practice. One day, Auerbach remarked: "Jesus Christ, Russ, you look like shit!" Russell did not argue. "Ok, don't scrimmage today." The great Celtics center saved all his energy for when it counted.

Bill Russell was an overwhelming force on the court, averaging better than 22 rebounds and 15 points per game in a 14-year NBA career. Credited with nearly single-handedly elevating defensive play in the league, he also won five MVP awards and was selected to the All-Star team 12 times. He is shown here on August 28, 1963, at the March on Washington. Photograph by Rowland Scherman (National Archives).

When Russell rested three minutes between quarters, Red understood.[28] Blessed with a big personality, Russ was a teaser, whose laugh or cackle, Red remarked, "sounded like a hyena in full throat."[29] In his last game as player/coach, at age 35, Russell directed his team to a victory over the Los Angeles Lakers. On the losing side again, Wilt Chamberlain suffered a double indignity. Lakers coach Bill van Breda Kolff benched Chamberlain in the final minutes of a gallant comeback effort, which fell short by a two-point margin, 108 to 106. In a charitable gesture, Russell comforted a distraught Jerry West. He also disparaged Chamberlain's play, causing a rift in a once amiable relationship. Finally, Russell failed to show up for the Celtics' victory celebration. He left cold turkey. Fans and journalists felt betrayed. Elected to the Hall of Fame in 1975, big Bill did not attend. According to his rationale, he did not want to share a podium with the bigoted Adolph Rupp or be the first Black player inducted rather than Chuck Cooper.[30]

Russell coached the Seattle Supersonics from 1973 to 1977 and later the Sacramento Kings from 1987 to 1988. Neither post proved gratifying. Anything after the Celtics' dynasty of 11 titles in 13 years, in which Russell played the pivotal role, would appear anticlimactic. Russell did apply his basketball knowledge to televised games as color commentator for CBS and TBS from the 1970s to the mid–1980s. Unable to engage in hype, he advised viewers to pay attention to the last minutes of each half

to understand the narrative of each game—unwelcome advice to sponsors hawk-
ing beer and deodorant. Russell published several autobiographies with co-authors
revealing much about his personal struggles. He also brokered a peace between Shaq
O'Neal and Kobe Bryant—no mean task—after their bitter feud as Lakers teammates. Eventually he agreed to accept formal entry into the Hall of Fame. Author
David Halberstam described Bill Russell as a proud man who refused to sign autographs or call Boston his home. Avoiding caricature, he played "with a special fury,"
arguably as an outlet for his Black rage. Before each game, he would throw up. In
racist cities like St. Louis, he played brilliantly.[31]

On November 17, 2006, the NCAA voted Bill Russell into the Collegiate Basketball Hall of Fame with John Wooden, James Naismith, Dean Smith, and the Big O—
Oscar Robertson. Since 2009, the NBA Most Valuable Player Award has been named
in Bill Russell's honor thanks to a Solomonic decision by David Stern, NBA commissioner at that time. Two years later, President Barack Obama bestowed on William
Fenton Russell the Presidential Medal of Freedom. At that celebratory event, President Obama said:[32]

> He marched with King; he stood by Ali. When a restaurant refused to serve black Celtics, he
> refused to play in a scheduled game....
> He endured insults and vandalism but kept focusing on making teammates who he loved
> better players, made possible the success of so many who would follow. I hope that one day in
> the streets of Boston children will look up at a statue built not only to Russell, the player, but
> Bill Russell the man.

In September 2017, Bill Russell joined the digital age. He opened a Twitter
account, on which he tweeted a photo of himself on bended knee in support of NFL
players and wrote "Proud to take a knee and to stand tall against racial injustice."[33]
He carried that righteousness to the end of his life, passing away after a long illness
on July 31, 2022. Upon his death the NBA took the extraordinary step of retiring his
number 6 throughout the league; only Jackie Robinson and Wayne Gretzky have
been similarly honored in major sports.

Oscar Robertson

One of the most misunderstood Black heroes in sports, Oscar Palmer Robertson,
the youngest of three sons, was born in Charlotte, Tennessee, on November 24, 1938,
to Henry and Mazell Robertson. The family Robertson moved to Indianapolis as
part of the Great Migration that started during World War I and gained momentum
during World War II. Growing up poor in a segregated part of town, young Oscar
learned to shoot by wrapping rags around a tennis ball with rubber bands and tossing his *ersatz* basketball into that James Naismith creation: a peach basket.[34] Because
hoops required less expenditure than other major sports, Oscar gravitated to basketball, honing his court skills at the local YMCA. Although Oscar's parents divorced
in 1949, he received guidance from older brother Bailey and found a father figure
in his coach at Crispus Attucks High School, Ray Crowe. The school had no gym,
and teams were denied competition with white schools until Robertson's star power

became apparent. In his sophomore year at Crispus Attucks High (named after the first martyr during the 1770 Boston Massacre, prelude to the American Revolution), Robertson played forward on a team that lost to the eventual state champs, Milan High School. That upset victory led to a book and later a feel-good film called *Hoosiers*. It was the "last hurrah" for all white teams in Indiana.[35] Returning to his point guard position, Oscar led his high school team to two consecutive state championships, the first for an Indianapolis high school. In 1955 Crispus Attucks went 31–1. Remarkably, this final contest featured two all-Black teams and two future professional basketball stars: Oscar Robertson's high school versus Dick Barnett's Gary Roosevelt High School, with the "Big O's team winning in a rout, 97–64."[36] Unwilling to risk a parade through the main street of Indianapolis, the victory procession was diverted to a marginal ghetto area. Oscar Robertson fumed at this indignity. Robertson's heroics resulted in a repeat performance with a perfect 31–0 record and a 45-win streak, carried over from the prior year. Robertson was named Indiana's "Mr. Basketball." Although the victory parade started at the town center, it ended in a park, again to allay white fears, based in racism, that Blacks would misbehave.[37] Again, Robertson felt disrespected. Because of Black dominance in high school basketball, Black students were sent to other schools, thereby integrating public education in Indiana.[38]

Repelled by Indiana coach Branch McCracken's indifferent attitude toward his brother Bailey and the insinuation that Robertson might want to be paid, Oscar decided to attend Cincinnati University, as the first African American to play basketball there.[39] Oscar captured national attention with his superlative play there. In his three years as a collegiate star, Robertson led his teams to three consecutive appearances in the NCAA's Final Four from 1959 to 1961. Twice defeated in the semi-finals by the University of California, Oscar's teams never achieved that elusive golden ring. Robertson averaged 33 points per game as a sophomore (tops in the nation), 35.1 as a junior, and 32.6 as a senior, guiding the Bearcats to a splendid 89–9 record. While at the university, Robertson worked part-time in a gas/electric company and endured racial slurs plus segregated facilities on road trips.[40] Ironically, his high profile brought other outstanding Black hoopsters to reach a title the year after his graduation as the Cincinnati Bearcats defeated a powerful Ohio State team, starring Bobby Knight, John Havlicek, and future pro teammates Jerry Lucas and Larry Siegfried.

Arguably, Oscar's biggest collegiate moment occurred on March 24, 1958, in New York City's Madison Square Garden, when he scored 56 points on 22 field goals and 12 out of 12 soul shots in demolishing Seton Hall 118 to 54.[41] His one-hand jump shot cradled from a flattened hand launched at a 45-degree angle above his right ear was a thing of beauty and a joy forever. Robertson's dribbling skills with either hand and no-look passes evoke poetry in motion too. He also witnessed the ugly thrust of racism on the road when hotels barred him from staying with white teammates until his junior year.[42] He led the nation in scoring throughout his college career, averaging 33.8 points per game, leading to All-American status as well as College Player of the Year. Co-captain with Jerry West of the U.S. Olympic team in Rome, the "Big O," as the leading scorer with 14.6 points per game, helped capture the gold medal in basketball. I remember the Olympic workouts from the balcony of the Columbia University gym, which offered a display of brilliant shooting by both

West and Robertson. After that triumph, West and Robertson were selected one-two in the NBA draft: West went to the Lakers of Minneapolis, Robertson to the Royals of Cincinnati.

Voted Rookie of the Year after the 1960–61 season, Robertson averaged 30.5 points per game that year. As a first-time All-Star, Oscar scored 23 points and dished out 14 assists to win the MVP Award. No sophomore slump befell the young star as he averaged a remarkable triple double in points, rebounds, and assists. At 6'5", Robertson was built like a power forward who played point guard, often outrebounding much taller opponents with strength, speed, and savvy. Despite his extraordinary gifts and outstanding statistics, Robertson could not drive his team to a championship because the Russell-led Celtics and the Chamberlain 76ers blocked the Royal road to a title. After a 10-year stint with the Royals, Robertson was at a bottleneck with the newly appointed coach, Bob Cousy, whose assist records Oscar had superseded. Perhaps motivated by envy, Cousy traded Robertson to Milwaukee, where finally the "Big O" could team up with a brilliant center then known as Lew Alcindor. In 1971 they brought the one and only NBA title to Milwaukee with Alcindor providing the firepower up front and Oscar orchestrating back-court play.[43]

According to Sam Smith in *Hard Labor*, Oscar Robertson's lawsuit initiated in 1970 marks the onset of the modern era in NBA history. As president of the players union, a post he inherited from Tom Heinsohn, Robertson temporarily blocked the proposed merger of the two leagues, the National Basketball Association and the American Basketball Association. Consequently, NBA owners went to Congress to seek an exemption from the Sherman Anti-Trust Act and various supplemental acts like pro baseball and football but failed. NBA players eventually settled in 1976 when the ABA countersued the NBA. This agreement constituted a giant though incremental step forward culminating in the 1990s. The average player salary in 2017 "rose to approximately eight million dollars per player in a movement for economic equality and personal dignity."[44] Oscar Robertson, as Sam Smith emphatically argues, had the most to lose as a highly paid player. Nevertheless, he accepted the challenge as players association chief. Pat Riley called Robertson "a man of conviction." Akin to Ida Tarbell on John D. Rockefeller, Oscar Robertson was a "muckraker." Bill Walton paid tribute to the heroic leadership of Roberson, Bill Bradley, John Havlicek, Jerry West, Dave DeBusschere, and Wes Unseld.[45] Tom Heinsohn, who preceded Oscar as players association leader, realized that players were reluctant to join, fearing loss of their jobs.

When the NBA decided to put a player on its logo designed by Alan Siegel, owners chose Jerry West even though the honoree considered Oscar as the superior player. Like Curt Flood, a litigant in baseball, Oscar was denied a coaching or front office job in basketball after he retired in 1974. A multi-year contract with CBS to telecast NBA games lasted only one year after Buffalo Braves owner Paul Snyder persuaded Commissioner Walter Kennedy to abrogate the contract because of the still-pending suit.[46] Wayne Embry, Oscar's teammate, blames the suit for that blacklist. A subsequent commissioner, David Stern, tried to laugh it off with a patronizing quip: "Oscar is a grouch."[47] Jeff Mullins observed that the NBA pays 10 NBA alums to appear at All-Star games and other promotional events "worth a couple of hundred thousand." Oscar is not on that list. Fiercely competitive, he refused to be replaced at the Maurice Stokes game at Kutcher's by a newspaper reporter, Peter Vecsey.[48]

A snarky reporter, Bill Simmons, also called Oscar a grouch. After reading Robertson's autobiography, Simmons piled on other weaponized adjectives: "angry, selfish, bitter."[49] Hated by coaches, referees, and owners, Simmons explains underlying reasons without condoning these traits. A victim of prejudice as well as a profile in courage, Oscar disdained authority. As mentioned above, in 1955 after his high school team won the state championship, a victory parade was rerouted to the ghetto.[50] He resented recruiters like Branch McCracken and teachers at Cincinnati University who belittled him in class. In Dallas, fans tossed a black cat into his locker room. In Houston, he had to sleep in a Texas Southern (all-Black college) dorm room. In North Carolina, the Klan Grand Wizard sent him a letter: "Don't come to the South." Most disturbing, in Cincinnati, they had colored-only water fountains and cinemas that refused entry to Negroes. Because of these experiences, Simmons avers, Oscar snapped and vented frustrations on others. Anticipating Michael Jordan, Robertson's perfectionism targeted teammates. Jerry Lucas, Wayne Embry, and Zelmo Beaty attested to this trait.[51]

Simmons degrades Robertson as CBS commentator (he marks Bill Russell with the same "poison pen"). Nobody hired Oscar for anything since 1975. Buried in footnote 32, Simmons quotes Bill Bradley: "Perhaps he (Robertson) doesn't give lesser players enough margin of error, but when they listen to him, he makes All-Stars of meager talents. He controls events on the court with aplomb and the authoritarian hand of a symphony conductor."[52] Prone to mockery, Simmons resumes his personal attack, tweeting in response to Oscar's complaints about being underpaid. Indeed, he was! When Bob Cousy, as Royals coach, traded Robertson to Milwaukee for two less-talented players, it was due to envy rather the alleged fading skills of the "Big O." Robertson had broken Cousy's assist records—hence, the trade. Robertson had enough energy in the tank to team up with brilliant young star Lew Alcindor to win the NBA title in 1971. After 14 stellar years as a pro, Robertson retired. In another footnote, #41, Simmons cites Jason Whitlock's criticism of his criticism. Whitlock claims that Oscar Robertson, like Bill Russell, suffered from racial injustice throughout the 1950s and 1960s. Unlike Bill Russell, however, Robertson did not play for a "creative visionary like Red Auerbach willing to construct an environment that catered to a black superstar's identity." Plus, Russell had more NBA crowns thanks to more talented teammates.[53]

In the final analysis, Bill Simmons conceded that Oscar Robertson ranks as the 10th best player on a list of 98 pro players. Besides, because of Robertson's donation of a kidney to a daughter suffering from lupus, his many benefactions to charity (NBA Legends Foundation, Boys Club of New York, the National Kidney Foundation, the International Prostate Cancer Foundation), and his vital contributions as players association president in attaining free agency for players, he most certainly deserves a high perch in our pantheon.[54]

16

Elgin Baylor,
Connie Hawkins, and Dr. J

Elgin Baylor

When I played competitive basketball—with more energy than talent—our coaches insisted that we never leave our feet when passing because that move can only lead to bad things. Conventional wisdom went the way of the horse and buggy as Black hoopsters, like the Tuskegee airmen, took flight. Novelist/poet—and former basketball star at University of Pennsylvania—John Wideman offers a cogent explanation[1]:

> When it's played the way it's "spozed" to be played, basketball happens in the air, the pure air; flying, floating, elevated above the floor, levitating the way oppressed people of this earth imagine themselves in their dreams, as I do in my lifelong fantasies of escape and power, finally, at last, once and for all, free.

Born on September 16, 1934, Elgin Gay Baylor was named after his father's favorite watch. He grew up in Washington, D.C., when it was highly segregated. African Americans washed the clothes and shined the shoes of white leaders in the 1950s, writes Nelson George. A mentor, Clarence Haynsworth, and two older brothers, Sal and Kermit, tutored him in basketball. Elgin honed his considerable hoop skills at the Southwest Boys Club and Brown Junior High School. Denied a spot on varsity teams initially, Elgin ultimately became a high school All-American.[2] Gifted in other sports, Baylor played baseball as well as football. Starting at Phelps Vocational High School for two years, 1951–52, Baylor's game rose through the air with the greatest of ease, when he scored 44 points in one game. He averaged 18.5 and 27.6 points each season. Beset by academic woes, Elgin dropped out to earn money as a worker in a furniture store but stayed in shape, sharpening his hoop skills in local recreational leagues. Returning to school in 1954, Baylor found a niche in newly built Spingarn High School. As a senior, he averaged 36 points per game. In one game against his former team, he scored a record-breaking 63 points and was named best basketball player in the D.C. metropolitan area.

Poor school grades precluded easy access to college. Through a friend's recommendation, Elgin managed to get a scholarship to the University of Idaho to play football as well as basketball. When the college reduced scholarship aid, Baylor left for another school in the far West. After a year of Amateur Athletic Union ball, Baylor matriculated at Seattle University, rejecting an offer from the Minneapolis Lakers. The explosive Baylor led Seattle to the NCAA title game in 1958, in a losing bid to topple the Kentucky Wildcats. He was featured in *Sports Illustrated* as a 6'5" wizard, unstoppable, like Connie Hawkins.[3] When the Lakers pursued him again as the first draft choice in the NBA draft, he accepted. As a three-year college star, Elgin Baylor averaged 31.3 points per game and, at only 6'5", he led the NCAA in rebounds during the '56–'57 season.

When Baylor joined the Lakers in 1958, the once dominant team in pro basketball had fallen on hard times, going a dismal 19–53 prior to Baylor's advent. Elgin signed for $20,000 per year. The hapless New York Knicks offered $200,000 for the rights to sign Baylor, buts Laker owner Bob Short, though strapped for cash, prudently rejected that offer.[4] Baylor flourished in a Lakers uniform. As a rookie, he averaged 34.9 points per game, hauled in 15 rebounds per game, and dished out 4.1 assists per game. In one game, he scored 55 points. At the end of his phenomenally successful first season, he was named Rookie of the Year as the Lakers went from last place to the NBA finals. In the next three seasons, Baylor averaged 34.8, 38.3, and 34 points per game. On November 15, he scored 71 points and nabbed 25 rebounds against the New York Knicks. He actually played for his team while serving in the U.S. Army on weekends. During that period, he scored 61 points in a finals contest against the seemingly invincible Celtics.[5]

How did Baylor do it? Jerry West, Baylor's longtime teammate and a heroic figure in his own right, remembers pivotal moments when he learned to admire his buddy. Elgin joined Oscar Robertson and Bill Russell in a threatened boycott of the 1964 All-Star game in the Boston Garden unless the owner agreed to recognize the players union.[6] The owners agreed. Later, Elgin Baylor scored 15 points for the losing West team while Oscar Robertson led the East with 26 points to a 111–107 victory.[7] Former teammate Gail Goodrich marveled at Baylor's skill. "He was the Julius Erving of the time, going to the hoop, hanging; moves Julius was doing later on. He was the first one, 6'5". Quicker than everyone, taking the ball off the backboard and going all the way with it."[8] Another incident in his rookie year showed Baylor's true grit in the aggressive mode. The Lakers were scheduled to play a regular-season game in Charleston, West Virginia. In "solidarity with their black teammates, the white players elected to stay in a rooming house for Negroes." When Baylor was refused service at a restaurant, he refused to play. In response to the urgent pleas of "Hot" Rod Hundley, a native of West Virginia, he adamantly refused, saying: "I am not an animal, I am a human being and I want to be treated like one." Hundley understood. So did Black leaders in Charleston because it led to change in their city.[9]

Baylor's stellar play was impeded by a series of knee injuries in 1963 and 1965, the latter in the Western division playoff series. His point-per-game average declined along with his lateral movement and jumping ability. Sadly, he was forced to retire in his 14th season, when the Los Angeles Lakers, the only team that he played for, went on to win the NBA title. Columbia College's star player Jim McMillan replaced him at small forward in 1971. Baylor's record of achievements with 23,149 points, 3,650 assists, and 11,643 rebounds continues to impress. He was elected to basketball's Hall of Fame in 1977 and many other teams of honor, including the dubious distinction of an NBA superstar who never won a championship—in the words of Bill Simmons, "the most underappreciated superstar in NBA history."[10]

As a coach, for the New Orleans Jazz, he was less successful. In 1986, he began working for the Los Angeles Clippers as vice president of basketball operations, a position he held for 22 years with only two winning seasons. Yet he was named the NBA Executive of the Year in 2006, two years before his ouster. He sued the feckless owner, Donald Sterling, who later would be forced to sell the Clippers for conduct unbecoming an owner, including blatantly racist remarks. Baylor claimed racism and ageism in his litigation but failed to prove his case. Still, as Mrs. Loman remarked about her husband Willy in Arthur Miller's 1949 Pulitzer Prize winning play, *Death of a Salesman*: "Attention must be paid." And it was on April 6, 2018, when a tearful Elgin Baylor witnessed his statue placed alongside of other Lakers greats—Shaquille O'Neal, Kareem Abdul-Jabbar, Magic Johnson, Jerry West, and Chick Hearn—in front of the Staples Center. On that occasion, Elgin Baylor said: "I certainly appreciate the wonderful things people have said about me. But without the wonderful teammates, this certainly would have been impossible. I'd just like to thank my teammates."[11] In saluting their fellow honoree, Magic Johnson, Kobe Bryant, and Jerry West sang the praise of Elgin Baylor. Magic admitted to stealing all of Elgin's moves except for the hang-time in the air, which few could emulate. The late Kobe Bryant also admitted to stealing Baylor's moves. A tearful Jerry West described Elgin Baylor as "one of the greatest men I've ever met in my life."[12] Baylor died on March 22, 2021.

Connie Hawkins

Some levitators flew high but could not "hang." Others are like the mythical Icarus, who flew too high and the sun burned his wings, causing this tragic figure to crash. Richard Goldstein's October 2017 *New York Times* obituary, "Connie Hawkins, Electrifying N.B.A. Forward Barred in His Prime, Dies at 75," illustrates the tragicomic arc of rise, fall, and rise again, pointedly, with a better outcome than that of poor Icarus.[13]

Born on July 17, 1942, the fifth of six children, Hawkins grew up in the Bedford-Stuyvesant section of Brooklyn. He slept on a cot with two brothers in a cold-water railroad flat with bugs on the table in the kitchen and squalor—except for two pictures of Christ on bare walls—everywhere. His mother, Dorothy, was a heavy-set, deeply religious woman who suffered from glaucoma and a drink-prone husband who deserted the family when Connie was nine. Dorothy made her children go to the Cornerstone Baptist Church Sunday School; Connie attended until he was 14 years old. At age 10, he was 5'10" and 115 pounds. In the seventh grade, he grew to 6'1" and 125 pounds, earning such nicknames as "Slim," "Bones," and "Long Tall Sally." Despite taunts questioning his masculinity and being the victim of bullies, Connie—a true Christian—refused to fight back. An ungainly adolescent, he pinched pennies and collected deposit bottles for survival money. If Jesus sustained his mother, Connie found salvation in basketball on asphalt courts and on hardwood floors, where he discovered individual talent and developed self-esteem.[14]

Connie learned basketball at a local YMCA recreation center under the tutelage of Gene Smith, a New York City police officer who served as a leader of recreational programs. A street-wise gritty little friend, Eddie Simmons, drew Connie out and toughened his game. This Brooklyn playground legend grew up poor and semi-literate in Bedford Stuyvesant. Because of his extraordinary talent and obedient behavior in public school, Hawkins was awarded "social promotion," even though he could barely read or write. His English teachers at Boys High failed to improve his minimal skills. Basketball would be his ticket, he hoped, for a better life. At age 11 and 6'2" but rail thin, he could dunk. As a high school sophomore, Hawkins rode the bench. He grew six inches while at Boys High School, where he awed spectators at basketball games with his huge hands and tremendous "slam dunks." Hawkins blossomed into an all-star in his junior year, scoring 15 points and skying for rebounds in a lopsided win over Commerce High School in the 1959 Public Schools Athletic League (PSAL) final 74–58. At 6'5", he could play up front with the city's best, and his remarkable ball-handling skills enabled him to double as a guard. In his senior year, he moved to center for those mano-a-mano confrontations with Wingate High School's ace, Roger Brown. Though Brown usually scored more points, Hawkins's versatility invariably led to team victories as in the PSAL semifinals, 62 to 59. In a bizarre final, Columbus High School coach Roy Rubin engineered a slow-down strategy that almost worked. Hawkins was held to two points and a single rebound as 7,000 fans watched in amazement. Boys High eked out a win 21–15. In New York City's all-star game, Connie regained his scoring touch with 15 points in his team's 64–48 romp. Scoring 16 points, however, Roger Brown won the MVP.[15]

Connie's Boys High coach, Mickey Fisher, proved masterful in molding championship teams and securing scholarships for his human "skyscrapers" but contributed little to ensure their readiness for college, a more secure road to social mobility.[16] Nearing high school graduation, Connie's IQ was quantified at 65 with a seventh-grade reading level. Through a massive tutoring effort, Mr. Mazer, the English department chair, raised Connie's IQ to 113. Certainly not dumb, Connie Hawkins was the victim of "compulsory miseducation," as one critic put it. According to David Wolf, the tragedy of this major improvement was that now Connie Hawkins was ready for high school, not college.[17] Recruiters were certainly ready for Hawkins. They rolled out red carpets. They spared no expense on meals and flights. As journalist Jimmy Breslin acidly commented, "Take," they said, "Take everything from everyone except from gamblers."[18] Connie finally decided to take the best offer from the University of Iowa: "$180 per month for a no-show job in addition to tuition, room, and board," all illegal under Big Ten rules because Connie Hawkins, regardless of his basketball genius, was on academic probation.[19] A splendid freshman year on the courts, primarily during intra-squad play, found no parallel in the classroom. Connie passed his physical education courses with an "A" and a "B." He flunked English and one other subject and received an "I" for "incomplete" in another. He slept for long stretches. Years later, Hawkins engaged in self-deprecating humor perhaps in confession of painful truths. When reporter Jim Goodrich asked him about honors he had won in college, his degree, his college minor, and his grade point average, Connie's tart replies were as follows: "I won the honor to leave," "Fifty points," "Sports," and "zero-zero."[20]

In an ESPN documentary about Connie Hawkins, the highly mercurial and multi-traveled coach Larry Brown enthused: "He was simply the greatest individual player I have ever seen." After Connie led his team twice to New York City championships, he was named to first-team All-American by *Parade* magazine in 1960.[21] He seemed destined for basketball Eden. Unfortunately, there was a snake under the asphalt. Brilliant, handsome, and totally corrupt, Jack Molinas slithered onto the scene, where heaven was a playground. A graduate of Stuyvesant High School and Columbia College (where I matriculated too, five years after Molinas), he became a habitual gambler, selling his Faustian soul to the mob. Wagering while a rookie sensation with the Fort Wayne Pistons in 1953–54, Molinas was caught on a wire repeatedly betting on games through a bookie/associate in the Bronx. Exposed, he was suspended indefinitely by NBA Commissioner Maurice Podoloff. Undaunted after legal attempts to beat the ban, Molinas went to Brooklyn Law School. Fortified with a degree and "dirty money," Molinas targeted young college hoopsters with favors, loans, and the use of his car. Molinas met Hawkins at Manhattan Beach Park. He lent the naïve Hawkins $200, later repaid by Connie's older brother. He also let Connie Hawkins and Roger Brown drive his big luxury car. Because Hawkins failed to mention these benefactions to the authorities, he became a victim of district attorney Frank Hogan's overreach. Conned into a confession of guilt by association, Hawkins became a pariah.[22]

As a freshman in Iowa, Connie outplayed Iowa's top player, future pro and coach Don Nelson. Before he could move up to the varsity, however, he was kicked out of school and, like Molinas several years prior, banned from the NBA for life, though he was never formally charged. So, Hawkins became a roving hoopster. Returning to the asphalt courts and netless rims of New York City, Hawkins found sustenance in countless pick-up games, which may have shortened his professional career through damage to his knees. Then, the Rucker tournament beckoned, where "the Hawk" went one-on-one with Wilt Chamberlain and dunked over the most prolific scorer in the NBA at that time. Whenever he appeared in East Harlem, fans shouted: "The Hawk, the Hawk, the Hawk is here."[23] Soon, Connie Hawkins, to echo a favorite Beatles song, "was here, there, and everywhere." An itinerant, he played one year in the American Basketball League until it folded, moved onto the road with the Globetrotters for two seasons, then joined the American Basketball Association with the Pittsburgh Pipers. Everywhere he went, anywhere he wandered, he excelled. Yet, for him, Nirvana meant the NBA.

Author David Wolf wrote a pivotal article in May 1969 about the injustice visited upon Connie Hawkins in *Life* magazine, a template for a later book and successful litigation. Wolf stated emphatically:

> Evidence recently uncovered indicates that Connie Hawkins never knowingly associated with gamblers, that he never introduced a player to a fixer, and that the only damaging statements about his involvement were made by Hawkins himself—as a terrified, semi-literate teenager who thought he'd go to jail unless he said what the D.A.'s detectives pressed him to say. Hawkins, in other words, did nothing that would have justified his being banned by the N.B.A.[24]

Three civil liberties lawyers—the husband-and-wife team of Roslyn and S. David Litman plus Howard Specter—sued the National Basketball Association for antitrust violations, arguing that the league, by barring Connie Hawkins, had denied him the "opportunity to earn a livelihood." They won.

Perhaps unwilling to incur further antitrust litigation, the NBA did not appeal but awarded Hawkins $1.3 million and dropped the ban. Hawkins signed with the Phoenix Suns as a rookie at age 27, with his best years left behind due to knee injuries after too many games all over the globe. Hawkins confided to a reporter that Elgin Baylor was his model. When Baylor played for the Lakers, first in Minneapolis, later in Los Angeles, Connie and friends used to sneak into the old Madison Square Garden to see him play. Before Elgin, Connie said, "basketball was a more stand-up-and-shoot game." After Elgin, it was more elevated with "superb body control."[25] Emulating Baylor's style, Hawkins averaged 24.6 points, 10.4 rebounds, and 4.8 assists per game in his rookie season. In the last game of that season, Connie scored 44 points, grabbed 20 rebounds, dished eight assists, and added five blocks and five steals. As broadcaster Mel Allen used to declare: "What a finish!"

Although overshadowed by the then Lew Alcindor in his NBA debut, Connie had a fine first season in the sun, which elevated the "Hawk" to an all-star perch and his Suns team to its highest finish (third) and best attendance in years.[26] Sadly, Connie's best "hoops" years were left behind in the wake of what poet Andrew Marvell described as "time's winged chariot." Unable to regain the form that prompted Bill Sharman to tout him as one of the seven best players in the world, Hawkins had several luminous if unspectacular seasons with Phoenix and Los Angeles and one forgettable season in Atlanta.

He had come a long way from poverty in Brooklyn. After retirement, Hawkins remained loyal to friends, family, and roots. Because of his successful litigation, he encountered difficulty in finding a suitable position in basketball as sportswriter Peter Vecsey reported in a *New York Post* article, "Connie Hawkins Still Needs a Home."[27] Lacking sufficient education also limited Connie's opportunities. Eventually, his former team, the Phoenix Suns, provided work in community relations. Connie Hawkins was inducted into the Basketball Hall of Fame in 1992. But where are his youthful friends, the boys of winter, who gained glory in play in abbreviated lives? For every Connie Hawkins, there are multitudes who fail to "make it." His buddy Eddie Simmons became a "methadone man" after being hooked on heroin; Sparky Donovan and Earl Manigault became junkies; Kenny Bellinger and Boobie Tucker became corpses in drug-related deaths. Biographer David Wolf lists Earl Wright and Hal Halliburton among the fallen stars of Rick Telander's "playground heaven." To the final question—what price mobility?—there is no easy answer.[28]

Julius Erving

Julius Erving's signature move was deftly described by Alexander Wolff in his book's excellent chapter on flight. Inspired by a soaring portrait of Dr. J, Wolff wrote:

In game 4 of the NBA Finals, the 76ers' Julius Erving navigates the right baseline, picking up his dribble outside the lane, a good 12 feet from the basket. Forced by the Lakers' Mark Landsberger and Kareem Abdul-Jabbar to drift beyond the backboard and over the baseline, he then reappears on the far side of the basket. Extending his arm as if hydraulically, he flips a reverse layup off the board and in. Erving's move will inspire Grover Washington, Jr., to write and record *Let it Flow* [*for Dr. J*].[29]

Born on February 22, 1950, in East Meadow, Long Island, Julius Erving was left fatherless at age three. To support her children, his mother worked as a domestic. They lived in public housing. Erving grew up on the "mean streets" of Hempstead and Roosevelt, Long Island. Early on, Julius must have realized that basketball provided an escape from trouble and a "ticket to a better life." Julius played for a Salvation Army team, averaging 11 points per game. His mother remarried when Erving was 13, moving her family to a middle-class lifestyle in Roosevelt. His academic performance improved in sync with his extraordinary basketball ability, especially in taking flight with artful drives to the hoops, culminating in signature slam dunks. Erving gained attention at Roosevelt High School.[30]

While in high school, Erving acquired his designation as Dr. J in exchange with a friend, whom he dubbed "the professor." Erving preferred Dr. J to other appellations like the Claw, Black Moses, Houdini, and Jewell from his glory days in Harlem's Rucker Park League. In the summer of his last year in high school, Erving ventured up to a basketball camp in the Catskills, where he urged Celtics backup center Wayne Embry to engage him in a one-on-one contest. As a 6'8", 275-pound center, Embry was reluctant to take on the 6'5" stringbean forward, but he relented. Erving, a veritable David, beat Goliath-like Embry three times in a row, then repeated the rout of "Jumping" Johnny Green as Embry vividly recalled.[31] After a competent if not superstar career in high school basketball, in 1968 Erving opted to enroll in a small-market college, the University of Massachusetts at Amherst, where, in two varsity seasons, he averaged a rare double-double: 26.3 points and 20.2 rebounds per game.[32] In the summer of his second year at the University of Massachusetts, Dr. J participated in an NCAA all-star team tour of Western Europe and the Soviet Union. Voted the MVP on this tour, Erving decided to go pro. His heroes were Oscar Robertson, Bill Russell, and Jerry West.[33]

Erving signed with the Virginia Squires of the fledgling American Basketball Association for $500,000, playing alongside high-scoring Charlie Scott. When he went by 7'2" Artis Gilmore and 6'9" Dan Issel for a tremendous slam dunk after they came down, Dr. J—at 6'7", a 210-pound small forward—knew that he had arrived.[34] In five ABA seasons, two with the Squires and three with the New York Nets, Erving gained All-Star recognition. He won three scoring titles, three MVP awards, and two championships with the Nets. In his rookie year in Virginia, he averaged 27.3 points per game. In his first ABA playoff series, he averaged 33.3 points per game. Unable to join the NBA, Julius remained with the Squires and led the league in scoring with his career-best record of 31.9 points per game. Being traded to the New York Nets proved profitable for Erving and his new team, which he led to a league title in 1974 with a 55–29 regular season record. In addition, Dr. J racked up another scoring title with 27.9 points per game. More than a high scorer, the good doctor displayed other gifts with an impressive record of assists (sixth best in the ABA) along with steals and blocked shots (third best in the league). Consequently, he acquired the first of three consecutive MVP Awards.[35] He applied the skills of Connie Hawkins—swooping dunks, improvisatory moves with "extended hangtime," and delicate grace plus pure power, like modern musical jazz—in every game that he played. In a desperate attempt to beef up attendance, the ABA created a slam-dunk contest in 1975–76 at the mid-season All-Star Game. Competing against great leapers Artis Gilmore, David Thompson, George Gervin, and Larry Kenon, Dr. J wowed the crowd with an amazing dunk that took off from the free-throw line to win the contest. Erving described his strategy:[36]

> For my dunk from the left side, I did what I call the Iron Cross. I'd jump by the basket, spread my arms as if I were flying then dunk the ball behind me without ever looking at the rim.
> For my standstill dunk under the basket, I took a basketball in each hand and then slammed one after the other.
> For my dunk from the right side, I drove under the basket, grabbed the rim with my right hand and slammed the ball with my left.

For the *pièce de résistance* or long dunk, Dr. J started from three quarters back, cradling the ball like it was a baseball. He moved "with long, majestic strides," Carl Scheer recalled, like a "graceful antelope…. Then he was off in the air, and he brought the ball back from behind himself as if he were a helicopter…. He rammed it through the rim. … The people just went crazy." ABA coaches Hubie Brown, Al Bianchi, and Kevin Loughery marveled at Erving's enormous talent, gigantic hands, excellent work ethic, and teamwork.[37]

Financial distress forced a merger of four ABA teams and the NBA despite Oscar Robinson's heroic efforts to block this action. Financial exigency also compelled Nets owner Roy Boe to auction off Erving to the highest bidder. The Knicks stupidly refused an offer to acquire Erving by waiving the Nets' required expansion fee of $4.8 million, demanded by the New York team, claiming territorial rights, for entry into the NBA. The 76ers of Philadelphia won the bidding war by purchasing Erving's contract for $3 million and another $3 million to cover the expansion fee. The Nets' loss of Erving proved a gain for the 76ers. Although injured knees due to incessant pounding and 'bounding reduced some of Dr. J's explosive moves, he still managed to lead his team to title contention. In his first year with the 76ers, fortified with high scorers, Erving could concentrate on other facets of his game: rebounding, passing, and steals. He also won the MVP award with 31 points, 12 rebounds, and four steals. The 76ers won the Atlantic Division title with a 50–32 record. Erving led his new team to the NBA title series against the Portland Trailblazers. After winning the first two games, a pivotal fight between Maurice Lucas and Darryl Dawkins (won by Lucas) and the outstanding play of Bill Walton resulted in four straight losses and a Blazers championship.[38]

An All-Star in all 11 seasons in the NBA, Dr. J had to curb his enthusiasm for flights to the rim among basketball's behemoths. Nevertheless, minus Michael Jordan's jump-shooting skills, he managed to rack up points and continued to wow his many fans. He also conducted clinics in conjunction with his corporate sponsors of athletic shoes and apparel. On one occasion, he came to Long Island University Brooklyn's gym, built in the bowels of the landmarked Brooklyn Paramount

Theater. As a tenured professor, I attended with a neighbor and his young son, among a thousand fans in the stands. Accompanied by former North Carolina Tar Heel hoopster turned sales executive York Larese, Erving demonstrated his warm-up techniques: stretching, walking on the corners of his feet, and shooting from all over the court. He played one-on-one with youngsters to their delight, fielded questions, and expounded on the art of basketball, eloquently. It was a Saturday to remember.

The 76ers reached the NBA finals again in 1980 with a 59–23 record. They beat Washington, Atlanta, and Boston (with rookie Larry Bird) to take on the Los Angeles Lakers, resurgent with the advent of Magic Johnson adding punch to the lineup, spearheaded by our next subject, Kareem Abdul-Jabbar. In the final of the six-game set, Magic, subbing at center for the injured Kareem, tossed in 42 points for the title. Lacking a dominant center, Philly lost once more. In 1981 Dr. J won the MVP award with a 24.3 points per game average plus career highs in assists (364) and steals (173). Tied with Boston in the regular season, 62–20, Philly took a 3–1 lead in the Eastern Conference finals. But Boston rallied, thanks to Larry Bird's sensational play, to win in seven games. A do-over occurred in 1982, beating the Celtics in seven games, only to succumb to the Lakers juggernaut in the finals.

To bolster their chances, the 76ers sent Caldwell Jones and a future first-round draft choice to Houston in exchange for Moses Malone. That deal paid immediate dividends, leading to a 65–17 regular season record. Supported by Mo Cheeks, Andrew Toney, and Bobby Jones, the 76ers breezed through the playoffs, taking eight of nine games. Happily for Julius Erving, they also breezed through the formidable Lakers in four straight, earning the only NBA championship for Dr. J, a moment he still savors. After five years in the ABA at the peak of his power and 11 years in the NBA, Julius Erving hung up his sneakers in 1987 at age 37. To reach the 30,000-point plateau, Dr. J had to score 36 points in his last game. Thanks to teammate Andrew Toney's 13 assists, he scored 38. Erving went out with a bang, not a whimper. In 1993, elected to the Naismith Memorial Basketball of Fame, he was immortalized.[39]

In retirement, Erving's skill coupled with his education brought success. He invested wisely in a Coca-Cola bottling plant in Philadelphia and cable stations in New Jersey and New York. Erving served as NBC studio analyst for basketball telecasts. He is also involved in a sports management company started by his son, Julius III. He even tried the executive suite in Orlando for six years. After pointing out his foibles on defense, outside shooting, weak opposition in the American Basketball Association, that he's a nice guy rather than a killer, the picayune critic Bill Simmons concedes Erving's brilliance, ranking him 16th on his so-called GOAT list, one behind his predecessor as a leaping lord—Elgin Baylor. Simmons ends his quirky summation with this encomium:

> And Julius Erving remains one of the most gripping, terrifying, and unforgettable players I have ever seen in person. If he was filling the lane on a break, your blood raced. If he was charging toward a center and cocking the ball above his head, your heart pounded. Over everything else, I will remember his hands—his gigantic, freak show Freddy Krueger fingers—how he palmed basketballs like softballs…. He did it easily and beautifully, like a golden gust of 110 mph wind, like nothing you have ever seen. His opponents would shake their heads in disbelief…. One of a kind![40]

17

Kareem Abdul-Jabbar
and Earvin "Magic" Johnson

Kareem Abdul-Jabbar

A public intellectual now with 11 books under his championship belt and two books about his life, Kareem Abdul-Jabbar has come a long way from his Harlem roots. An only child born Ferdinand Lewis Alcindor on April 16, 1947, one day after his hero, Jackie Robinson, arrived in Brooklyn, he moved with parents Ferdinand and Cora to the Inwood Public Housing Project, where he grew up. Like his hero, young Lew played baseball and once pitched a no-hitter in a sandlot game, but a growth spurt shifted his attention to basketball. In the seventh grade, Lew was already 6'5" tall. By age 14, he grew another five and half inches when he entered Power Memorial High School, a Catholic all-male school on the west side of mid-town Manhattan. During his three years of varsity hoops in high school, his team lost only one game, to Washington, D.C., powerhouse DeMatha High School 46–43, in which Lew was held to 16 points. As a 7'2" gazelle, Alcindor was highly recruited by St. John's, Holy Cross, Boston College, Michigan, Columbia, and UCLA. Lew might have chosen Holy Cross, where his high school coach, Jack Donohue, became head coach, but in a clumsy attempt to motivate the young star in a close game, he used the "N" word. This ugly incident occurred in his junior year in a game against St. Helena's quintet. At halftime, the volatile Coach Donohue laced into the whole team, finally fixing on his star players: "And you, Lew, you go out there and don't hustle ... you're Lew, you're acting like a n----r!"—alienating the young giant.[1] Alcindor did not respond as he buried his fury that festered. After the game, Coach Donahue brought Lew to his office, crowing that his strategy worked to justify his abhorrent use of words, which broke Alcindor's heart. Many years later, Jabbar and his former coach reconciled. Lew finished his brilliant high school career with 2,017 points and 2,002 rebounds.

Alcindor chose UCLA because it was co-ed and primarily because of Coach John Wooden. According to NCAA rules then, he could not play varsity ball. Nevertheless, Lew scored 31 points in a win over the varsity, which had won the NCAA title two years before the advent of Alcindor. One year later, he led UCLA to a 30–0 record and a new streak of three consecutive NCAA basketball championships, followed by four after his graduation. In a rule revision that many thought was motivated by racism, NCAA officials banned the dunk shot. So, Alcindor polished his unstoppable skyhook shot. Two more titles followed with an 88–2 record, the only two losses to Houston and the University of Southern California.[2]

Academically, Alcindor also starred as a history major. Mesmerized by Malcolm X's autobiography, Lew converted to Islam in 1968. That plus his refusal to join the U.S. Olympic team generated controversy. Drafted number one by the Milwaukee Bucks, he won Rookie of the Year honors as he helped to raise the Bucks from ineptitude with a 27–55 record the prior year to an impressive 56–26 record.[3] I recall raucous Knicks fans chanting derisively "Bye, bye Louie, we hate to see you go" during the playoff series, which the New Yorkers won en route to their first NBA championship. In his second year with Milwaukee, abetted by the addition of legendary star Oscar Robertson, Kareem Abdul-Jabbar (newly named in 1971, the name signifying "servant of God" in Arabic), led the Bucks to a 66–16 record and four-game sweep of the Baltimore Bullets for the NBA title. It was a banner year for Kareem with a league-leading 31.7 points per game and a double MVP for season and playoffs.

Several successful seasons ensued for Abdul-Jabbar, but no more titles for Milwaukee. After his first losing season with the Bucks, he requested a trade to the Los Angeles Lakers. In exchange for four Lakers players, Jabbar went to Los Angeles. With the Lakers, he continued to star. Thanks to the 1979 acquisition of "Magic" Johnson, the Lakers won titles in 1980, 1982, 1985, 1987, and 1998. Jabbar finished his lengthy career with 38,387 points, a record that still stands. Voted the greatest college player by ESPN, KAJ (in short) went on to star in different fields: history and literature. From NBA Rookie of the Year (1970) through six NBA MVPs to his Hall of Fame induction in 1995, Kareem Abdul-Jabbar had quite a career, something to cheer about.

Marcus Hayes, a reporter for the *Philadelphia Inquirer*, wrote an illuminating article on Abdul-Jabbar's literary output.[4] He noted that the great hoopster had written 15 books, appeared in two films, and is a community activist to boot. His 2015 book *Mycroft and Sherlock: The Empty Bird Cage*, is the third in a series featuring Sherlock's older brother, Mycroft. Perhaps Kareem, an only child, projected his need for an older brother as protector. Hayes speculates that Abdul-Jabbar's literary output is a search for "redemption for a life led in haughty judgment of a word he resented, feared, or both."[5] Jabbar's long career required toughness and discipline. For toughness, he studied martial arts under Bruce Lee in the late 1960s and cites yoga for his productivity in the 1980s. In his own words, Jabbar wrote the Holmes trilogy because "I'm passionate about history. I am particularly fond of the Victorian Era when one superpower ruled the waves."[6] Two months of intense research went into *Mycroft and Sherlock: The Empty Bird Cage*, which includes a Black mentor, Cyrus Douglas, age 40, who assists Mycroft Holmes, age 23.

Abdul-Jabbar also writes editorials. His April 2019 article for *The Guardian*, "The Way Americans Regard Sports Heroes versus Intellectuals," speaks "volumes."[7] He begins with a stark contrast. While France mourned Jean-Paul Sartre, a winner of the Nobel Prize in Literature who refused the award because he believed that it would compromise his independent mind, Americans responded to the 1995 death of Russian immigrant Joseph Brodsky, also a Nobel laureate in literature, with barely a nod. Yet Babe Ruth's death elicited 150,000 mourners and Ali's death drew 100,000 bereft admirers. Sadly, Kareem observes that Kardashian is a more familiar name. He notes that recent surveys indicate that 93 percent of American males are spectators while 60 percent are fans, as is Jabbar. Disturbed by the rise of anti-intellectualism regarding facts, science, and logic—think anti-vaxxers and climate change deniers—Kareem decries the current conservative ethos, which he equates with shared ignorance and fake patriotism in the playbook of Trump, the 45th president, who loves dictators and ignores facts. In this populist miasma, junk science reigns as measles (and COVID-19) rates rise, fortified by nutty conspiracy theories. Because they push boundaries, run faster, and jump higher, admired athletes unleash untapped potential. The poorly educated American can read a box score but cannot read an article on melting ice caps. Abdul-Jabbar urges intellectuals not to demean popular culture as a measure of intelligence. Athletic prowess, he argues, can be elegant and balletic. Thus, Kareem seeks a synthesis of two cultures somewhat like the efforts of C.P. Snow to bridge two cultures—science and humanities—over 50 years ago.

Sportswriter Alexander Wolff took the measure of the "new" KAJ as a public intellectual in *Sports Illustrated* (July 14, 2015). Unable to become an assistant coach in the NBA, he shifted comfortably to intellectual pursuits. KAJ put it succinctly (as quoted by Wolff): "I have a platform and a voice, so I might as well use it."[8] *On the Shoulders of Giants* pays tribute to his predecessors in basketball, especially the Harlem Renaissance Five (see prior chapter), and became the template for his film. No longer the target or aloof, he wants to communicate for the greater good. Each story, poem, or play—KAJ insists—can illuminate the dark cave of our existence. Did he have Plato in mind when he shared these ideas with Wolff? Always a reader and thinker, KAJ shares a Malcolm X wish not to be defined by others. In his early years of basketball ascendency, he felt imprisoned by an image. As a gangly 6'10" 14-year-old freshman at Power Memorial High School, he became an object of ridicule, a laughingstock. So, he developed political awareness and joined the debate team. He supported civil rights, CORE, and SNCC. At age 17, he spent the summer at Harlem Youth Opportunities Unlimited (HARYOU), a city-funded program to identify young African Americans with leadership potential.

At HARYOU, Kareem found a mentor in historian John Henrik Clarke, who introduced him to W.E.B. DuBois and Marcus Garvey. KAJ went to the Schomburg Center's collection of Harlem Renaissance writers. After attending a Martin Luther King, Jr., press conference, he was caught in the Harlem riots sparked by the killing of black teenager James Powell by a white police officer. The incident raised Kareem's consciousness, as he wrote: "I was born in Harlem in the summer of 1947. I was reborn in Harlem in the summer of 1964."[9] His sentimental education continued at UCLA when his teacher read aloud in class something he had written about a night with a friend at a jazz club. "Maybe, I could write." What impressed Lew Alcindor about Coach John Wooden, besides his brilliant strategy, was his ability to quote Langston Hughes's poetry by heart. Wooden taught Lewis, as he called him, a lot about "becoming a man as intelligent human being." In 1969, Alcindor began reading Arthur Conan Doyle, becoming in the process a devotee of detective fiction. He read voraciously. A fire in January 1983 in California destroyed his prize possessions as a Los Angeles Laker. KAJ was also finishing his first book, the autobiographical *Giant Steps*. The book revealed a persona, once carefully concealed behind sullen silence. The destructive fire served as a spur to creativity. A second book, *Brothers in Arms*, painted a vivid picture of a highly decorated all-Black 761st tank battalion in World War II. All of his books are co-authored. More books on a variety of subjects followed. He writes three hours each morning. He admires John le Carré and Edgar Allan Poe and uses Elmore Leonard and Ross Thomas for dialogue.[10]

KAJ has five children: Habiba, Sultana, and Kareem Jr. from his marriage with Habiba (1971–78) and two, Adam and Amir, with two different partners. Kareem Jr., at 6'7", played college basketball and with a minor league pro team, the Oklahoma Storm, coached by his famous father. His younger half-brother Amir, as a medical student during one of Kareem Sr.'s medical crises, was able to diagnose his father's leukemia condition in 2008, early enough to save his life. Novartis manufactured a drug, Gleevec, that stabilized his condition. Amir is now an orthopedic surgeon.[11] In 2012, Secretary of State Hillary Clinton appointed Abdul-Jabbar cultural ambassador to promote racial tolerance and multicultural appreciation. Three years later, KAJ required quadruple bypass open-heart surgery. Despite these challenges, he soldiered on. President Barack Obama bestowed the Presidential Medal of Freedom on Kareem Abdul-Jabbar in 2016 before leaving office.

Several years ago, I was introduced to Kareem Abdul-Jabbar in the Long Island University Brooklyn Gym, the home court of the Brooklyn Kings quintet, then situated in the old Brooklyn Paramount Building. At that time, KAJ was coaching a minor league basketball team from Oklahoma. His son Kareem Jr. was a one of the players. After the game, the league commissioner, Ed Krinsky, son of basketball pioneer Nat Krinsky and former basketball captain at Brooklyn's James Madison High School and Cambridge's Harvard College, brought us together for a photo op and a brief chat. I stood in awe, up to Kareem's midsection, captured in a photograph now sitting as a relic on a piano I never play. Unlike his public persona, cultivated for many years,

Kareem Abdul-Jabbar, shown here alongside the author in the 1990s, retired in 1989 as the NBA's all-time leading shot blocker and, according to many of his opponents, the greatest player in league history. In the years since, he has become an author and cultural critic, publishing several books on African American history (author collection).

KAJ seemed gracious and friendly. Until I researched his personal narrative, I could not fathom why he was denied a future in NBA basketball after his retirement until 2007. Kareem's conversion to Islam did not help his cause. Nor did his refusal to participate in the 1968 Olympics, which triggered negative reaction. Most compelling was his outspoken advocacy of civil rights while most of his peers chose silence like Michael Jordan, a silence that KAJ disdained. Enraged by the 1963 Baptist church bombing in Birmingham that killed four young girls and injured 22, he could no longer sit silent on the sidelines. So, he paid a price before others through social media and increased clout found their voice. His criticism of Michael Jordan for refusing to support the senatorial bid of Harvey Gantt against the ultra-reactionary Jesse Helms resonated with progressives if not the political establishment. True, Republicans also buy sneakers, as Jordan rationalized but, in that dispute, Jabbar bent the arc of history towards social justice.

Earvin "Magic" Johnson

Earvin "Magic" Johnson's heroic status is frequently paired with his longtime rival but current friend Larry Bird.[12] That pair started in college when both Johnson and Bird squared off in the 1978 NCAA Final, in which Johnson's Michigan State Spartans beat Bird's Indiana State Sycamores. Truth be told, although my wife Eileen is a Sycamore alumna, I rooted for the Spartans. That said or written, I admire both Bird and Johnson, both of whom left imprints on basketball history. As Martin Gitlin put it, elegantly[13]:

> Two men put the madness into March. Two men popularized a floundering NBA, two men whose friendship off the court eventually matched the intensity of their rivalry on it will be forever linked in the history of basketball.

Born on August 14, 1959, Earvin Johnson, Jr., grew up in Lansing, Michigan, the fourth child in a nuclear family with 10 children. Earvin Johnson, Sr., worked in a General Motors plant by day and collected garbage by night to augment family income while Earvin's mother worked as a school custodian who supervised student lunches. Singing on street corners with friends, Earvin earned the nickname "June Bug" from neighbors. He gravitated to basketball, often playing at 7:30 a.m. and dribbling with both hands as he went on errands. Reluctant at first to attend a predominantly white school in Lansing, Johnson relented. Later, he acknowledged the benefits of integration. "It got me out of my own little world and taught me how to understand white people, and how to communicate with them."[14] His favorite player and winner was Bill Russell, followed by Earl Monroe and Marques Haynes. "Magic" became his moniker when a local reporter, Fred Stabley, Jr., was so awed by Johnson's phenomenal skills—the high school player scored 36 points, collected 15 rebounds, and dished out 16 assists in a single game—that he described them as magical. In his senior year at integrated Everett High School, Johnson led his team to a 27–1 record while averaging 28.8 points and 16.8 rebounds per game. His team won the Michigan state championship.[15]

Though recruited aggressively by Indiana's controversial coach Bobby Knight, Johnson chose to stay close to home at Michigan State University. There, as a freshman, he helped the Spartans go from a losing record to a 25–5 record with 17 points per game, 7.9 rebounds per game, and 7.4 assists per game. The Spartans, however, lost to a more talented Kentucky team in the NCAA Finals. Magic achieved national recognition for his stellar play as a 6'8½" point guard who also played power forward when needed to garner more rebounds. In his sophomore and last year in college, Magic's MSU team got off to a slow start with a 4–4 record. After a soul-searching session with Coach Jud Heathcote, in which Magic led a mini-rebellion to change the half-court offense to a quick up-tempo fast-break run-and-gun attack, the coach relented. It worked. The Spartans finished the season with a 15–1 run; the only loss came as a result of a 55-foot buzzer beater in the final seconds by Wisconsin's Wes Matthews.[16] In the playoffs, Michigan State cruised past Lamar, Louisiana State, and Notre Dame. In the semifinals, the Spartans defeated Ivy League champions, University of Pennsylvania. Now came a showdown with the Larry Bird–led Indiana State Sycamores. Preparing for its undefeated quintet, Coach Heathcote had Magic Johnson imitate Larry Bird.[17] Roughly 18 million households furnished with 40 million viewers, the largest audience ever to watch an NCAA Final, witnessed the success of coach Heathcote's preparation.[18] Smothered by two MSU defenders and controlling all the passing lanes, the great Larry Bird could only score seven buckets in 21 attempts for 19 points, dish only two assists, and commit six turnovers.[19] Conversely, Johnson led all scorers with 24 points on 8-of-15 shooting and seven rebounds followed by Greg Kelser's 19 points and eight rebounds that led Michigan State to victory over Larry Bird's Indiana State quintet for the NCAA basketball championship, 75–64.[20] As Johnson exulted, beaming his signature smile, Bird buried his face in a towel, sobbing salty tears.[21] They resumed their rivalry as NBA professionals.

After his sensational sophomore year in college, Magic decided to turn pro. To decide a joint claim to the first pick in the 1979 NBA draft between Chicago and Los Angeles, Commissioner Larry O'Brien tossed a coin, which the Lakers won. Had they lost, Magic Johnson would have returned to Michigan State.[22] Johnson and his father negotiated a lucrative contract from owner Jack Kent Cooke over lunch. To assert his dominant alpha role, Cooke ordered fish for everyone but himself. Politely, Earvin Johnson, Jr., demurred. He wanted—and got—a hamburger with fries. Cooke offered $400,000. Magic rejected that order, insisting on $600,000, despite his father's willingness to accept the first offer. After a hiatus to think things over, they returned to a pizza lunch and final negotiations. Cooke and Magic compromised at $500,000, making him the richest rookie in NBA history and second only to Lakers veteran star Kareem Abdul-Jabbar's $650,000.[23] Worth every dollar, Johnson had a magical year in 1980. Fortunately for both Johnson and his team, they started another dynasty. Despite resentment from Lakers veterans on lesser salaries, Johnson became NBA Rookie of the Year and Finals MVP and played a brilliant game at center in the absence of Abdul-Jabbar due to injury in game six versus Philadelphia with a spectacular 42 points, 17 rebounds, and seven assists.[24]

Injury marred Magic's second Lakers year as the team failed to repeat while

Larry Bird's Celtics beat the Houston Rockets in six games. After the season, which ended in an early playoff loss to the Houston Rockets, two games to one, Johnson signed a then record contract for $25 million over a 25-year period. In 1982, the Lakers rebounded and beat the 76ers again in six games as Pat Riley, at Magic's behest, replaced Coach Westhead and his slowdown half-court offense with an up-tempo one more in tune with Johnson's genius. Thus, Magic found his groove in arguably his greatest season with 18.6 points per game, 9.6 rebounds per game, and 9.5 assists per game, though he still had to share point guard duties with teammate Norm Nixon.[25] In a third crack at Philadelphia for the title, the Lakers lost in four straight games. Fortified with a new center in Moses Malone, the 76ers prevailed, conferring a singular NBA championship for their star player, Julius Erving, commonly known as Dr. J.

In their first title contest since college, Larry Bird got revenge as the Celtics defeated the Lakers in seven games. In game two, the Lakers led with 31 seconds to play and possession of the ball. James Worthy inbounded the ball with a risky cross-court pass, which was intercepted by Gerald Henderson, who scored to tie the game, which went into overtime. The Celtics won 124–121 and tied the series.[26] In a second pivotal moment, Kevin McHale clobbered Kurt Rambis with impunity on the way to an easy basket, establishing the Celtics' physical superiority in game four.[27] Unusual poor play by Magic in clutch moments during several games also contributed to the Laker loss, providing a put-down by Celtics forward Kevin McHale who altered the epithet to "Tragic" Johnson.[28] Consoled by friends Isiah Thomas and Mark Aguirre after the loss, Magic could take comfort in his overall performance: 18 points per game, 13.6 assists per game, 7.7 rebounds per game, and a .560 shooting percentage. Nevertheless, Johnson regretted this 1984 championship season as the one that got away. Sweet revenge, however, came the following season. Although the Lakers were blown out in game one, 148–114, often referred to as "The Memorial Day Massacre," they regained their mojo in game two as Kareem Abdul-Jabbar defied "Father Time" with a stellar performance of 30 points and 17 rebounds at the age of 38. The Lakers took the next three of four games as Johnson also found redemption in 18.3 points, 6.8 rebounds, and 14.0 assists per game. Revenge was particularly enjoyable for coach Pat Riley, who hated the Celtics.[29] Both Abdul-Jabbar and Johnson claimed it was the highlight of their careers.

The agony of defeat followed the ecstasy of victory as the Houston Rockets ousted the Lakers in a five-game Western Finals playoff series in 1986. So, the following year, a hard-working Magic diligently prepared to pull off his best Lakers season yet. When an eye infection sidelined Abdul-Jabbar, Magic began to increase his scoring output. With 23.0 points per game, 12.2 assists per game, and 6.3 rebounds per game, Magic won his first MVP Award. A third battle with the Boston Celtics produced another high. The Lakers took game one as Magic scored 29 points, grabbed 13 rebounds, dished 8 assists, and had no turnovers in a 126–113 win. In the second-game Lakers win, 141–122, Magic had 22 assists and 20 points. Bird's 30 points helped the Celtics take game three. On Boston's parquet floor, Celts and Lakers faced off for game four. Trailing by 16 points in the fourth quarter, Magic led the charge back. Down one point with seconds remaining, Magic took an inbound pass and drove laterally to the bucket with Parrish and McHale ready to swat whatever shot Johnson put up. He fooled everybody with a sky hook shot borrowed from Kareem's toolbox, leaving his opponents swatting air, as he deftly curled in the winning shot, leading to a 107–106 win. Larry Bird had two seconds to retaliate, but his desperate heave missed the mark. Bird regained his touch in game five, resulting in a Celtic win, 123–108. Game six belonged to the Lakers, 106–93. A rejuvenated Abdul-Jabbar scored 32 points and Magic 16, but more important were Johnson's 19 assists. Averaging 26.2 points, 13 assists, 8 rebounds, and 2.33 steals per game, Magic deservedly won his third Finals MVP Award. A gracious Larry Bird conceded that "Magic is a great, great basketball player … the best I've ever seen."[30]

Could the Lakers repeat as Coach Riley predicted? Yes, they could. The Lakers repeated their victory lap as Coach Riley predicted. In the finals, Magic's Lakers did battle with brawling Detroit Pistons, although love seemed to be in the air as Isiah Thomas and Magic Johnson exchanged kisses prior to game one. A new hero emerged. Former North Carolina Tar Heel James Worthy had a career triple double to lead the Lakers to victory with Johnson now in a supporting role, marking his fifth and final NBA title. The next year belonged to the Detroit Pistons, who took four straight from the Lakers, beset with an injury to their Magic man. Spent, Pat Riley retired to the broadcasting booth, and, showing his age, Kareem also hung up his sneakers. Under new coach Mike Dunleavy, the now vulnerable Lakers lost to a new dynastic team in the making, the Chicago Bulls, and their emergent stars, Michael Jordan and Scottie Pippen, who shadowed Magic throughout the series, which the Bulls won, four games to one.

Though the aging process began to affect Johnson's play, the Lakers star wished to continue. During the pre-season training period, Johnson's insurance policy required a medical exam. Then, in a bombshell disclosure, the word went out, inaccurately, that Magic Johnson had AIDS, tantamount to a death sentence. Fortunately for Magic, family, and millions of fans, he was infected with HIV, not full-blown AIDS. Among the first to know was Johnson's longtime rival Larry Bird. During that fateful conversation, a worried Bird was consoled by Magic with assurances that he would be fine. Once fierce rivals, they bonded in friendship.[31] Advised by his doctors to retire, Johnson agreed and held a press conference on November 7, 1991, assuring viewers that his wife, Cookie, and the unborn child she was carrying were HIV-free. Magic promised to do battle with this potentially deadly disease. In his autobiography, *My Life*, Magic insisted that he was not gay and that he contracted this virus through unsafe sex with multiple partners in a variety of combinations. Some critics found fault with his account as a bit of braggadocio and a tad of homophobic posturing. Whatever his motives—good or bad—he became a public figure who brought attention, like Rock Hudson, to this new epidemic. Unlike the prominent actor, Johnson survived with AZT medication. Thus, Earvin Johnson, Jr., became a hero for the second time in his adventurous life. Acclaimed as such by the first President Bush, Magic won new friends and influenced many people. And he continued the play the game that he loved with several (if unsuccessful) comebacks.

Despite Karl Malone's disinclination, shared by A.C. Green and Byron Scott, to play with or against Magic, thereby incurring danger of contamination,

Johnson—overwhelmingly elected by fans—insisted on playing. And play he did! The West walloped the East with Johnson scoring 25 points, dishing nine assists, grabbing five rebounds, and winning the All-Star MVP. Amazing! And the Magic was not finished. Selected to represent the United States in the Olympics as part of the "Dream Team," arguably the greatest collection of talent—including Michael Jordan, Charles Barkley, and Larry Bird—since Thomas Jefferson dined alone in the White House (to borrow a quip from President Kennedy), Johnson excelled, despite sore knees, with 8 points per game, evoking tremendous love and booming cheers from attendees, becoming in the process the positive face of HIV fighters for their survival.

In retirement, Earvin "Magic" Johnson found new outlets for his extraordinary energy. He joined NBC as a color commentator. To match much-admired Julius Erving's eloquence, Magic took elocution lessons. He bought and sold movie theaters and Starbucks stores in minority neighborhoods to provide employment for inner-city denizens and sold these enterprises to fill deep pockets as a progressive capitalist. He bought into the Los Angeles Dodgers franchise as minority owner. He assumed a similar position with the Lakers in 1994, even serving briefly as coach and, until recently, president of basketball operations for his former team, helping the Lakers to sign LeBron James and acquire Anthony Davis. Johnson barnstormed with former NBA players to Asia and Australia. Magic wrote books and raised money for the United Negro College Fund through his foundation from 1985 to 2005. He got involved in politics as a Democrat, supporting Hillary Clinton in 2016 and other candidates. While writing this summation, I noted his tweets on August 11, 2020:

> Cookie and I are very happy with Presidential candidate Joe Biden's decision to select Senator@KamalaHarris as his running mate. We have happily supported Kamala throughout her career over the years!
>
> Best of all, history was made tonight. The first woman of color was nominated for national office by a major political party. I'm excited that Senator Harris accepted the nomination for Vice President. Her speech was strong, direct, & moving.[32]

Earvin "Magic" Johnson has come a long way from his early morning garbage collection chores in Lansing, Michigan. He found profound joy and huge success through the agency of basketball, invariably flashing that signature smile. Clearly, the charismatic Magic Johnson brought "Showtime" to Los Angeles, from where it beamed a thousand points of light to distant places, appealing to basketball *aficionados* of all races, colors, and creeds. Author James Michener wrote that sports should promote fun, health, and entertainment. Magic Johnson fulfilled that mandate.[33]

18

Charlie Scott
and Michael Jordan

Charlie Scott

Preeminent anthropologist Claude Lévi-Strauss argued that popular hero myths serve to resolve unwelcome contradictions in order to restore equilibrium. In this vital task, the hero functions as healer, savior, deliverer, scapegoat, and quester. Heroes mediate among competing forces in society with which they must also synchronize. In the Jim Crow era, Black hero/leaders had to play role models that were both attractive and non-threatening. Hence, they experienced the constraints of accommodation and the temptations of avoidance. World War II, however, erected a door of opportunity through which Joe Louis and Jackie Robinson ran, opening up boxing and baseball, respectively, to African Americans. A few years later, integration came, too, to basketball, a sport that Blacks would come to dominate.

I was exposed to racial integration at summer camps and through the political activity of a left-leaning family. An African American classmate in junior high school saved me from a sucker punch in the gym, for which I am forever grateful to Milford Dyches. When I became a teacher 12 years later, the student body at Harlem's James F. Cooper Junior High School 120, where I taught, was 85 percent Black and 15 percent Hispanic. Most students had never been beyond the confines of their ghettoized existence. In a basketball game that students played with faculty, an annual ritual, we barely eked out a win against the young teenagers. Of course, it helped that one faculty member, Ralph Bacote, after a stellar college career, played with the Harlem Globetrotters. One mixed-raced 13-year-old student named Cotto, red-haired and freckled, was actually scouted by "Biggie Munn," former football coach at Michigan State and currently its athletic director. Unfortunately, Cotto (I do not remember his first name) succumbed to drugs at an early age and never fulfilled his early promise.

That spring, I was offered a job at my alma mater, Stuyvesant High School, arguably the best academic high school in our country. Before you can say Jackie Robinson stole second base, I flew downtown to 345 East 15th Street and First Avenue to teach alongside my former mentors. Quite an honor and somewhat intimidating, I was in academic nirvana. My euphoria was short-lived as I was fired at term's end by a hostile principal, Leonard Fliedner, who was booed at graduation and scorned by students as well as many faculty as "The Flea" for his disturbing dictatorial ways. Here is the main reason for my ouster. Assigned three classes in American History and two in European History, I had many brilliant students and two outstanding athletes, both African American. One would go on to integrate North Carolina "Tar Hell" basketball and earn fame and fortune in the NBA. He was at that time 6'1" of thin, wiry frame. Blessed with a good mind and a fine sense of humor, he earned an 85 in my class despite difficulty, it turned out, in several other classes. Dr. Fliedner, the principal, summoned me to his office and questioned my grade for Charlie Scott. Because Charlie was failing other classes, Fliedner directed me to change Scott's grade to an F. With the rationale that Charlie's performance in other classes had no bearing on mine, I absolutely refused and indicated that I would file a grievance with our fledgling teachers' union, the United Federation of Teachers. Later, he observed a class that I taught on imperialism and wrote a predictably negative evaluation. Two other incidents invite mention. Fliedner entered my homeroom class during the obligatory Pledge of Allegiance each morning. Some of the students were talking and indifferent to this solemn ritual. Fliedner pounced on one offender, Thomas Musliner, who happened to be the number one student with the highest average in the senior class and already accepted at Harvard. The apoplectic principal threatened to deprive Thomas of his diploma. Deeply aggrieved at the shabby treatment of their son and well appointed in their community, armored with political clout, Musliner's parents apparently threatened to sue the feckless principal. He relented but found an easy target in this untenured teacher. I was fired and Charlie Scott left school that summer.

Many years later, I attended a panel discussion at the NBA store. Larry Doby and Charlie Scott were the guest attendees. During the Q&A, I reminded Charlie Scott about our dual departure from Stuyvesant High School. He confided that family woes and enormous pressure caused him to drop out. His father had died and his mother abandoned him at age 14 according to Cody Cunningham.[1] The Stuyvesant High School basketball coach gave Charlie a hard time because he was Black, even though he was already gaining attention as an Amateur Athletic Union player and exciting fans in Rucker League competition. One of my colleagues told me that in one game, Scott scored 11 baskets in 12 attempts, for which he was benched as a "chucker" by the basketball coach. Nevertheless, Charlie Scott, gifted with a scholarship, attended Laurinburg Institute High School in North Carolina, where nothing could be finer when you are both a star athlete and a high-achieving scholar, a compelling dyad of brains and brawn.[2] Valedictorian of his high school class, he proved me right and Fliedner wrong.

Avidly scouted by the then Davidson coach "Lefty" Driesell, Scott opted for North Carolina rather than Duke, Wake Forest, and Davidson after Coach Dean Smith brought him to his integrated church. Charlie attended a "Jubilee Weekend" on campus, which featured Smokey Robinson and the Miracles. Also recruited by Assistant Coach Larry Brown and encouraged by his high school coach, Frank McDuffie, Scott chose Chapel Hill. A pioneer, he became the first African American to earn an athletic scholarship at the University of North Carolina in 1966. Scott led his team to the NCAA Final Four in consecutive years, 1968 and

1969.[3] While watching a final game for the NCAA title on my black and white TV, I spotted a familiar face, only four inches taller than the student that I remembered. "That's Charlie Scott!" I shouted to one in particular in my bachelor apartment, all alone with memories. Overlooked for best player awards, Scott averaged 27.1 points per game in his senior year. Despite Harry Edwards's advocacy of an Olympic boycott, Scott, along with high school phenom Spencer Haywood, helped the USA team win gold in Mexico City in 1968, shades of Jesse Owens and Ralph Metcalfe. Despite his success, Scott experienced the loneliness of a pioneer on the basketball frontier. On the court, however, Scott soared, especially in the traditional rivalry pitting UNC against Duke. As Cunningham describes this epic struggle in 1968, Scott led the Tar Heels back from a deficit at halftime to a stunning victory, 85–74. He scored 40 points on 17 field goals in 23 attempts. While everyone celebrated, Scott returned to his hotel room because of racial restrictions.[4] In his senior year, Scott averaged 27.1 points, 8.6 rebounds, and 3.1 assists per game.

Drafted by Boston's Celtics, Charlie chose to go pro with the Virginia Squires of the American Basketball Association, as did Julius Erving. In 1971, he led the league in scoring with a 34.6-points-per-game average. He made the all-ABA team and tied Dan Issel for the league's rookie of the year.[5] One year later, he entered the NBA with the Phoenix Suns, leading to a championship final with the Celtics, who had traded him for Paul Silas. Unable to defeat the Celtics, he joined them in a trade for another Paul—Westphal—and two draft picks. Consequently, he earned a title ring as the Celtics defeated the Suns in 1976 for the world title. He hung up his sneakers in 1980 with a hefty scoring total of 14,937 points. Voted into the Basketball Hall of Fame in 2018, he enjoyed a successful career after basketball in business, initially at Champion Apparel, later with a telemarketing firm. Unlike many athletes, he did not pursue "the high life" and squander his money. More to the point of this book, he paved the way for other outstanding athletes to thrive under Dean Smith at UNC.

A solid family man, Charlie Scott married twice. With his first wife, Margaret, he had a daughter named Holly. With second wife, Trudy, he has three children: daughter Simone, and two sons, Shawn and Shannon. The latter played for Ohio State, bringing the family north. Early life for Charlie, to echo poet Langston Hughes, was "no crystal stair." He kept climbing as a proud Black man to glory. Never easy, it was the right path as he asserted in his eloquent Hall of Fame induction speech in 2018 with his family in attendance. These names spring to mind: Sam Perkins, James Worthy, Kenny Smith, Raymond Felton, Rasheed Wallace, Brad Daugherty, Jerry Stackhouse, Walter Davis, Bob McAdoo, Antawn Jamison, Vince Carter (still playing at 41), and Ty Lawson. Lest we forget, one of the greatest players in the NFL, Lawrence Taylor, also hailed from UNC. And of course, at the pinnacle stands the GOAT who jumps into a later frame as Michael Jordan. Tar Heel star and highly regarded pro hoopster Walter Davis paid tribute to Charlie Scott with these words[6]:

> I never had to go through what he had to go through. You admire people on how they handle bad things in their life. And he played great. He was All-American and played pro. When I got to Carolina, I just had to play ball, listen to coach and go to class. That was it. He took all the heat. He made that possible for all of us to do that at Carolina.

Basketball legend Charlie Scott (left) and 13-time U.S. sabre champion Peter Westbrook at the NBA Store, New York, in 2000. Westbrook participated in every Olympiad from 1976 to 1996, winning a bronze in 1984 to become the first African American to medal in fencing. Scott starred at the University of North Carolina, where he became the first African American on a full athletic scholarship in a once-segregated institution. He led the Tar Heels to two NCAA Finals before moving on to the ABA for two seasons and the NBA for eight. Scott was inducted in the Basketball Hall of Fame in 2018 (author collection).

Michael Jordan

When assessing the astronomical ascent of Michael Jordan, we enter a brave new world. Arguably, the world's most recognized and admired athlete—in the French idiom, *basketeur*—he attracted huge crowds the last time he saw Paris. Idolized not unlike *Le Roi Soleil*, Jordan reached the pinnacle of fame in 1998, earning a grand total of $78 million. In his definitive study of Mr. Jordan, David Halberstam cited a variety of sources.[7] Even the social critic Harry Edwards, not given to hyperbole when discussing Black athletes, whom he often equates with "gladiators" in white America, regards Jordan as the quintessence of human achievement on par with Gandhi, Einstein, and the other Michael—Michelangelo. Coach Phil Jackson tried to lay a guilt trip on Jordan by referring to his extraordinary talent as a form of artistic genius, which belongs to the millions for their pleasure. Heeding his inner voice, Jordan departed into the sunset in the mythic manner of Shane, Charlie Chaplin, and Jim Brown. "God's child," "Jesus in Nikes," "Ten": the Chicago Bull icon has earned his rubrics and spurs.[8]

The advent of this miracle worker on the hardwood floor did not occur in a vacuum. In contrast to baseball, basketball started in the upper reaches of African

American society. One can trace this development to the prestigious St. Christopher Club of New York and say the sport sprouted from the roots of "muscular Christianity." Sponsored by the wealthiest Black congregation in America—St. Philip's Protestant Episcopal Church, founded in 1809—basketball flourished. Promoting "physical vigor, mental alertness and moral soundness," the program attracted 1,000 members and spurred competition with other social/athletic clubs.

Basketball games complemented dances in "hot" social events, which both sexes enjoyed at the Manhattan Casino on 155th Street. In 1913–14, a white coach, Jeff Wetzler, tutored the first of many great Black players: Clarence "Fats" Jenkins. As a 16-year-old, Jenkins won the city championship in the 100-yard dash while attending Commerce High School. Lean and compact, belying his nickname, Jenkins also excelled as a left-handed hitting outfielder and as a superb basketball player. He led the St. Christopher quintet to triumph in 1914. He went on to star in the Black baseball circuit. Later, Paul Robeson lent his enormous athletic talent to this team. A Rutgers All-American in football and track, the future singer/actor played center in basketball. His 6'2" frame provided strength in the middle flanked by the Jenkins brothers. Basketball in Harlem proved a pleasant diversion for young Paul.

The center of gravity in basketball shifted to Pittsburgh under the leadership of Cum Posey, Jr., who assembled a dream team called the Loendi Big Five. This quintet featured college stars: George Gilmore from Howard and the Young brothers—Ulysses and William—from Lincoln University and their childhood friend, James "Pappy" Ricks.[9] Looming above the rest was the tallest player of that era: 6'7" James "Legs" Sessoms. They dominated inter-city play until the emergence of the Harlem Renaissance Big Five, arguably the best Black team in history under the aegis of Bob Douglas. The Rens owner emigrated from St. Kitts in 1901. He fell in love with "the city game." More adroit as promoter than player, Mr. Douglas worked as a doorman and later as a tireless organizer of sporting events featuring the Caribbean Athletic Club, which competed in cricket as well as in basketball. He joined forces with an immigrant from Montserrat, William Roche, who became a successful realtor. With capital generated from real estate, he built the Harlem Renaissance Casino, a two-story center that presented films downstairs and basketball games upstairs. Allied with Roche, Douglas hit pay dirt in 1923 with the Harlem "Rens." Evidently named after this new casino in Harlem rather than the cultural explosion that rocked New York City in the 1920s, the center served as home base for the famous quintet, which won its first game against the Chicago Collegians by a score of 28–22 on November 30, 1923. Soon the best team in Black basketball—perhaps all basketball—the Rens featured Leon Monde, Hy Monte, Zack Anderson, Clarence "Fat" Jenkins (also a fine Negro League baseball player), and Frank Forbes (later the first black boxing judge).

Douglas pioneered on the urban frontier. He offered the players monthly contracts and a customized bus. This vehicle, loaded with modern amenities, toured the South bringing the city game to rural America. But Douglas cooked up the hottest rivalries in cities where fans turned out in large numbers to watch the Rens take on the Young Men's Hebrew Association of South Philadelphia or the Original Celtics at home. With the elimination of the center jump and the introduction of a smaller ball minus the laces, which had impaired dribbling, the game shifted into high gear with speed and jumping ability at a premium. Powered by this new style, the Rens crested during the 1930s. Playing center, a new recruit, Wee Willie Smith—who towered above opponents and teammates alike at 6'5"—led this team to 88 consecutive wins during the 1932–33 season. Joining veteran Fat Jenkins and Smith, James "Pappy" Ricks, Eyre Saitch, Bill Yancey, Johnny Holt, and "Tarzan" Cooper racked up a phenomenal record, from 1932 to 1936, of 473–49. Traveling in southern comfort on the custom Blue Goose bus, the Rens added Pop Gates, a local star at Benjamin Franklin High who attended Xavier College in Louisiana, and Johnny Isaacs. A hothead with a hot hand, Gates was a brilliant shooter who complemented the outstanding playmaking skills of Rens survivor Johnny Isaacs. Each player earned a monthly salary of $145 plus a stipend of three dollars per day meal money. Coach and impresario Bob Douglas insisted on proper deportment and neat attire. He cultivated a sense of professionalism on and off the court. In a showdown contest, the Rens copped the vaunted world title by defeating the Harlem Globetrotters in 1939. After that high point, players shifted to other franchises in quest of further glory and a little gold.[10]

Many players built a real bridge to the mythical El Dorado. Chuck Cooper, Earl Lloyd, and Nat "Sweetwater" Clifton are credited with being the first Blacks to enter the National Basketball Association in 1950 as part of the Boston Celtics, Syracuse Nationals, and New York Knickerbockers, respectively. Despite initial quotas and setbacks through scandal, many more would follow—too numerous to delineate here. Attention must be paid, however, to Maurice Stokes, whose career—indeed life—was tragically shortened by an attack of encephalitis. As a collegiate star at Saint Francis College in Loretto, Pennsylvania, Stokes could do it all: shoot, pass, rebound, and win. Earlier, due to a point-fixing scandal that rocked New York City basketball, America's premier college player at Long Island University, Sherman White, was banned for life. The most dominating force in modern basketball, no doubt, was Bill Russell. In his mano-a-mano duels with another giant, Wilt Chamberlain, the wiry Celtic center transformed the game with superhuman defensive skills—rebounding and shot blocking. With a superior supporting cast of role players, the great Russell led his team to 11 world championships in 13 seasons. The last two titles came during his dual tenure as player/coach. Oscar Robertson of the Cincinnati Royals and Elgin Baylor of the Los Angeles Lakers deserve mention for their extraordinary gifts as well. So do Earvin "Magic" Johnson and Kareem Abdul-Jabbar for their stellar play in Los Angeles. Like the last act in basketball, however, time is running short. So, let us fast forward to Michael Jordan.

Reputedly the best and the brightest of the modern cohort, Michael Jordan was born in Brooklyn, the fourth of five children, on February 17, 1963. His parents moved to North Carolina in search of a better life in 1970. This future star endured the trials of Hercules. He survived a severe electric shock at age two. He nearly drowned at age seven. He had cause to be phobic about water. His college girlfriend drowned in a flood.[11] His parents, solidly middle-class, raised the children with mainstream values. His father, James, an air force veteran, encouraged his children not to overreact to the "N" word. His mother, Delores, a bank teller, realized that education was the gateway to social betterment. Growing up, Michael competed with older brother Larry, built like a fireplug, all muscle but only 5'7" in height. A tremendous leaper, Larry pushed Michael to the limit and beyond. During his sophomore year at Laney High School, Jordan experienced a profound setback: he was dismissed from the varsity basketball squad.[12] He cried a river.

Then, he enjoyed a major growth spurt: four inches in a few months. Always fast, he could now dunk. Young Michael worked tirelessly to perfect his craft. As a junior, he returned to the varsity, which compiled a 13–10 record. This record improved to 19–4 in his senior year. Spurred by his father and Coach Clifton "Pop" Herring, he shot more. Recruiters took note. Initially, Jordan favored North Carolina State. A trip to Chapel Hill, however, exposed Michael to a minority support program, Project Uplift. He was impressed. Roy Williams, then a poorly paid assistant to Dean Smith, actively wooed Jordan. His parents liked Williams too.[13] In his senior year, averaging 27 points, six assists, and 12 rebounds per game, Jordan was invited to the 1981 McDonald's All American Game, where he scored 30 points and gained national attention.[14]

So, he headed for North Carolina. In the first game, he scored 12 points against Smith's former team, the Kansas Jayhawks. The culmination of a dream season came on March 29, 1982, when Jordan calmly canned a 16-foot jumper with 15 seconds left to defeat a Patrick Ewing–led Georgetown for the NCAA title. No sophomore slump followed, but his team, the Tar Heels, faltered. Jordan sank another buzzer beater to best Tulane in a game North Carolina won in triple overtime. Against a top-rated Syracuse team, Jordan scored 18 points, amassed seven rebounds, and made a key block while the game was on the line.[15]

A Maryland opponent described his play this way: He "roams like a madman." Madly, he pursued perfection. After a loss, he worked extra hard on defense and improving his shots. He developed a close bond with Coach Dean Smith, who advised him to turn pro. Following his junior—and last—year at North Carolina, Jordan led the American Olympic team to victory with a 37.1 points per game average, gaining international attention. Joining the professional ranks as a Chicago Bull (he was not the first pick in the NBA draft: that distinction went to a Kentucky underachiever named Sam Bowie), he quickly developed "the blackest game of all." He could do it all: jump, shoot, defend, pass, rebound, and drive.[16] In a spectacular career, he won 10 scoring titles, five MVP awards, six NBA championships, and two Olympic gold medals, not to mention several all-star contests where he won trophies for being the best player on the court. Nelson George argues that the bald Michael Jordan, like Jack Jackson, redefined American masculinity. His winning smile and his spectacular feats on the hard court propelled him onto another planet.[17] If women are from Venus and men from Mars, then MJ is from the sun. Born in Brooklyn, Jordan is now a global citizen. So brilliant and dazzling, when he failed in baseball, many fans—this writer included—felt relieved. No one, not even Michael Jordan, is perfect or comparable to Jackie Robinson in diversity of talent. In 15 seasons as a hoopster interrupted by a strange interlude in baseball, Jordan became an iconic figure and a billionaire to boot, earning $30 million a year playing basketball and twice that amount from personal businesses and endorsements.[18]

Though his swagger and early endorsements may have alienated teammates as well as opponents, Jordan drove the Chicago Bulls out of mediocrity and bolstered NBA coffers. In his first year, Jordan averaged 28.2 points per game with a shooting percentage of 51.5 and appeared on the cover of *Sports Illustrated*. Thus, a star was born.[19] A quick study, Michael added humility to his playbook in his second season and led the Bulls into the playoffs once he returned to play (contrary to medical orders) after a broken left foot put him on the deactivated list for 64 games. Despite losing to the championship-bound Celtics, Jordan electrified fans with an outburst of 63 points in game two. He even elicited praise from a victorious Larry Bird, who proclaimed: "I think he's God disguised as Michael Jordan."[20]

Under new ownership, management, and personnel, the Bulls began to build towards a championship. Jordan had another great regular season—average 37.1 points per game, 48.2 shooting percentage, 200 steals, and 100 blocks—but they were swept by the Celtics again. General Manager Jerry Krauss, "the gerbil," brought in Bill Cartwright and Craig Hodges through trades and drafted Scottie Pippen to bolster the team. Nevertheless, for the next three years, the Bulls could not get past the "Bad Boys" from Detroit whose goon tactics and "Jordan Rules" (three defenders converge on Jordan whenever he gets the ball) effectively stymied the Bulls. With the addition of power forward Horace Grant, guard John Paxson, and coach Phil Jackson in 1987, however, the Bulls managed to beat the Pistons, finally. Jackson applied the principles of selflessness, compassion, love, and the triangle offense (from Tex Winter), which Jordan bought into gradually. Phil Jackson installed his own rules, including an emphasis on defense, brought over from his playing days as a New York Knick.[21]

According to sportswriter Sam Smith, everyone was unhappy during the 1990–91 season. Coach Jackson was struggling to get Jordan to accept the triangle offense. Underpaid, Scottie Pippen was pissed off. Horace Grant, Stacey King, and Will Perdue wilted under Jordan's withering criticism. As Jim Paxson remembered: "Here we are winning and no one is happy" as revealed in the *The Last Dance*, ESPN's 10-part documentary.[22] Yet, Jordon persevered and bore no grudges. Having the final say on the ESPN series, which caused a number of arguments among dissenting voices, Michael approved the appearance of Sam Smith, though he knew that the sportswriter was not going to burnish his image, a major concern of the incomparable *basketeur*.[23]

In their first NBA final, the Bulls beat the formidable Los Angeles Lakers after losing game one. In the pivotal second game, Jordan scored 33 points, leading the Bulls to a rout, 107–86. They won the next three games and the title. Holding the trophy, his head buried in wife Juanita's arms, Michael Jordan cried as millions watched.[24] He also laughed all the way to the bank from promoting Chevrolet, McDonald's, Coca-Cola, Gatorade (source of the "Be Like Mike" slogan), Johnson & Johnson products, and Nike. He became the first basketball player to appear on the "Breakfast of Champions," the Wheaties cereal box.[25]

The Bulls' second championship pitted Jordan against Clyde Drexler's Portland Trailblazers, who fumbled their chance to claim Jordan in the 1984 draft. In 1992, the Bulls had set a regular season record, winning 67 of 82 games. Jordan won his second consecutive MVP Award. During the 1992 Super Bowl, his commercial with Bugs Bunny, called "Hare Jordan," won an award for the best commercial of that extravaganza, adding more money and exposure to the Jordan brand. The year of 1992 marked Jordan's second triumph in the Olympics. Possibly the greatest assemblage of hoopsters, aptly named the "Dream Team," won gold easily. Jordan joined Larry Bird, Scottie Pippen, David Robinson, Charles Barkley, Patrick Ewing, Christian Laettner (the only amateur), Chris Mullen, and Magic Johnson, recently retired due to his HIV diagnosis, to beat their opponents by an average of 44 points per game. Public adulation followed Jordan everywhere.[26]

Gambling issues dogged Jordan throughout the 1992–1993 season. He wrote a $57,000 check to an unsavory character named James "Slim" Bouler to cover gambling debts. Sports executive Richard Espinas wrote a book claiming that he won $1.25 million in a 10-day golf and card-playing spree, proving that Jordan was less than god-like. Jordan insisted that he never bet on basketball. Charles Barkley, now playing for the Phoenix Suns, won the NBA MVP Award that year. He also led his team to the NBA title series against Jordan's Bulls. Seeking to eclipse Jordan's commercial success at Nike, Barkley posed a challenge to Jordan's supremacy on and off the court. In a six-game series, Jordan bested Barkley, scoring 31 points in game one, which resulted in a Bulls win, 100–92. He scored 55 points in game four, shooting the winning shot directly over "Sir Charles" on the way to a third successive Bulls' championship.[27]

Jordan's beloved father was murdered on July 23, 1993, at a highway rest area. Depressed and exhausted, Michael announced his retirement on October 6, 1993. As a tribute to his late father, Michael established a Chicago Boys & Girls Club. He then ventured into another field of dreams, one evoking happy times with his father, James, at baseball games. He became a baseball player in the Chicago White Sox organization, starting with the Double A Birmingham Black Barons, a city and name harking back to Willie Mays's Negro League debut. In 1994 he played in the Arizona Fall League, lifting his batting average to .252, up from .202 in 1993.[28]

Lion-hearted, he retreated into his den after his father, James, was murdered. Absent from basketball for 21 months, he played lackluster baseball for 1.5 years, cut short by a threatened Major League Baseball strike in his second season. Late in 1994–95, he announced: "I am back!" Jordan proceeded to average 27.9 points in a late 17-game stretch, in which the Bulls went 13–4. To prove he was indeed back with a long-range jump shot, he scored 55 points against the Knicks in his sixth game in Madison Square Garden, the most famous arena in basketball. Although Jordan averaged 31.5 points per game in the semifinals, the Orlando Magic, featuring massive Shaq O'Neal, trash-talker Nick Anderson, and former teammate Horace Grant, won the series, four games to two.[29]

Like the "hero of 1000 faces" of that imaginative if anti–Semitic scholar, Joseph Campbell, Jordan dropped out then returned to lead the Bulls to three more championships in the next four years after losing to the Orlando Magic in the play-offs. To replace Grant, the Bulls traded for the quixotic Dennis Rodman, a great rebounder and an unselfish defensive wizard. Steve Kerr and Trent Tucker replaced the departed three-point shot-makers, Jim Paxson and B.J. Armstrong. Despite injury-plagued knees, Ron Harper added necessary defense. With the restoration of his old number 23 in place of 45, Jordan and Pippen led the Bulls to a new record of 72 victories during the regular season. They rolled through the playoffs, beating Miami in three straight, the Knicks in five, and the Magic, for sweet revenge, in four straight. Rodman outplayed Grant at power forward. In the NBA Finals, the Bulls took three straight from the Supersonics of Seattle, who responded with two victories. In game six, the Bulls demonstrated mental toughness, heart, and talent, as Sonics coach George Karl observed, and won handily, 87 to 75.[30] After the final game ended, appropriately, on Father's Day, Jordan clutched the ball and unashamedly wept openly, no doubt with father James Jordan on his mind.

Chicago continued to win in 1996–97. Dennis Rodman went berserk in one contest, kicking a photographer in the groin, a flagrant foul, which led to an 11-game suspension, followed by an injury that benched him for another 13 games, leading to several losses. Activated, the mercurial Rodman led the Bulls to a 48–4 record. Again, the Bulls breezed through the playoffs in order to take on the Utah Jazz for the title. Malone had superseded Michael Jordan as the MBA's MVP in the 1996–1997 season, but the Bulls beat his Utah Jazz in six games for their fifth crown. A pivotal game five brought out the best in the heroic Jordan. Suffering from a stomach virus that had kept him awake the prior evening, Jordan willed himself into play. In that crucial moment, viewed globally, Jordan scored 38 points, 15 in the last quarter. He was helped off the court by Scottie Pippen.[31]

The climax of this meteoric career is dramatically recounted in David Halberstam's definitive book. Ailing and fatigued, Sir Michael girded on his armor for a last campaign in 1997–98. The Bulls finished with a 60–22 record in the regular season. In the playoffs, they took the New Jersey Nets in three straight, the Charlotte Hornets in five, and the Pacers in seven hard-fought games. The Utah Jazz, on paper at least, led by the mountainous Karl Malone and the speedy John Stockton, had a distinct edge, particularly in reserve strength. The Bulls lost the first game and were on the verge of losing the second. Jordan put in an offensive rebound to bring the Bulls back in the fourth quarter while Malone disappeared. Enervated by flu, Jordan went into high gear to lead Chicago to the brink of victory, three games to two. Playing on the Jazz's home court, the Bulls trailed but stayed close. In the waning minutes, Jordan snatched victory from the jaws of defeat. Driving to the hoop, he was fouled repeatedly and sank the foul shots in the clutch. With a little over two minutes remaining, Utah held an 83 to 79 lead. Jordan sank two foul shots with 2:07 remaining. Fouled again with 59.2 seconds on the clock, Michael calmly buried two foul shots. Stockton then hit a "trey," giving the Utah quintet a three-point lead 41.9 seconds before the end. Then Jordan took Bryan Russell to school with a blitz along the baseline. High off the glass the ball went in, putting his team one point short of a tie. With 37 ticks left, the Jazz held the ball for a Malone maneuver. Anticipating the pass, Jordan came around Karl's blind side and cleanly swiped the ball. Instead of calling for a time-out, the magnificent Mr. Jordan pushed the pellet to the goal with only 19 seconds left. Working the clock down to eight seconds, Jordan suddenly darted to a spot, isolating Bryan Russell one on one. Russell went for the fake. Jordan pulled up, jumped on tired legs, and swish—the ball fell through the hoop. Michael's mechanics were perfect. Finally, the Bulls had forged ahead. The Jazz could not capitalize on their six-second possession. Stockton's shot missed the mark. The Bulls won 87–86. Jordan had scored 45 points: 22 in the second half, 8 (all that the Bulls could muster) in the game's final minutes. A world watched in awe as Michael proved that he was indeed immortal, at least in the world of basketball. A star of international dimensions, Michael Jordan produced good vibrations for America from sports to politics.[32]

Subsequently, Jordan put on a Washington Wizards uniform in 2001 as player/part owner in a deal designed with owner Abe Pollin. Somewhat below his prior superstar performance and primarily positioned at small forward, Jordan still scored 20 or more points per game until a knee injury reduced him to a mere mortal. As a judge of talent, his first-round pick of high school star Kwame Brown proved painfully poor. Fired by Pollin, Jordan felt betrayed.[33] As the third richest African American behind Oprah Winfrey and Robert Smith, Jordan is well fixed at $1.7 billion. A majority owner of the Charlotte Hornets since 2010, Michael Jordan was awarded the Presidential Medal of Freedom in 2016 by our first African American president, Barack Obama. Both flying high exemplify the fulfillment of the America Dream.

Who, in the Gershwin groove, could ask for anything more? Perhaps courage. Jordan's refusal to use his fame as a force for social and political change invited criticism. Dave Zirin wrote: "Much is also expected of those with power. And no athlete who has ever had more and has done less than Michael Jeffrey Jordan has done."[34] Most athletes, like Jordan, looked away when Rodney King was beaten by police. Jordan refused to endorse African American Harvey Gantt's effort to unseat notorious racist Jesse Helm, joking—according to Sam Smith—because "Republicans buy sneakers too." More outspoken Black athletes—Craig Hodges, Hank Aaron, Arthur Ashe, and Jim Brown—have questioned Jordan's rules of neutrality. In 1992, Jim Brown complained that he (Air Jordan) "is more interested in his image for shoe deals than helping his own people."[35] In defense of Jordan, African American sportswriters argued that Jordan has a right to be silent but he missed a golden opportunity to promote racial justice. Discreetly, "His Airness" did contribute money to the Gantt campaign as well to the Obama campaign. His numerous charities—noted elsewhere in this book—speak to a more compassionate, civic-minded person than the one portrayed in the 2020 documentary *The Last Dance*. Clearly, Michael Jordan will be remembered for his basketball genius and carefully crafted image, reflected in the many honors he has earned, especially in his induction into the Naismith Memorial Basketball Hall of Fame in 2009. Humbly—an attitude nurtured over a long career—Michael acknowledged his debt to predecessors in a co-authored autobiography, *For the Love of the Game*, in which he stated:

> There is no such thing as a perfect basketball player, and I don't believe there is only one greatest player either. Everyone plays in different eras. I built my talents on the shoulders of someone else's talent. I believe greatness is an evolutionary process that changes and evolves era to era. Without Julius Erving, David Thompson, Walter Davis, and Elgin Baylor there would never have been a Michael Jordan. I evolved from them.[36]

19

LeBron James
and Kobe Bryant

LeBron James

Arguably the greatest basketball player of our time, LeBron James was born on December 10, 1984, to a 16-year-old mother, Gloria, and an absent father, Anthony McClellan, who had a criminal record. LeBron and his mother moved seven times during his first five years. His love for basketball started in elementary school. By the time that he had reached the eighth grade, he gained a wide reputation in Amateur Athletic Union ball with the Northeast Ohio Shooting Stars. In his first season at St. Vincent–St. Mary High School in Akron, Ohio, he averaged 18 points per game and led his team to the state title. He also played football as a wide receiver. During his remarkable sophomore season, LeBron averaged 25.2 points per game, 7.2 rebounds per game, 5.5 assists per game, and 3.3 steals per game, leading his team to another state championship. ESPN closely followed his promising career, as did *The Sporting News*. Because he had accepted gifts from a Cleveland sporting goods store, he was declared ineligible. Evoking angry protest, that suspension lasted only one day. In his senior year, LBJ (James not Johnson) rose to new heights with 31.5 points and 10 rebounds per game, leading his team to a third state title in four years. Dubbed Ohio's "Mr. Basketball," James attracted national attention. During his four high school years, James scored 2,657 points, corralled 892 rebounds, and made 523 assists.[1] Spurning any and all college scholarship offers, James, like his predecessor Kobe Bryant, went straight to the pros: he was drafted by the Cleveland Cavaliers in 2003 as their first selection.[2]

James's debut yielded 25 points. Later, he scored 41 points against the New Jersey Nets. Throughout his rookie season, he averaged 20 points, five rebounds, and five assists. Only Michael Jordan and Oscar Robertson had amassed comparable totals. Thanks to the advent of LeBron, Cleveland upped its win total from 17 to 25. At 6'8" and 260 pounds with speed, agility, savvy, desire, and dedication, he soared in the public eye. He was the youngest player at age 20 to score more than 50 points in an NBA game.[3] He added strength to his arsenal using weights, improved his long-distance shooting, and developed superior defense. In the 2006 playoffs, he scored 32 points, corralled 11 rebounds, and plied 11 assists in his first game. Two years later, he won the scoring title playing mostly at guard. James led Cleveland to

233

its best record in the NBA and won MVP honors with 28.4 points, 7.6 rebounds, and 7.2 assists per game. Disappointment followed, however, as underdog Orlando plied its magic to take a playoff series in six games. Daunted by defeat, LBJ, now a free agent, signed with Miami, joining Chris Bosh and Dwayne Wade to create a formidable *troika* for pursuit of an elusive NBA title. This move elicited charges of betrayal by Cavaliers owner Dan Gilbert. Many fans regarded James as a mercenary; James responded in kind, claiming that the blowback was tinged with racism.

Regardless of his motive, James found success with his new team after a slow start. When he returned to Cleveland with the Heat, he was loudly booed. Perhaps his 38 points and Miami's win that night may have added oxygen to the flames of furious fans. LeBron averaged 26.7 points per game with the Miami Heat. In the semifinal playoffs, they defeated the once mighty Celtics in five games largely due to LeBron's will to win, scoring the last 10 points during crunch time of the final game. The Heat, however, lost to the Dallas Mavericks, who benefited from their German import, Dirk Nowitzki, and recent acquisitions, including Tyson Chandler from the Charlotte Bobcats and Jason Kidd from the New York Nets, in advantageous trades. Ever resilient, James and teammates rebounded the following years. Off to a fast start, the Heat again reached the finals with James leading the charge with 27.1 points, 7.9 rebounds, 6.2 assists, and 1.9 steals per game. In the playoffs, the Heat dispatched the Indiana Pacers quickly and the Celtics less quickly in seven hard-fought games. With LeBron at this best, the Miami Heat disposed of Oklahoma City in five games. In the mano-a-mano struggle with Oklahoma City's best player, Kevin Durant, James was chosen MVP, a laurel now named after the great Bill Russell. In game five, James scored 26 points, garnered 11 rebounds, and dished out 13 assists. That victory marked LBJ's first title.

The Miami Heat repeated in 2012–2013. In February, LeBron's team won 27 straight games. After beating the Indiana Pacers in the semis, the Heat faced the San Antonio Spurs. Once again, James rallied his team to defeat the Spurs in seven games, winning the MVP for his all-round play at both ends of the court. Gaining revenge, the Spurs defeated the Heat in five games the following year. As a free agent, LeBron, in a surprise move, returned to Cleveland to the delight of Cavaliers fans and detractors, including owner Dan Gilbert, who welcomed the itinerant star with open arms and deep pockets.

Along with Kyrie Irving and a new player, Kevin Love, whom the Cavs acquired at LeBron's urgent request in a trade for Andrew Wiggins and Anthony Bennett, Cleveland had a new dynamic *troika* to drive for an NBA title in 2015. Irving was an excellent passer as point guard who could shoot with both hands while driving to the bucket, Love a power forward who could rebound and shoot from outside with the best, and King James who did everything brilliantly. Their goal appeared possible as Cleveland defeated the Bulls and Hawks in successive rounds to reach the finals against an emerging juggernaut, the Golden State Warriors. Despite jumping to a 2–1 lead, the Cavs lost the next three games due to the absence of Love and Irving to injury and their opponents' superior depth. Clearly, James's greatest accomplishment occurred in the 2016 finals. After leading the Cavs to 57 wins and engineering the ouster of Coach David Blatt in favor of former teammate Tyronn

Lue, LeBron helped his team sweep through the playoffs for another try at a title against the seemingly invincible Warriors with outstanding long distance "gunners" Klay Thompson and Steph Curry reaching new heights. Down three games to one, LeBron helped engineer a reversal in two ways. He continued his powerful inside and outside game, scoring 41 points in the next two games to knot the series. In game four, he induced opposing defensive ace Draymond Green into a foolish flagrant foul punctuated by a kick that caused Green to be suspended from game five, in which Cleveland staged an unprecedented three-game comeback to take the exciting seven-game series. James also made a pivotal play near the end of that final game. With game and series on the line, tied 89 all, Andre Iguodala broke free for an apparently easy layup. Out of nowhere, King James streaked across the court and blocked the shot against the backboard. Cleveland controlled the rebound with 1:51 remaining on the clock.[4] They took time off the clock to set up the winning shot, a clutch three-pointer by Kyrie Irving with time elapsing. Steph Curry missed a three-pointer at the 10-second mark; James grabbed the rebound. With three seconds left, Draymond Green fouled James en route to a dunk shot; James made one of two foul shots, icing the game. In that game LeBron James scored a triple double in points, rebounds, and assists. Joy erupted in Cleveland (not far from Mudville). The city had not won a championship in a major sport in many years: the Indians took the World Series in 1948, the Browns the NFL Championship in 1964.

The following two years resulted in Warrior victories as Cleveland lacked the depth and firepower of their opponents, who were strengthened by the addition of Kevin Durant through free agency. Durant played James evenly on defense as well as on offense, while Curry and Thompson rained three-pointers from well beyond the arc. After the 2018 season, LeBron James opted again as a free agent to move, signing with a once dominant franchise, the Los Angeles Lakers. The years of 2018 and 2019 were a rebuilding—hence, disappointing—period for the Lakers. The next season, before Covid-19 halted play in March 2020, proved fruitful with the addition of center Anthony Davis in a trade with the New Orleans Pelicans. James welcomed Davis and refused to sit out games like Kawhi Leonard because he wanted to impress youngsters who might have never seen him play. He played in 60 of 63 games, averaging 26 points per game, 8 rebounds per game, plus 11 assists per game.[5] When play was suspended on March 11, 2020, the Lakers touted a 49–14 record, with James averaging 30 points, on 55 percent shooting, 82 rebounds, and a league-leading 9.4 assists after the All-Star break.[6]

In assessing LeBron's greatness, Howard Bryant waxed eloquently over his return to Cleveland culminating in a long-awaited championship.[7] When he departed for Miami, white fans burned his uniform in 2010. Owner Gilbert added a nasty letter condemning LeBron's move. When James returned, he was greeted as a prodigal returned to the fold almost, I believe, in synchronicity with Joseph Campbell's hero paradigm of initiation, departure, and return. *New York Times* sportswriter Scott Cacciola recently summarized his amazing resume.[8] As of March 2020, he had played 17 seasons, 248,000 minutes. At age 35, he was the 10th oldest active player in the NBA. Before closing up shop for sequestration, basketball fans were treated to vintage LeBron with a victory over their Staples Center rivals, the Los Angeles Clippers, 112–103. In this hotly contested game for bragging rights in Los Angeles, James scored 28 points, collared seven rebounds, and dished out nine assists. A few days earlier, the Lakers beat the Bucks of Milwaukee, a team with last year's MVP Giannis Antetokounmpo and the best record for the 2019–2020 season, as LeBron scored 37 points with eight rebounds and eight assists and ably defended Milwaukee's best player at crunch time. Lakers coach Frank Vogel extolled James's unbelievable dominance. After his team's loss to the Lakers, Clippers coach Doc Rivers called attention to LeBron's intelligence, which makes him great. As the Lakers leader, LBJ inspires his teammates. At the end of the Clippers game mentioned above, an exhausted LeBron went to the bench, where he was crowned by teammate Kyle Kuzma for giving his mates "great looks and inspiration." And he refused to slow down.[9] Any doubts about LeBron James as this generation's "GOAT" were dispelled when he led the Los Angeles Lakers to victory over the Miami Heat for the 2020 NBA championship. Scoring 28 points, corralling 14 rebounds, dishing 14 assists, and shutting down Jimmy Butler, the Heat's best player, in game six, James earned his fourth finals MVP.[10]

One day before he succumbed in that tragic helicopter crash, Kobe Bryant called LeBron James to congratulate him for passing Bryant's record as the third highest scorer in NBA history. Both expressed mutual admiration and respect. Both also had labored under the shadow of Michael Jordan. As a teenager, LeBron copied Kobe in going directly from high school to instant stardom in pro basketball. Both became Lakers icons, strengthening their bond. At Kobe's memorial service, LeBron tore up his prepared speech and spoke from the heart, embracing Kobe as hero, the Lakers as family, and promising to continue his legacy. Before his untimely death, Kobe Bryant asked Lakers fans to embrace LeBron James too.[11]

Beyond stats, wins, losses, and records, LeBron James deserves credit for his actions outside the basketball arena. In response to ultra-conservative Fox host Laura Ingraham's rant commanding athletes to shut up and dribble, James responded in kind: "Who is this woman?" Ingraham's comment followed a James endorsement of Hillary Clinton at a Cleveland campaign rally in 2016, wherein LeBron "repeatedly blasted" the Republican candidate. Earlier, James had supported Barack Obama's bid for the presidency and actively promoted the Black Lives Matter movement, warming up with these words emblazoned on his T-shirts.[12] Author Perry Bacon, Jr., starkly contrasted the liberal orientation of basketball fans to conservative football fans. LeBron and 23 athletes publicly denounced police brutality on the field with many wearing T-shirts like LeBron's. When Trump denounced Steph Curry and teammates who refused to visit the White House after winning the NBA title in 2018, LeBron defended the Warriors' decision. The president, he pushed back, "made it fashionable to hate." Stirred by the president's penchant for mendacity, race baiting, and blame-shifting, James famously tweeted: "U Bum!" Coaches Steve Kerr, Gregg Popovich, Stan Van Gundy, and football star Chris Long supported the "refuseniks," while most athletes remained silent, fearful of financial reprisals.[13] Trump also insulted Don Lemon who, like LeBron James, spoke truth to power. Rather than engage in a hostile chat or verbal pissing match with 45, James preferred to let his actions to do the talking. Because he grew up poor with a single mom, he decided to pay back those who had helped him. James established a public, non-charter school for at-risk youth in his hometown of Akron, Ohio. There, his foundation " committed tens of millions of dollars to help provide college scholarships for Akron public school graduates."[14] He also plans to give every child a bike and a helmet as a symbol of freedom that he used to explore the larger world, including white kids, whom he befriended.[15] Moreover, King James recently invested $20 million through his foundation to erect a new school, three residential buildings of affordable housing, and a sports-entertainment complex in the neighborhood in which he grew up. Thus, James has used his financial and moral capital to build a better, more just America.[16]

Kobe Bryant

Born in Philadelphia on August 23, 1978, to Joe "Jellybean" Bryant and Pam Bryant, Kobe Bryant's career on and off the court transmitted mixed messages. Like his predecessor, Michael Jordan, he relentlessly drove himself and his teammates to victory. He won fans but antagonized other members of his winning team. He forced Shaq O'Neal out of town to a championship for the Miami Heat in 2006. More problematic in this era of #MeToo was his alleged rape of a 19-year-old hotel worker. After she dropped charges, followed by a financial settlement, Kobe confessed to a sexual encounter. Several of his commercial sponsors—Nutella and McDonald's, but not Nike—disengaged. But questions remained regarding his status. Was he a hero or an antihero? When he died along with daughter Gianna and associates in that tragic helicopter crash on January 26, 2020, different appraisals emerged. The genuine display of grief by participants and countless viewers on television prompted a reevaluation of his short life and enormous accomplishments.[17]

At age six, his family moved to Italy, where his father prolonged his professional career in basketball. In Italy, young Kobe grew fluent in Italian, Spanish, soccer, and basketball, thanks to NBA videos that his grandfather sent to Reggio Emilia, the last Italian residence of his nuclear family.[18] At age 13, Kobe and his family moved back to Philadelphia. He attended a 90 percent white high school. He matured on the hoops court at Ardmore's Lower Merion High School, leading his school to the state title in 1996 and gaining recognition as the leading scorer. Despite his excellent grades, this scholar-athlete shunned college basketball for a direct move to the NBA. Los Angeles Lakers general manager Jerry West traded for him, with center Vlade Divac going to the Charlotte Hornets. As a rookie coming off the bench, he averaged 7.6 points per game. During the All-Star weekend, Kobe participated in the Rookie Challenge. In 1997, he won the Slam Dunk Contest, the youngest champion in that event at age 18.[19]

In his sophomore year, he became the youngest ever All-Star. His scoring average doubled to 15.4 points per game. Often paired with two starting guards, Nick Van Exel and Eddie Jones, Bryant played small forward, earning more minutes of hoop action. In 1998, both starting guards were traded, providing more time for Bryant as shooting guard. In the lockout-shortened 50-game season, Kobe signed a $70 million salary extension for six years. Sportswriters began to take notice. When the Lakers hired coach Phil Jackson and acquired Shaq O'Neal in 1996, a new dynasty was about to emerge in the so-called City of Angels. Finally, the Lakers won NBA titles in 2000, 2001, and 2002, powered by Tex Winter's triangle offense and inspired by Phil Jackson's Zen psychology. The streak ended in 2003 when the Lakers lost to the San Antonio Spurs.[20] After Shaq's departure, propelled by the antagonistic Kobe, the Lakers rebounded. Phil Jackson returned as coach and persuaded Bryan to fully buy into his triangle offense. Despite Kobe's sexual assault incident in 2005, he won the scoring title in 2005–2006 with 35 points per game. That year, Kobe scored 81 points against the Toronto Raptors on January 2, followed by MVP honors in 2006–2007. That prodigious output was second highest in NBA history. Only Wilt Chamberlain's 100 points against the hapless Knicks in 1962 topped Kobe's effort. Along with his amazing offense, Bryant played tenacious defense that led to two more Lakers championships in 2009 and 2010, totaling five during Bryant's 20-year career with only one team, a rarity in this age of free-agency.[21] Injuries diminished Bryant's performance in his final years as an active player, though he did manage to score 60 points in this final game on April 16, 2016.

Kobe Bryant wrote a book, *The Mamba Mentality: How I Play*, in 2018 that displays, in glorious color, his rigorous workouts, careful study of opponents' strengths as well as weaknesses, and that powerful will to win. In one segment, he pays tribute to the players who inspired him. He is seen with Kareem Abdul-Jabbar, who informs Kobe that he held him high, when he was two-year-old toddler, while Kobe's dad, Joe, then a player with the Los Angeles Clippers, gleefully watched.[22] Abdul-Jabbar talked about playing with Oscar Robertson, another Kobe idol, and under Coach Pat Riley against the Boston Celtics. Another idol, Muhammad Ali, advised him to "work hard to shine in the light." Kobe confided that he emulated Ali's strategy of "rope-a-dope" and applied the psychology behind it. Kobe learned lessons from Bill Russell and his autobiography.[23] Bryant talked with Byron Scott, who played with Kareem and Magic. As Lakers coach, Scott and Kobe were like brothers.[24] More than a coach, Phil Jackson was a visionary. Good coaches are teachers. Kobe praises Tex Winter for devising the triangle offense. "Now, I coach my daughter's team and we run the triangle."[25] Bryant details his major challenge: playing through pain. He showed a splint on a damaged finger, which forced him to change his shooting form in 2009–2010. He suffered his worst injury, a torn Achilles, in 2013. His attention to detail is displayed in the design of Nike sneakers bearing his name.[26]

In agreement with Michael Jordan and LeBron James, Bryant aimed to kill the opposition. He willingly assumed the role of alpha male in the locker rooms of national teams in international competition. That led to three gold rings. In the locker room, Kobe welcomed silence to engage in meditation and to observe everything, minus music. Tex Winter gave him the green light to call shots, putting Kobe in control. Kobe admitted that he was hard on younger Lakers players D'Angelo Russell, Larry Nance, Jr., and Jordan Clarkson. The Lakers formed an extended family that permitted Bryant to exhibit his "Mamba Mentality." More than a catchy phrase, it embodied the ability to strike opponents with the stealth, speed, and lethal strike of a snake. It is derived from a code name of an assassin in a Quentin Tarantino film.[27]

B.J. Armstrong's recollection—recently published—of a Bryant-Jordan encounter is fascinating.[28] A threesome of basketball stars went to lunch in 2014; two talked, one listened. Kobe and Michael discussed and debated strategy. How would you play defense, for example, if a ball were delivered to a certain spot? What's your pivot foot? What's the score of the game? Enthralled by this mental chess game applied to basketball, the listener, B.J. Armstrong, concluded that these two superstars "could actually play in their mind." Demonstrating great respect for each other, Kobe and Michael could only agree on one thing: that Michael Jordan had bigger hands. Hating to lose, neither Bryant nor Jordan would concede to any other deficit. Bryant admitted that he had stolen all his moves from several predecessors: he learned to freeze defenders from Oscar Robertson, to create space for pull-up jumpers from Jerry West, to post-up shake and go from Hakeem Olajuwon, to spin right for a crossover dribble from Jimmy Jackson, and to ward off defenders with a left hand while dribbling in for layups from John Battle. He cited Elgin Baylor as the inspiration for his expert footwork. Bryant expressed adoration of Magic Johnson for his pinpoint passing and expert court vision and admiration, belatedly, of Michael Jordan because "His Airness" took the game "to a whole new level with his athletic ability, determination and fundamentals." Besides, their height and body types were comparable, and he wanted to know "how he got his shot off against bigger players."[29]

The January 26, 2020, news of Kobe's death along with 13-year-old daughter Gianna and friends in that dreadful helicopter crash sent shockwaves throughout the globe and evoked A.E. Housman's several stanzas of his poignant poem: "To an Athlete Dying Young."

> The time you won your town the race
> We cheered you through the market-place;
> Man and boy stood cheering by.
> And home we brought you shoulder-high.
>
> Today, the road all runners come,
> Shoulder-high we bring you home,
> And set you at your threshold down,
> Townsman of a stiller town.
>
> Eyes that shady night has shut
> Cannot see the record cut,
> And silence sounds no worse than cheers
> After earth has stopped the ears.

At the Staples Center's public memorial for Kobe and Gianna held on February 24, 2020, Michael Jordan spoke. Teary-eyed, Jordan described the close bond he had with Bryant. He called him "little brother" at one point. Kobe would call or text at all hours, "talking about post-up moves, footwork, and sometimes the triangle…. At first it was an aggravation. But then it turned into a certain passion. This kid had passion like you would never know."[30] Conversely, the stirring documentary *The Last Dance* revealed belatedly this confession from Kobe Bryant: "What you get from me is from him. I don't get five championships here without him because he guided me so much. He gave me so much great advice."[31]

20

Ora Washington, Lynette Woodard, Cheryl Miller, Lisa Leslie, Cynthia Cooper-Dyke, and Maya Moore

While completing this section on basketball, I felt a pang of guilt over the absence of women. Was it part of my cultural DNA to exclude females followed by a categorical need to atone? Whatever the reason, my discussions with two women, Val Ackerman and Ernestine Miller—recollected in tranquility—compel me to add Black female heroes in basketball to this narrative. I met Val Ackerman at a basketball conference at St. Francis College in Brooklyn, where she shared her experience as president of the fledgling NBA since its inception in 1997. After commending NBA Commissioner David Stern for his support, she eloquently extolled the virtues of female hoopsters, delineating their challenges and explaining their hard-won success stories. A former hoopster at University of Virginia, a lawyer, and sports executive, she added *gravitas* as well as grace to our conclave.

I met Ernestine Miller at another conference—this time on baseball—in Cooperstown. An expert on the life of Babe Ruth, director of our annual Society for American Baseball Research Casey Stengel Chapter in New York prior to the Covid epidemic, Ms. Miller is also a strong advocate of feminist causes, which is apparent in her book, *Making Her Mark*, cited below. As I finished this chapter, I wondered what Ernestine would think about the absent women. Perhaps English playwright William Congreve had the appropriate answer, evoking the fury of rejection. Hence, I seek redemption through addition.

Failure to address the role of women was endemic in a culture of gender discrimination. In 1931, however, historical records indicate the presence of two early all-Black, all-female basketball clubs, one in Philadelphia, led by multitalented Ora Washington, called the Tribune Girls, and the other, in Chicago, named the Romas. The Romas were undefeated in six years spanning 1939–1945. Their best players were identified as Corinne Robinson, Virginia Willis, Lola Porter, Mignon Burns, and Isadore Channels.[1] Little is known about this all-but-forgotten quintet. Ora Washington, however, emerged from obscurity.

Ora Washington

Skin color prevented Ora Washington from equaling Babe Didrikson's fame. A peerless tennis player and hoopster, she was confined to the "chitlin'" or segregated circuit. She was "Serena William before Serena Williams," and "Maya Moore before Maya Moore," lamented reporter Frank Fitzpatrick. Helen Wills Moody refused to play her because Ora was black, Frank Fitzpatrick observed.[2] Born in rural Virginia in 1898, Ora moved to Philadelphia at age 14 to live with an aunt.[3] She found refuge in a local YWCA in Germantown, Pennsylvania. She turned to tennis after her sister died. Tennis was considered more suitable for women because it seemed less taxing "on the fragile female body" and less corruptible as a predominantly amateur sport according to sports historian Jennifer H. Lansbury.[4] Black women benefited from a new era of expanding leisure following World War I. The local YWCAs gave Ora and her peers opportunities to learn and play. Being unable to compete against white tennis players proved advantageous in a way. White women were constrained by rules of gentility and femininity while Black women, unencumbered by such restraints, developed a game that put a premium on power rather than finesse. Competing in American Tennis Association tournaments, Ora found her groove.

In these tournaments, Washington won eight straight tennis titles from 1929 to 1936. In 12 years, she never lost a tennis match. Denied a chance to challenge Helen Wills Moody, Ora turned to basketball to satisfy her competitive urges during wintertime. Perhaps even better in basketball, Ora played center, 5'11", on the Germantown Hornets, sponsored by the YWCA. The Hornets won 45 games in a row, 66 of 68 victories, as Ora averaged 16 points per game in a low-scoring era. Her team captured the 1930–31 Colored Women's National Championship. A sports reporter enthused: "She passes and shoots with either hand. She is a ball hawk. She has stamina and speed."[5]

The Hornets turned professional in 1931 successfully. Their two star players, Washington and Lulu Ballard, joined the Philadelphia Tribunes, a pro team sponsored by a Black newspaper. According to Arthur Ashe, "the Tribunes became America's first premier female sports team." Ashe touted Washington as possibly "the best female ever."[6] She played with men, competitively. Her team was "ranked number one in the country with Ora leading the way from 1931 to 1943, basically creating Black female athletic stardom," according to sports historian Pamela Grundy.[7] Unable to earn much money in her athletic endeavors, Ora had to earn a living as a domestic worker. When she died in 1971, Ora had slid into obscurity. Perhaps her alternative lifestyle—shunned by religious members of her community—contributed to her recession into the shadows. Resurrected by successors like Arthur Ashe, Ora reclaimed public recognition, marked by inductions into the Naismith Memorial Basketball of Fame, Black Athletes Hall of Fame, and Black Tennis Hall of Fame. Chanté Griffin concludes her illuminating biographical sketch with a paean to "Queen Ora," who "will always be the queen of two courts."[8]

Lynette Woodard

Thanks to the civil rights movement and Title IX of the 1972 Education Amendments Act, female hoopsters of color were spared the indignities that befell Ora Washington. One beneficiary, Lynette Woodard, broke barriers when she played for the Harlem Globetrotters. Born on August 12, 1959, Woodard started her basketball career tossing rolled-up socks into a basket under the direction of her older brother. At age 10, she captained a team of mostly male players. After a coach at Wichita North High School advised her to join the junior varsity team as a "freshwoman," Lynette opted to join the varsity as a sophomore. No slump for this sophomore; Woodard led her team to the Kansas state championship in 1975. As a senior, she earned national recognition.[9]

At the University of Kansas from 1978 to 1981, Woodard helped the Lady Jayhawks to three consecutive Big Eight titles, posting a 108–32 record, during which she scored 3,649 points. Unable to play in the 1980 Olympics because of our country's boycott of the games held in Soviet Russia, she had to wait until 1984 to strut her stuff in pursuit of gold in basketball. Her reward—or punishment, if you prefer—was to join the Harlem Globetrotters for a two-year tour. Excited by her exposure to pro basketball abroad, Woodard played professionally in Japan as well as in Italy. Returning to America, she was inducted into the Kansas Hall of Fame in 1990. Though past her prime, Lynette came out of retirement to play for two more years (1997–1998) in the WNBA with the Cleveland Rockers and the Detroit Shock. She subsequently became assistant, then head coach at Winthrop University. Woodard was inducted into the Basketball Hall of Fame in 2004 and the Women's Basketball Hall of Fame in 2005.[10]

Cheryl Miller

"For of all sad words of tongue or pen," John Greenleaf Whittier wrote presciently, "The saddest are these: 'It might have been!'" This lament certainly applies to the sudden end of Cheryl Miller's brilliant career due to a torn ACL incurred during a meaningless pickup game at USC in 1986. This epic saga of rise and fall is vividly depicted in a HBO documentary *Women of Troy*, released on March 10, 2020.[11] Cheryl D. Miller was born on January 3, 1964, the middle child of Saul and Millie Miller. She grew up in Riverside, California. Her dad, a musician in the military, demanded excellence from his children in school as well as in sports arenas, as evidenced in the work ethics that molded the basketball careers of Cheryl and her younger brother, Reggie. Playing against her brothers, Cheryl developed her game, even beating Reggie, one on one, in many games. Reaching a height of 6'2" helped. In Riverside High School, she scored 3,405 points, almost 37 points per game. Most biographical accounts list her one-game performance of 105 points against a much weaker team in a rout, minus any criticism of Cheryl or her amoral coach. Perhaps the basketball gods would later exact retribution by aborting Cheryl's career before she could turn pro. She set a single-season record in high school with 1,156 points.

Riverside Polytechnical High School sported a 132–4 record during Miller's time there from 1978 to 1982.[12]

Miller's time at USC proved equally fruitful. Recruited by more than 250 schools, she chose to stay close to home at the University of Southern California, where Cheryl joined several outstanding players, including twins Pam and Paula McGee, Cynthia Cooper, and Rhonda Windham. She averaged 23 points and 11.9 rebounds per game. This outstanding team won two consecutive NCAA championships in 1983 (season record of 31–2) and 1984 (season record of 29–4) against Louisiana Tech and Tennessee University, respectively. Perhaps Miller's best time occurred in the 1984 Los Angeles Olympics. In front of family as well as a friendly crowd, she dominated play, leading the United States to a gold medal. She opened the first contest against Yugoslavia scoring 23 points in a 83–55 win. In the second game against Australia, Miller caged 70.8 percent of her shots in a rout, 81–47. Against South Korea in game three, Miller shared double-figure scoring with Lynette Woodard and Janice Lawrence. The United States topped China 91 to 58. In the semifinals, Team USA defeated Canada led by Anne Donovan's 14 points. In the final game, Miller resumed leadership in scoring with 16 points and 12 rebounds as the United States defeated South Korea 85–55. Now, with Olympic gold added to wins in the Pan American Games and the World University Games, Cheryl had attained international stature. The world was her oyster, and she emerged as the pearl. *Sports Illustrated* named her National Player of the Year in 1985.[13]

All athletes, ABC television mogul Roone Arledge proclaimed, experience the agony of defeat along with the ecstasy of victory. Cheryl Miller was no exception. In victory, Miller excelled as a multiple award winner with a record number of steals, free throws, and points. She also exuded "attitude" and engaged in "trash-talk." Unwilling to join the Globetrotters like Lynette Woodard or go pro in Europe, she ventured into broadcasting and coaching. The ACL tear, absent current advances in surgery, ended her basketball career and any hope of reprising her glory in the 1988 Olympiad.

In a controversial move, she returned to her alma mater, USC, to coach women's basketball. She replaced Marianne Stanley, who had demanded equal pay with George Raveling, the men's coach, and was suing USC for sex discrimination. Unruffled by criticism, Miller enjoyed two successful years as head coach. She was voted into the Naismith Memorial Hall of Fame in 1995. She later coached at Langston University in Oklahoma for two years, followed by a four-year stint as coach and general manager with the Phoenix Mercury. Recently, she was recruited by former USC football star Mike Garrett—who had previously hired her at USC—to coach the women's basketball team at Cal State Los Angeles. Miller accepted. President William A. Covino of Cal State Los Angeles said that "Cheryl embodies the kind of athlete and human being who will lead our students to successful futures beyond what they imagined."[14]

Lisa Leslie

Another outstanding basketball star, Lisa Leslie, shares a distinction with Cheryl Miller. Both could dunk a basketball in high school. Born on July 7, 1972, in Gardenia, California, to 6'3" mother Christine and father Walter Leslie, who left the family while her mother was pregnant, Lisa Leslie grew up with two sisters and a brother named Elgin, named after the basketball player who flew through the air with the greatest of ease. Six feet tall in the seventh grade, she was reluctant to play basketball at first. Later, it became a labor of love in middle school where she learned to shoot with both hands. In junior high school, she joined the boys' team in the absence of one for girls. At age 14, she entered Morningside High School, where she did track and field (high jump) and played volleyball as well as basketball. In the latter sport, she led team to a state title in 1989 as a sophomore.[15] In her senior year, she averaged 27 points per game. As a high school sophomore, she could dunk basketballs, a rarity among women at that time. Leslie attended USC from 1990 to 1994, where she earned a BA degree and basketball glory. Later, she earned an MBA at the University of Phoenix. She tore up what broadcaster Red Barber called "The Pea Patch" over 120 games. She averaged 20.1 points per game with a 54.4 percent field goal record, a 70 percent free throw percentage, 1,214 rebounds, and 391 blocks. Her USC team notched 89 victories as opposed to 31 losses in a highly competitive conference.[16]

After graduation, Leslie turned pro with the Los Angeles Sparks in the fledgling Women's National Basketball Association, where she starred but failed to win a title until 2001. She was the first pro female player to dunk. She also made history with a triple double, scoring 29 points, grabbing 15 rebounds, and blocking 10 shots. Before she retired in 2009, Lisa Leslie appeared in four Olympiads, winning four gold medals while leading the United States team in scoring, rebounding, and shot blocking.

A Renaissance woman, Lisa Leslie is a fashionista who models and designs clothes, a movie and television actress, and a sports commentator and analyst for Turner Sports, CBS Sports Network, and ABC. She has written an autobiography, *Don't Let the Lipstick Fool You*. Recently she worked the Orlando Magic games on Fox TV. Married to Michael Lockwood on November 6, 2005, Lisa took time off to give birth to a daughter in 2007. She returned to the WNBA one year later. A close friend of Kobe Bryant, she mourned his loss. Heroic in stature as well as achievement, Lisa Leslie is a role model for all women, regardless of race, color, or creed.[17]

Cynthia Cooper-Dyke

Cynthia Cooper played alongside of and often in the shadow of Cheryl Miller at the University of South Carolina during their championship seasons. Nevertheless, this 5'10" point guard enjoyed a longer and more productive career. To fulfill her dreams, she had to travel up from poverty and far from home. No stranger to challenges along that journey, she made it to the top. One of seven children, she was born in Chicago, Illinois, on April 13, 1963. Like so many other athletes profiled in this book, her parents, Kenny and Mary Cooper, separated when she was young. Her mother moved with seven children to Los Angeles. She grew up in the Watts section of the city. Cynthia attended Locke High School, where she excelled in track—relays and hurdles—and basketball.[18] Awarded a sports scholarship, she enrolled in the University of Southern California (USC), where she led her team to conference titles and the finals in the NCAA tournament in 1983 and 1984. She left college before graduation to turn pro in Europe, first to Spain, then to Italy for nine years. At USC, Cooper averaged 12.7 points, 4 rebounds as a stellar point guard. During her fours at USC, her team went 114–15. During her senior (and best) year, 1986, she averaged 17.2 points, nine assists, and four rebounds per game with a 50.6 percent field goal average and 74.8 percent free throw record.[19] In 1983, she led the United States team to a 84–82 victory over the Soviet team in Moscow. She repeated a rout of the "Russkies" in 1986, 108–88. Cooper went 17 for 34, hitting on 50 percent of her shots, setting up high-scorer USC teammate Cheryl Miller, who went 47 for 89 or 52.8 percent in seven games.[20]

When the WNBA formed in 1997 under the presidency of Val Ackerman, she played for the Houston Comets. She was a rookie at 34 years old. And her contributions to that team were meteoric. She led her Houston team to four straight titles, winning the MVP all four times. After a short break, she returned to Houston as the oldest player to compete in the 2003–2004 season at age 40. In her five-year WNBA career, this aging wonder averaged 21 points, 4.9 assists, 1.5 steals, and 3.2 rebounds per game. Her free-throw average was 87.1 percent.[21] Quite an accomplishment! Unaware of her extraordinary skills until I witnessed her brilliant ball handling and explosive moves to the basket in the *Women of Troy* documentary film, I became a believer.[22]

Cooper turned to coaching and to completing her college degree at Prairie View College. Cooper coached at various schools subsequently, including the University of North Carolina Wilmington, Texas Southern, and back at her alma mater, USC. Cynthia returned to coach the Phoenix Mercury in 2001–2002. In 2007, she became assistant coach of the United States women's team. Because of her linguistic skills in Italian, Spanish, and English, she regularly hosted the WNBA commentary room during international contests. Her popularity led to a lucrative two years as pitchwoman for General Motors.[23] After a failed first marriage, Cynthia Cooper married Brian Dyke in 2001. One year later, she gave birth to twins, a son and a daughter. In her autobiography, *She Got Game: My Personal Odyssey*, she charts her roadmap from poverty to glory.[24] She won a gold medal with the United States Olympic team in 1988 in Seoul. In addition, Cynthia won gold medals in various international events. Her list of extraordinary accomplishments serves as a beacon of hope for underprivileged youngsters the world over.

Maya Moore

Sports Illustrated named Maya Moore the greatest winner in the history of women's basketball in 2017. Born on June 11, 1989, in Jefferson, Missouri, to Kathryn Moore and an absent father, Mike Dabney, who reentered her life in her senior year in high school, she has won basketball championships in many different countries, venues, and levels. What makes her heroic, however, may not derive from her considerable basketball prowess. As *New York Times* reporter Kurt Streeter points out, Ms. Moore stepped away from a glorious basketball career in 2019 to help free a prisoner wrongfully convicted and jailed for 23 years of a 50-year sentence for burglary and assault.[25] Thanks in large measure to her gallant and unrelenting efforts, Jonathan Irons was freed recently. In a jubilant moment, Maya and Jeremy embraced. Female athletes don't get the same limelight as men like LeBron James, Streeter argues. Whatever the reason for benign neglect, Maya Moore used her bully pulpit to advance the cause of social justice, which she prioritized over winning championships.

From high school on, that's what Moore has accomplished. Attending Collins Hills High School, she led her teams to a 125–3 record in four years. She dunked at age 16. As a junior, this six-foot, 165-pound star scored 23 points, grabbed 11.3 rebounds, 4.5 assists, and 5.4 steals per game. She improved in her senior year to 25.5 points, 12.1 rebounds, four assists, and 4.3 steals per game. Maya's high school team won four consecutive state championships. She also engaged in track and field (high jump). To put the icing on her high school cake, she graduated with a 4.0 GPA—a true scholar-athlete. While in high school, she competed in Amateur Athletic Union tournaments on travel teams, which sharpened her skills. As a "freshwoman" at University of Connecticut under coach Geno Auriemma, she continued to flourish. The Huskies went 36–2 while she averaged 17.8 points per game, 42 percent in three-pointers, 7.6 rebounds per game, 2.0 steals per game, and 2.3 blocks per game. Moore continued to improve along with UConn, which won two NCAA titles in two consecutive, undefeated seasons. In her senior year, even though Maya Moore averaged 36 points per game, UConn lost a semifinal to Notre Dame, precluding a "threepeat." During her four-year college career, UConn compiled a 150–4 record.[26]

Tabbed number one in the WNBA draft by the Minnesota Lynx, she was the first female hoopster to gain a Jordan brand. As a rookie, she helped the Lynx win the first of several league titles and was named Rookie of the Year in 2011. In 2012, Moore's team went 27–7 but lost to the Indiana Fever in the finals. In her third year, the Lynx regained their winning touch with Moore leading the league in three-pointers and percentage with a 26–8 record. Thanks in large measure to Maya Moore, the Lynx copped four WNBA titles in 2011, 2012, 2015, and 2017. In the summer of 2016, Maya was jolted out of complacency with the deaths of Philando Castile and Alton B. Sterling, both shot by police officers. Five Dallas police officers were killed by a sniper during a protest of police brutality. During that summer, Maya and Lynx teammates wore black T-shirts with "Change Starts with Us. Justice and Accountability" on the front and "Black Lives Matter" on the back, along with the names of victims.[27] Then she turned her lens on prison reform in order to help Jonathan Irons, who she felt was wrongfully convicted and serving a 50-year sentence.[28] Her voluntary hiatus from pro basketball in pursuit of social justice puts Ms. Moore at the pinnacle of praxis, the ability to combine theory and action. Willing to sacrifice a lucrative career in basketball for a just cause, Maya Moore is a genuine hero. As she recently explained:

I am really in a good place right now with my life, and I don't want to change anything now. Basketball has not been foremost in my mind. I've been able to rest, and connect with people around me, actually be in their presence after all these years on the road. And I've been able to be there for Jonathan.[29]

Now that Jonathan Irons is a free man and married to his savior, will Maya Moore be free to return to basketball? On July 5, 2022, she gave birth to a son, Jonathan Irons, Jr., putting hoops aside for motherhood as she continued her work for reform in the justice system.

SECTION 7

GOLF,
HOCKEY,
GYMNASTICS

21

Tiger Woods, Willie O'Ree, and Simone Biles

For reasons of class, status, race, and gender, the sports of golf, hockey, and gymnastics did not welcome Black participants. The historical origins of golf have several claimants among early civilizations in Rome, China, Persia, and later in Europe. The name derives from the Dutch word for club. Rules of the game were printed in Dutch and Latin in the sixteenth century according to golf historian Maggie Lagle.[1] Modern golf, however, can be documented in Scotland circa 1450, probably the result of active trade between Holland and Scotland.

The 18-hole course was started at St. Andrews in 1764, with the first major tournament held in 1860 at Scotland's Prestwick Golf Club. The Scottish railway system wrought by the industrial revolution provided transportation for English tourists eager to play on holiday trips. Begun by Dutch settlers in America between 1650 and 1660 in upstate New Amsterdam, later New York, the modern version owes its origin to Scottish immigrants in New York, the Carolinas, and Georgia during the 1770s. Dormant after the War of 1812, golf experienced a resurgence in the 1880s. By 1895 the U.S. Open, the U.S. Amateur, and the U.S. Women's Amateur golf tournaments had been established.[2] One year later, however, Plessy v. Ferguson proclaimed the hoary doctrine of "separate but equal" as the racist law of our land.

Theodore Rhodes is regarded as the first African American professional golfer. Starting out as a caddie at a time when Blacks were not allowed to play golf or be members of country clubs, Rhodes practiced in local Nashville parks. After a stint in the U.S. Navy during World War II, Rhodes became a serious golfer on the alternative Black circuit known as the United Golfers Association (UGA), founded in 1926 as a response to segregation, strictly enforced. Rhodes won 150 UGA tournaments as well as the Negro National Open title in 1957. As his career ended by 1960, he began mentoring Charlie Sifford and Lee Elder. Failing health led to his early death on July 4, 1969, at age 55.[3]

Before Tiger Woods, Charlie Sifford, like Ted Rhodes, served as a pioneer when he became the first African American to join the Professional Golfers' Association (PGA) tour in 1961. Starting as a 13-year-old caddie, he became a player in Philadelphia, competing against other Black golfers. Sifford turned pro in 1948, winning six championships in competition with Black peers. Rejected by whites-only protocols until 1957, when he won the Long Beach Open, a PGA-sponsored event. He later won two Opens in Hartford in 1967 and Los Angeles in 1969. His greatest victories, however, occurred in 2004, when he was inducted into World Golf Hall of Fame, and in 2014, when he received the Presidential Medal of Freedom at age 92 from President Barack Obama.[4]

Writing in *The New York Times*, Karen Crouse complained that the "Augusta National has always existed in a bubble ... maintaining practices, that throughout is storied history, were exclusionary and racist." She added that, historically, "golf has practiced segregation by class, gender, race, and religion." In a litany of grievances, she noted that the Masters, begun in 1934, denied entry to Black players until 1975, rejected club membership till 1990 and refused female membership until 2012.[5] Augusta's national chair, Fred Ridley, announced plans to honor the 86-year-old Lee Elder along with Arnold Palmer and Jack Nicklaus for the first ceremonial tee shot on April 8, 2021. The decision was based, Ridley stated, on Elder's "'courageous life" and "all he has done in his career to help eliminate barriers and inspire Black men and women in the name of gold and beyond." Lee Elder was delighted to receive this honor, but does this gesture go far enough to atone for our sins? Karen Crouse wonders. "But in honoring one Black player, it also shines a new light on those it continues to ignore."[6] Lee Elder died on November 28, 2021.

Tiger Woods

Hero or antihero? That is the question one asks in pondering the roller-coaster career of America's richest athlete with the possible exception of Michael Jordan. Eldrick Tont "Tiger" Woods was born on December 30, 1975, in Orange County, California, to Earl and Kultida Woods. Lieutenant Colonel Earl Woods had been married before and fathered three children prior to his famous son. The nickname Tiger honored Earl's Vietnamese buddy who had saved his life twice.[7] At age nine months, Tiger swung a golf club. At 18 months, he went to a driving range with his dad, who had only recently taken up the game (at age 40) that would make both father and son famous. A television crew followed little Eldrick at age two and captured the young phenom on film. Tiger shot a 48 on a nine-hole golf course that year.[8] Featured on *The Mike Douglas Show* in 1978, Tiger putted with Bob Hope to the delight of television viewers. Fame had its downside. Probably inflamed with envy, older boys tied him to a tree and threw stones at him along with verbal insults. Consequently, he preferred solitude unless involved in tournament play. At age eight, he won the Junior Golf (age 10 and younger) World Championship. Obsessed with golf, he dropped Little League baseball. Earl Woods denied pushing young Tiger into an embrace with golf. "Everything," he argued, "came from him." He added: "I treated Tiger as an equal. We transcended the parent-child relationship and became best friends a long time ago."[9]

Moving up in the age brackets, Tiger won six junior championships and was named his high school's top athlete. In 1990 he faced racism in PGA events, particularly in Alabama. Preferring to be called American rather than Black, he was the third African American (on his father's side) to cross over after O. J. Simpson and Michael Jordan. Woods, however, considered African American pioneer golfer Charlie Sifford his hero, along with father Earl, who was the only Black athlete on scholarship at Kansas State in the then Big Seven as a baseball catcher.[10] Later Earl and Tiger gave free golf clinics to inner-city youngsters.

In 1994, Tiger enrolled in Stanford University. As a freshman, he won his first tournament and the U.S. Amateur Title. Despite a six-hole deficit, he rallied to become the youngest player to win that coveted award. Tiger went on to cop nine of the 13 NCAA tournaments, winning three consecutive amateur titles from 1994 to 1996, which led to a five-year, $40-million endorsement deal with Nike.[11] During his first year as a pro, he won six of 25 events and earned a record $2,066,833.[12] In 1997, he won the Masters by 12 strokes with a record low of 18 below par, attaining the world's number one ranking in less than a year since turning pro. After his stunning victory, as 43 million viewers watched, Earl gave Tiger a bear hug. As Earl said "I love you, son," tears streamed down the cheeks of both father and son.[13] Woods was the youngest golfer to take the four majors: the Masters, PGA Championship, U.S. Open, and British Open.[14] Tiger roared to the top and stayed there until 2004. After a brief hiatus he was tops again from June 2005 to October 2010. At his peak, Tiger Woods won nine tournaments in a single year, earning $9 million in prize money en route to grand total of $1.5 billion with endorsements coupled with tournament pay-offs. In 2002, Woods easily won the Masters and U.S. Open. After a slight drought in 2003–2004, Tiger bounced back in a series of triumphs from 2005 to 2007. Thanks to endorsements, Woods became a money machine. The first endorsement with Nike for $100 million led to other deals, all, it appears, for five years: $30 million with General Motors, $30 million with EA Sports, $45 million with Upper Deck; $20 million with Disney, $25 million with Asahi Beverages, $26 million with American Express, $40 million with Buick, and other deals with TLC Laser Eye Centers, TAG Heuer, Wheaties, Coca-Cola, and *Golf Digest*.[15]

Did Tiger Woods sell his soul to the corporate devil? With Nike, he made a far-out commercial, "Hello World," that contrasted his spectacular accomplishments with his inability to play on certain golf courses because of race. When the ad flopped, causing a nasty backlash that threatened diminished shoe sales, Woods and Nike took their relationship in another direction.[16] The irony that Woods was multi-racial was lost on his detractors, who shared Earl Woods's contention that one drop of Black blood determined racial identification.[17] Earl and Tiger launched a foundation to foster social mobility among inner-city youth through golf lessons and core lessons à la Horatio Alger through education.[18] That commitment was one of Tiger's excuses for refusing an invitation to celebrate Jackie Robinson's 50th anniversary of Major League Baseball barrier-breaking at Shea Stadium in the company of President Bill Clinton and Baseball Commissioner Bud Selig, among other dignitaries. He was too busy to honor a race hero and true pioneer.

Tiger and his father established the Tiger Woods Foundation (TWF) with a donation of $500,000. Shortly thereafter, a whole host of corporate sponsors and board members signed on. In a web address beamed at visitors, Tiger explained his motivation.[19]

> When I was younger, my Dad encouraged me to change the world. He taught me that anything was possible and he showed me how to use my talents to reach my goals. Golf has been good to me, but the lessons I've learned transcended the game. I'm now trying to pass these

lessons and show kids how they can be applied to every aspect of life. Do your best. Play fairly. Embrace every activity with ingenuity, honesty, and discipline. Be responsible for your actions. And above all have fun.

Tiger applied the last words but not the full program of his TWF tenets to his own life. His Horatio Alger platform was built on support from the corporate world, more inclined to value their "bottom line" rather than meaningful social change. Critics of Wood fixed on this dichotomy. His self-identification as multicultural also troubled other critics as disingenuous. For most observers of his great ascent, blackness was the operative word. Did he sell his birthright for a mess of potage or a pot of gold? The jury of public opinion has suspended judgment. As a sports fan, I admire his great skill. As a social historian, I find it hard to "wrap my head around" this enigma.

In 2000, I was invited to give a keynote lecture on "Black Heroes in Sports" at the Annual "Pop" Lloyd Conference. Covered in the local press, the conference expected Tiger Woods to appear, but he had a conflict that precluded his attendance. The lecture was well received and, despite a recent spell of dizziness, my head swelled with pride instead of vertigo. The following day, however, light-headedness returned. Therefore, I asked conference co-director Lawrence Hogan (no relation to Maryland's governor) to give me a lift from our motel to the casino for our big banquet in Atlantic City. The van was filled with guests when I entered a rear door. Rush-hour traffic impeded our progress. Nervously, I started small talk. Larry Hogan and I were the only whites in the van. As the premier golfer in the world, Tiger Woods was the best advertisement for interracial marriage and children, I said. Everyone in the van seemed to agree. That reminds me, I added, of a Chinese couple named Wong who had trouble conceiving a child. So, they went to a fertility clinic and, after multiple tries, Mrs. Wong gave birth to a son. Happy but perturbed, Mr. Wong thought that their new baby boy looked Caucasian. He began to doubt his paternity and complained to his wife. Mrs. Wong reassured her husband that the baby was his son.

"No!" Mr. Wong shouted.

"Yes!" Mrs. Wong shouted back.

Finally, Mr. Wong exclaimed: "You cheated on me, Mrs. Wong! You can't fool me, Mrs. Wong, because I know two Wongs don't make a white!!"

Fortunately, everyone laughed. Emboldened after my silly joke landed, I asked the handsome, well-muscled man sitting directly in front of me close to a beautiful, much younger woman to his left, who had been talking about Tiger Woods: "Are you connected to Tiger Woods, as his business manager or in some other capacity?" Amid a chorus of laughter, he replied: "I am his father."

Our driver interjected: "Joe, do you have any medicine for vertigo?" A certified hypochondriac, I always carry medicine wherever I go. "Earl Woods is speaking tonight, and he too has vertigo." "Sure!" I responded with glee. No one in the van, however, carried water as we do now. So, as we got to the hotel, I asked an employee to fetch water for Tiger Woods's father. He gulped down a Meclizine tablet and thanked me. During the festivities, I read the contents on the label of Meclizine. It was "not to be taken with alcohol." Looking over at the adjacent able where Earl Woods and his party were seated, I saw the senior Mr. Woods downing screwdrivers. Fearing a dire outcome with my complicity, I rushed over to Mr. Woods, my newly minted friend and partner in dizziness, and showed him the warning label. Earl smiled at me again and downed another vodka and orange juice. One hour later, Earl Woods got up and delivered a powerful secular sermon on his rise from seg-regated poverty to success and philanthropy in concert with his famous son. Earl Woods recalled how Black athletes who came to his hometown—Manhattan, Kan-sas—were denied access to hotels and restaurants. He preached the gospel of golf coupled with education as the roadmap to the good life. Moreover, he and Tiger had set up a foundation to help youngsters in inner cities to rise and shine fortified with the proper values and assistance from their foundation. He explained Tiger's absence and received a standing ovation.

Injuries began to slow Tiger in 2008, leading to knee surgery. Yet he managed to win the U.S. Open, to score his 14th Major Tournament for a total of 67 victories to that point. On the top of golf world if not the entire world as his late father had predicted, Tiger Woods had a precipitous fall from grace. First came the death of his father on May 3, 2006, due to a "body weakened by cancer and his longtime affec-tion to alcohol and cigarettes," according to authors Jeff Benedict and Armen Ketey-ian.[20] Their relationship was extremely tight, yet fractured by his father's infidelities. Tiger shared his feelings about his father with a girlfriend.[21] Years later, while on a tour in Africa—father and son frequently travelled together on golf tours—he "caught his father in a room with 'escorts' or ladies of commercial affection."[22] Tiger's mother, Kul-tida, the real disciplinarian in the Woods family, encouraged her son to reconcile with his estranged father. The ambivalent relationship among all three impacted Tiger's personality. Driven by guilt, he replicated his father's rigorous training as an officer in the Special Forces unit of the U.S. Army, causing bodily wear and tear that eventu-ally adversely affected his golf game. The absence of his loving if unfaithful father left a vacuum in his troubled soul. Disdaining his father's philandering, he repeated his lustful overtures with multiple women. Exposed, he suffered his wife's wrath. In an account laced with various interpretations, she attacked Tiger's car, forcing him to flee. In his state of shock and/or inebriation, he crashed the car near his house. The gos-sips had a field day with this scandal, as did the comedians. Tiger became the target of vicious punchlines; indeed, he morphed into a verbal punching bag.

After a long spell of inactivity coupled with subpar performance on the links, Wood's great comeback victory in the 2019 Masters "is the stuff that dreams are made of," to quote Humphrey Bogart as Sam Spade in *The Maltese Falcon*. Fans and sportswriters called it "the greatest comeback in sports history."[23] Following four back surgeries and sundry sex scandals that rocked his reputation and diminished his endorsements, he came from several shots behind leader Francesco Molinari in the first 10 holes of the final round. After his chief rival bogied on hole 12, Tiger scored birdies on holes 13, 15, and 16 to forge a stroke lead at hole 18. A par on hole 18 sealed the deal, giving Woods his fifth Masters crown and a fifth green jacket. This remarkable win marked his 81st PGA triumph.[24] Still chasing Jack Nicklaus's record of 18 major titles, Tiger moves on. Recently Tiger teamed up with Peyton Manning versus Phil Mickelson and Tom Brady in a charity event on May 24, 2020. Conse-quently, $10 million went to coronavirus relief. A fierce competitor, Tiger avenged a prior loss to Mickelson.

Has Tiger gained full redemption from salacious scandal? Does his serial philandering impair his once heroic stature? Another knotty question remains unanswered. Is Tiger a Black hero or one that embodies Asian fusion and multiculturalism? Largely, middle-class white fans still adore Tiger. Conservatives view him as proof of American inclusion into a white man's upper-class game. Trump conferred the American Medal of Freedom on Woods not long after his surprise win in the Masters. In receiving this coveted honor from a leader with a dubious record on race, Tiger thanked his fans for their support through his highs and lows. He hailed his late father and acknowledged his mother along with his two children and current lady friend, Erica. Woods also thanked Arnold Palmer, Jack Nicklaus, and "Grandpa" Charles Sifford, the Black pioneer in golf after whom his son Charlie is named.

Writing 15 years ago and before the sex scandal, S.W. Pope concluded that Eldrick "Tiger" Woods stands as a sporting hero for a variegated, often polarized American society. He is the perfect icon for a white world: "black, handsome, athletic, well-spoken and respectable, with a clear commitment to the Protestant work ethic." In short, Woods is an ideal postmodern sports hero who represents and embodies multiple narratives in late twentieth- and early twenty-first-century culture.[25] Writing 15 years later, Martin Gitlin offers a more critical assessment in the negative. He questions Tiger's ability to learn from sexual escapades, citing the breakup with ski champ Lindsey Vonn "after a rumored affair." Will Tiger's almost compulsive reenactment of his father's frailties ruin his career, his recent comeback notwithstanding? The answer may be written in the winds of future events.

Tiger Woods's 2021 rendezvous with destiny in a car crash on Tuesday, February 23, nearly resulted in death. Speeding in a Genesis GV80 SUV on his way to a film shoot, he evidently lost control, hitting a center median, then a tree, turning over multiple times, and ending in a bush. First responders had to pull him from the wreck with a pry bar and ax. His right leg suffered fractures in the tibia and fibula bones, requiring major surgery.[26] After a long recuperation, the resilient Woods returned to the PGA Tour in the 2022 Masters, finishing 47th. Whether he can draw closer to Jack Nicklaus's record 18 majors victories remains to be seen, but his will to win and desire to fulfill father Earl's prophecy cannot be ignored.

Willie O'Ree

Willie O'Ree was a pioneer in professional hockey as a one-eyed African American pioneer. He attended a Pop Lloyd conference as one of the honorees, and before that event I did not realize his historical significance. In 2018, he was voted into the National Hockey League Hall of Fame. No stranger to violence embedded in this sport—described by one sportscaster as a fight in which a hockey game broke out—Willie had to be rescued from a bunch of thuggish Rangers fans who tried to yank him into the stands. In Chicago, the police had to escort O'Ree from the ice after a brawl, in which his front teeth were deliberately and forcibly removed by the butt-end of an opponent's stick.[27]

As Willie recalled this ugly incident with the sardonic detachment of an 83-year-old survivor, he added pertinent painful details. His Chicago Blackhawks opponent stood 6'4" and weighed 235 pounds, 45 pounds heavier than the shorter Willie. So he hit the bully over the head with his stick, cut his forehead, and exchanged punches with the aggressor. Then, he grabbed on and waited for the benches to clear. The brawl resulted in 80 minutes of assessed penalties. O'Ree had his bloody nose plugged, ready to resume play, but Boston Bruins coach Milt Schmidt, sensing imminent danger, wisely summoned police to protect for him in the visitor's dressing room.[28] This was in 1958, 11 years after Jackie Robinson made history in baseball.

Canadian born in Fredericton, New Brunswick, Willie met his idol Jackie Robinson on a trip to New York City with his youth baseball team. He told the Dodgers star that, in addition to baseball, he also played hockey. Surprised by this information that Black youngsters played, Jackie encouraged young Willie. Years later they met again in Los Angeles at an NAACP luncheon. Robinson recognized O'Ree from their meeting 13 years prior in Brooklyn.[29] O'Ree cherished both meetings. Willie made his debut as a Boston Bruin on January 18, 1958, earning distinction as the league's first Black player in a Bruin victory over the Montréal Canadiens.[30] He only played two games. In 1960–61, however, Willie was recalled by the Bruins, playing 43 games. He scored four goals, 10 assists, and lifelong memories as a pioneer.[31]

Chicago proved to be the most hostile of all six cities in which O'Ree played. Yet, he realized that he could not fight every time that he heard a racial slur because that would land him in the penalty box or the hospital at a time when hockey players wore no helmets. Maintaining his cool enabled Willie to play pro hockey—mostly in the minors—for 21 years. Stoically and heroically, O'Ree played hockey, blind in one eye. It happened early in his career at age 19 when a puck ricocheted off a stick and stuck him in his right eye. The puck shattered the retina. Had his condition been known by hockey officials, it would have terminated Willie's career. So, he continued to practice with a well-kept secret. As a left-handed left winger, he made major adjustments. Happily for O'Ree, he received a call from coach of the Québec Aces, inviting him to training camp. Despite the disability, he made the team. That year (1956–57), Willie scored 22 goals, helping his team to a championship.[32]

In 1956, at age 21, Willie was offered a tryout with the Milwaukee Braves in Waycross, Georgia. Despite family warnings about southern inhospitality, he went. He was shocked by that brief encounter with overt racism in Atlanta's airport, particularly the restroom signs for White Only and Colored Only. A cab driver drove him to a Black hotel in the Black part of town. At tryout camp, he was assigned to a "colored" dorm. Racist epithets flew freely. After two weeks, he returned to Canada in the back of the bus. As he edged closer to home, Willie moved forward on the bus, reaching the first row on the last leg from Bangor, Maine, to home in Canada. "Free at last," O'Ree bade farewell to baseball in favor of hockey.[33]

Hockey, unlike baseball, was not segregated. In fact, early in the twentieth century, an all-Black team played hockey and probably introduced the slapshot and butterfly goaltending style, writes Andrew Knoll.[34] Regarded as the best Black hockey player minus an NHL pedigree, Herb Carnegie preceded O'Ree on the Québec Aces team. Offered a minor league contract with the New York Rangers, he turned it down because he earned more money with his minor league team.[35] Nevertheless, it took 16 years before another Black, Mike Marson, entered the NHL as a Washington Capital. Bill Riley became the third in 1973. These three prepared the ice for Grant Fuhr, the Hall of Fame Edmonton Oiler goalie of their dynastic years. Though racial taunts continue—as Philadelphia Flyer Wayne Simmonds and Washington Capitals forward Devante Smith-Pelly attest—more Blacks have entered the NHL, skating and lashing when necessary. Simmonds, who won the MVP Award in the 2017 NHL All-Star game, cites Willie O'Ree as a source of inspiration. Present at his game in Los Angeles's Staples Center, O'Ree beamed with pride. He also inspired P. K. Subban, the first Black winner of the coveted Norris Trophy, awarded to the league's best defenseman.[36]

O'Ree ended his career in the Western Hockey League in San Diego, where he now lives. He became the director of youth development for the NHL/USA Hockey Diversity Task Force, a nonprofit program that encourages youngsters to play hockey and stay in school. Recipient of many awards, O'Ree claimed that he was on "Cloud Nine" about his 2018 induction into the NHL Hall of Fame. This award recognizes his role as pioneer and his noble efforts on behalf of the service rendered to youths, ages five to 18, which he regarded as a labor of love. NHL Commissioner Gary Bateman defined Willie O'Ree as a hero, forcefully[37]:

> Willie O'Ree devoted his life to our sport and our young people. His words of encouragement and the lessons that he has taught, have inspired thousands not only to play hockey but to incorporate our game's values and ideals to their lives. We marvel at Willie's strength and courage, at his willingness to blaze a trail for future generations of players, and we are honored by his continuing presence as a role model, mentor and ambassador for our sport.

Simone Biles

Like Tiger Woods and O. J. Simpson, both of whom refused to serve as African American role models or identify with the Black Power movement, the world's greatest female gymnast, Simone Biles, insists that she is not a race woman, "just Simone." She blocks out race when she competes. And competes to win, as her medal tally attests. She has amassed a total of 30 Olympic and World Championship medals as America's most decorated gymnast. Although her grandfather/adoptive father considers her "an inspiration for the African American community," he "is not sure Simone sees it that way."[38]

Simone Arianne Biles was born on March 14, 1997, in Ohio State University Hospital, the third youngest of four children to Sharon Biles and a deadbeat father, Kelvin Clemons, who abandoned the family. Unable to care for her children due to drugs and alcohol, Sharon gave up her four children to foster care in 2001. Two years later, Simone's grandfather Ron Biles stepped in to thwart the imminent adoption of his four children to "strangers." He and his second wife adopted Simone and her younger sister Adria and sent two older siblings, Tevin and Ashley, to live with Ron's sister in Ohio. Despite this harrowing early childhood—or perhaps because of it—Simone was driven to succeed. According to author Danyel Smith, citing psychologist Ellen Winner, Simone has the "rage to master" or "enhanced capacity to self-directed learning, common to unusually gifted children." Simone had it, Smith asserts, at age six.[39]

To escape the sweltering summer heat, Simone and her daycare class took refuge in local air-conditioned Bannon's Gymnastix for four hours. There, Simone tumbled to eventual glory.[40] At age 12, her birth mother attempted to reenter her life. It knocked Simone for a loop and into depression. Her performance suffered. Therapy in 2013 helped. She also drew closer to her grandparents, who had taken charge of Simone and younger sister Adria. Recharged, she won every all-around competition she entered through 2021 (her withdrawal from the Olympics notwithstanding).[41] In winning the gold at the 2013 National Championships, Biles created a new trick—a double flip in a straight body position with a half turn at the end. This new move is called "the Biles."[42] That initial international victory was marred by a racial slur. A sore-loser Italian gymnast complained to reporters: "Next time we should paint our skin black, so we could win, too."[43] After winning her 15th gold medal, she draped 14 gold medals around her neck on an Instagram "selfie" with a caption: "Work hard in silence, let your success be the noise." Her reward for an outstanding performance in Rio, where Biles won five golds, was carrying the American flag during the ceremonial climax.[44]

Biles's disinclination to serve as a Black role model begs analysis. In responding to a question posed at a public appearance on New York City's Lower East Side, where she promoted a Japanese skin care product of a company that underwrote the forthcoming Olympics, she addressed several barbs tossed her way. Simone revealed that her hair, her legs, and her race had entered the conversation. On the latter issue, Biles admitted that while growing up, she did not know of many Black gymnasts. But, she added, that she was inspired by Gabby Douglas's victory in the 2012 Olympics, sensing "if she can do it, I can do it" (as quoted by Aguirre). When asked about sexual abuse in gymnastics, Biles showed the true color of heroism.

That dark period in her life as with other aspiring gymnasts began in Texas. At the age of 12, Simone was invited to the 2,000-acre Karolyi Ranch in Walker County. Pushed beyond her limits, Simone hated her experience. All work and no play all day from 8 a.m. to 7 p.m., most ambitious gymnasts followed the rules. After all, the Karolyis trained Nadia Comăneci to be a perfect 10 before Bo Derek claimed that number—at least on film. They also trained Mary Lou Retton. "The Karolyis," Danyel Smith wrote, "have been accused of beating and scratching young athletes, of withholding food, and of aiding and abetting Larry Nassar."[45] On January 15, 2018, Simone broke her silence. She publicly charged the infamous trainer with sexual abuse in a tweet. Coming from arguably the best gymnast—male or female—it had instant impact. Like a hot potato, USA Gymnastics dropped the Karolyi Ranch as a training facility. When Mary Bono, former Congresswoman and widow of her predecessor husband, Sonny, "dissed" Nike for its endorsement of Colin Kaepernick, Simone Biles used her athletic clout to force the ouster of Bono as interim president of USA Gymnastics. *C'est-ce si bon sans Bono.* Abby Aguirre admires Biles's ability "to bend both space and time" as she conquers gravity to be sure, but what elevates her to iconic status alongside of Muhammad Ali is "her willingness to speak out from within the sport" on sexual abuse.[46]

After the murders of Ahmaud Arbery and George Floyd, Biles became more vocal on social and political issues. "We need change. We need justice for the Black community." No longer on the sidelines, Biles hailed the peaceful protestors. On July 3, 2020, Simone Biles posted photos with her new boyfriend, Houston Texas safety Jonathan Owens. One wishes that Simone Biles finds equal success in the game of love.

Conclusion

Blacks lives do matter. In the wake of COVID-19 coupled with the cases of brutality and excessive force by police, we search for solutions. Though we have come a long way from when lynching with impunity was operative in the South as the mutilated body of Emmett Till in 1955 brutally testifies, the quest for justice continues. When Kobe Bryant and his daughter Gianna succumbed with associates in that horrible and preventable helicopter crash, millions across the globe expressed grief and disbelief. Black lives mattered. Racism and social injustice remain, so our fight continues. But how do we account for the progress we've seen? What prompted the change "from stumbling block to steppingstone, from the outhouse to the White House," in the words of Jesse Jackson?

Clearly, the civil rights movement propelled major change. No doubt. Dr. King, Malcolm X, and, lest we forget, supportive white allies and political leaders sped the plow to social parity. My purpose in writing this book highlights the role of Black athletes, often confronting major hurdles, who strove heroically to bend the arc of history, in concert with Dr. King, to achieve justice. Black athletic lives had a significant impact in this quest. True, my thesis invites debate. Dr. Harry Edwards, for example, has waxed eloquent on the exploitation of Black athletes, who he claims function as modern gladiators. He famously wrote that "on the field blacks are supposed to be superhuman; off the field they are regarded as subhuman."[1] Edwards went on to note that a Black hoopster who cannot jump or a halfback with average speed does not play. In his 1970 book, *Black Students*, Edwards painted a dark picture of Blacks recently recruited to white schools who endured "Mickey Mouse" courses and were subjected to "stacking" positions. In football, they were denied quarterback positions. In baseball, they were assigned to middle infield, pitcher-catcher roles. In short, they were used and cast aside despite the enormous revenue that stars like Lew Alcindor at UCLA and O. J. Simpson at USC generated.[2] Many athletes fail to graduate. They are debased, Edwards argued, as "Niggers, coons, jigaboos" six days a week despite the façade of team spirit once a week. Moreover, they are prohibited from dating whites.[3] Years later, football star Michael Bennett in conjunction with Dave Zirin equated the NCAA quest for profit to a "gangster operation." Unduly harsh words perhaps, but Bennett and Zirin make a strong case that college players should be paid.[4]

Howard Bryant agrees that great Black athletes such as Jim Brown, Bill Russell, Wilt Chamberlain, Elgin Baylor, and Lew Alcindor integrated college sports and in the process created a billion-dollar industry "undermining the economic power of traditionally black colleges." As commodities, Bryant contends, they were taken, but the power positions—coaches, executives, and athletic directors—fell to whites. Black minds lagged behind their bodies in opportunities.[5] Magic Johnson has reiterated an earlier Arthur Ashe exhortation for Black youngsters to concentrate more on education than sports. In "Epilogue: A Message for Black Teenagers" inserted at the end of his autobiography, Earvin Johnson writes:

> Basketball is not the best way to get ahead. It's probably the most difficult path you could take.... You have to understand that your chances of playing basketball for a living are minuscule.
>
> The black community already has enough basketball players. And enough baseball players, and football players.... We need more teachers. We need more lawyers. We need more doctors. We need more accountants. We need more nurses. We need more pilots and more scientists. And more carpenters. And more professors. And more police officers. And more bankers.... And more politicians. And every single one of these professions—including doctor and lawyer—is easier to get into than the NBA....
>
> Racism exists, but too often we use it as an excuse. I'm not saying it isn't there, because it definitely is. But if you get your education, you can look beyond that. I don't care what somebody calls you. You can still walk proud because of who you are.... We have to go to college. Think about business. Work hard. Support one another, like other groups do.[6]

Journalist/writer William Rhoden, a former football player at Morgan State, provides a template for this coda in his important book, *Forty Million Dollar Slaves: The Rise, Fall, and Redemption of the Black Athlete*. The title strikes me as not at all incongruous. Power still resides in the white establishment, which presides over—metaphorically—the sports plantation.[7] Despite this feudal condition, or because of it, Black athletes developed a unique style according to Howard Bryant as well as Bill Rhoden. The latter cites chest bumps, high fives, shakes, and shimmies as basic components of this "black style." More than gestures, it is a state of mind. Duke Ellington had it right: "It don't mean a thing if it ain't got that swing!" Author Ralph Ellison captured the beat when writing, "Without the presence of Negro American style, our jokes, folk tales, even our sports would be lacking in the sudden turns, shocks, the swift changes of pace ... that serve to remind us that the world is ever unexplored, and that while a complex mastery of life is mere illusion the real secret of the game is to make it swing."[8]

And swing it did with Willie Mays's basket catch; Miles Davis's trumpet solo in jazz; Jackie Robinson's dancing off the bases; R. C. Owens's "alley oop" catch; Jim Brown running over would-be tacklers; Elgin Baylor hanging in the air along with Russell, Chamberlain, Jabbar, Dr. J; Miami romping over Texas in the 1991 Cotton Bowl.[9] Rhoden charts the waves of African American progress. First came Jackie Robinson, a belated rookie at age 28 in 1947. Willie Mays launched the second wave in 1951, bringing both youthful vitality and Black style with his signature basket catch and his flying cap. Despite initial progress, the human stain of racism persisted. When the New York Giants—may they rest in peace—displayed an all-Black outfield with Mays in center, Monte Irvin in left, and Hank Thompson in right, residual racist white fans felt uncomfortable, their malaise captured by the doggerel of an anonymous sportswriter who hissed:

> Willie Mays is in a daze
> And Thomson's lost his vigor
> But Irvin whacks for all the Blacks
> Ain't it good to be a nigger

My progressive-minded family loathed the N-word, and I absolutely forbade its use in my classes, heavily populated by students of color. I recall that Mickey Mantle received more press coverage than Willie Mays, though this once ardent Yankee fan concedes that Mays, less injury prone, was the superior player. He was detached, cool, resigned, Rhoden observed, yet joyful.[10] He put soul into play, but was powerless and deferential to Manager Durocher, a man he called "Mr. Leo." Indeed, when Durocher heckled adversary Jackie Robinson, applying the N-word after Robinson questioned Leo's masculinity, Mays and Irvin refused to speak up in protest because they acted as "team players."[11]

Rhoden's third wave included Bill Russell, Jim Brown, Curt Flood, and Elgin Baylor, all acknowledged in this book. Rules changes were implemented to curb Black style. R. C. Owens not only devised the alley-oop catch on "Hail Mary" throws into the end-zone usually at crucial moments in a football game, but he also used his great leaping ability to block long field goals. That defensive strategy was jettisoned by the NFL rule makers. To curtail Black dominance on offense, the NCAA officials widened the lane from eight to 12 feet. And at one point, 1966 to be precise, the NCAA banned the dunk shot to thwart Lew Alcindor's superior play. On defense, in response to Bill Russell's amazing ability to block shots, they banned goal tending. Holding the firm line at foul shooting disabled Wilt Chamberlain from flying through the air with the greatest of ease to dunk foul shots.

In baseball, as we have shown, Curt Flood challenged baseball's reserve cause. Rather than report to the Philadelphia Phillies, a $90,000 "slave," he sat out the 1970 season. Supported by Bob Gibson and Jackie Robinson, Flood was abandoned by many others, including Black peers; therefore he went into exile. While in Spain, he learned that two white players, Andy Messersmith and Dave McNally, qualified as free agents. Though Flood had paved the way for others, he remained essentially "blackballed," unable to secure work in Major League Baseball until a broadcasting job in Oakland in 1978 opened briefly.[12]

Historian John Hope Franklin questioned the notion of sports as "the promised land for African Americans." Pessimistic but a bit also hopeful, this pioneer Black academic wanted to believe that a better day was coming for people of color. I have attempted to offer a counter-argument to the pessimists cited above. Indeed, I concur with Bill Rhoden's more optimistic view, thanks to Jack Johnson's joy of defiance, Jackie Robinson's open door to access and to opportunity, Muhammad Ali's inspiration with conviction, the Williams sisters' power of self-definition, LeBron James's bully pulpit, Colin Kaepernick's kneeling tribute to victims of police violence—all contribute to a great chain of being and becoming.[13]

Just a few years prior, defiant athletes became pariahs, thrust out of their professional positions, often blackballed for life. When Denver Nugget sharpshooter Mahmoud Abdul-Rauf né Chris Jackson refused to salute the flag before games in 1996, he was blacklisted, and later his Mississippi home was burned to the ground. Similarly,

Chicago Bulls three-point specialist and union rep Craig Hodges, a 10-year NBA veteran, protested the treatment of minorities in a letter, hand-delivered to President George H. W. Bush, and he too was blackballed while his famous teammate Michael Jordan said nothing.[14] Dramatic changes followed the murder of Trayvon Martin in 2012 in Sanford, Florida, and the unrest brought on by Michael Brown's killing in Ferguson, Missouri, in 2014. During the antebellum era, it is appropriate to note, Florida and Missouri were slave states. These and other examples of questionable police actions brought LeBron James and other highly visible athletes out of their luxury cars, but they came up against a heightened patriotism, spawned by 9/11.[15] If Samuel Johnson was correct in his observation that "patriotism is the last refuge of the scoundrel," then anyone who questioned the behavior of one's nation was a traitor. This mindset became grist for the mills of demagoguery. Author Howard Bryant asserts[16]:

> With the opportunistic demagoguery that won him the presidency, Donald Trump engaged in a twenty-first-century version of McCarthyism by demanding that protesters receive the Robeson treatment. "Wouldn't you love to see one of those NFL owners, when somebody disrespects our flag, to say, 'Get that son of a bitch off the field right now? Out. He's fired! Fired!'"

Spoken more like a TV emcee than a president, these words resonated at a rally in Huntsville, Alabama, on September 22, 2017. POTUS 45 threatened owners to blacklist non-compliant players. "Make them stand," he demanded.[17]

Though dissenters were equated with traitors, even Colin Kaepernick, the target of this invective, had support from military members and Black police organizations committed to eradication of police brutality. On a collision course, sports owners were committed to commercialized nationalism, while NFL Players Association members balked. Until she was banned for her minstrel songs, Kate Smith resounded at sundry stadiums belting out Irving Berlin's "God Bless America." One person tried to make his way to a restroom as the song played during a seventh inning stretch at Yankee Stadium. Stopped by an NYPD officer, he demanded relief and he was ejected from the ballpark, a somewhat better option than a bullpen in prison. Bradford Campeau-Laurion then sued the Yankee organization and the city for religious and political discrimination with the help of the New York Civil Liberties Union. Eleven months later he won the case, $10,000 from the city, and the right of free movement during the "Fat Lady's" song.[18]

When Colin Kaepernick called attention to police misbehavior, most white fans, who preferred entertainment, did not get the message.[19] They regarded Kaepernick as "ungrateful." Rich Black athletes were instructed to be quiet. Media commentariat played it both ways. They praised "Ali with one hand," especially after his death, "and slapped Kaepernick with other," according to Dave Zirin.[20] That double standard was evident when Baltimore Ravens star linebacker Ray Lewis pled guilty to obstruction of justice in a murder case and was fined $250,000 and allowed to play in the 2000 Super Bowl but Kaepernick was blacklisted for a silent protest.[21] And Ray Lewis had the chutzpah to advise Kaepernick to "Shut your mouth." And Michael Irvin, after cocaine issues and alleged rape, was welcomed back to telecasting at the behest of Dallas owner Jerry Jones. Former Black football stars were evidently useful pawns in the game to checkmate Colin Kaepernick.[22]

Trump's strategy may have backfired. New England Patriots owner Robert Kraft, who donated $1 million to his 2016 campaign plus a Super Bowl ring to the president, stated on September 24, 2017, that players have the right "to peacefully affect social change." Thus Kraft, my contemporary at Columbia College, reaffirmed the value of our liberal arts education. Moreover, that Sunday, we witnessed a dozen Baltimore Ravens and Jacksonville Jaguars kneeling in protest.[23] A compromise was reached on May 23, 2018, in which players must stand during the opening ceremony but could opt to remain in the locker room, an option condemned by Trump. An arbitrator ruled in favor of Kaepernick 21 days later. Nike introduced a "Just Do It" campaign with Colin as the face and voice of this effort. In February 2019, during Super Bowl month, he posted athletes wearing #imwithkap jerseys on social media. On February 15 Kaepernick and Eric Reid won settlements of their suit in a confidential agreement.[24] Whatever his motives, Colin Kaepernick had compelled Black athletes to reclaim their historical heritage and assert their political influence.[25]

Athletes as activists owe a debt to their predecessors. Earning far less money, the early pioneers took far greater risk. Consider the treatment meted out to Paul Robeson after his unrelenting pressure to end Jim Crow laws and his favorable view of Stalin's Russia. After baseball, Jackie Robinson received no offers to manage or to coach. Similarly, Oscar Robertson was exiled following his litigating against the NBA to prevent a merger with the ABA. Kareem-Abdul Jabbar became a pariah, unable to latch on to a career in coaching following his glory days and nights as a player. The establishment had no room for Black rebels with a cause. Something positive, however, happened with the attempt to stifle dissent over perceived injustice by current athletes. Steph Curry refused to participate in White House ceremonies after his team, the Golden State Warriors, won an NBA title because of the hostile atmosphere, laced with racism, emanating from the Oval Office. Warriors coach Steve Kerr supported his players who protested, as did San Antonio Spurs coach Gregg Popovich. LeBron James, as noted above, joined the fray and jousted with the president.

Today, conditions seem more favorable to the rebels in an aggressive mode due to increased salaries, social media, globalization, and unionization. Money is power. Formerly neutral—because "Republicans also buy sneakers"—global icon and billionaire Michael Jordan stepped up to the plate. He formed a foundation with his second wife, Juanita, donating $2 million for relief efforts after Hurricane Florence wreaked havoc. After 9/11, Jordan donated $1 million—his Wizards salary—to victims, with $100,000 to children who lost parents in that tragedy. He worked for the Make-A-Wish Foundation from 2001 to 2004, managing $5 million. His Michael Jordan Celebrity Invitational Golf Tournament featuring Wayne Gretzky, Michael Phelps, Samuel L. Jackson, and Mark Wahlberg raised $7 million for charity. Quite a *pushke* (collection box)! Jordan donated a combined $17 million (over four years) to Family Health Clinics and $5 million to the Smithsonian African American History and Culture Museum in Washington, D.C. To prove that he is still a man in the middle, Michael donated $1 million to the NAACP Legal Defense Fund and $1 million to the Institute for Community-Police Relations.[26]

Contemporary athletes rejected the earlier apolitical template of Michael Jordan. O. J. Simpson and Tiger Woods, eager for Madison Avenue appeal, deracinated themselves as crossover artists. New militants followed the road paved by Jackie Robinson and Bill Russell. Howard Bryant points to antihero Allen Iverson, bedecked in blue jeans and gold chains, sporting cornrows, proudly indifferent to "greenwash."[27] Suddenly, in response to recent events, Carmelo Anthony, Chris Paul, and Dwayne Wade formed the Social Change Fund, which reporter Sopan Deb describes as "a philanthropic effort to invest in organizations that support people of color from a political perspective—such as advancing causes like criminal justice reform and expanded voting rights—and at a community level by targeting racial inequities in housing and education."[28] Earlier, in 2016, Anthony had joined with LeBron James and Chris Paul to use the ESPYs as a stage for denouncing racism and police brutality. While Anthony had refused to get involved in the 2020 election, his peers did not share his reluctance. They are engaged, regardless of consequences. The gloves are off. Howard Bryant closes his powerful tome by invoking Muhammad Ali, who famously said in 1971: "I just love the freedom and the flesh and blood of my people more than I do the money.… You can take your show and play it right in Washington, let Nixon hear it. And I'll be happy. So this boldness and telling the truth overshadows sports greatly."[29]

Unable to gain victories in the 2020 election cycle, red-state legislatures with one exception, Kentucky, passed retrograde legislation to turn back the political clock on voting rights. Black athletes of renown contributed to the quest for leveling the political playing field along with their quest for social justice. Their efforts with supportive white peers brought pressure to bear on this volatile issue. Opposition to Georgia's attempt to suppress voter rights through recent legislation intensified. Consequently, two CEOs of major corporations with corporate headquarters in Atlanta—Coca-Cola and Delta Airlines—expressed their displeasure. Baseball Commissioner Rob Manfred decided to switch the All-Star Game venue, originally slated for Atlanta, to Denver, Colorado, where the Rockies play and my distant cousin Jared Polis serves as Governor. Though controversial, this move illustrates the growing influence of "woke" athletes, their ability to turn the wheels toward political as well as social justice. In the *New York Times,* James Wagner stressed this significant act in baseball, where most of the owners are conservative in sync with a sport steeped in tradition, as a major step forward. Former Atlanta Braves star and current Houston Astros manager Dusty Baker invoked his late friend and superstar Hank Aaron to hail Major League Baseball's stance. He told reporters: "This is what Hank would have wanted, even if it was his own town. He always had the rights of the people in the forefront of his mind and in his heart."[30]

Academics no longer scoff at sports history as they did when I introduced the first course at Long Island University Brooklyn in 1976. David Hollander, assistant dean at New York University, sensing that the world is broken, introduced a new course, "How Basketball Can Save the World." In the prism of basketball, he believes we can mend this fractured world, appealing to all classes, sections, races, and ethnicities.[31] Perhaps Dean Hollander is both too narrow in focus (basketball) and too expansive in remedy. All sports provide access and mobility, as our study has demonstrated. The Black athlete as hero has illustrated the high purpose of *tikkun olam*, derived from the Mishna's rabbinical texts, to promote social justice and thereby repair the world. Champions can be dethroned, but heroes are forever, as Jesse Jackson reminded us at Sugar Ray Robinson's funeral: "Champions win events. Heroes win people. Champions are of short duration—you can be stripped of champion stature. Heroes cannot be. Heroes are needed. They give us security and confidence."[32] Thanks to the many athletes profiled in this book, democracy is advancing in the USA.

Chapter Notes

Introduction

1. Ray Browne and Marshall Fishwick, eds., *The Hero in Transition* (Bowling Green, OH: Bowling Green University Press, 1983), 5–14, 60–61.

2. See Jim Holt's review of the Hoberman book in the *New York Times*, April 16, 2000, BR 11.

3. John Hoberman, *Darwin's Athletes: How Sport Has Damaged Black America and Preserved the Myth of Race* (Boston: Houghton Mifflin Mariner, 1997), 3–51. See also Christopher's balanced critique in *The Chronicle of Higher Education*, March 7, 1997, A15–16.

4. Gerald R. Gems, in David Wiggins, ed., *Out of Our Shadows: A Biographical History of African American Athletes* (Fayetteville: University of Arkansas Press, 2008), 59.

5. William Rhoden, *Forty Million Dollar Slaves: The Rise, Fall, and Redemption of the Black Athlete* (New York: Random House, 2006), 79–84.

6. Sidney Gendin, "Moses 'Fleetwood' Walker," in *Jackie Robinson: Race, Sports and the American Dream*, eds. Joseph Dorinson and Joram Warmund (Armonk, NY: M.E. Sharpe, 1998), 22–29.

7. C.E. Lincoln, *Black Muslims in America* (Boston: Beacon, 1968), 33–40.

8. W.E.B. Dubois, *The Souls of Black Folk* (New York: Dover, 1994; originally published 1903), 2.

9. Peter Saharko, "Ex-mayor Usry Gets Hero Award," *The Press of Atlantic City*, October 8, 2000, MM, 282.

10. Tom Hawkins, "Jackie, Do They Know?" in *Jackie Robinson: Race, Sports, and the American Dream*, xv. See also Bonnie DeSimone, "Intense, Inspirational … Indispensable," *Chicago Tribune*, March 31, 1997.

11. Howard Bryant, *The Heritage: Black Athletes, a Divided America, and the Politics of Patriotism* (Boston: Beacon, 2018), 192–193.

12. Richard Sandomir, "Irv Cross, First Black Network TV Sports Analyst, Dies at 81," *New York Times*, March 2, 2021, B9. See also Richard Goldstein, "Elgin Baylor, 86, Hall of Famer Who Sent the N.B.A. Skyward, Is Dead," *New York Times*, March 23, 2021, B11.

Chapter 1

1. John T. Talamini and Charles H. Page, eds., *Sport and Society: An Anthology* (Boston: Little, Brown, 1973), 242.

2. Rhoden, *Forty Million Dollar Slaves*, 47, 52.

3. C. Vann Woodward, *Reunion and Reaction: The Compromise of 1877 and the End of Reconstruction* (Boston: Little, Brown, 1951), Chapter 11.

4. As cited by Juan Haines's book review of Rhoden's *Forty Million Dollar Slaves, San Quentin News*, March 26, 2017, sanquentinnews.com.

5. Joseph J. Vecchione, ed., *The New York Times Book of Sports Legends* (New York: Random House, 1991), 136–138.

6. The appalling conditions that confronted African Americans are chronicled in many sources. The most readable in my judgment is Lerone Bennett, Jr., *Before the Mayflower*, 5th ed. (New York: Penguin, 1984), especially chapters 9 and 11.

7. David K. Wiggins, *More Than a Game: A History of the African American Experience in Sport* (Lanham, MD: Rowman & Littlefield, 2018), 39–40.

8. Introduction, *My Soul's High Song: The Collected Writings of Countee Cullen*, edited by Gerald Early (New York: Doubleday, 1991), 25.

9. Lawrence W. Levine, *Black Culture and Black Consciousness* (New York: Oxford Univ. Press, 1977), 430–433; Al-Tony Gilmore, *Bad Nigger! The National Impact of Jack Johnson* (Port Washington, NY: Kennikat, 1975), 46.

10. Gilmore, *Bad Nigger!*, 52–53.

11. Quoted in Gilmore, 52. See also Gerald R. Gems, "Jack Johnson and the Quest for Racial Respect," in Wiggins, *Out of the Shadows*, 64.

12. Gilmore, *Bad Nigger!*, Chapter 3.

13. Brad Herzog, *The Sports 100: The One Hundred Most Important People in American Sports History* (New York: Simon & Schuster, 1995), 68–69.

14. Herzog, 69. See also James Slater, "105 Years Ago Today—Jack Johnson Takes a 'Dive' Against Jesse Willard," Boxing News 24/7, April 5, 2020, www.boxing247.com.

15. Jack Orr, "The Black Boxer: Exclusion and Ascendance," in *Sport and Society: An Anthology*,

eds. John T. Talamini and Charles H. Page (Boston: Little, Brown, 1973), 247–248.

16. Levine, *Black Culture,* 430–433; David K. Wiggins, "The Notion of Double-Consciousness and the Involvement of Black Athletes in American Sport," in *Ethnicity and Sport in North American History and Culture,* ed. George Eisen and David K. Wiggins (Westport, CT: Greenwood, 1994), 140–142.

17. W.E.B. DuBois, "The Prize Fighter," *The Crisis* 8, no. 4 (August 1914): 181.

18. Randy Roberts, *Papa Jack: Jack Johnson and the Era of White Hopes* (New York: Free Press, 1983), 218-230.

19. Kenneth Shropshire, *In Black and White: Race and Sports in America* (New York: NYU Press, 1998), 146–147.

20. Jack Orr, "The Black Boxer: Exclusion and Ascendance," in Talamini, *Sport and Society,* 250.

21. James P. Dawson, "Louis Evens Score with Schmeling," in Allison Danzig and Peter Brandwein, eds., *The Greatest Sport Stories from* The New York Times (New York: A.S. Barnes, 1951), 488–490.

22. Dominick J. Capeci, Jr., and Martha Wilkerson, "Multifarious Hero: Joe Louis, American Society and Race Relations During World Crisis, 1935–1945." In Paul J, Zingg, ed., *The Sporting Image: Readings in American Sport History* (Lanham, MD: University Press of America, 1988).

23. Levine, *Black Culture,* 433.

24. Levine, 434.

25. Capeci and Wilkerson, "Multifarious Hero," 302, 313.

26. As quoted in Robert Lipsyte and Peter Levine, *Idols of the Game: A Sporting History of the American Century* (Atlanta: Turner, 1995), 149.

27. Lipsyte and Levine, 149, 157.

28. Lipsyte and Levine, 160–161.

29. As cited in Richard O. Davies, *Sports in American Life: A History* (Malden, MA: Wiley-Blackwell, 2017), 199. See also Herzog, *The Sports 100,* 41.

30. Kenneth Shropshire, *Being Sugar Ray: The Life of Sugar Ray Robinson, America's Greatest Boxer and the First Celebrity Athlete* (New York: Hatchette, 2007), 56.

31. Ron Flatter, "The Sugar in the Sweet Science," ESPN Classic, Mar. 1, 1999, https://www. espn.com; Dave Anderson, "Sugar Ray Robinson, 1921–1989," in Vecchione, *New York Times Book of Sports Legends,* 267.

32. Anderson, "Sugar Ray Robinson," 264; "Sugar Ray Robinson," Biography.com, Oct. 20, 2020, https://.biography.com/athlete/sugar-ray-robinson.

33. Nick Parkinson, "Rewind to 1951: The St. Valentine's Massacre," *ESPN,* Feb. 14, 2016, www. espn.com.

34. Shropshire, *Being Sugar Ray,* 120–121. See also Lipsyte and Levine, *Idols of the Game,* 159.

35. Shropshire, *Being Sugar Ray,* 122–123.

36. Shropshire, 61–64, 127–129.

37. Anderson, "Sugar Ray Robinson," 266.

38. James P. Dawson, "Robinson Knocks Out

LaMotta in 13th Round for World Middleweight Title," *New York Times,* Feb. 15, 1951, 43.

39. For details of Cerdan's fatal crash, see Aviation Safety Network, Oct. 28, 1949, https://aviation-safety.net/database/record.php?id=19491028-0.

40. "Sugar Ray Robinson in 1950s Paris," *Entrée to Black Paris Blog,* Nov.1, 2018, www. entreeyoblackparis.com.

41. "Sugar Ray Robinson in 1950s Paris." Also see Shropshire, *Being Sugar Ray,* 155–157.

42. "Sugar Ray Robinson in 1950s Paris."

43. "Sugar Ray Robinson in 1950s Paris." Also see Robert Portis, "Sept. 12, 1951: Robinson vs. Turpin," Boxiana (website), Sept. 20, 2020, www. thefightcity.com.

44. Michael Carbert, "June 25, 1952: Maxim vs Robinson," Boxiana (website), June 25, 2020, www. thefightcity.com.

45. Anderson, "Sugar Ray Robinson," 266 and 268. See also Marty Mulcahey, "Forgotten Champ: Paul Pender," ESPN Boxing, accessed May 16, 2022, http://a.espncdn.com/boxing/a/2002/0618/1396276.html.

46. Thomas Hauser, "Sugar Ray Robinson Revisited," *Boxing Forum,* Nov. 21, 2010, https:// www.boxingscene.com. See also the documentary *Sugar Ray Robinson: The Bright Lights and Dark Shadows of a Champion,* HBO Sports of the 20th Century series, first aired Dec., 8, 1998.

47. Tim Graham, "Documentary Exposes the Real Sugar Ray Robinson," *Las Vegas Sun,* Dec. 2, 1998, https://lasvegassun.com.

48. Hauser, "Sugar Ray Robinson Revisited."

49. Graham, "Documentary Exposes Real Sugar Ray Robinson." Also see Will Haygood, *Sweet Thunder: The Life and Times of Sugar Ray Robinson* (New York: Lawrence Hill, 2009), 94.

50. Sugar Ray Robinson with Dave Anderson, *Sugar Ray* (Boston: DaCapo Press, 1994), 380, Appendix.

51. Shropshire, *Being Sugar Ray,* 206–208.

52. Shropshire, 206–208.

53. Browne and Fishwick, *Hero in Transition,* 5–7.

54. Douglas A. Noverr and Larry E. Ziewacz, *The Games They Played: Sports in American History, 1865-1980* (Lanham, MD: Rowman and Littlefield, 1983), 24.

55. Orr, "The Black Boxer," 253, 259–261.

56. Wiggins, 146.

57. Joyce Carol Oates, "Muhammad Ali: The Greatest," in *ESPN SportsCentury,* ed. Michael MacCambridge (New York: Hyperion, 1999), 202, 204.

58. Wiggins, 147; Jonathan Eig, *Ali: A Life* (Boston: Houghton Mifflin Harcourt), 272–273; Lipsyte, *SportsWorld,* 264–265.

59. Hauser, *Muhammad Ali: His Life and Times* (New York: Touchstone, 1991), 280–281.

60. Jaher, "White America Views Jack Johnson, Joe Louis, Muhammad Ali," in *Sport in America,* edited by Donald Spivey (Westport, CT: Greenwood, 1985), 180; Hauser, *Muhammad Ali,* 282–283, 286–287.

61. Hauser, *Muhammad Ali,* 259–260, 457–458.

62. Hauser, 206–207.

63. Jaher, "White America," 182.

64. Gary Harmon, "Tarzan and Columbo," in Browne and Fishwick, *The Hero in Transition,* 115.

65. Lincoln, *Black Muslims,* 37–41.

66. Oates, "Muhammad Ali," 220.

67. President Obama's Statement on Muhammad Ali, *New York Times,* June 4, 2016 from nytimes.com.

Chapter 2

1. David Goldblatt, *The Games: A Global History of the Olympics* (New York: W. W. Norton, 2016), 30–37.

2. As quoted in Dave Zirin, *A People's History of Sports in the United States: 250 Years of Politics, Protest, and Play* (New York: New Press, 2008), 88.

3. Zirin, 79; Jules Tygiel, *Baseball's Great Experiment: Jackie Robinson and His Legacy* (New York: Oxford University Press, 1998), 61.

4. Jennifer H. Lansbury, *A Spectacular Leap: Black Women Athletes in Twentieth-Century America* (Fayetteville: University of Arkansas Press, 2014), 4–10.

5. Lansbury., 44.

6. Bernard McFadden, "Fred Thompson, 85, Champion of Women in Track and Field, Dies," *New York Times,* January 26, 2019, B15.

7. William Baker, *Jesse Owens: An American Life* (New York: Free Press, 1986), 74.

8. Baker, 74.

9. Baker, 25.

10. Baker, 84.

11. Vecchione, *New York Times Book of Sports Legends,* 235, puts the number of Black Olympians at 10, while John A. Lucas & Ronald A. Smith, *Saga of American Sport* (Philadelphia: Lea and Febiger, 1978), 379, mention 18.

12. Arthur Daley, "U.S. Captures 4 Events," *New York Times,* August 5, 1936, 1.

13. Baker, *Jesse Owens,* 103–105, and Vecchione, *Sports Legends,* 235.

14. Eisen and Wiggins, *Ethnicity and Sports,* 142–143.

15. Baker, *Jesse Owens,* Ch. 12–14.

16. Daniel McGraw "The Forgotten Fastest Man," Andscape, July 12, 2016, https://andscape.com/features/the-forgotten-fastest-man/.

17. McGraw "Forgotten Fastest Man."

18. Frank Litsky, "Harrison Dillard: World's Best Hurdler in the 1940s, Dies at 96," *New York Times,* Nov. 18, 2019, D7.

19. Litsky, "Harrison Dillard."

20. McGraw, "Forgotten Fastest Man."

21. McGraw, "Forgotten Fastest Man,"and Litsky, "Harrison Dillard."

22. McGraw, "Forgotten Fastest Man,".

23. McGraw, "Forgotten Fastest Man."

24. Litsky, "Harrison Dillard."

25. Frank Litsky, "Mal Whitfield, Olympic Gold Medalist and Tuskegee Airman, Dies at 91," *New York Times,* Nov. 20, 2015, B14.

26. Litsky, "Mal Whitfield."

27. Elaine Woo, "Mal Whitfield Dies at 91," *Los Angeles Times,* Nov. 29, 2015, https://www.latimes.com/local/obituaries/la-me-mal-whitfield-20151121-story.html.

28. Fredricka Whitfield, "My Dad, Marvelous Mal," CNN.com, November 22, 2015, https://www.cnn.com/2015/11/22/opinions/whitfield-marvelous-mal/index.html.

29. Bill Dwyre, "Rafer Johnson Was a Humble Champion Who Put Others in the Spotlight," *Los Angeles Times,* Dec. 5, 2020, https://www.latimes.com/sports/story/2020-12-05/rafer-johnson-humble-olympic-champion.

30. Rafer Johnson and Philip Goldberg, *The Best That I Can Be: An Autobiography* (New York: Doubleday, 1998), xiv–xv.

31. Larry Schwartz, "From Rags to Sport Riches," ESPN.com, https://www.espn.com/sportscentury/features/00016405.html.

32. Schwartz, "Rags to Sport Riches." Also see Jayne Kamin-Ocea, "Rafer Johnson, 1960 Olympic Decathlon Champion, Dies at Age 86," SI.com, Dec. 2, 2020, https://www.si.com/olympics/2020/12/02/rafer-johnson-death-olympic-decathlon-champion.

33. Johnson and Goldberg, *Best That I Can Be,* 136–141, and David Maraniss, *Rome 1960: The Olympics That Changed the World* (New York: Simon & Schuster, 2008), 35–37.

34. Kurt Streeter, "Remembering Rafer Johnson in a Long Year of Lost Sports Legends," *New York Times,* December 7, 2020, D1. Also consult News and Notes, at NPR.org, for Farai Chideya's interview of David Maraniss, who discusses his book *Rome, 1960: The Olympics That Changed the World.* July 3, 2008, available at https://www.npr.org/templates/story/story.php?storyId=92192195.

35. Streeter, "Remembering Rafer Johnson," and Johnson and Goldberg, *Best That I Can Be,* 150–155. See also Richard Goldstein, "Rafer Johnson, Winner of a Memorable Decathlon in 1960, Is Dead at 86," *New York Times,* December 4, 2020, B14.

36. Maraniss, *Rome 1960,_____.* See also Johnson and Goldberg, *Best That I Can Be,* 138.

37. Johnson and Goldberg, *Best That I Can Be,* 170–181.

38. Johnson and Goldberg, *Best That I Can Be.* Also see "Special Olympics Southern California Mourns the Passing of Rafer Johnson," December 2, 2020, https://wearesosc.org/2020/12/02/special-olympics-southern-california-mourns-the-passing-of-founder-rafer-johnson/.

39. Johnson and Goldberg, *Best That I Can Be,* 199–201.

40. Johnson and Goldberg, *Best That I Can Be,* 240–251.

41. Johnson and Goldberg, *Best That I Can Be,* 12–16, 53–54, 73, 257.

42. Johnson and Goldberg, *Best That I Can Be,* 262.

Chapter 3

1. Nathan Aaseng, *African American Athletes* (New York: Infobase Publishing Facts on File, 2011), 205; Frank Litsky, "Wilma Rudolph, Star of the 1960 Olympics, Dies at 54," *New York Times*, November 13, 1994, 53.

2. Litsky, "Wilma Rudolph."

3. "Wilma Rudolph," Biography.com, January 19, 2018, https://www.biography.com/athlete/wilma-rudolph.

4. Arlisha R. Norwood, "Wilma Rudolph," National Women's History Museum, accessed May 20, 2022, https://www.womenshistory.org/education-resources/biographies/wilma-rudolph.

5. From Rudolph's autobiography, *Wilma*, as quoted by Litsky, "Wilma Rudolph."

6. Litsky, "Wilma Rudolph."

7. Lansbury, *A Spectacular Leap*, 137–145; Johnson and Goldberg, *Best That I Can Be*, 149; and Maraniss, *Rome 1960*, 420.

8. Maraniss, *Rome 1960*, 421.

9. Maraniss, 421.

10. Maraniss, 421.

11. Martin Gitlin, *Powerful Moments in Sports: The Most Significant Sporting Events in American History* (New York: Rowman & Littlefield, 2017), 109.

12. John Carlos and Dave Zirin, *The John Carlos Story: The Sports Moment That Changed the World* (Chicago: Haymarket Books, 2011), xiii–xv.

13. Gitlin, *Powerful Moments*, 113.

14. Erin Blakemore, "How the Black Power Movement…" October 19, 2018, www.history.com.

15. Gitlin, *Powerful Moments*, 109–111.

16. Gitlin, 111–112.

17. Kenny Moore "A Courageous Stand," *Sports Illustrated*, August 6, 1991, https://vault.si.com/vault/1991/08/05/the-1968-olympics-a-courageous-stand-first-of-a-two-part-series-in-68-olympians-tommie-smith-and-john-carlos-raised-their-fists-for-racial-justice.

18. Carlos and Zirin, *John Carlos Story*, 81.

19. Carlos and Zirin, 82.

20. Carlos and Zirin, 82.

21. Gitlin, *Powerful Moments*, 113.

22. Carlos and Zirin, *John Carlos Story*, 114.

23. Gitlin, *Powerful Moments*, 114.

24. Carlos and Zirin, *John Carlos Story*, 113–114.

25. Carlos and Zirin, 84–85.

26. Carlos and Zirin, 86.

27. Carlos and Zirin, 89, 92.

28. Carlos and Zirin, 130.

29. Carlos and Zirin, vviii.

30. Carlos and Zirin, 130.

31. Carlos and Zirin, 139–142.

32. Roxanne Jones and Jessie Paolucci, *Say It Loud: An Illustrated History of the Black Athlete* (New York: Ballantine, 2010), 220.

33. Belson, "Tommie Smith's Fist Is Still Raised: 'We Still Need to Fight,'" *New York Times*, June 14, 2020, Sp 23.

34. "Florence Joyner," January 30, 2020, updated from April 18, 2014, https://www.biography.com/athlete/florence-joyner.

35. Avery Yang, "Black History Month: Florence Griffith Joyner Smashed Records and Stereotypes," *Sports Illustrated*, Feb.1, 2020, https://www.si.com/olympics/2020/02/01/black-history-month-florence-griffith-joyner.

36. "Jackie Joyner-Kersee," Biography.com, updated May 5, 2021, https://www.biography.com/athlete/jackie-joyner-kersee.

37. "Jackie Joyner-Kersee."

38. "Jackie Joyner-Kersee."

39. Jere Longman, "Goodwill Games; A Queen Retires the Way She Ruled: With Class," *New York Times*, July 21, 1998, C5.

40. "Carl Lewis," Biography.com, updated April 14, 2021, https://www.biography.com/athlete/carl-lewis.

41. "Carl Lewis."

42. "Carl Lewis."

Chapter 4

1. Alden T. Vaughan, *New England Frontier: Puritans and Indians, 1620–1676*, 3d ed. (Norman, OK: University of Oklahoma Press, 1995), 50.

2. Murray Rose, "Football and Baseball in America," in *Sports & Society: An Anthology*, ed. John T. Talamini and Charles H. Page (Boston: Little, Brown, 1973), 107.

3. Daniel P. Finney, "A Dirty Hit, A Broken Jaw and the Day Drake and Oklahoma A&M Changed College Football Forever," *Des Moines Register*, updated Dec. 16, 2019, https://www.desmoinesregister.com/in-depth/sports/history/2019/10/18/johnny-bright-incident-still-echoes-player-safety-issues-today/3942341002/.

4. James H. Grey and D. Stanley Eitzen, "Sport & Society," *Annual Review of Sociology* 16 (1991): 513–516. See also D. Stanley Eitzen & Norman R. Yetman, "Immune from Racism? Blacks Still suffer from Discrimination in Sports," *Civil Rights Digest* 9 (Winter 1977): 3–13.

5. See Derrick E. White, *Blood Sweat and Tears: Jack Gaither. Florida A&M and the History of Black College Football* (Chapel Hill: University of North Carolina Press, 2019).

6. A brief list, culled from "African-American Pioneers," Pro Football Hall of Fame, accessed May 22, 2022, https://www.profootballhof.com/news/2004/02/news-african-american-pioneers/. Also see Jordan James, "First Black Player in History of Major College Football Programs,"247 Sports, Feb. 13, 2009, https://www.247sports.com.

7. Michael Gray, *Hand Me My Walkin' Shoes: In Search of Blind Willie McTell* (Chicago: Chicago Press Review, 2009), 248–249.

8. "Gideon 'Charlie' Smith (1994)," Michigan State University Athletics, https://msuspartans.com/honors/hall-of-fame/gideon-charlie-smith/123; "Gideon Smith," Hampton Athletics Hall of Fame, https://hamptonpirates.com/

hof.aspx?hof=11&path=&kiosk=; and Charles K. Ross, *Outside the Lines: African Americans and the Integrations of the National Football League* (New York: New York University Press, 2000), 18.

9. Todd Peterson, *Early Black Baseball in Minnesota: The St. Paul Gophers, Minneapolis Keystones and Other Barnstorming Teams of the Deadball Era* (Jefferson, NC: McFarland, 2010), 43.

10. Todd Peterson, "Can You Hear the Noise?," *Baseball Research Journal* 36 (2007): 33–43.

11. Steven Wine, "Duke Slater, NFL's First Black Lineman, Is Now Hall of Famer," APNews.com, July 21, 2021, https://apnews.com/article/sports-nfl-europe-football-race-and-ethnicity-300e805a7c1e9915e4a19d7d41b6c572.

12. "Boston Honors John Shelburne '19," *Dartmouth Alumni Magazine,* January 1973, 47.

13. "Solomon Butler ('19)," University of Dubuque Athletics Hall of Fame, accessed February 22, 2022, https://www.dbq.edu/athletics/athleticshalloffame/solomonbutler/.

14. Paul Waggoner, "Sol Butler: Hutchison's Greatest Athlete," *Legacy: Journal of the Reno County Historical Society* 17 (Winter 2005), 7.

15. "Liberty-Snyders, Redwood Falls to Clash," *Minneapolis Star Tribune*, October 21, 1923, 39.

16. Neal Rozendaal, "African American Pioneers in Hawkeye History," Neal Rozendaal (personal website), accessed June 15, 2021, http://nealrozendaal.com/black-hawkeye-sports-pioneers/.

17. "Alston's Death Stuns Campus," *Daily Collegian* (Penn State University newspaper), Aug. 18, 1942, https://www.blackhistory.psu.edu/assets/timeline/African_American_Chronicles_Alston1.pdf.

18. Judith Ann Schiff, "Levi Jackson: Hometown Hero," *Yale Alumni Magazine* 63, no. 1 (Oct. 1999), http://archives.yalealumnimagazine.com/issues/99_10/old_yale.html. See also Richard Goldstein, "Levi Jackson, A Pioneer at Yale, Is Dead at 74, *New York Times*, Dec. 29, 2000, 10.

19. Goldstein, "Levi Jackson."

20. Goldstein, "Levi Jackson."

21. Amanda Prahl, "Biography of Mary Jackson, NASA's First Female Black Engineer," *Thought Co.*, updated June 3, 2019, https://www.thoughtco.com/mary-jackson-4687602.

22. Gary Webster, *The League That Didn't Exist: A History of the All-American Conference* (Jefferson, NC: McFarland, 2019), 1–2.

23. Paul Zimmerman, *The New Thinking Man's Guide to Pro Football* (New York: Simon & Schuster, 1984), 393–401.

24. Zimmerman, 393–401.

25. Frank Litsky, "Marion Motley, Bruising Back for the Stories Browns, Dies at 79," *New York Times*, June 28. 1999, B7.

26. Chris Murray, "On 100th Birthday, Legacy of Nevada's Marion Motley More Important than Ever," Nevada Sportsnet, June 5, 2020, https://nevadasportsnet.com/news/reporters/on-100th-birthday-legacy-of-nevadas-marion-motley-more-important-than-ever.

27. Richard Goldstein, "Bill Willis, 86, Racial Pioneer in Pro Football, Dies," *The New York Times*, Nov. 29, 2007, B7.

28. Goldstein, "Bill Willis."

29. "Salute 2021 Nominee: Emlen Tunnell, New York Giants," NFL, Oct. 27, 2021, https://www.nfl.com/news/salute-2021-nominee-emlen-tunnell-new-york-giants. See also Pat Eaton-Robb, "The Coast Guard Honors Black Veteran, NFL Great Emlen Tunnell," Feb. 6, 2021, https://www.navytimes.com/news/your-navy/2021/02/08/coast-guard-honors-black-veteran-nfl-great-emlen-tunnell/#:~:text=Before%20he%20became%20the%20first,two%20shipmates%20in%20separate%20incidents.

30. Robert Siegel, "Emlen Tunnell: A Largely Unknown NFL Great," *All Things Considered*, NPR, Dec. 30, 2011, https://www.npr.org/2011/12/30/144491425/emlen-tunnell-a-largely-unknown-nfl-great.

31. Robert W. Cohen, *The 50 Greatest Players in New York Giants Football History* (Lanham, MD: Rowman & Littlefield, 2014), 15–18.

32. Richard Sandomir, "The 'Greatest Game' in Collective Memory," *New York Times,* Dec. 4, 2008, B11; Don McGrath, "Books Tackle Landmark Game," *Chicago Tribune,* Dec. 13, 2008, https://www.chicagotribune.com/news/ct-xpm-2008-12-13-0812120227-story.html. See also Frank Gifford and Peter Richmond, *The Glory Game: How the 1958 NFL Championship Changed Football Forever* (New York: Harper Collins, 2009).

33. Associated Press, "Coast Guard Honors Black Veteran, Emlen Tunnell," *Independent*, https://www.independent.co.uk/news/coast-guard-honors-black-veteran-nfl-great-emlen-tunnell-black-grant-coast-guard-story-service-b1798594.html.

34. Matthew Thieme, "'Offense on Defense'": Football Legend Was a Coast Guard Hero," My CG, Feb. 5, 2021, *https://www.mycg.uscg.mil/News/Article/2495256/offense-on-defense-football-legend-was-a-coast-guard-hero/.*

35. Cohen, *50 Greatest Players*, 13–17.

36. Cohen, 19.

37. Cohen., 19–20.

38. Cohen, 20; Frank Litsky, "Roosevelt Brown, 71, Dies; Hall of Fame Giants Tackle," *New York Times,* June 11, 2004, B10.

39. As quoted in Richard Whittingham, *We Are the Giants! The Oral History of the New York Giants* (Chicago, IL: Triumph, 2014), 99.

40. Cohen, *50 Greatest Players*, 21.

41. Cohen, 22.

42. Wayne Stewart, *Remembering the Stars of the NFL Glory Years: An Inside Look at the Golden Age of Football* (Lanham, MD: Rowman and Littlefield, 2017), 108–109.

43. Stewart, 108–109.

44. "Dick Lane Biography," *Encyclopedia of World Biography*, accessed May 23, 2022, https://www.notablebiographies.com/supp/Supplement-Ka-M/Lane-Dick.html.

45. Associated Press, "Wally Triplett, N.F.L. Trailblazer, Is Dead at 92," *New York Times,* Nov.

9, 2018, https://www.nytimes.com/2018/11/09/obituaries/wally-triplett-dead.html#:~:text=Wally%20Triplett%2C%20one%20of%20the,not%20say%20where%20he%20died. See also Terrence F. Ross, "The Fire That Drove Wally Triplett, the First Drafted Black Player in the NFL," Guardian, Mar. 10, 2021, https://www.theguardian.com/sport/2021/mar/10/wally-triplett-detroit-lions-first-black-drafted-player-nfl-football-penn-state.

46. Paul Guggenheimer, "Story of Wally Triplett, 1st Black Football Player to Start for Penn State, To Be Made into Movie," Trib Live, Mar. 20, 2021, https://triblive.com/sports/story-of-wally-triplett-penn-states-first-black-football-player-to-be-made-into-movie/.

47. Ross, *"Fire That Drove Wally Triplett."*

48. Ross, *"Fire That Drove Wally Triplett."*

49. Darryl P. Daisy, "Wally Triplett, *African American Chronicles; Black History at Penn State* from blackhistory.psu.edu. See also "Former Nittany Lion Standout, First African American NFL Player Passes," Penn State website, June 20, 2021, https://www.psu.edu/news/athletics/story/former-nittany-lion-standout-first-african-american-nfl-player-triplett-passes/, and Scott DeCamp, "This is Wally Triplett: A Lions Legend Hidden in Plain Sight," MLive, https://www.mlive.com/lions/page/this_is_wally_triplett_a_lions_2.html.

50. "Wally Triplett, N.F.L. Trailblazer."

51. William C. Rhoden, "Wallace Triplett Is an NFL Legend: Honoring the First African American to Play Pro Ball," Andscape, November 11, 2018, https://andscape.com/features/wallace-triplett-is-an-nfl-legend-honoring-the-first-african-american-to-play-pro-ball/.

52. Charles K. Ross, *Outside the Lines: African Americans and the Integration of the National Football League* (New York: New York University Press, 1999), 62–63; Valerie J. Nelson, "Pasadena Civic Leader Was Teammate of Jackie Robinson, *Los Angeles Times,* June 28, 2008, https://www.latimes.com/archives/la-xpm-2008-jun-28-me-bartlett28-story.html.

53. Rebecca Gibian, "Before Jackie Robinson There Was Kenny Washington," Inside Hook, Jan.3, 2018, https://www.insidehook.com.

54. Ross, *Outside the Lines*, 65–67.

55. Ross, 65–67.

56. Ross,65,83–84.

57. Charlayne Hunter, "Woody Strode? He Wasn't the Star but He Stole the Movie," *New York Times,* Sept. 19, 1971, B7; David Shipman, "Obituaries: Woody Strode," Independent, https://www.independebt.co.uk; and Associated Press, "Woody Strode, 80, Character Actor," *New York Times,* Jan.4, 1995, D18.

58. "Kenny Washington," Pro-Football-Reference, from https://www.pro-football-reference.com.

59. Ross, *Outside the Lines,* 112,139; Alexander Wolff, "The NFL's Jackie Robinson," *Sports Illustrated*, Oct. 12, 2009, https://vault.si.com/vault/2009/10/12/the-nfls-jackie-robinson.

60. Ken Belson, "Raiders Defensive End Becomes First Active Player to Announce He's Gay," *New York Times,* June 22, 2021, B9.

61. For an excellent discussion of this challenge, see Joram Warmund, "On the Eve of the Storm," in Dorinson and Warmund, eds., *Jackie Robinson*, 3–12.

62. Charles K. Ross, *Mavericks, Money and Men: The AFL, Black Players, and the Evolution of Modern Football* (Philadelphia: Temple University Press, 2016), 10–14.

63. Ross, 93–94.

64. As quoted in Ross. 95–98, 99. Much of the above substance was culled from Ross's excellent book.

Chapter 5

1. Stephen Fox, *Big Leagues: Professional Baseball, Football, and Basketball in National Memory.* New York: William Morrow, 1994, 317–319.

2. Jere Longman,. "A Stadium Says His Name: Jack Trice," *New York Times*, July 20, 2020, D1, D3.

3. Fox., *Big Leagues,* 319–320.

4. Carroll, *Fritz Pollard,* 9; Ross, *Outside the Lines*, 23–24.

5. Carroll, *Fritz Pollard,* 19, 21, 27

6. Carroll, 29.

7. Ross, *Outside the Lines*, 23–24.

8. Carroll, *Fritz Pollard,* 101–105.

9. Ross, *Outside the Lines*, 26–27.

10. Carroll, *Fritz Pollard,* 130–131.

11. Ross, *Outside the Lines*, 31–32.

12. Carroll, *Fritz Pollard,* 147.

13. Peterson, *Pigskin,* 176–177.

14. Carroll, *Fritz Pollard,* 236.

15. Carroll, 238–239.

16. Carroll, 96. 184, 196.

17. Carroll, 239.

18. Carroll, 240.

19. Paul Robeson, *Here I Stand* (Boston: Beacon, 1971; first published 1958), 22.

20. Lloyd Brown, *The Young Paul Robeson: "On My Journey Now"* (New York: Basic Books, 1997), 46.

21. Brown, *Young Paul Robeson,* 46–47.

22. Brown, *Young Paul Robeson,* 61–62; Robert Van Gelder, "Robeson Remembers," *New York Times,* June 16, 1944, 2, 7.

23. Martin B. Duberman, *Paul Robeson,* 1988, 21; L. Brown, 62.

24. Duberman, 21–22.

25. Duberman, 21–22.

26. Lenwood G. Davis, comp., *Paul Robeson Research Guide* (Westport, CT: Greenwood, 1982), #609, 309.

27. Robeson, *Paul Robeson Speaks,* ed. Philip S. Foner (New York: Brunner/Mazel, 1978), 45–53.

28. Robeson, 45–53.

29. "Fordham Crushed by Rutgers Power," *New York Times,* Oct. 28, 1917, 5.

30. Taylor, "Maroon Grid Warriors Smothered by Rutgers," *New York Tribune,* October 28, 1917, 1.

31. As quoted in Davis, *Robeson Research Guide*, #700, 309.

32. As quoted in Duberman, *Paul Robeson,* 23.

33. Duberman, 23.

34. "NYU Defeats Columbia; Rutgers Beats Newport Navy," *New York Sunday Tribune,* Nov. 25, 1917, sec. 2, p. 1.; as quoted in Davis, *Robeson Research Guide,* #702, 310.

35. Robeson, *Robeson Speaks,* 51–53; Davis, *Robeson Research Guide,* #102, 66–67.

36. Brown, *Young Paul Robeson,* 81–82.

37. Francis C. Harris, "Paul Robeson," in Jeffrey Stewart, ed., *Paul Robeson Artist & Citizen,* 1998, 41–44.

38. Davis, *Robeson Research Guide,* #711, 313.

39. Brown, *Young Paul Robeson,* 95–96.

40. Paul Robeson, "The Scarlet Letter," *Rutgers University Yearbook, 1919,* 167, as cited in Davis, *Robeson Research Guide,* #714, 314.

41. Lester Rodney, "Robeson, the Athlete: A Remembrance," a recollection from the *Daily Worker,* May 8, 1953, in Dorinson and Pencak, eds., *Paul Robeson ...* Jefferson, NC: McFarland, 2004, 78.

42. Harris, "Paul Robeson," 44–45.

43. Albert Britt, "The Dusky Rover," *Outing* (Jan. 1918), as cited in Davis, *Robeson Research Guide* #711, 313.

44. Murray Kempton, *Part of Our Time: Some Ruins and Monuments of the Thirties* (New York: Simon and Schuster, 1955), 233–260.

45. Kempton, *Part of Our Time,* 238.

46. Paul Robeson, "Here's My Story," *Freedom* 1, no. 7 (Nov. 1951), as cited in Davis, *Robeson Research Guide,* #197, 67.

47. Lamont Yeakey, "A Student Without Peer: The Undergraduate College Years of Paul Robeson," *Journal of Negro History* 42, no. 4 (Fall 1973): 489–503.

48. Lamont Yeakey, "The Early Years of Paul Robeson," master's thesis, Columbia University, 1971.

49. Yeakey, "Early Years of Paul Robeson," 28, 49.

50. Yeakey, "Early Years of Paul Robeson," 53.

51. Yeakey, "Early Years of Paul Robeson," 39–40.

52. Yeakey, "Early Years of Paul Robeson," 56–57.

53. Duberman, *Paul Robeson,* 760, n8; 763, n21.

54. Harris, "Paul Robeson," 45–47.

55. Jeffrey C. Stewart, "The Black Body: Paul Robeson As a Work of Art and Politics," in J. Stewart, ed. *Robeson, Artist and Citizen,* 135–155.

56. Jackie Robinson as told to Alfred Duckett, *I Never Had It Made: An Autobiography of Jackie Robinson.* New York: Putnam, 1972, 82–86. See also Paul Drier, "We are Long Overdue for a Paul Robeson Revival," May 8, 2014, *Los Angeles Review of Books,* https://lareviewofbooks.org/article/long-overdue-paul-robeson-revival-talented-person-20th-century/.

57. Drier, "Paul Robeson Revival."

58. Peter Applebone, "From the Valley of Obscurity, Robeson's Baritone Rings Out; 22 Years After His Death, Actor-Activist Gets a Grammy." *New York Times,* Feb. 25, 1998, E1.

Chapter 6

1. Transitional pro football players following World War II are discussed in several sources: Andy Piascik, *Gridiron Gauntlet: The Story of the Men Who Integrated Pro Football in Their Own Words* (Lanham, MD: Taylor Trade, 2009), 69–76; Peterson, *Pigskin,* 185–200; Dave Zirin, *People's History,* 108–110.

2. Dave Zirin, *Jim Brown: The Last Man Standing,* 2018, 259. For other biographical information, consult Brad Herzog, *The Sports 100: The One Hundred Most Important People in American Sports History* (New York: Macmillan, 1995), 232–233; Mike Freeman, *Jim Brown: The Fierce Life of an American Hero* (New York: HarperCollins, 2009), 16–17.

3. J. Thomas Jable, "Jim Brown: Superlative Athlete, Screen Star, Social Activist," in Wiggins, ed., *Out of the Shadows,* 243.

4. Freeman, *Jim Brown,* 1–2.

5. Freeman, *Jim Brown,* 1–2, 12–14.

6. Freeman, *Jim Brown,* 4–5.

7. Freeman, *Jim Brown,* 39–40.

8. Charles Heaton, "Browns Win with Collins, Brown Out," *Cleveland Plain Dealer,* December 20, 1965; republished Dec. 19, 2011, Cleveland.com, https://www.cleveland.com/datacentral/2011/12/cleveland_browns_defeat_st_lou.html. See also Freeman, *Jim Brown,* 39–40.

9. Freeman, *Jim Brown,* 5–8, 8–10.

10. Jable, "Jim Brown," in Wiggins, *Out of the Shadows,* 248.

11. Jable, 248–249.

12. Freeman, *Jim Brown,* 14–16.

13. Freeman, 18–20.

14. Freeman, 20–21.

15. Freeman, 22–23.

16. Freeman, 263 266.

17. Jim Brown, "Football Has Forgotten the Men Who Made It Great," *New York Times,* Dec. 7, 2019, SR 10.

18. As cited in Zirin, *Jim Brown,* 257.

19. Zirin, 259.

20. Jeff Adler, "Serving Time on His Own Terms," *Washington Post,* April 13, 2000, https://www.washingtonpost.com/archive/politics/|2002/04/13/serving-time-on-his-own-terms/f617519e-8d47-478c-a27f-4723db27f9d0/; Freeman, *Jim Brown,* 18.

21. Freeman, *Jim Brown,* 18.

22. Zirin, *Jim Brown,* 294–295.

23. Chase Stuart, "The 101-Year History of Black Quarterbacks in the NFL," *Football Perspective* (blog), June 23, 2012, https://www.footballperspective.com/the-101-year-history-of-black-quarterbacks-in-the-nfl/. See also Jerry Rice and Randy O. Williams, *America's Game: The NFL at 100* (New York: HarperCollins, 2019), 103–106 .

24. Rice and Williams, *America's Game*, 103–106.

25. Terry Bledsoe, "Black Dominance in Sports: Strictly from Hunger," in D. Stanley Eitzen, ed., *Sport in Contemporary Society* (New York: St, Martin's Press, 1979), 362.

26. Stuart, "101-Year History."

27. John Feinstein, *Quarterback: Inside the Most Important Position in the National Football League* (New York: Doubleday, 2018), 25–26.

28. Rice and Williams, *America's Game: The NFL at 100*, 2019, 104.

29. Samuel G. Freedman, "Football's Quiet Farewell to James Harris," *New Yorker*, March 13, 2015, https://www.newyorker.com/sports/sporting-scene/footballs-quiet-farewell-to-james-harris.

30. Feinstein, *Quarterback*, 24–25.

31. Feinstein, 24–25.

32. Feinstein, 25–26.

33. John Feinstein, "Doug Williams," *Washington Post,* Oct. 1, 1980, https://www.washingtonpost.com/archive/sports/1980/10/01/doug-williams/5972e48b-7d12-4082-b231-2e2395b9c4a6/.

34. Sam Smith, "Survival's Reward, Doug Williams Endures Disaster and Gets a Big Opportunity," *Chicago Tribune* reprinted in *South Florida Sun Sentinal*, Jan. 6, 1988, 33.

35. "Doug Williams Leads Redskins to Super Bowl Victory," History.com, Jan.31, 1988, https://www.history.com/this-day-in-history/doug-williams-leads-redskins-to-super-bowl-victory.

36. Liz Clarke, "Doug Williams's Super Bowl Win 30 Years Ago Changed the Game for Black Quarterbacks," *Washington Post*, Jan. 30, 2018, https://www.washingtonpost.com/sports/doug-williamss-super-bowl-win-30-years-ago-changed-the-game-for-black-quarterbacks/2018/01/30/6a5f2d06-05f0-11e8-b48c-b07fea957bd5_story.html.

37. Stuart, "101-Year History."

38. Stuart.

39. Jason Reid, "The Rise of Black Quarterbacks," accessed May 30, 2022, https://andscape.com/features/the-rise-of-black-quarterbacks/.

40. Ken Belson, "Mahomes's Record Extension: $503 Million Over 10 Years," *New York Times*, July 7, 2020, B6.

41. Larry Fitzgerald, "Year of the Black Quarterback," *Minnesota Spokesman-Recorder*, Sept. 11, 2019, https://spokesman-recorder.com/2019/09/11/year-of-the-black-quarterback/.

42. Alex Didion, "Roger Goodell Apologizes to Colin Kaepernick, Wishes NFL Had Listened." Aug. 23, 2020, https://www.nbcsports.com/bayarea/49ers/goodell-apologizes-kap-wishes-nfl-had-listened-earlier.

43. "Limbaugh's Comments Touch off Controversy" ESPN.com, Oct. 1, 2003, https://www.espn.com/nfl/news/story?id=1627887.

44. "Colin Kaepernick," Pro-Football-Reference.com, accessed May 30, 2022, https://www.pro-football-reference.com/players/K/KaepCo00.htm.

45. "Colin Kaepernick (1987–)," Biography, updated January 26, 2021, https://www.biography.com/athlete/colin-kaepernick.

46. "Colin Kaepernick (1987–)."

47. Victor Mather, "The Anthem Uproar Goes into Overtime," *New York Times*, Feb. 16, 2019, B8.

48. Victor Mather and Ken Belson, "Dolphins Policy and Union Talks Rekindle Anthem Protest Dispute," *New York Times*, July 21, 2018, D5.

49. Jeré Longman, "An Echo of 1968 Follows Kaepernick," *New York Times*, Sept. 7, 2018, B9.

50. Longman.

51. Ken Belson, "Years Later, More in the N.F.L. Are Joining Kaepernick's Calls for Justice." *New York Times*, June 6, 2020, D4.

52. John Lewis, "Together, You Can Redeem the Soul of Our Nation," *New York Times*, July 30, 2020, A23.

53. Jeré Longman, "Athletes and the Anthem: How Trump Lost Sports as a Political Strategy," *New York Times*, Nov. 12, 2020, B9.

Chapter 7

1. Murray Ross, "Football and Baseball in America," in Talamini and Page, *Sport and Society*, 100, 102–106.

2. Geoffrey C. Ward and Ken Burns, *Baseball: An Illustrated History* (New York: Alfred A. Knopf, 1994), 314.

3. D. Stanley Eitzen and George H. Sage, *Sociology of North American Sport*, 3d ed. (Dubuque, IA: Wm. C. Brown, 1986), Table 11.3, 273.

4. James Diamond, "Baseball's Dearth of Black Catchers Helps Explain Its Dearth of Black Managers," *Wall Street Journal, Nov.* 12, 2020, https://www.wsj.com/articles/baseballs-dearth-of-black-catchers-helps-explain-its-dearth-of-black-managers-11605193200.

5. Diamond.

6. Jack Harris, "MLB to Give Negro Leagues 'Long Overdue Recognition' as a Major League," *Los Angeles Times*, Dec. 16, 2020, https://www.latimes.com/sports/story/2020-12-16/mlb-negro-leagues-major-league-status.

7. I refer to Jon Entine's *Taboo* and John Hoberman's *Darwin's Athletes*, cited earlier.

8. Most of the biographical data comes from Robert Peterson, *Only the Ball Was White*, especially chapters 3–5.

9. John Holway, *Blackball Stars: Negro League Pioneers* (Westport, CT: Meckler, 1988). 1–7.

10. Sol White, *Sol White's History of Colored Baseball, with Other Documents on the Early Black Game, 1886–1936* (Lincoln: University of Nebraska Press, 1995). See also Peterson, *Only the Ball,* 26–39.

11. Bruce Chadwick, *When the Game Was Black and White: The Illustrated History of Baseball's Negro Leagues* (New York: Abbeville Press, 1992), 28–29.

12. Peterson, *Only the Ball,* 72.

13. Chadwick, *When the Game,* 34.

14. G. Edward White, *Creating a National Pastime: Baseball Transforms Itself, 1903–1953.* Princeton, NJ: Princeton University Press, 1996), 128.

15. White, 129–130.

16. White, 131–132. See also Michael Lomax's important study that calls attention to the entrepreneurial and community-building contributions of Negro League baseball in his dissertation, "Black Baseball, Black Entrepreneurship, Black Community," (PhD. Dissertation, Ohio State University, 1996), ii–iii, 3–40.

17. Fox, *Big Leagues: Professional Baseball, Football, and Basketball in National Memory* (New York: William Morrow, 1994), 307–308.

18. Gardner and Shortelle, *The Forgotten Players: The Story of Black Baseball in America* (New York: Walker, 1993), 23–23; White, *Creating a National Pastime,* 131.

19. White, *Creating a National Pastime,* 132; Lomax, "Black Baseball," 362, 370–380.

20. Peterson, *Only the Ball,* 109–110.

21. Gardner and Shortelle, *Forgotten Players,* 27.

22. White, *Creating a National Pastime,* 133.

23. Holway, *Blackball Stars,* 24.

24. Fox, *Big Leagues,* 312–314.

25. Fox, 313.

26. White, *Creating a National Pastime,* 137.

27. White, 137–138.

28. White, 137–138.

29. White, 139.

30. White, 141–142.

31. White, 143.

32. Janet Bruce, *The Kansas City Monarchs: Champions of Black Baseball* (Lawrence: University Press of Kansas, 1985), 72–76.

33. John B. Holway, *Voices from the Great Black Baseball Leagues* (New York: Da Capo, 1993), *passim.*

34. Gardner & Shortelle, *Forgotten Players,* 38–40.

35. Donn Rogosin, *Invisible Men: Life in Baseball's Negro Leagues* (Lincoln: University of Nebraska Press, 2020), 76–77.

36. Campanella, *Good to Be Alive* (Boston: Little, Brown, 1959), 84.

37. Ralph Berger, "Buck Leonard," SABR Biography Project, accessed May 30, 2022, https://sabr.org/bioproj/person/buck-leonard/.

38. Fox, *Big Leagues,* 333.

39. Fox, 333–334.

40. White, *Creating a National Pastime,* 134.

41. White, 135–136.

42. Ribowski, *A Complete History of the Negro Leagues* (Secaucus, NJ: Citadel, 1995), 315–316.

43. Chadwick, *When the Game,* 94–96.

44. Chadwick., 94–95.

45. Peterson, *Only the Ball Was White,* 129.

46. Peterson, 129. See also Riley, *Biographical Encyclopedia,* 598–600; Dick Clark & Larry Lester, eds., *The Negro Leagues Book* (Cleveland: Sosciety for American Baseball Research, 1994), 328.

47. Benjamin Rader, *Baseball: A History of America's Game* (Urbana: University of Illinois Press, 1992), 147.

48. Peterson, *Only the Ball,* 140.

49. Rader, *Baseball,* 148.

50. Peterson, *Only the Ball,* 130.

51. Introduction to John B. Holway, *Blackball Stars,* ix.

52. Holway., ix.

53. Rob Ruck, *Sandlot Seasons: Sport in Black Pittsburgh* (Pittsburgh: University of Pittsburgh Press, 1993), ix–xviii, 3–7.

54. Leslie Heaphy, "Black Women in Baseball," *Sport in American History* (blog), March 21, 2016, https://ussporthistory.com/2016/03/21/black-women-in-baseball/. See also Michelle Y. Green, *A Strong Right Arm: The Story of Mamie "Peanut" Johnson* (New York: Puffin, 2004), and Jason Lewis, "Black Women Have a Long History in Professional Baseball," *Our Weekly,* Mar. 10, 2016, https://ourweekly.com/news/2016/03/10/black-women-have-long-history-professional-basebal/.

55. Both quotes are cited in Lipsyte and Levine, *Idols of the Game,* 162–164.

56. Lipsyte and Levine, 165.

57. James A. Michener, *Sports in America* (New York: Random House, 1976), 24–25.

58. Lipsyte & Levine, *Idols of the Game,* 170.

59. Lipsyte & Levine, 170–172.

60. John "Buck" O Neil with Steve Wulf & David Conrads, *I Was Right on Time: My Journey from the Negro Leagues to the Majors* (New York: Simon & Schuster, 1996), 2–3.

61. Rogosin, *Invisible Men,* 34–36.

Chapter 8

1. Jules Tygiel borrowed this observation from fellow sports historian Steven Riess and repeated it at LIU Brooklyn's Jackie Robinson Conference on April 5, 1997. See his afterword in *Baseball's Great Experiment,* 345.

2. Spender's poem appears in Oscar Williams, ed., *Immortal Poems of the English Language* (New York: Washington Square, 1969), 589–590.

3. Maury Allen, "Pepper Street, Pasadena," in Tygiel, ed., *Jackie Robinson Reader,* 15–24; Woody Strode & Sam Young, "Goal Dust Gang," in *Robinson Reader,* 25–37.

4. Robinson's early years are traced in several sources, Among the best are found in biographies by Maury Allen and Arnold Rampersad. Julies Tygiel's essay collection *The Jackie Robinson Reader: Perspectives on an American Hero* (New York: Dutton, 1997) offers multiple views of this transformative hero; the introduction and chapters by Maury Allen, Woody Strode, Red Barber, and Tygiel, the editor, in particular, are noteworthy. Rachel Robinson's compelling *Jackie Robinson: An Intimate Portrait* (New York: Harry N. Abrams, 1996), provides wonderful photographs and personal recollections, 14–41.

5. Jules Tygiel, "The Court-Martial of Jackie Robinson," in *Robinson Reader,* 39–51; Arnold

Rampersad, *Jackie Robinson: A Biography,* 1997, 102–112. See also Jackie's recollection his autobiography, *I Never Had It Made,* updated in 1995, 18–23.

6. Rampersad, *Jackie Robinson,* 116–117. R. Robinson, *Intimate Portrait,* 33–35.

7. Glen Stout and Dick Johnson, *Jackie Robinson: Between the Baselines* (Emeryville, CA: Woodford Press, 1997), 35–36.

8. Stout and Johnson, 36–40; Rampersad, *Jackie Robinson,* 119–120.

9. Stout and Johnson, *Jackie Robinson,* 41–42.

10. O'Neil with Wulf and Conrads, *Right on Time,* 163–164; Jonathan Eig, *Opening Day: The Story of Jackie Robinson's First Season* (New York: Simon & Schuster, 2007), 17.

11. Stout and Johnson, *Jackie Robinson,* 42–43.

12. Rampersad, *Jackie Robinson,* 118–119; Peterson, *Only the Ball,* 186.

13. Jack Jedwab, *Jackie Robinson's Unforgettable Season in Montreal* (Montr996, 7–11.

14. Jedwab., 23–26; Rampersad, *Jackie Robinson,* 146–147.

15. Wendell Smith, "It Was a Great Day in Jersey," in Tygiel, *Robinson Reader,* 96–100; Rampersad, *Jackie Robinson,* 149–150.

16. Jedwad, *Robinson's Unforgettable Season,* 30; Rampersad, *Jackie Robinson,* 153: Tygiel, *Great Experiment,* 121.

17. Robinson, *I Never Had It Made,* 50.

18. Robinson, 31–39; Stout and Johnson, *Jackie Robinson,* 58: Tygiel, *Great Experiment,* 140.

19. Stout and Johnson, *Jackie Robinson,* 59; Rampersad, *Jackie Robinson,* 154–156.

20. Stout and Johnson, *Jackie Robinson,* 59–62; Rampersad, *Jackie Robinson,* 156–157.

21. Tygiel, *Great Experiment,* 143.

22. As quoted in Stout and Johnson, *Jackie Robinson,* 62. For the record, Sam Maltin was a Canadian Jewish socialist. See Rampersad, *Jackie Robinson,* 152.

23. Tygiel, *Great Experiment,* 200. Robinson's rookie year is comprehensively covered in Rampersad, *Jackie Robinson,* Chapter 8, and in Eig, *Opening Day.*

24. Joseph Dorinson, *Jackie Robinson: New York Times Newspaper in Education Curriculum Guide* (New York: New York Times, 1997), 1–3.

25. Rampersad, *Jackie Robinson,* 220–221.

26. Arnold Schechter, "The Diabetic Athlete: His Toughest Component Is His Own Metabolism," *Sports Illustrated,* Apr. 22, 1985, https://vault.si.com/vault/1985/04/22/the-diabetic-athlete-his-toughest-opponent-is-his-own-metabolism.

27. Robinson, *I Never Had It Made,* 82–87.

28. Robinson, 275.

29. Dixie Walker, a former teammate and initial adversary, made this stunning observation as quoted in Eig, *Opening Day,* 267.

30. These observations are culled from an op-ed essay that I wrote: "Jackie's a Hero Now—But He Wasn't Always," *New York Daily News,* March 28, 1997, 41.

31. Dorinson, "Jackie's a Hero."

32. Rampersad, *Jackie Robinson,* 185.

33. Dorinson "Jackie's a Hero"; Daniel Boorstin, "Hero to Celebrity: Human Pseudo Event," in Harold Lubin, ed., *Heroes and Anti-Heroes: A Reader in Depth* (San Francisco: Chandler, 1959), 325–340.

34. Roger Rosenblatt, "Keynote Address," in Dorinson and Warmund, *Jackie Robinson,* 245.

35. As quoted in Stout and Johnson, *Jackie Robinson,* 193. See also "Thousands Mourn Jackie Robinson," *Amsterdam News,* Nov. 4, 1972, reprinted in Tygiel, *Robinson Reader,* 278.

36. Brian Carroll, "It Couldn't Be Any Other Way: The Great Dilemma for the Black Press and Negro League Baseball," *Black Ball* 5, no. 1 (Spring 2012): 5–23. See also Lawrence. D. Hogan, *Shades of Glory: The Negro Leagues and the Story of African American Baseball* (Washington, DC: National Geographic, 2006), 342–345.

37. Spender, in Williams, *Immortal Poems,* 590.

Chapter 9

1. Irwin Silber, *Press Box Red: The Story of Lester Rodney, the Communist Who Helped Break the Color Line in American Sports* (Philadelphia: Temple University Press, 2003), 156–157.

2. Moffi and Kronstadt, *Crossing the Line: Black Major Leaguers, 1947–1959* (Jefferson, NC: McFarland, 1994), 27.

3. As cited in Jack B. Moore, "Monte Irvin: Up from Sharecropping," in Dorinson and Warmund, *Jackie Robinson,* 30–31.

4. "Big Man from Nicetown," *Time,* Aug. 8, 1955, 51.

5. Rick Swaine, "Roy Campanella," SABR Biography project, https://www.sabr.org/bioproj/person/roy-campanella; Golenbock, *Bums,* 198.

6. Tygiel, *Great Experiment,* 145–146.

7. Swaine, "Roy Campanella."

8. "Big Man from Nicetown," 54.

9. Swaine, "Roy Campanella."

10. Swaine.

11. Golenbock, *Bums,* 201.

12. Swaine, "Roy Campanella."

13. Golenbock, *Bums,* 448.

14. Kahn, *Boys of Summer,* 330–331.

15. Dave Anderson, "In Roy Campanella, the Heart of a Hero," *New York Times,* June 28, 1993, C8.

16. Swaine, "Roy Campanella."

17. Robert M. Thomas, Jr., "Roy Campanella, 71, Dies; Was Dodger Hall of Famer," *New York Times,* June 28, 1993, B8; Philip Quarles, "Roy Campanella," Annotations: The NEH Preservation Project, https://www.wnyc.org/story/roy-campanella/.

18. Quarles; Leroy Watson, Jr., "Forgotten Stories of Courage and Inspiration: Roy Campanella," https://bleacherreport.com/articles/166177-forgotten-stories-of-courage-and-inspiration-roy-campanella.

19. Richard Goldstein, "Don Newcombe," *New York Times,* Feb. 19, 2019, B10, B14.

20. Goldstein.

21. Nancy Scannell, "Newcombe's Biggest Victory Was Over the Bottle," *Washington Post*, May 22, 1977, https://www.washingtonpost.com/archive/sports/1977/05/22/newcombes-biggest-victory-was-over-the-bottle/b4b9934c-4e4a-4d58-96fe-8dd188da73ab/.

22. Riley, *Biographical Encyclopedia*, 583.

23. Tygiel, *Great Experiment*, 68.

24. Golenbock, *Bums,* 233–235.

25. Tygiel, *Great Experiment*, 166.

26. Gene Schoor, *The Complete Dodgers Record Book* (New York: Facts on File, 1984), 342.

27. Bob McGee, *The Greatest Ballpark Ever: Ebbets Field and the Story of the Brooklyn Dodgers* (New York: Rivergate, 2005), 219.

28. Ralph Branca, *A Moment in Time: An American Story of Baseball, Heartbreak and Grace* (New York: Scribner, 2011), 3, 205, 207.

29. Peter Williams, "The Interborough Iliad," in Dorinson and Warmund, *Jackie Robinson*, 56–57.

30. Branca, *A Moment in Time*, 150–152; McGee, *Greatest Ballpark Ever*, 223.

31. Schoor, *Dodgers Record Book,* 351–356.

32. Scannell, "Newcombe's Biggest Victory."

33. Russell Bergtold. "Don Newcombe," SABR Biography Project, https://sabr.org/bioproj/person/don-newcombe/.

34. Bertgold; Liz Roscher, "All-Time Great Dodgers Pitcher Don Newcombe Dies at 92," Feb. 19, 2019, https://www.yahoo.com/video/time-great-dodgers-pitcher-don-newcombe-dies-92-201751922.html; Richard Goldstein, "Don Newcombe," *New York Times*, Feb. 20, B10, B14.

35. Goldstein, B10.

36. Perry Dayn, "Don Newcombe, Former Dodger Great and Inaugural Cy Young Award Winner, Dead at 92," https://www.yahoo.com/video/time-great-dodgers-pitcher-don-newcombe-dies-92-201751922.htmlv.

37. Biographical information is from Monte Irvin and James A. Riley, *Nice Guys Finish Last: The Autobiography of Monte Irvin* (New York: Carroll & Graf, 1996); Larry Hogan, "Monte Irvin," SABR Biography Project, https://sabr.org/bioproj/person/monte-irvin/; Jack B. Moore, "Monte Irvin: Up from Sharecropping," in Dorinson and Warmund, *Jackie Robinson*, 30–40. Internet sites: http://www.nlbpa.com/irvin_monte.html; also consult James A. Riley, *The Biographical Encyclopedia of the Negro Baseball League* (New York: Carrol & Graf, 1994).

38. Moore, "Monte Irvin," 35.

39. Riley, *Biographical Encyclopedia,* 408.

40. Moore, "Monte Irvin," 36–37. Monte's daughter Pamela Irvin related the intercepted letter incident in a conversation with me at the Pop Lloyd Conference. See also Peter Golenbock, *In the Country of Brooklyn* (New York: HarperCollins, 2008), 149.

41. Moore, "Monte Irvin," 36–37. See also Riley, *Biographical Encyclopedia,* 408–409; Moffi and Kronstadt, *Crossing the Line,* 40; and James Overmyer, *Queen of the Negro Leagues: Effa Manley and the Newark Eagles* (Metuchen, NJ: Scarecrow, 1993), 240–243.

42. Moore, "Monte Irvin," 34–35.

43. Riley, *Biographical Encyclopedia*, 409.

44. Brad Snyder, *Well-Paid Slave*, 140.

45. Moore, "Monte Irvin," 39, makes this salient point.

46. John McMurray, "Larry Doby," SABR Biography Project, accessed June 6, 2022, https://sabr.org/bioproj/person/larry-doby/; Riley, 241–242, Joseph Thomas Moore, *Larry Doby: The Struggle of the American League's First Black Player* (Mineola, NY: Dover, 2011), 7–8.

47. Ira Berkow, "He Crossed the Color Barrier, but in Another's Shadow," *New York Times*, Feb. 23, 1997, 1.

48. Moore, *Larry Doby*, 19–25, 38; Overmyer, 236–237.

49. Moore, 49. In an interview with Fran Healey on the Baseball Hall of Fame telecast, Doby recalled his encounter with the Cleveland Indians.

50. Moore, 61, 67, 78.

51. Moffi and Kronstadt, *Crossing the Line*, 15–17; "Larry Doby Stats" in *Baseball Almanac*, baseball-almanac.com.

52. Riley, *Biographical Encyclopedia*, 241; McMurray, "Larry Doby."

53. Moore, *Larry Doby*, 114–115.

54. Moore, 170.

55. Moore, 171.

56. Moore, 172 .

57. Moore, 172–175; McMurray, "Larry Doby"; Ken Kurson, "Larry Doby: Courage and Life," *Montclair Times,* June 26, 2003, A12; Claire Smith, "Larry Doby Dies at 79," *New York Times*, June 19, 2003, B11.

Chapter 10

1. Jacobson, *Carrying Jackie's Torch*, xix–xx.

2. Peter Williams, "The Interborough Iliad," in Dorinson and Warmund, *Jackie Robinson*, 57.

3. Jacobson, *Carrying Jackie's Torch*, xii.

4. Jacobson, xv.

5. Aaseng, *African American Athletes*, 157–159. Additional biographical information can be found in John Saccoman, "Willie Mays," SABR Biography Project, accessed June 6, 2022, https://sabr.org/bioproj/person/willie-mays/; Riley, *Biographical Encyclopedia*, 523–524; Charles Einstein, *Willie's Time: A Memoir* (Carbondale: Southern Illinois University Press, 2004).

6. Bryant, *Legends*, 24–25.

7. Bryant, 27–28.

8. Tyler Kepner, "Willie Mays at 89: 'My Thing Is Keep Talking and Keep Moving.'" *New York Times*, May 12, 2020, B9.

9. Phil Pepe, "Mays' Hit Keys 10–7, 12-Inning Win," *Daily News*, Oct. 15, 1973, 74, 78 and 81.

10. John Shea, "Willie Mays '24" book: excerpt: The Story of the Absurdity of Racism," *San Francisco Chronicle* May 9, 2020, https://www.sfchronicle.com/giants/article/Willie-Mays-24-book-excerpt-The-Story-of-15259067.php.

11. Kepner, "Mays at 89."

12. "Willie Mays All-Star Stats, Baseball Almanac, https://www.baseball-almanac.com/players/playerpost.php?p=mayswi01&ps=asg.

13. Williams quoted in Bryant, *Legends*, 28.

14. Bill Rhoden, *40 Million Dollar Slaves*, 144, 147–150.

15. Rhoden, 149–151.

16. Robert Frost, "The Road Not Taken," accessible at Poetry Foundation, https://www.poetryfoundation.org/poems/44272/the-road-not-taken.

17. Kepner, "Mays at 89."

18. Peter Golenbock *Bums: An Oral History of the Brooklyn Dodgers* (New York: G.P. Putnam's Sons, 1984), 135–136.

19. Golenbock, 165

20. Sid Jacobson, *Carrying Jackie's Torch,* 39, 41, 42–43; Allen, *Jackie Robinson*, 42–43. See also Golenbock, *Bums*, 166.

21. Ed Hoyt, "Ed Charles," SABR Biography Project, https://sabr.org/bioproj/person/ed-charles/.

22. Jacobson, *Carrying Jackie's Torch,* 45–46. 47; Ed Hoyt, "Ed Charles."

23. Lori Martin, *White Sports/Black Sports: Racial Disparities in Athletic Programs* (Santa Barbara, CA: ABC-Clio, 2015), 74–75.

24. Hoyt, "Ed Charles."

25. Hoyt.

26. Hoyt.

27. Hoyt.

28. Hoyt.

29. As quoted in Jacobson, *Carrying Jackie's Torch,* 57.

30. Hoyt, "Ed Charles."

31. See Pete Williams's description that inspired this antic in "The Interborough Iliad," an article in Dorinson and Warmund, *Jackie Robinson*, 57.

32. As quoted by Bill Madden, "Ed Charles, Beloved Third Baseman and Poet Laureate of 1969 'Miracle Mets,' dies at 84," *New York Daily News,* May 15, 2018, https://www.nydailynews.com/sports/baseball/mets/ed-charles-member-1969-miracle-mets-dead-84-article-1.3877376. For the poem, see Andy Esposito, "Ed Charles:1933–2018," *NY Sports Day, https://www.nysportsday.com/2018/03/17/esposito-ed-charles-1933-2018/.*

33. Howard Bryant, *Last Hero: A Life of Henry Aaron* (New York: Anchor, 2011), 11, 16–17, 21–26.

34. Bill Johnson, "Henry Aaron."

35. Bryant, *Last Hero,* 29.

36. As quoted by Peter Levine, "A Ten-Year-Old Dodger Fan Welcomes Jackie Robinson to Brooklyn," in Dorinson and Warmund, *Jackie Robinson,* 63–64.

37. Levine, 64.

38. Bryant, *Last Hero,* 23.

39. Johnson, "Henry Aaron."

40. As cited in George Will, "Hank Aaron's Record May Fall but His Greatness Will Stand," *San Jose Mercury News,* May 6, 2007, https://www.mercurynews.com/2007/05/06/hank-aarons-record-may-fall-but-his-greatness-will-stand/.

41. Johnson, "Henry Aaron."

42. Johnson.

43. Bryant, *Last Hero*, 69.

44. Johnson, "Henry Aaron."

45. Johnson.

46. Bryant, *Last Hero*, 79–80, 119.

47. Gitlin, *Powerful Moments,* 188–189.

48. Gitlin, 192.

49. Gitlin, 193.

50. Gitlin, 193.

51. George Will, *Men at Work: The Craft of Baseball* (New York: Macmillan, 1990), as cited by Bill Johnson, "Henry Aaron," SABR Biography Project, updated Dec. 8, 2021, https://sabr.org/bioproj/person/hank-aaron/. See also "Vin Scully's Call on Hank Aaron's 715th Home Run, *Atlanta Journal-Constitution,* Jan. 22, 2021, https://www.ajc.com/sports/atlanta-braves/vin-scullys-call-on-hank-aarons-715th-home-run/KX565A7ACZGH5BEST5PBTWPAMY/.

52. Bryant, *Last Hero*, 396; Gitlin, *Powerful Moments,*198.

53. Bill Johnson, "Henry Aaron." See also Richard Goldstein, "With 755 Home Runs, Dealing Racism a Blow," *New York Times,* Jan. 23, 2021, 1, 24–25.

54. Maxwell Kates, "Frank Robinson," SABR Biography Project, https://sabr.org/bioproj/person/frank-robinson/.

55. Kates.

56. Kates.

57. Richard Justice, "Frank Robinson, Legend and Pioneer, Dies," MLB.com, Feb. 7, 2019, https://www.mlb.com/news/frank-robinson-dies-c303656538.

58. Justice.

59. Richard Goldstein, "Frank Robinson, Hall of Fame Slugger and First Black Manager, Dies at 83," *New York Times,* Feb. 7, 2019, A1.

60. Goldstein, "Frank Robinson."

61. Kates, "Frank Robinson."

62. Goldstein, "Frank Robinson."

63. Joseph Wancho, "Ernie Banks," SABR Biography Project, https://sabr.org/bioproj/person/ernie-banks/.

64. "Ernest (Ernie) Banks," in Riley, *Biographical Encyclopedia*, 54.

65. Golenbock, *Wrigleyville*, 1996, 349.

66. Richard Goldstein, "Ernie Banks, the Eternally Hopeful Mr. Cub, Dies at 83," *New York Times* Jan. 23, 2015

67. Golenbock, *Wrigleyville*, 399.

68. Goldstein, "Ernie Banks."

Chapter 11

1. Bill White with Gordon Dillow, *Uppity: My Untold Story About the Games People Play* (New York: Grand Central, 2011), 46–47.

2. Warren Corbett, "Bill White," SABR Biography Project, https://sabr.org/bioproj/person/bill-white-3/. Much of the biographical information can be found in White, *Uppity*, 2011.

3. White, *Uppity*, 7.

4. White, 4.

5. White, 29.

6. White, 36–37; Corbett, "Bill White."

7. White, *Uppity*, 45.

8. White, 51–55.

9. White, 59–60; Bill Ladson, "A Diverse Life in Baseball: White Has Done It All," MLB. com, Jan. 31, 2017, https://www.mlb.com/news/bill-white-thankful-for-his-life-in-baseball-c214862220.

10. Brad Snyder, *Well-Paid Slave*, 2006, 54–60; White, *Uppity*, 71–79.

11. White, *Uppity*, 84–87, 90–95.

12. White, 98–100.

13. White, 98–102.

14. White, 80–82, 106–114.

15. White, 125.

16. White, 146–147.

17. White, 149–156.

18. White, 181–184.

19. White, 195–200, 238–250.

20. White, 277–279.

21. Richard Sandomir, "Away from the Rat Race, but Writing Bluntly About It," *New York Times*, April 2, 2011, SP2.

22. Sandomir, "Away from the Rat Race."

23. Brad Snyder, *Well-Paid Slave*, 33; Alan Barra, "How Curt Flood Changed Baseball and Killed His Career in the Process," *Atlantic*, July 12, 2011, https://www.theatlantic.com/entertainment/archive/2011/07/how-curt-flood-changed-baseball-and-killed-his-career-in-the-process/241783/.

24. Snyder, *Well-Paid Slave*, 34.

25. Snyder, 34–37.

26. Snyder, 38.

27. Steve Jacobson, *Carrying Jackie's Torch*, 79–80.

28. Jacobson, 42–43.

29. Snyder, *Well-Paid Slave*, 56–57.

30. Snyder, 60–61.

31. Mark Tomasik, "Should Curt Flood Have Caught Jim Northrup's Drive?," *Retrosimba* (blog), June 12, 2011, https://retrosimba.com/2011/06/12/should-curt-flood-have-caught-jim-northrups-drive/. In that losing cause, Flood, who batted third in the starting line-up, got two hits and stole the only base. See also Aaseng, *African American Athletes*, 80.

32. Snyder, *Well-Paid Slave*, 69–71, 77. See also Lee Lowenfish, *The Imperfect Diamond: A History of Baseball's Labor Wars*, revised edition (New York: Da Capo, 1991), 207–217.

33. Snyder, *Well-Paid Slave*, 76–77.

34. Snyder, 94–95

35. Rhoden, *40 Million Dollar Slaves*, 231.

36. Snyder, *Well-Paid Slave*, 105.

37. Snyder, 121.

38. Snyder, 111–112; Lowenfish, *Imperfect Diamond*, 216.

39. Lowenfish, *Imperfect Diamond*, 255.

40. Rhoden, *40 Million Dollar Slaves*, 234–235: Lowenfish, *Imperfect Diamond*, 212.

41. Snyder, *Well-Paid Slave*, 285–296.

42. Lowenfish, *Imperfect Diamond*, 207–201; Snyder, *Well-Paid Slave*, 284, 296.

43. Snyder, *Well-Paid Slave*, 312.

44. As quoted in Snyder, 324–325.

45. Snyder, 309; Lowenfish, *Imperfect Diamond*, 216.

46. Snyder, *Well-Paid Slave*, 309.

47. Snyder, 333–334.

48. Snyder, 336.

49. Snyder, 344.

50. Snyder, 345.

51. Snyder, 346.

52. Snyder, 348–349. See also "Flood Eulogized as Man Who Changed Baseball," *St. Louis Post-Dispatch*, Jan. 28, 1997, 66.

53. Jenisha Watts, "Why Everyone Should Know and Remember Former Baseball Player Curt Flood," *Black Enterprise*, https://www.blackenterprise.com/why-everyone-should-know-remember-former-baseball-player-curt-flood/.

Chapter 12

1. Samuel O. Regalado cites Robert Peterson for this quote in Dorinson and Warmund, *Jackie Robinson*, 160.

2. According to Brad Snyder, *Beyond the Shadow of the Senators* (New York: McGraw-Hill, 2003), 220–232.

3. Peter C. Bjarkman, "Dark-Tempered and Great," *La Vida*, May 17, 2017, https://www.lavidabaseball.com/adolfo-luque-first-latino-superstar/.

4. Rogosin, *Invisible Men*, 158–160.

5. See Adrian Burgos, "El Profe: Jackie Robinson Day to Latinos," *La Vida*, April 16, 2018, https://www.lavidabaseball.com/jackie-robinson-day-latinoes/.

6. "Jose Mendez," National Baseball Hall of Fame, accessed June 9, 2022, https://baseballhall.org/hall-of-famers/mendez-jose.

7. Peter C. Bjarkman, "Jose Mendez," SABR Biography Project, accessed June 9, 2022, https://sabr.org/bioproj/person/jose-mendez/.

8. Ira Thomas, "How They Play Our National Game in Cuba," *Baseball Magazine* 10, no. 5 (1913), 61–65, as quoted in Roberto González Echevarría, *Pride of Havana*, 133–134.

9. Holway, *Blackball Stars*, 132.

10. Bill James, *The New Bill James Historical Abstract* (New York: Free Press, 2001), 365.

11. "Friendship First, Competition Second—An Amateur Sport Website," Amateur Sport, accessed June 9, 2022, https://www.amateursport.com.

12. Hogan, *Shades of Glory*, 164–165, 386–387, 404–405.

13. "Minnie Miñoso" History Makers, historymakers.org, and Joe Posnanski, "The Wonder of Minnie," NBC Sports.com, https://sportsworld.nbcsports.com/remembering-minnie-minoso/.

14. Dania Santana, "Afro-Latinos and Baseball's Color Line: 5 Pioneers in the Post-Segregation

Era,"#BlackHistoryMonth dania@embracingdi-versity.us blog.

15. "Minnie Miñoso," the player page at baseball-reference.com, lists .262, .277, and .403 for 1946–1948, whereas Mark Stewart, in "Minnie Miñoso," at the SABR Biography Project website, posits .260 in 1946 and .294 in 1947 and the Negro League Museum records .309 in 1946.

16. Stewart, "Minnie Miñoso."

17. Stewart, "Minnie Miñoso."

18. Joseph Wancho, "Vic Power," SABR Biography Project , https://sabr.org/bioproj/person/vic-power/.

19. Roger Kahan, *The Era, 1947–57* (New York: Ticknor and Fields, 1993), 45, as cited by Wancho, "Vic Power."

20. Richard Goldstein, "Vic Power, 78, Pioneer Latino and First Baseman with Flair," *New York Times*, Nov. 30, 2005, C19.

21. David Maraniss, *Clemente: The Passion and Grace of Baseball's Last Hero* (New York: Simon & Schuster 2006), 35, and David Maraniss, "Roberto Clemente Was No Gentle Saint," Andscape, May 31, 2016, https://andscape.com/features/roberto-clemente-was-a-fierce-critic-of-both-baseball-and-american-society/.

22. Maraniss, *Clemente,* 35.

23. Samuel Octavio Regalado, *Viva Baseball! Latin Major Leaguers and Their Special Hunger* (Urbana: University of Illinois Press, 1998), 161.

24. Wancho, "Vic Power."

25. Rich Marazzi and Les Fiorito, *Baseball Players of the 1950s* (Jefferson, NC: McFarland, 2004), 311–312.

26. Goldstein, "Vic Power, 78."

27. David Maraniss, *Clemente: The Passion and Grace of Baseball's Last Hero* (New York: Simon and Shuster, 2006), 24.

28. Maraniss, 24–25; review of David Maraniss's *Clemente: The Passion and Grace of Baseball's Last Hero,* WBUR (NPR Boston), June 1, 2006. See also David Maraniss, "No Gentle Saint."

29. Maraniss, *Clemente,* 24.

30. Regalado, *Viva Baseball!,* 70.

31. Maraniss, "The Last Hero Roberto Clemente, Baseball's Latino Legend," *Washington Post,* April 2, 2006 https://www.washingtonpost.com/archive/opinions/2006/04/02/the-last-hero-span-classbankheadroberto-clemente-baseballs-latino-legendspan/7c38584c-a70d-4ff1-9eea-1febd1c05402/.

32. George Will, "Fielder of Dreams," *New York Times,* May 7, 2006, sec. 7, p. 13.

33. Maraniss, "The Last Hero."

34. Maraniss.

35. Will, "Fielder of Dreams."

36. Maraniss, *Clemente,* 120–136.

37. Maraniss, 241–267, and Bryant, *Legends,* 157–158.

38. Maraniss, *Clemente,* 354.

39. Maraniss, 353.

Chapter 13

1. Tom Ferraro, "Tennis and Social Class in America," *New York Tennis Magazine* 8, no. 1 (Jan./Feb. 2018): 64–67.

2. Rhiannon Walker, "Black Tennis History," July 31, 2017, Undefeated (now Andscape.com), https://andscape.com/features/black-tennis-history-timeline/.

3. Walker.

4. Cindy Shmerler, "Overlooked No More: Jimmie McDaniel, Tennis Player Who Broke Barriers," Feb. 15, 2021, D6.

5. D'Arcy Maine, "For Serena Williams and Naomi Osaka, Nothing but Respect—and a Desire to Win," *ESPN,* Feb. 16, 2021, https://www.espn.com/tennis/story/_/id/30910888/for-serena-williams-naomi-osaka-respect-desire-win.

6. Mary Jo Festle, "'Jackie Robinson Without the Charm': The Challenges of Being Althea Gibson," in Wiggins, *Out of the Shadows,* 189.

7. Sally Jacobs, "She Achieved Many Firsts. She's Getting Her Due at Last," *New York Times,* Aug. 26, 2019, D1.

8. Katharine Q. Seelye, "Angela Buxton, Half of an Outcast Duo in Tennis History, Dies at 85," *New York Times,* Aug. 27, 2020, A24.

9. Festle, "Robinson Without the Charm," 199–200.

10. Quoted in Festle, 202.

11. As cited by Jacobs, "She Achieved Many Firsts," D1.

12. Jacobs, D4.

13. Seelye, "Angela Buxton."

14. As quoted in Jones and Paolucci, *Say It Loud,* 166.

15. Jones and Paolucci, 169.

16. Jones and Paolucci, 169.

17. Damon Thomas, 279.

18. See John McPhee, *Levels of the Game* (New York: Farrar, Straus and Giroux, 2011), 28–29.

19. Arthur Ashe, *Advantage Ashe* (New York: Coward-McCann, 1967), 90.

20. Thomas, 289–293.

21. As quoted by Laurel Graeber, "New & Noteworthy Paperbacks," *New York Times,* Jan.23, 1994, sec. 7, 24.

22. David K. Wiggins, "Symbols of Possibility: Arthur Ashe, Black Athletes and the Writing of a Hard Road to Glory," *Journal of African American History,* 99 (4), 379.

23. Thomas, 289–293.

24. Richard Williams with Bart Davis, *Black and White: The Way I See It* (New York: Atria, 2014), 5.

25. Wiggins, *Out of the Shadows,* 353.

26. L. Jon Wertheim, *Venus Envy: Power Games, Teenage Vixens, and Million Dollar Egos on the Women's Tennis Tour* (New York: Harper, 2002),13.

27. Elizabeth Weil, "Venus Williams, the Pioneer," *New York Times Magazine,* Aug. 25, 2019, 46.

28. Williams, *Black and White,* 212.

29. As cited in R. Pierre Rodgers and Ellen

Drogin Rodgers, "Ghetto Cinderellas," in Wiggins, *Out of the Shadows*, 355.

30. Rodgers and Rodgers, 363.

31. Louisa Thomas, "Serena Williams's Extraordinary Wimbledon and Ordinary Motherhood," *New Yorker*, July 12, 2018, https://www.newyorker.com/sports/sporting-scene/serena-williams-extraordinary-wimbledon-and-ordinary-motherhood.

32. Elizabeth Weil, "Venus Williams," 65.

33. Karen Crouse, 'To Push Forward, Williams Hits Rewind," *New York Times*, Feb. 15, 2021, D1, D5.

34. Gerald Mazorati, "How to Watch Serena Williams at the U.S. Open Where She Has Nothing Left to Prove," *New Yorker,* Aug. 30, 2020, https://www.newyorker.com/sports/sporting-scene/the-best-way-to-watch-serena-williams-at-the-us-open-where-she-has-nothing-left-to-prove/amp.

35. Mikael McKenzie, "Jennifer Brady Insists Naomi Osaka Not 'God' Like Serena Williams After Final Defeat," *Express,* Feb. 20, 2021, https://www.express.co.uk/sport/tennis/1400379/Jennifer-Brady-Naomi-Osaka-Serena-Williams-Australian-Open-final.

36. "'Before I'm an Athlete, I'm a Black Woman': Naomi Osaka Quits US Tournament in Protest Over Jacob Blake Shooting," *RT, https://www.rt.com/sport/499158-osaka-tennis-boycott-jacob-blake/.*

37. Brook Larmer, "Naomi Osaka's Breakthrough Game," *New York Times,* Aug. 23, 2018, MM24.

38. Katherine J. Igoe, "Naomi Osaka's Parents, Leonard Francois and Tamaki Osaka, Are Her Biggest Fans," *Marie Claire,* Sep. 10, 2020, https://www.marieclaire.com/celebrity/a33979330/naomi-osaka-parents/.

39. D'arcy Main, "For Serena Williams and Naomi Osaka, Nothing but Respect ... and a Desire to Win," *ESPN,* Feb. 16, 2021, https://www.espn.com/tennis/story/_/id/30910888/for-serena-williams-naomi-osaka-respect-desire-win.

40. Main.

41. Karen Crouse, "Naomi Osaka Beats Jennifer Brady at Australian Open for Her 4th Grand Slam Title," *New York Times,* Feb. 21, 2021, A35.

Chapter 14

1. Bill Bradley, *Values of the Game* (New York: Artisan Workman, 1998), 17.

2. "Dolly King: L.I.U. Star Athlete and a Collegiate Coach, Dies at 51," *New York Times,* Jan. 30, 1969, 35.

3. Stephen Fox, *Big Leagues: Professional Baseball, Football, and Basketball in National Memory* (New York: William Morrow, 1994), 324–326; Susan Rayl, "The New York Renaissance Professional Black Basketball Team, 1923–1950," unpublished Ph.D. dissertation, Penn State University, 1996, 18–19.

4. Robert W. Peterson, *Cages to Jump Shots: Pro*

Basketball's Early Years (New York: Oxford University Press, 1990), 43–45.

5. Susan Rayl, "The Real Renaissance Men," unpublished paper presented at the St. Francis College Conference on the History and Cultural Significance of Basketball, Nov. 3, 2001, 1. Rayl cites several sources, including Howie Evans, "Blacks Who Made History in the Basketball World," *New York Amsterdam News*, Feb. 17, 1973, D-28, and an unsigned article in the *New York Age,* Nov. 4, 1922, 6.

6. Rayl, "Real Renaissance Men," 2, and "Professional Black Basketball Team" (Ph. D. Dissertation), 33–44.

7. Rayl, "Professional Black Basketball Team," 57; Peterson, *Cages to Jump Shots,* 97; and Nelson George, *Elevating the Game: Black Men and Basketball* (New York: HarperCollins, 1992), 35.

8. *Ibid.,* 63.

9. Rayl, "Real Renaissance Men," 2.

10. Rayl, "Professional Black Basketball Team," 28–30.

11. Rayl, "Real Renaissance Men," 3; Peterson, *Cages to Jump Shots,* 98.

12. Rayl, "Real Renaissance Men," 3–4, citing *Pittsburgh Courier,* Feb. 11, 1928, sec. 2, 4.

13. Rayl, "Real Renaissance Men," 4–5.

14. George, *Elevating the Game,* 38; Peterson, *Cages to Jump Shots,* 98.

15. Rayl, "Professional Black Basketball Team," 56; Rayl, "Real Renaissance Men," 6.

16. Rayl, "Real Renaissance Men," 6–7.

17. Vincent M. Mallozzi, "John Isaacs, Star for the Rens Basketball Team, Dies at 93." *New York Times,* Feb. 2, 2009, https://www.nytimes.com/2009/02/03/sports/basketball/03isaacs.html?searchResultPosition=1; George, *Elevating the Game,* 39.

18. Mallozzi, "John Isaacs"; George, *Elevating the Game,* 39–40.

19. George, *Elevating the Game,* 7–8; Fox, *Big Leagues,* 331–332; Peterson, *Cages to Jump Shots,* 99–100.

20. Peterson, *Cages to Jump Shots,* 100; Rayl, "Real Renaissance Men," 9; Fox, *Big Leagues,* 329–332.

21. Rayl, "Real Renaissance Men," 10–12.

22. Gus Alfieri, *Lapchick: The Life of Legendary Player and Coach in the Glory Days of Basketball* (Guilford, CT: Lyons Press, 2006), 154; Zelda Spoelstra, an NBA Alumni executive, shared this view in her presentation of the early NBA Black players' role designated for defense, setting picks, and grabbing rebounds at our St. Francis College Basketball Conference, Nov. 3, 2001.

23. Alfieri, *Lapchick,* 152–154.

24. Alfieri, 139.

25. Alfieri, 141.

26. Ron Thomas, *They Cleared the Lane: The NBA's Black Pioneers* (Lincoln: University of Nebraska Press, 2004), 44.

27. Thomas, 148–149; Peterson, *Cages to Jump Shots,* 170–173; Fox, *Big Leagues,* 343.

28. Alfieri, *Lapchick,* 149.

29. Alfieri, 150.
30. Alfieri, 159–160.

Chapter 15

1. Bill Russell with Taylor Branch, *Second Wind: The Memoirs of an Opinioned Man*, New York" Ballantine Books, 1979, 25–26; Jones & Paolucci, *Say It Loud*, 72.
2. Russell with Branch, 37.
3. Russell with Branch, 43.
4. Russell with Branch, 44–45.
5. James W. Johnson, *The Dandy Dons: Bill Russell, K.C. Jones, Phil Woolpert, and One of College Basketball's Greatest and Most Innovative Teams* (Lincoln: University of Nebraska Press, 2009), 3–4.
6. Johnson, 6–7.
7. Johnson, 7.
8. Johnson, 17.
9. Johnson, 52–55.
10. R. Goldstein, "Willie Naulls, 84, Dies; Among First Black N.B.A. Stars, Won 3 Rings With Celtics," *New York Times*, Nov. 27, 2018, B11.
11. Jones and Paolucci, *Say It Loud*, 72; Packer's concession is found in J. W. Johnson, *Dandy Dons*, xxiii–xxiv.
12. "Bill Russell," Biography.com, https://www.biography.com/athlete/bill-russell.
13. "Bill Russell"; Johnson, *Dandy Dons*, 55.
14. Russell with Brand, *Second Wind*, 130–132.
15. Gary M. Pomerantz, *The Last Pass: Cousy, Russell, the Celtics, and What Matters in the End.* New York: Penguin, 2018 (New York: Penguin, 2018), 74–77, 85–87; Fox, *Big Leagues*, 404.
16. As quoted in Johnson, *Dandy Dons*, xi.
17. Tony Kornheiser, "Bill Russell, Nothing but a Man," in Michael MacCambridge, ed., *ESPN Sports Century* (New York: Hyperion ESPN Books, 1999), 181.
18. Bill Simmons, *The Book of Basketball: The NBA According to the Sports Guy.* (New York: Ballantine, 2009), 607–611.
19. Jackie McMullen, Rafe Bartholomew and Dan Klores, *Basketball: A Love Story* (New York: Random House Penguin, 2018), 38; Pomerantz, *Last Pass*, 271–273, 298.
20. Pomerantz, *Last Pass*, 125–126, Sam Smith, *Hard Labor*, 54–56.
21. Pomerantz, *Last Pass*, 123–125.
22. Pomerantz, *Last Pass*, 123–126.
23. Russell with Brand, *Second Wind*, 204–07.
24. Russell with Brand, 209–10, 216.
25. Russell with Brand, 213–15.
26. Pomerantz, *Last Pass*, 121–122.
27. Maureen M. Smith, "Bill Russell: Pioneer and Champion of the Sixties," in Wiggins, *Out of the Shadows*, 237. See also Dave Zirin, *People's History*, 152–153.
28. Bill Russell and Allen Steinberg, *Red and Me: My Coach, My Lifelong Friend* (New York: HarperCollins, 2009), 100–101.
29. Pomerantz, *Last Pass*, 125–126.

30. Ryan Young, "44 Years Later, Bill Russell Finally Accepts His NBA Hall of Fame Ring," Nov. 15, 2009, https://www.yahoo.com/video/nba-bill-russell-finally-accepts-hall-of-fame-ring-induction-ceremony-boycott-boston-celtics-first-black-player-chuck-cooper-222834792.html.
31. Halberstam, *The Fifties* (New York: Villard, 1993), 697–698.
32. Pomerantz, *Last Pass*, 279– 280.
33. Pomerantz, 281.
34. "Legends Profile: Oscar Robertson," NBA.com, https://www.nba.com/news/history-nba-legend-oscar-robertson; Aaseng, *African American Athletes*, 196.
35. George, *Elevating the Game,* 120.
36. George, 121
37. "Legends Profile: Oscar Robertson."
38. George, *Elevating the Game,* 121.
39. Bill Simmons, *Book of Basketball*, 555.
40. Aaseng, *African American Athletes*, 197.
41. As recalled by Oscar Robertson, "When the Big O First Played the Garden: 56 in '58," *New York Times*, March 9, 2008, SP9. See also George, *Elevating the Game*, 122.
42. "Legends Profile: Oscar Robertson."
43. Salient biographical information can be culled from "Oscar Robertson: Player of the Century," from oscaarrobertson.com.
44. Smith, *Hard Labor*, 2–4.
45. Smith, 6.
46. Smith, 10–11.
47. Smith, 13.
48. As quoted in Smith, 15.
49. Simmons, *Book of Basketball*, 554.
50. Simmons, 555.
51. Simmons, 556–557.
52. Simmons, 557.
53. Simmons, 562–563.
54. "Oscar Robertson: Player of the Century."

Chapter 16

1. As quoted in Alexander Wolff, *Basketball: A History of the Game* (New York: Bishop Books, 1997), 73.
2. George, *Elevating the Game*, 124–125; Smith, *Hard Labor*, 51.
3. George, 125–126.
4. Smith, *Hard Labor*, 52.
5. Simmons, *Book of Basketball*, 526; Smith, 50.
6. "NBA Players Threaten Strike in Dispute Over Pension Plan," *New York Times*, Jan.15, 1964, 34.
7. "Players Threaten Strike."
8. Smith, *Hard Labor*, 50.
9. Smith, 58.
10. Simmons, *Book of Basketball*, 531; Wolff, *Basketball*, 118.
11. Alex Vejar, "Lakers Unveil Statue of Elgin Baylor outside the Staples Center," April 5, 2018, https://www.seattletimes.com/sports/lakers-unveil-statue-of-elgin-baylor-outside-staples-center/.
12. Vejar.

13. Richard Goldstein, "Connie Hawkins: Electrifying N.B.A. Forward Barred in His Prime, Dies at 75," *New York Times*, Oct. 7, 2017, B5.

14. Details of Hawkins' early life are found in David Wolf, *Foul! The Connie Hawkins Story* (New York: Warner, 1972), 15–45.

15. Wolf, 35–64; Gordon S. White, Jr., "Boys High Tops Wingate, 62–59, and Reaches P.S.A.L. Final," *New York Times*, March 16, 1960, 45; Robert M. Lipsyte, "Boys High Beats Freeze, Takes Final, 21–15," *New York Times,* March 18, 1960, 29.

16. Wolf, 51; Robert Lipsyte, *SportsWorld: An American Dreamland* (New York: Quadrangle, 1975), 148–149.

17. Wolf, 73–74.

18. Jimmy Breslin, "The Fix Was On," *Saturday Evening Post* 35, Feb. 23, 1963, 19.

19. Wolf, *Foul!*, 76–77.

20. Jim Goodrich, "The Sun Finally Rises for Connie Hawkins," *Ebony* 25 (Feb. 1970): 40.

21. Goldstein, "Connie Hawkins."

22. Wolf, *Foul!,* 105–121; Lipsyte, *SportsWorld*, 147–148.

23. Pete Axthelm, *The City Game: Basketball in New York from the World Champion Knicks to the World of the Playgrounds* (New York: Harper's Magazine Press, 1970), 6–8.

24. David Wolf as quoted by Jonathan B. Segal in his review of Wolf's *Foul! The Connie Hawkins Story, New York Times Book Review*, March 26, 1972, 38.

25. Goldstein, "Connie Hawkins."

26. Tex Maul, "A Coming Out Party for Lew and Connie," *Sports Illustrated*, 31 Oct. 6, 1959, 27; Wolf, *Foul!*, 365.

27. Peter Vecsey, "Connie Hawkins Still Needs a Home," *New York Post*, Aug. 8, 1977, 56.

28. Wolf, *Foul!*, 508–510; Rick Telander, *Heaven Is a Playground* (New York: St. Martin's Press, 1976), 279–282; Axthelm, *City Game,* 125–144.

29. A. Wolff, *Basketball*, 74–75.

30. Aaseng, *African American Athletes*, 72.

31. Terry Pluto, *Loose Balls: The Short, Wild Life of the American Basketball Association* (New York: Fireside, 1990), 230–231.

32. "Legends Profile: Julius Irving," NBA.com, accessed June 13, 2022, https://www.nba.com/news/history-nba-legend-julius-erving.

33. "Julius Erving: The Wondrous Dr. J," Academy of Achievement, accessed June 13, 2022, https://achievement.org/achiever/julius-erving/; "Exclusive Interview with Julius Erving," NBA.com, September 8, 2011, https://www.nba.com/sixers/features/exclusive_interview_with_julius_erving_110908.html.

34. "Legends Profile: Julius Erving."

35. "Legends Profile: Julius Erving."

36. As recalled by Carl Sheer in Pluto, *Loose Balls*, 28–29.

37. Pluto, 24, 227, 229, 313, 317–318, 420.

38. Legends profile: "Julius Erving"; "Dr. J" in Zander Hollander, ed., *The NBA's Official Encyclopedia of Pro Basketball* (New York: New American Library, 1977), 245–247.

39. "Exclusive Interview with Julius-9/8/2011 from nba.com Erving.

40. Simmons, *Book of Basketball,* 524–525.

Chapter 17

1. Spencer Stueve, *UCLA Basketball Encyclopedia: The First Hundred Years* (New York: Simon & Schuster, 2019), retrieved from Google Play, https://books.google.com/books.

2. Jerry Crowe, "His USC Team Stood Around and Beat UCLA," *Los Angeles Times*, Feb. 2, 2009, https://www.latimes.com/archives/la-xpm-2009-feb-02-sp-crowe-nest2-story.html.

3. Aaseng, *African American Athletes*, 5–6.

4. Marcus Hayes, "In His Writing, Abdul-Jabbar Has a Lot to Say," *Philadelphia Inquirer,* March 26, 2015, https://www.inquirer.com/philly/sports/sixers/20150326_In_his_writing__Abdul-Jabbar_has_a_lot_to_say.html.

5. Hayes.

6. Hayes.

7. Kareem Abdul-Jabbar, "The Way Americans Regard Sports Heroes versus Intellectuals Speaks Volumes," *Guardian*, April 15, 2019, https://www.theguardian.com/sport/2019/apr/15/the-way-americans-regard-sports-heroes-versus-intellectuals-speaks-volumes.

8. Alexander Wolff, "Kareem Abdul-Jabbar as Comfortable as Ever as a Public Intellectual, *Sports Illustrated*, July 14, 2015, https://www.si.com/more-sports/2015/07/14/kareem-abdul-jabbar-where-are-they-now.

9. Wolf.

10. Much of the above was culled from Jay Caspian Kang, "What the World Got Wrong about Kareem Abdul-Jabbar," *New York Times*, Sept. 17, 2015, https://www.nytimes.com/2015/09/20/magazine/what-the-world-got-wrong-about-kareem-abdul-jabbar.html.

11. Wolf, "Kareem Abdul-Jabbar."

12. "Legends Profile: Magic Johnson," NBA.com, Sept. 14, 2021, https://www.nba.com/news/history-nba-legend-magic-johnson.

13. Gitlin, *Powerful Moments*, 213.

14. Ervin "Magic" Johnson with William Novak, *My Life* (New York: Fawcette, 2009), 26.

15. Johnson with Novak, 30, 42–44.

16. Johnson with Novak, 84.

17. Johnson with Novak, 89.

18. Excerpt from Mark Mehler and Charles Paikert, *Madness: The Ten Most Memorable NCAA Basketball Finals* (New York: Skyhorse, 2018), https://www.si.com/college/2018/02/07/magic-johnson-larry-bird-michigan-state-indiana-state-1979-excerpt.

19. Gitlin, *Powerful Moments*, 218–219.

20. "Legends Profile: Magic Johnson."

21. Johnson with Novak, *My Life*, 91; Michael Wilbon, "Bird vs. Magic 1979 NCAA Championship Game Launched March Madness," *Washington Post*, March 26, 2009, 2.

22. Gitlin, *Powerful Moments*, 220.

23. Jeff Pearlman, *Showtime: Magic, Kareem, Riley and the Los Angeles Lakers Dynasty of the 1980s* (New York: Gotham, 2014), 11–16.

24. Pearlman, *Showtime*, 99–101; Simmons *Book of Basketball*, 592.

25. Simmons, 593.

26. Johnson with Novak, *My Life*, 171.

27. Johnson with Novak, 212.

28. Gitlin, *Powerful Moments*, 222.

29. Gitlin, 222–224; Johnson, *My Life.*, 195; Pearlman, *Showtime*. 261–265.

30. As quoted in Gitlin, *Powerful Moments*, 224.

31. Gitlin, 224–225.

32. Earvin "Magic" Johnson Twitter Account, @MagicJohnson from mobile.twitter.com.

33. James Michener, *Sports in America*, 23–26.

Chapter 18

1. Cody Cunningham, "Charlie Scott. Paving the Way for Future Generations," NBA.com, Feb. 29, 2020, https://www.nba.com/suns/features/charlie-scott-paving-way-future-generations.

2. Cunningham.

3. Cunningham; "Charles Scott," Naismith Memorial Basketball Hall of Fame website, accessed June 13, 2022, https://www.hoophall.com/hall-of-famers/charles-scott/.

4. Cunningham.

5. Terry Pluto, *Loose Balls*, 201.

6. As quoted in Cody Cunningham, "Charlie Scott."

7. David Halberstam, *Playing for Keeps: Michael Jordan and the World He Made* (New York: Broadway, 2000), 4–13.

8. David Halberstam, *Playing for Keeps*, 8–9.

9. Claude Johnson, "'Pimp and 'Lyss": The Immortal Young Brothers," *Black Fives Foundation*, Nov. 20, 2015, https://www.blackfives.org/pimp-and-lyss-the-immortal-young-brothers/.

10. More details can be found in Susan Rayl, "Professional Black Basketball Team"; David Halberstam, *Playing for Keeps*; and Nelson George, *Elevating the Game*.

11. Janet Lowe, *Michael Jordan Speaks: Lessons from the World's Greatest Champion* (New York: Wiley, 1999), 1–4.

12. "Legends Profile: Michel Jordan," NBA.com, Sept. 14, 2021, https://www.nba.com/news/history-nba-legend-michael-jordan; Walter LaFeber, *Michael Jordan and the New Global Capitalism* (New York: W.W. Norton 1999), 29–30.

13. Halberstam, *Playing for Keeps*, 67–68.

14. Roland Lazenby, *Michael Jordan: The Life* (New York: Little, Brown, 2014), 145–146.

15. Lazenby, 145–146; Lowe, *Michael Jordan Speaks*, 7–13; Halberstam, *Playing for Keeps*, 18–22, 77–95; LaFeber, *Michael Jordan*, 49–50.

16. Halberstam, *Playing for Keeps*, 149–157.

17. Nelson George, "Michael Jordan: The Head and the Heart," in Michael MacCambridge, ed., *ESPN SportsCentury*, 267–269.

18. LaFeber, *Michael Jordan*, 28.

19. Jordan appeared on the Dec. 10, 1984, cover of *Sports Illustrated*.

20. As quoted by LaFeber, *Michael Jordan*, 51.

21. LaFeber, *53*; Phil Jackson and Hugh Delehanty, *Sacred Hoops: Spiritual Lessons of a Hardwood Warrior* (New York: Hyperion, 1995), 80. See also Peter Richmond, *Phil Jackson: Lord of the Rings* (New York: Blue Rider, 2013), 143.

22. Jamal Collier, "What Was the Reaction from Michael Jordan, the Chicago Bulls and f=Fans After Sam Smith wrote *Jordan Rules?*," *Chicago Tribune*, May 3, 2020, https://www.chicagotribune.com/sports/bulls/ct-chicago-bulls-michael-jordan-last-dance-20200503-pglv7j7lurhqfjknhzrjughp6i-story.html.

23. Collier.

24. LaFeber, *Michael Jordan*, 77–78.

25. LaFeber, 75.

26. LaFeber, 84–85.

27. LaFeber, 113–118.

28. "Michael Jordan Chronology," CNN/SI, Jan. 12, 1999, web.archive.org.

29. Halberstam, *Playing for Keeps*, 330–335; "Legends Profile: Michael Jordan."

30. Halberstam, 352–353; "Legends Profile: Michael Jordan."

31. Halberstam, 355–356; Marty Burns, "Michael Jordan Retires—23 to Remember," *Sports Illustrated*, Jan. 16, 1999, CNN/SI web.archive.org.

32. Halberstam, 383–397, provides a sparkling description of Jordan's "Last Dance" to an NBA championship; LaFeber, *Michael Jordan*, 132–133.

33. Mike Wise. "Jordan Surprised and Inflamed As Wizards Show Him the Door," *New York Times*, May 8, 2003, D1.

34. Zirin. *People's History*, 237.

35. Zirin, 237–238. See also Howard Bryant, *The Heritage*, 82–90 and 130–132, for criticism of Jordan's silence on other controversial issues and Smith's explanation.

36. As quoted in "Legends Profile: Michael Jordan."

Chapter 19

1. "LeBron James," Biography.com, updated August 31, 2021, https://www.biography.com/athlete/lebron-james.

2. "LeBron James."

3. "LeBron James."

4. Dylan Murphy, "The Art of the LeBron James Chase-Down Block," *Bleacher Report*, Jan. 2, 2014, *https://bleacherreport.com/articles/1908022-the-art-of-the-lebron-james-chasedown-block*.

5. Bill Plaschke, "LeBron James Goes from Shunned to Beloved in L.A., a Remarkable Image Makeover," *Los Angeles Times*, April 17, 2020, https://www.latimes.com/sports/lakers/story/2020-04-17/lebron-james-los-angeles-favorite-athlete-lakers-image-makeovers.

6. Statistics from ESPN.com, Mar. 16, 2020, retrieved from Google.

7. Bryant, "The Legacy of LBJ," ESPN, 12.

8. Scott Cacciola, "LeBron James Is Reminding Everyone He's the King," *New York Times*, March 9, 2020, B12, B15.

9. Cacciola.

10. Scott Cacciola, "Hollywood Royalty," *New York Times*, Oct. 13, 2020, D1, D6.

11. Plaschke, "Remarkable Image Makeover."

12. Perry Bacon, Jr., "Why LeBron Can Say Whatever He Wants About Politics, FiveThirtyEight, July 31, 2018, https://fivethirtyeight.com/features/page/562/?sa=X&ved=0CCwQ9QEwCmoVChMIl9TY8fzxxgIVCTWICh2vYQpT%2F.

13. Bryant, *The Heritage*, 18. See also Michael Bennet with Dave Zirin, *Things That Make White People Uncomfortable* (Chicago: Haymarket, 2018), 204.

14. Michael Powell, "Why Does Trump Attack Black Athletes? It's Quite Clear," *New York Times*, Aug. 6, 2018, D1.

15. Powell.

16. Keith Schneider, "A Hometown Hero Using His Power for Good," *New York Times,* March 10, 2020, B7.

17. Thomas Curwen and David Wharton, "Kobe Bryant, from the Start, Was an Athlete Like No Other," *Los Angeles Times,* Jan. 26. 2020, https://www.latimes.com/sports/lakers/story/2020-01-26/lakers-kobe-bryant-obit.

18. Meagan Flynn, "'My Story Began in This Town': Kobe Bryant Mourned in Italy, Where He Learned to Play Basketball," *Washington Post*, Jan. 27, 2020, https://www.washingtonpost.com/nation/2020/01/27/kobe-italy-death/.

19. Flynn; Curwen and Wharton, "Kobe Bryant."

20. Aaseng, *African American Athletes*, 38–39.

21. Laker Season Capsules, "Three Peat, 1998–2004" and "Back to Back 2004–2012," NBA.com.

22. Kobe Bryant, *The Mamba Mentality*: *How I Play* (New York: Farrar, Straus & Giroux, 2018), 58.

23. Bryant, 59–60.

24. Bryant, 61.

25. Bryant, 62–63.

26. Bryant, 74–77.

27. Bryant, 84–89, 91–92; Curwin & Wharton, "Kobe Bryant."

28. Jill Painter Lopez, "Michael Jordan and Kobe Bryant Once Played a Mental Game of One-on-One Over Dinner," *Sports Illustrated*, https://www.si.com/nba/lakers/news/michael-jordan-and-kobe-bryant-once-played-a-virtual-game-of-one-on-one-over-dinner.

29. Jackie MacMullan, "Kobe Bryant: Imitating Greatness," *ESPN*, June 4, 2010, https://www.espn.ph/nba/playoffs/2010/columns/story?columnist=macmullan_jackie&page=kobefilmstudy-100604.

30. Lopez, "Jordan and Kobe Bryant."

31. As quoted by Lopez.

Chapter 20

1. "Black History in Women's Professional Basketball: A Story," African American Registry, accessed June 13, 2022, https://aaregistry.org/story/black-women-are-changing-pro-basketball/.

2. Frank Fitzpatrick, "A Philadelphian Who Shone in the Shadows of Frank's Place," *Philadelphia Inquirer*, Oct. 21, 2017, https://www.inquirer.com/philly/sports/other_sports/a-philadelphian-who-shone-in-the-shadows-franks-place-20171021.html.

3. Pamela Grundy, "Ora Washington: The First Black Female Star," in Wiggins, *Out of the Shadows,* 79–92.

4. Jennifer H. Lansbury, *A Spectacular Leap: Black Women Athletes in Twentieth Century America* (Fayetteville: University of Arkansas Press, 2014), 24.

5. Fitzpatrick, "A Philadelphian"; Steven J. Niven, "Queen of the Courts: How Ora Washington Helped Philly 'Forget the Depression.'" *Root*, Mar. 14, 2016, https://www.theroot.com/queen-of-the-courts-how-ora-washington-helped-philly-1790854634.

6. Arthur Ashe, "View of Sport: Taking the Hard Road with Black Athletes," *New York Times*, Nov. 13, 1988, sec. 8, 11.

7. Chante Griffin, "Before Althea Gibson, There Was Ora Washington," *OZY*, https://www.ozy.com/true-and-stories/the-forgotten-black-athlete-who-crushed-two-sports-at-once/288784/.

8. Griffin.

9. "Lynette Woodard," *Kansapedia*, Kansas Historical Society, modified August 2013, https://www.kshs.org/kansapedia/lynette-woodard/12244.

10. "Lynette Woodard," Women's Basketball Hall of Fame, https://www.wbhof.com/famers/lynette-woodard/.

11. As discussed by Saroya Nadia McDonald, "Cheryl Miller's Career As a Baller May Have Been Cut Short, but Her Story Is Big," Andscape, https://andscape.com/features/cheryl-millers-women-of-troy/.

12. "Miller, Cheryl (1964–)," Encyclopedia.com, accessed June 13, 2022, https://www.encyclopedia.com/women/encyclopedias-almanacs-transcripts-and-maps/miller-cheryl-1964.

13. "Miller, Cheryl (1964–)"; Allison Ellwood, dir., *Women of Troy*, HBO Documentary Film, Mar. 10, 2020.

14. "Cheryl Miller to Coach Women's Basketball at Cal State LA," Cal State LA website, May 20, 2016, https://www.calstatela.edu/univ/ppa/publicat/cheryl-miller-coach-womens-basketball-cal-state-la#:~:text=Cheryl%20Miller%20is%20the%20new,as%20a%20player%20and%20coach.

15. "Lisa Leslie (1972–)," Biography.com, April 2, 2014, https://www.biography.com/athlete/lisa-leslie.

16. "Lisa Leslie (1972–)"; "Lisa Leslie," Women's Basketball Hall of Fame website, accessed June 14, 2022, https://www.wbhof.com/famers/lisa-leslie/.

17. Maya A. Jones, "Broadcaster Lisa Leslie Remembers Prince, Loves Nilla Wafers—and 'Gidget,'" Andscape, July 15, 2017, https://andscape.com/features/cultureplay-lisa-leslie/.

18. Fran Sypak, "Hall of Fame Inductee Cynthia Cooper Blazed Trail for Women," *Springfield (MA) Republican*, Mar. 25. 2019 updated from Aug. 1, 2010, https://www.masslive.com/sports/2010/08/hall_of_fame_inductee_cynthia.html.

19. "Women's Basketball Finest" (PDF), NCAA.org, Oct. 2, 2017, http://fs.ncaa.org/Docs/stats/w_basketball_RB/misc/wbbfinest.pdf, 20 (of 166).

20. "Tenth World Championship for Women," USA Basketball, August 14, 2013, https://www.usab.com/history/national-team-womens/tenth-world-championship-for-women-1986.aspx.

21. "Cynthia Cooper WNBA Stats," Basketball-Reference.com, accessed June 14, 2022, https://www.basketball-reference.com/wnba/players/c/coopecy01w.html.

22. Ellwood, *Women of Troy.*

23. Kathy Jackson, "GM Helps Hoop Star Cooper Toward a Seat in the Press Box," *Automotive News*, July 21, 1999, https://www.autonews.com/article/19990621/ANA/906210815/gm-helps-hoop-star-cooper-toward-a-seat-in-the-press-box.

24. Cynthia Cooper, *She Got Game: My Personal Odyssey* (New York: Warner Books, 1999), Chapter One.

25. Kurt Streeter, "As Athletes Pursue Justice, Women Are a Force Without Fanfare," *New York Times,* July 3, 2020, A1.

26. "About Maya," MayaMoore.com, accessed June 14, 2022, https://mayamoore.com/about/; "Maya Moore," USA Basketball, Oct. 24, 2013, https://www.usab.com/bio/maya-moore.aspx.

27. Editorial Board, "Maya Moore Is a Hero on (and in) the Court," *Minneapolis Star Tribune,* July 11, 2020, https://www.startribune.com/maya-moore-is-a-hero-on-and-in-the-court/571712072/.

28. Kurt Streeter, "Maya Moore Left Basketball. A Prisoner Needed Help," *New York Times*, June 30, 2019, https://www.nytimes.com/2019/06/30/sports/maya-moore-wnba-quit.html.

29. Kurt Streeter, "W.N.B.A.'s Maya Moore to Skip Another Season to Focus on Prisoner's Case," *New York Times,* Jan. 23, 2020, B7.

Chapter 21

1. Jackson Wald, "Who Invented Golf, and How Did It Become so popular," *Golf News,* Sept. 20, 2020, golf.com.

2. Wald.

3. "About Ted Rhodes: Pearl High Graduate and Pro Golfer," *Metro Schools,* Feb. 18, 2020, https://www.mnps.org/news/featured-stories/about-ted-rhodes-pearl-high-graduate.

4. "Charlie Sifford: the First Black Member of the PGA Tour,"Andscape, Feb. 22, 2018, https://andscape.com/whhw/charlie-sifford-the-first-black-member-of-the-pga-tour/.

5. Karen Crouse, "At Augusta National, Not Talking About Race Is Tradition," *New York Times,* Nov. 10, 2020, B8.

6. Crouse.

7. Aaseng, *African American Athletes,* 259.

8. Martin Gitlin, *Powerful Moments,* 239; Frank Litsky, "Earl Woods, 74, Father of Tiger Woods, Dies," *New York Times,* May 4, 2006, A29.

9. Litsky.

10. Litsky.

11. Gitlin, *Powerful Moments,* 241.

12. S.W. Pope, "'Race,' Family and Nation: The Significance of Tiger Woods in American Culture," in Wiggins, *Out of the Shadows,* 326.

13. Jeff Benedict and Armen Keteyian, *Tiger Woods,* 2018, xiv–xv.

14. Benedict and Ketevian.

15. Pope, "'Race,' Family and Nation," 339–340.

16. Pope, 347–348.

17. Pope, 339.

18. Pope, 342–343.

19. Pope, 343.

20. Benedict and Keteyian, *Tiger Woods,* 2018, xiv.

21. Gitlin, *Powerful Moments,* 241.

22. Gitlin, 243.

23. Jeff Schrock, "Tiger Woods Completes the Impossible Comeback," *NBC Sports,* April 14, 2019, https://www.nbcsports.com/bayarea/golf/tiger-woods-completes-improbable-comeback-wins-2019-masters-championship.

24. Victor Mather, "A Masters Victory That Ranks Among the Greatest Comebacks," *New York Times,* April 16, 2019, B7.

25. Pope, "'Race,' Family and Nation," 351.

26. Andrew Beaton, "What We Know About Tiger Woods's Injury and Car Accident," *Wall Street Journal,* updated April 7, 2021, https://www.wsj.com/articles/tiger-woods-car-crash-cause-11614186728.

27. Andrew Knoll, "A Builder of the Game Couldn't Be Torn Down," *New York Times*, Nov. 11, 2018, D1.

28. Tony Paige, "Trailblazer: O'Ree, Who Was Blinded in One Eye, Was the Jackie Robinson of hockey," *New York Daily News.* Dec. 23, 2018, 74.

29. Knoll, "Builder of the Game," D6.

30. Eric Russo, "O'Ree, A Vital Part of Hockey History," NHL.com, Jan. 17, 2018, https://www.nhl.com/bruins/news/oree-a-vital-part-of-hockey-history/c-295030080.

31. Daryl Bell "The NHL's First Black Player, Willie O'Ree, Had a Short but Pathbreaking Stint with the Boston Bruins," Andscape, Feb. 14, 2017, https://andscape.com/features/nhl-first-black-player-willie-oree/.

32. Paige, "Trailblazer," 74.

33. Paige, 75.

34. Knoll, "Builder of the Game," D6.

35. Bruce Deachman, "Herb Carnegie: The Best Black Player to Never Play in the NHL," *Ottawa Citizen,* Aug. 26, 2017, https://ottawacitizen.com/news/national/herb-carnegie-the-best-black-hockey-player-to-never-play-in-the-nhl.

36. Knoll, "Builder of the Game," D6.

37. Daryl Bell, "Willie O'Ree."

38. Lonnae O'Neal, "The Difficulty in Being Simone Biles," *Andscape*, July 6, 2016, https://andscape.com/features/the-difficulty-of-being-simone-biles/.

39. Danyel Smith, "The Most Dominant Athlete of 2018," *ESPN the Magazine*, Dec. 2018/Jan. 2019, 5, 52–54.

40. Smith, 54.

41. Abby Aguirre, "Training During a Pandemic," *Vogue*, July 9, 2020, https://www.vogue.com/article/simone-biles-cover-august-2020.

42. Aguirre.

43. Aguirre.

44. Aguirre.

45. Smith, "Most Dominant Athlete," 54.

46. Aguirre, "Training During a Pandemic."

Conclusion

1. Edwards, *Black Students,* 151.

2. Edwards, 144–154.

3. Edwards, 147–150.

4. Bennett and Zirin, *White People Uncomfortable,* 22–24.

5. Bryant, *The Heritage*, 42–44.

6. Johnson and Novak, *My Life,* 356.

7. Rhoden, *Forty Million,* 206, xi–xii.

8. As quoted by Rhoden, 144.

9. Rhoden, 147–163.

10. Rhoden, 155.

11. Jack B. Moore, "Monte Irvin: Up from Sharecropping," in Dorinson and Warmund, *Jackie Robinson*, 38.

12. Rhoden, *Forty Million,* 236–237.

13. Rhoden, 269–270.

14. Wiggins, *More Than a Game,* 188–189; Bryant, *Heritage*, 189.

15. Bryant, xii.

16. Bryant, xiii.

17. Bryant, xiii.

18. Bryant, 153–164.

19. Bryant, 3–4.

20. As quoted by Bryant, 10.

21. Bryant, 25–26.

22. Bryant, 226–227.

23. Samuel G. Freedman, "Politics and Football Go Together," *New York Time*, Sept. 25, 2017, A23.

24. Victor Mather, "The Anthem Uproar Goes into Overtime," *New York Times*, Feb. 16, 2019, B8.

25. Bryant, *Heritage.* 23–24.

26. Khadean Coombs, "Michael Jordan Donates $10 Million to Open New Medical Clinics in His North Carolina Hometown," CNN, February 15, 2021, https://www.cnn.com/2021/02/15/us/michael-jordan-clinics-donation-trnd/index.html; "Smithsonian Announces $5 Million Gift From Michael Jordan to the National Museum of African American History and Culture," Smithsonian, August 9, 2016, https://www.si.edu/newsdesk/releases/smithsonian-announces-5-million-gift-michael-jordan-national-museum-african-american-histor; Jonah Engel Bromwich, "Michael Jordan Says He Is 'Deeply Troubled' by Recent Police-Related Violence," *New York Times*, July 25, 2016, https://www.nytimes.com/2016/07/26/sports/basketball/michael-jordan-statement-on-police-related-violence.html?searchResultPosition=1.

27. Bryant, *Heritage*, 188–191.

28. Sopan Deb, "Anthony Commits to Social Justice," *New York Times*, Aug. 12, 2020, B9.

29. Bryant, *Heritage,* Epilogue, 238.

30. James Wagner, "A Conservative Sport Receives Applause for Taking a Stand," *New York Times*, April 7, 2021, B9. See also David Gelles, "Delta and Coca-Cola Reverse Course on Georgia Voting Law, Stating 'Crystal Clear' Opposition," *The New York Times,* April 1, 2021, B1.

31. Kevin Armstrong, "Lamenting a World in Turmoil, a Scholar Thinks One Sport Can Save It," *New York Times*, Sept. 21, 2020, D3.

32. Shropshire, *Being Sugar Ray,* 206–208.

Bibliography

Newspapers

Chicago Tribune
Los Angeles Times
Minneapolis Star Tribune
Montclair (NJ) Times
New York Times
New York Post
Press of Atlantic City
Springfield (MA) Republican
Wall Street Journal
Washington Post

Books and Dissertations

Aaron, Henry, with Lonnie Wheeler. *I Had a Hammer: The Hank Aaron Story*. New York: Harper-Collins, 1991.

Aaseng, Nathan. *African American Athletes*. New York: Infobase Publishing Facts on File, 2011.

Abdul-Jabbar, Kareem. *Coach Wooden and Me: Our 50-Year Friendship on and Off the Court*. New York: Grand Central, 2017.

Abdul-Jabbar, Kareem, with Mignon McCarthy. *Kareem*. New York: Random House, 1990.

Adelson, Bruce. *Brushing Back Jim Crow: The Integration of Minor-League Baseball in the American South*. Charlottesville: University of Virginia Press, 1999.

Alfieri, Gus. *Lapchick: The Life of Legendary Player and Coach in the Glory Days of Basketball*. Guilford, CT: Lyons Press, 2006.

Ali, Muhammad, with Thomas Hauser. *Muhammad Ali: His Life and Times*. New York: Simon and Schuster, 1991.

Allen, Maury. *Jackie Robinson: A Life Remembered*. New York: Franklin Watts, 1987.

Allen, Ray, with Michael Arkush. *From the Outside: My Journey Through Life and the Game I Love*. New York: HarperCollins, 2018.

Arsenault, Raymond. *Arthur Ashe: A Life*. New York: Simon and Schuster, 2018.

Ashe, Arthur, Jr. *Advantage Ashe*. New York: Coward-McCann, 1967.

Ashe, Arthur, Jr. *Hard Road to Glory: A History of the African American Athlete Since 1946*. New York: Warner, 1988.

Ashe, Arthur, with Arnold Rampersad. *Days of Grace: A Memoir*. New York: Alfred A. Knopf, 1993.

Axthelm, Pete. *The City Game: Basketball in New York*, 1970

Baker, William. *Jesse Owens: An American Life*. New York: Free Press, 1986.

Benedict, Jeff, with Armen Keteyian. *Tiger Woods*. New York: Simon and Schuster, 2018.

Bennett, Michael, with Dave Zirin. *Things That Make White People Uncomfortable*. Chicago: Haymarket, 2018.

Biles, Simone, with Michelle Burford. *Courage to Soar: A Body in Motion, a Life in Balance*. Grand Rapids, MI: Zondervan, 2018.

Bradley, Bill. *Values of the Game*. New York: Artisan Workman, 1998.

Branca, Ralph. *A Moment in Time: An American Story of Baseball, Heartbreak and Grace*. New York: Scribner's, 2011.

Brown, Lloyd. *The Young Paul Robeson: "On My Journey Now."* New York: Basic Books, 1997.

Browne, Ray, and Marshall Fishwick, eds. *The Hero in Transition*. Bowling Green, OH: Bowling Green University Press, 1983.

Bruce, Janet. *The Kansas City Monarchs: Champions of Black Baseball*. Lawrence: University Press of Kansas, 1985.

Bryant, Howard. *The Heritage: Black Athletes, a Divided America, and the Politics of Patriotism*. Boston: Beacon, 2018.

_____. *The Last Hero: A Life of Henry Aaron*. New York: Pantheon, 2010.

_____. *Legends: The Best Players, Games, and Teams in Baseball*. New York: Penguin Group Philomel, 2015.

Bryant, Kobe. *The Mamba Mentality: How I Play*. New York: Farrar, Straus and Giroux, 2018.

Burgos, Adrian, Jr. *Playing America's Game: Baseball, Latinos, and the Color Line*. Berkeley: University of California Press, 2007.

Campanella, Roy. *It's Good to Be Alive*. Boston: Little, Brown, 1964.

Campbell, Joseph. *Hero with a Thousand Faces*. New York: Pantheon, 1949.

Carlos, John, with Dave Zirin. *The John Carlos Story: The Sports Moment That Changed the World*. Chicago: Haymarket, 2011.

Carroll, John M. *Fritz Pollard: Pioneer in Racial Advancement*. Urbana: University of Illinois Press, 1998.

Chadwick, Bruce. *When the Game Was Black and White: The Illustrated History of Baseball's Negro Leagues*. New York: Abbeville, 1992.

Cherry, Robert. *Wilt: Larger Than Life*. Chicago: Triumph, 2004.

Clark, Dick, and Larry Lester, eds. *The Negro Leagues Book*. Cleveland: SABR, 1994.

Danzig, Allison, and Peter Brandwein, eds. *The Greatest Sport Stories from* The New York Times. New York: A.S. Barnes, 1951.

Davies, Richard O. *America's Obsession: Sports and Society Since 1945*. Orlando, FL: Harcourt Brace Publishers, 1994.

_____. *Sports in American Life: A History*. Malden, MA: Wiley Blackwell, 2017.

Dewey, Donald, and Nicholas Acocella. *The Biographical History of Baseball*. New York: Carroll and Graf, 1995.

Dorinson, Joseph, ed. *Jackie Robinson: New York Times Newspaper in Education Curriculum Guide*. New York: New York Times, 1997.

Dorinson, Joseph, and William Pencak, eds. *Paul Robeson: Essays on His Life and Legacy*. Jefferson, NC: McFarland, 2002.

Dorinson, Joseph, and Joram Warmund, eds. *Jackie Robinson: Race, Sports and the American Dream*. Armonk, NY: M.E. Sharpe, 1998.

Draper, Deborah Riley, and Travis Thrasher. *Olympic Pride, American Prejudice: The Untold Story of 18 African Americans Who Defied Jim Crow and Adolf Hitler to Compete in the 1936 Berlin Olympics*. New York: Simon and Schuster, 2020.

Duberman, Martin Bauml. *Paul Robeson*. New York: Alfred A. Knopf, 1988.

Du Bois, W.E.B. *The Souls of Black Folk*. New York: Dover, 1994. First published 1903.

Echevarría, Roberto González. *The Pride of Havana: A History of Cuban Baseball*. New York: Oxford University Press, 1999.

Edgerton, Gary, Michael T. Madsen, and Jack Nachbar, eds. *In the Eye of the Beholder: Critical Perspectives in Popular Film and Television*. Bowling Green, OH: Bowling Green University Press, 1997.

Edwards, Harry. *Black Students*. New York: Free Press, 1970.

Ehrlich, Scott. *Paul Robeson: Athlete, Actor, Singer, Activist*. Los Angeles: Melrose Square, 1989.

Eig, Jonathan. *Ali: A Life*. Boston: Houghton Mifflin Harcourt, 2017.

_____. *Opening Day: The Story of Jackie Robinson's First Season*. New York: Simon and Schuster, 2007.

Einstein, Charles. *Willie's Time: A Memoir*. Philadelphia: Lippincott, 1979.

Eisen, George, and David K. Wiggins, eds. *Ethnicity and Sports in North American History and Culture*. Westport, CT: Praeger, 1995.

Entine, Jon. *Taboo: Why Black Athletes Dominate Sports and Why We're Afraid to Talk About It*. New York: Public Affairs, 2000.

Epstein, Joseph. *Masters of the Game: Essays and Stories on Sport*. Lanham, MD: Rowman and Littlefield, 2015.

Feinstein, John. *Quarterback: Inside the Most Important Position in the National Football League*. New York: Doubleday, 2018.

Fleischer, Nat. *The Heavyweight Championship: An Informal History of Heavyweight Boxing from 1719 to the Present*. New York: G.P. Putnam's Sons, 1949.

Foner, Philip S., ed. *Paul Robeson Speaks: Writings, Speeches, Interviews, 1918–1974*. New York: Brunner/Mazel, 1978.

Fox, Larry. *The Illustrated History of Basketball*. New York: Grosser and Dunlap, 1974.

Fox, Stephen. *Big Leagues: Professional Baseball, Football, and Basketball in National Memory*. New York: William Morrow, 1994.

Freeman, Mike. *Jim Brown: A Hero's Life*. New York: HarperCollins, 2009.

Frommer, Harvey. *Rickey and Robinson: The Men Who Broke Baseball's Color Barrier*. New York: Macmillan, 1982.

George, Nelson. *Elevating the Game: Black Men and Basketball*. New York: HarperCollins, 1992.

Gibson, Bob, Reggie Jackson, and Lonnie Wheeler. *Sixty Feet, Six Inches: A Hall of Fame Hitter and a Hall of Fame Pitcher Talk About How the Game Is Played*. New York: Random House Doubleday, 2009.

Gilmore, Al-Tony. *Bad Nigger! The National Impact of Jack Johnson*. Port Washington, NY: Kennikat, 1975.

Gitlin, Martin. *Powerful Moments in Sports: The Most Significant Sporting Events in American History*. Lanham, MD: Rowman and Littlefield, 2017.

Glickman, Marty, with Stan Isaacs. *The Fastest Kid on the Block: The Marty Glickman Story*. Syracuse, NY: Syracuse University Press, 1996.

Goldblatt, David. *The Games: A Global History of the Olympics*. New York: W.W. Norton, 2016.

Golenbock, Peter. *Bums: An Oral History of the Brooklyn Dodgers*. New York: G.P. Putnam's Sons, 1984.

Gutman, Bill. *The Pictorial History of College Basketball*. New York: W.H. Smith Gallery, 1989.

Guttmann, Allen. *A Whole New Ball Game: An Interpretation of American Sports*. Chapel Hill: University of North Carolina Press, 1988.

Halberstam, David. *The Fifties*. New York: Villard, 1993.

_____. *The Teammates: A Portrait of a Friendship*. New York: Hyperion, 2003.

Hauser, Thomas. *Muhammad Ali: His Life and Times*. New York: Touchstone, 1991.

Haygood, Will. *Sweet Thunder: The Life and Times of Sugar Ray Robinson*. New York: Lawrence Hill, 2009.

_____. *Tigerland: A City Divided, a Nation Torn Apart*. New York: Alfred A. Knopf Borzoi, 2018.

Heaphy, Leslie. "The Growth and Decline of the Negro Leagues." MA thesis, University of Toledo, 1986.

_____. *The Negro Leagues, 1869–1960.* Jefferson, NC: McFarland, 2003.

Herzog, Brad. *The Sports 100: The One Hundred Most Important People in American Sports History.* New York: Macmillan, 1995.

Hoberman, John. *Darwin's Athletes: How Sport Has Damaged Black America and Preserved the Myth of Race.* Boston: Mariner, 1997.

Hogan, Larry, ed. *Shades of Glory: The Negro Leagues and the Story of African American Baseball.* Washington, D.C.: National Geographic, 2006.

Holway, John B. *Blackball Stars: Negro League Pioneers.* Westport, CT: Meckler, 1988.

_____. *Josh and Satch: The Life and Times of Josh Gibson and Satchel Paige.* Westport, CT: Meckler, 1991.

_____. *Voices from the Great Black Baseball Leagues.* New York: Da Capo, 1993.

Hoose, Phillip M. *Necessities: Racial Barriers in American Sports.* New York: Random House, 1989.

Hutchinson, George. "The Black Athletes' Contribution Towards Social Change in the United States." Unpublished PhD dissertation, United States International University.

Huyghue, Michael. *Behind the Line of Scrimmage: Inside the Front Office of the NFL.* New York: Hachette, 2018.

Irvin, Monte, with James A. Riley. *Nice Guys Finish First: The Autobiography of Monte Irvin.* New York: Carroll and Graf, 1996.

Isaacs, Neil D. *Vintage NBA: The Pioneer Era, 1946–1956.* Indianapolis: Masters Press, 1986.

Jackson, Phil, and Hugh Delehanty. *Sacred Hoops: Spiritual Lessons of a Hardwood Warrior.* New York: Hyperion, 1995.

Jacobson, Steve. *Carrying Jackie's Torch: The Players Who Integrated Baseball—and America.* Chicago: Lawrence Hill, 2007.

James, Bill. *The New Bill James Historical Abstract.* New York: Free Press, 2001.

Jedwab, Jack. *Jackie Robinson's Unforgettable Season of Baseball in Montreal.* Montreal: Les Editions Images, 1996.

Johnson, Jack. *In the Ring—and Out.* Chicago: National Sports, 1927.

Johnson, James W. *The Dandy Dons: Bill Russell, K.C. Jones, Phil Woolpert, and One of College Basketball's Greatest and Most Innovative Teams.* Lincoln: University of Nebraska Press, 2008.

Johnson, Earvin "Magic," and William Novak. *My Life.* New York: Fawcette, 1992.

Johnson, Rafer, with Philip Goldberg. *The Best That I Can Be: An Autobiography.* New York: Doubleday, 1998.

Jones, Roxanne, and Jessie Paolucci. *Say It Loud: An Illustrated History of the Black Athlete.* New York: ESPN, 2010.

Kahn, Roger. *The Boys of Summer.* New York: Signet, 1971.

Kashatus, William. *Jackie and Campy: The Untold Story of Their Rocky Relationship and the Breaking of Baseball's Color Line.* Lincoln: University of Nebraska Press, 2014.

Kass, D.A. "The Issue of Racism at the 1936 Olympics." *Journal of Sports History* 3, no. 3 (Winter 1976): 222–235.

Kempton, Murray. *Part of Our Time: Some Ruins and Monuments of the Thirties.* New York: Simon and Schuster, 1955.

LaFeber, Walter. *Michael Jordan and the New Global Capitalism.* New York: Little, Brown, 2014.

Lansbury, Jennifer H. *A Spectacular Leap: Black Women Athletes in Twentieth Century America.* Fayetteville: University Arkansas Press, 2014.

Lapchick, Richard, et al. *100 Pioneers: African Americans Who Broke the Color Barrier in Sports.* Morgantown, WV: Fitness Information Technology, 2008.

Lazenby, Roland. *Michael Jordan: The Life.* New York: Little, Brown, 2014.

Lincoln, C.E. *Black Muslims in America.* Boston: Beacon, 1968.

Lipsyte, Robert. *SportsWorld: An American Dreamland.* New York: Quadrangle, 1977.

Lipsyte, Robert, and Peter Levine. *Idols of the Game: A Sporting History of the American Century.* Atlanta: Turner, 1995.

Lomax, Michael, ed. *Sports and the Racial Divide: African American and Latino Experience in an Era of Change.* Jackson: University Press of Mississippi, 2008.

Lowe, Janet. *Michael Jordan Speaks: Lessons from the World's Greatest Champion.* New York: Wiley, 1999.

Lowenfish, Lee. *Imperfect Diamond: A History of Baseball's Labor Wars.* Rev. ed. New York: Da Capo, 1991.

Lubin, Harold, ed. *Heroes and Anti-Heroes: A Reader in Depth.* San Francisco: Chandler, 1959.

Lucas, John A., and Ronald A. Smith. *Saga of American Sport.* Philadelphia: Lea and Febiger, 1978.

MacCambridge Michael, ed. *ESPN SportsCentury.* New York: Hyperion, 1999.

MacMullan, Jackie, Rafe Bartholomew, and Dan Klores. *Basketball: A Love Story.* New York: Crown, 2018.

Mandell, Richard. *The Nazi Olympics.* New York: Macmillan, 1972.

Maraniss, David. *Rome 1960: The Olympics That Changed the World.* New York: Simon and Schuster, 2008.

_____. *Clemente: The Passion and Grace of Baseball's Last Hero.* New York: Simon and Schuster, 2005.

Marazzi, Rich, and Len Fiorito. *Baseball Players of the 1950s: A Biographical Dictionary of All 1,560 Major Leaguers.* Jefferson, NC: McFarland, 2004.

Margolick, David. *Beyond Glory: Joe Louis Vs. Max Schmeling, and a World on the Brink.* New York: Alfred A. Knopf, 2005.

Martin, Lori Latrice. *White Sports/Black Sports:*

Racial Disparities in Athletic Programs. Denver: Praeger, 2015.

McGee, Bob. *The Greatest Ballpark Ever: Ebbets Field and the Story of the Brooklyn Dodgers*. New York: Rivergate, 2005.

McKissack, Fredrick, Jr. *Black Hoops: The History of African Americans in Basketball*. New York: Scholastic, 1999.

McPhee, John. *Levels of the Game*. New York: Farrar, Straus and Giroux, 2011.

McRae, Donald. *Heroes Without a Country: America's Betrayal of Joe Louis and Jesse Owens*. New York: Ecco, 2002.

Menefee, Curt, with Michael Arkush. *Losing Isn't Everything: The Untold Stories and Hidden Lessons Behind the Toughest Losses in Sports History*. New York: HarperCollins, 2016.

Michaels, Al, with Jon Wertheim. *You Can't Make This Up: Miracles, Memories, and the Perfect Marriage of Sports and Television*. New York: William Morrow, 2014.

Moffi, Larry, and Jonathan Kronstadt. *Crossing the Line: Black Major Leaguers, 1947–1959*. Jefferson, NC: McFarland, 1994.

Moore, Joseph T. *Pride Against Prejudice: The Biography of Larry Doby*. Westport, CT: Greenwood, 1988. Republished 2011 (as *Larry Doby: The Struggle of the American League's First Black Player*) by Dover.

Nash, Roderick. *The Nervous Generation: American Thought 1917–1930*. Chicago: Rand McNally, 1970.

Noverr, Douglas A., and Larry E. Ziewacz, *The Games They Played: Sports in American History, 1865–1980*. Lanham, MD: Rowman and Littlefield, 1983.

O'Neil, John "Buck," with Steve Wulf and David Conrads. *I Was Right on Time: My Journey from the Negro Leagues to the Majors*. New York: Simon and Schuster, 1996.

Overmyer, James. *Queen of the Negro Leagues: Effa Manley and the Newark Eagles*. Lanham, MD: Scarecrow, 1998.

Papineau, David. *Knowing the Score: What Sports Can Teach Us About Philosophy (And What Philosophy Can Teach Us About Sports)*. New York: Basic Books, 2017.

Pearlman, Jeff. *Showtime: Magic, Kareem, Riley, and the Los Angeles Lakers Dynasty of the 1980s*. New York: Gotham, 2014.

Peterson, Robert. *Cages to Jump Shots: Pro Basketball's Early Years*. New York: Oxford University Press, 1990.

———. *Only the Ball Was White: A History of Legendary Black Players and All-Black Professional Teams*. New York: Gramercy, 1970.

———. *Pigskin: The Early Years of Pro Basketball*. New York: Oxford University Press, 1997.

Piascik, Andy. *Gridiron Gauntlet: The Story of the Men Who Integrated Pro Football in Their Own Words*. Lanham, MD: Taylor Trade, 2009.

Plimpton, George, ed. *The Best American Sports Writing 1997*. Boston: Houghton Mifflin, 1997.

Plowden, Martha Ward. *Olympic Black Women*. Gretna, LA: Pelican, 1966.

Pluto, Terry. *Loose Balls: The Short, Wild Life of the American Basketball Association*. New York: Fireside, 1990.

Pomerantz, Gary. *The Last Pass: Cousy, Russell, the Celtics, and What Matters in the End*. New York: Penguin, 2018.

Raab, Scott. *You're Welcome, Cleveland: How I Helped Lebron James Win a Championship and Save a City*. New York: HarperCollins, 2017.

Rader, Benjamin. *Baseball: A History of America's Game*. Urbana: University of Illinois Press, 1992.

Rampersand, Arnold. *Jackie Robinson: A Biography*. New York: Alfred A. Knopf, 1997.

Rayl, Susan. "The New York Renaissance Professional Black Basketball Team 1923–1950." PhD diss., Pennsylvania State University, 1996.

Regalado, Samuel Octavio. *Viva Baseball! Latin Major Leaguers and Their Special Hunger*. Urbana: University of Illinois Press, 1998.

Reisler, Jim. *Black Writers/Black Baseball: An Anthology of Articles from Black Sportswriters Who Covered the Negro Leagues*. Jefferson, NC: McFarland, 1994.

Rhoden, William C. *Forty Million Dollar Slaves: The Rise, Fall, and Redemption of the Black Athlete*. New York: Random House, 2006.

Richmond, Peter. *Phil Jackson: Lord of the Rings*. New York: Blue Rider, 2013.

Riess, Steven. *City Games: The Evolution of American Urban Society and the Rise of Sports*. Urbana: University of Illinois Press, 1991.

Riley, James A. *The Biographical Encyclopedia of the Negro Baseball League*. New York: Carrol and Graf, 1994.

Roberts, Randy. *Papa Jack: Jack Johnson and the Era of White Hopes*. New York: Free Press, 1983.

Roberts, Randy, and James Olson. *Winning Is the Only Thing: Sports in America Since 1945*. Baltimore: Johns Hopkins University Press, 1989.

Robeson, Paul. *Here I Stand*. Boston: Beacon, 1971. First published 1958.

Robinson, Jackie, as told to Alfred Duckett. *I Never Had It Made: An Autobiography of Jackie Robinson*. New York: Putnam, 1972.

Robinson, Rachel, with Lee Daniels. *Jackie Robinson: An Intimate Portrait*. New York: Harry N. Abrams, 1996.

Robinson, Sharon. *Stealing Home: An Intimate Family Portrait by the Daughter of Jackie Robinson*. New York: HarperCollins, 1996.

Robinson, Sugar Ray, with Dave Anderson. *Sugar Ray*. Boston: DaCapo, 1994.

Rogosin, Donn. *Invisible Men: Life in Baseball's Negro Leagues*. Lincoln: University of Nebraska Press, 2020.

Romero, Patricia W., ed. *In Black America 1968: The Year of Awakening*. New York: International Publishers, 1969.

Ross, Charles K. *Outside the Lines: African Americans and the Integration of the NFL*. New York: NYU Press, 1998.

Rob Ruck, *Sandlot Seasons: Sport in Black Pittsburgh*. Pittsburgh: University of Pittsburgh Press, 1993.

Russell, Bill, with Alan Steinberg. *Red and Me: My Coach, My Lifelong Friend.* New York: Harper-Collins, 2009.

Russell, Bill, with David Falkner. *Russell Rules: Lessons on Leadership from the Twentieth Century's Greatest Winner.* New York: New American Library, 2001.

Russell, Bill, with Taylor Branch. *Second Wind: The Memoirs of an Opinionated Man.* New York: Ballantine, 1979.

Rust, Art, Jr., and Edna Rust. *Art Rust's Illustrated History of the Black Athlete.* New York: Doubleday, 1985.

Sammons, Jeffrey. *Beyond the Ring: The Role of Boxing in American Society.* Urbana: University of Illinois Press, 1988.

Schiot, Molly. *Game Changers: The Unsung Heroines of Sports History.* New York: Simon and Schuster, 2016.

Shropshire, Kenneth. *Being Sugar Ray: The Life of Sugar Ray Robinson, America's Greatest Boxer and the First Celebrity Athlete.* New York: Basic Books, 2009.

Silber, Irwin. *Press Box Red: The Story of Lester Rodney, the Communist Who Helped Break the Color Line in American Sports.* Philadelphia: Temple University Press, 2003.

Simmons, Bill. *The Book of Basketball: The NBA According to the Sports Guy.* New York: Ballantine, 2009.

Snyder, Brad. *Beyond the Shadow of the Senators: The Untold Story of the Homestead Grays and the Integration of Baseball.* Chicago: Contemporary, 2003.

——. *A Well-Paid Slave: Curt Flood's Fight for Free Agency in Professional Sports.* New York: Plume, 2007.

Spivey, Donald, ed. *Sport in America: New Historical Perspectives.* Westport, CT: Greenwood, 1985.

Stewart, Jeffrey, ed. *Paul Robeson: Artist and Citizen.* New Brunswick, NJ: Rutgers University Press, 1998.

Stout, Glen, and Dick Johnson. *Jackie Robinson: Between the Baselines.* Emeryville, CA: Woodford, 1997.

Stueve, Spencer. *UCLA Basketball Encyclopedia: The First 100 Years.* New York: Simon and Schuster, 2019.

Talamini, John T., and Charles H. Page, eds. *Sport and Society: An Anthology.* Boston: Little, Brown, 1973.

Taylor, John. *The Rivalry: Bill Russell, Wilt Chamberlain and the Golden Age of Basketball.* New York: Random House, 2005.

Thomas, Ron. *They Cleared the Lane: The NBA's Black Pioneers.* Lincoln: University of Nebraska Press, 2004.

Tutko, Thomas, and William Bruns. *Winning Is Everything and Other American Myths.* New York: Macmillan, 1976.

Tygiel, Jules. *Baseball's Great Experiment: Jackie Robinson and His Legacy.* New York: Oxford University Press, 1997.

Tygiel, Jules, ed. *A Jackie Robinson Reader.* New York: Dutton, 1997.

Vaughan, Alden T. *New England Frontier: Puritans and Indians, 1620–1676.* 3d ed. Norman: University of Oklahoma Press, 1995.

Vecchione, Joseph J., ed. *The New York Times Book of Sports Legends.* New York: Random House, 1991.

Ward, Geoffrey C., and Ken Burns. *Baseball: An Illustrated History.* New York: Alfred A. Knopf, 1994.

Wecter, Dixon. *The Hero in America: A Chronicle of Hero-Worship.* Introduction by Robert Penn Warren. New York: Charles Scribner's Sons, 1972.

Wertheim, L. Jon. *Venus Envy: Power Games, Teenage Vixens, and Million Dollar Egos on the Women's Tennis Tour.* New York: Harper, 2002.

White, Bill, with Gordon Dillow. *Uppity: My Untold Story About the Games People Play.* New York: Grand Central, 2011.

White, G. Edward. *Creating the National Pastime: Baseball Transforms Itself, 1903–1953.* Princeton, NJ: Princeton University Press, 1996.

Wiggins, David K. *Glory Bound: Black Athletes in White America.* Syracuse, NY: Syracuse University Press, 1997.

——. *More Than a Game: A History of the African American Experience in Sport.* Lanham, MD: Rowman and Littlefield, 2018.

——, ed. *Out of the Shadows: A Biographical History of African American Athletes.* Fayetteville: University of Arkansas Press, 2008.

Wiggins, David K., and Ryan Swanson, eds. *Separate Games: African American Sport Behind the Walls of Segregation.* Fayetteville: University of Arkansas Press, 2016.

Wigginton, Russell T. *The Strange Career of the Black Athlete: African Americans and Sports.* Westport, CT: Praeger, 2006.

Williams, Richard, with Bart Davis. *Black and White: The Way I See It.* New York: Atria, 2014.

Windhorst, Brian, and Dave McMenamin. *Return of the King: LeBron James, the Cleveland Cavaliers and the Greatest Comeback in NBA History.* New York: Grand Central, 2017.

Wolf, David. *Foul! The Connie Hawkins Story.* New York: Warner, 1972.

Wolff, Alexander. *Basketball: A History of the Game.* New York: Bishop Books, 1997.

Woodward, C. Vann. *Reunion and Reaction: The Compromise of 1877 and the End of Reconstruction.* Boston: Little, Brown, 1951.

Zirin, Dave. *Jim Brown: Last Man Standing.* New York: Blue Rider, 2018.

——. *A People's History of Sports in the United States: Years of Politics, Protest, and Play.* New York: New Press, 2008.

Index